T0336372

HOW IT HAPPENED

Fig. 1   Portrait of Ernő Munkácsi, 1943

ERNŐ MUNKÁCSI

HOW IT HAPPENED

Documenting the Tragedy of Hungarian Jewry

Translated from the Hungarian by Péter Balikó Lengyel
Edited by Nina Munk
Annotated by László Csősz and Ferenc Laczó

McGill-Queen's University Press
Montreal & Kingston • London • Chicago

© Nina Munk 2018

ISBN 978-0-7735-5512-9 (cloth)
ISBN 978-0-7735-5581-5 (EPDF)
ISBN 978-0-7735-5582-2 (EPUB)

Legal deposit fourth quarter 2018
Bibliothèque nationale du Québec

Printed in Canada on acid-free paper that is 100% ancient forest free (100% post-consumer recycled), processed chlorine free

Funded by the   Financé par le
Government   gouvernement   Canadä   Canada Council   Conseil des arts
of Canada   du Canada   for the Arts   du Canada

We acknowledge the support of the Canada Council for the Arts, which last year invested $153 million to bring the arts to Canadians throughout the country.

Nous remercions le Conseil des arts du Canada de son soutien. L'an dernier, le Conseil a investi 153 millions de dollars pour mettre de l'art dans la vie des Canadiennes et des Canadiens de tout le pays.

Library and Archives Canada Cataloguing in Publication

Munkácsi, Ernő
[Hogyan történt? English]
    How it happened : documenting the tragedy of Hungarian Jewry / Ernő Munkácsi ; translated from Hungarian by Péter Balikó Lengyel ; edited by Nina Munk ; annotated by László Csősz and Ferenc Laczó.

Translation of: Hogyan történt?
Includes bibliographical references and index.
Issued in print and electronic formats.
ISBN 978-0-7735-5512-9 (cloth).–ISBN 978-0-7735-5581-5 (EPDF).
–ISBN 978-0-7735-5582-2 (EPUB)

    1. Holocaust, Jewish (1939–1945) – Hungary – Personal narratives.
I. Munk, Nina, editor II. Title: Hogyan történt? English

DS135.H9M8613 2018   943.9'004924   C2018-903578-1
                                              C2018-903579-X

This book was designed and typeset by Peggy & Co. Design Inc. in 10.5/14 Sabon.

Contents

List of Illustrations

Editor's Preface

A few years ago, while rummaging through his desk drawers, my father, Peter Munk, found a tattered copy of a Hungarian book written in 1947 by his cousin Ernő Munkácsi. My father sat down, read the book in one sitting, and called me. "This book," he began urgently. "It has to be published in English."

Leading scholars of the Holocaust in Hungary have long been influenced by Ernő Munkácsi's remarkable book of 1947. Notably, *How It Happened* served as a vital source for Randolph L. Braham's encyclopaedic *The Politics of Genocide*. But, as my father understood immediately, *How It Happened* is not only an important historical record of the Holocaust in Hungary; it is an extraordinary first-hand account of the atrocity, written by a "privileged" eyewitness and victim. Memoirs of war are almost always affected by hindsight bias. *How It Happened* was written right after the Second World War, when the wounds were still raw. That immediacy magnifies the horrors Munkácsi describes: the barrage of increasingly preposterous demands made by Adolf Eichmann's special operations unit in Budapest (Sondereinsatzkommando Eichmann); the complicity of the Hungarian authorities; the disagreements that unfolded behind closed doors among frantic members of the Hungarian Judenrat; the mind-numbing swiftness and barbarity with which hundreds of thousands of Hungary's Jews were rounded up, robbed of their property and civil rights, herded into ghettos, and murdered in Nazi concentration camps.

My father and Ernő Munkácsi were first cousins once removed (my father's grandfather was Munkácsi's uncle). The Munk family was big and tightly knit and comfortably bourgeois. In Budapest in the years leading up to the war, family members gathered frequently at their local coffee house (*Országház kávéház*), at their synagogue on what was then Csáky Street, and for Shabbat dinners at my great-grandfather Gábor Munk's well-appointed apartment in Lipótváros. Ernő, born in 1896, was thirty-one years older than my father. My father, born in 1927, remembered his older cousin as serious, dutiful, and "rather dull." By all accounts, Ernő was all that and more. He was a member of Budapest's Jewish intelligentsia, a highly respected jurist, cultured, and committed to doing right by his community. As Susan Papp argues in her biographical essay (page lvii), by acting as secretary for the Judenrat or Jewish Council, Ernő Munkácsi surely believed he could act as a bulwark against the Nazis.

The reality was something very different, of course, as revealed by a disquieting joke that Ernő recounts in *How It Happened*:

> A Jew is woken up in the middle of the night by a banging on his door.
> "Who's there?" he calls out.
> "The Gestapo," comes the answer.
> "Thank God," says the Jew, with obvious relief. "I thought it was the Jewish Council!"

To read *How It Happened* is to understand that the Budapest-based Judenrat, an administrative body established by the SS immediately after the invasion of Hungary in March 1944, inadvertently facilitated the Nazis' "wholesale extermination of Hungarian Jews" (Ernő's words). Even today, this is a deeply unsettling, controversial topic. The tragic role played by the Jewish councils in Hungary, Poland, and other Nazi-occupied nations is often defined in terms of "impossible choices" or, to quote the Holocaust scholar Lawrence L. Langer, "choiceless choices." In *The Politics of Genocide*, Braham describes the Hungarian Judenrat as naïve, ineffective, and "almost completely oblivious of the inferno around it."[1] Rudolf Vrba, an escapee whose detailed report of April 1944 first documented the extent of the horrors at Auschwitz, went further in his critique of the Jewish elite who composed the Judenrat, charging them in his later memoirs with complicity in the Nazis' crimes: "It is my contention that a small group of informed people, by their silence, deprived others of the possibility or privilege of making their own decisions in the face of mortal dangers."[2]

Ernő Munkácsi wrote *How It Happened* well before Braham or Vrba questioned the role of Jewish leaders in Hungary; yet already in the immediate aftermath of the war he and other members of the Judenrat were confronted by intense hostility and outrage from fellow survivors, many of whom had lost their whole family and community to the gas chambers. Why didn't the Judenrat do more to save their people? How did the Judenrat and their families manage to emerge largely unscathed from the war even while more

Fig. 2   Ernő Munkácsi addresses a gathering at his cousin Peter Munk's bar mitzvah in
Budapest in 1940. In the centre is Peter Munk (1927–2018), whose grandfather Gábor Munk
(1865–1955) was a younger brother of Ernő Munkácsi's father, Bernát Munkácsi (1860–1937,
born Munk). In the background are Peter's classmates at Budapest's Neolog Jewish High
School (Pesti Izraelita Hitközség Gimnáziuma), and in the foreground far left is their
teacher Fülöp Grünvald (1887–1964), a distinguished historian. Next to Grünvald are two of
Ernő Munkácsi's first cousins: Peter's father, Lajos Munk, and Ilona Resofsky.

than 400,000 Hungarian Jews were murdered? In his perceptive introduction
to this volume, Ferenc Laczó suggests that in writing *How It Happened*, Ernő
had a personal stake in denying how much he knew about the Holocaust
by mid-1944; he needed to defend himself against accusations of having
done too little too late. Fülöp (Pinchas) Freudiger was another member of
my family who served on the Hungarian Judenrat in 1944. Years later, as a
witness at the Eichmann Trial, Freudiger was asked what he did to prevent
the mass deportations in Hungary. "What could we have done?" he asked.

Ernő Munkácsi and Fülöp Freudiger weren't the only members of my
family who wrestled with their wartime records. In June 1944, as the cattle
cars rolled from Hungary to the Auschwitz-Birkenau death camp at peak
capacity, fourteen members of my immediate family – including my father,
grandfather, and great-grandfather – fled Budapest on what we now know
as the Kasztner Train, the result of secret negotiations with the Nazis that
permitted 1,687 select Jews to flee to safety in Switzerland. To be blunt: my
family used its connections and money to escape the inferno, while others

with less money and fewer connections were murdered. That unspoken, unsavoury fact has caused lingering rifts, even within my own family, because less-wealthy or less-lucky branches of the family were trapped in Hungary and slaughtered by the Nazis or the Arrow Cross.

What was the right thing to do during the Holocaust? In *How It Happened*, Munkácsi offers readers a new understanding of the lamentable, impossible balancing act that he and his fellow members of the Judenrat performed. They were not heroes. They were dutiful, "rather dull" members of the establishment who implicitly or conveniently trusted in the established order that had permitted them to thrive in Hungary. Even as increasingly severe anti-Jewish measures robbed them of their property, their jobs, and their civil rights, the Jewish elite in Budapest rationalized that if they kept their heads down, they would emerge from the war relatively unscathed. Even after the Nazis arrived in 1944 and Hungary's Jews began to be herded into ghettos and deported, they stayed the course, perhaps because they "entertained the illusion that Hungary would be the exception, a tiny foothold of an island in the sea of Jewish devastation," as Munkácsi argues, or perhaps because they felt they had no other option. To quote Ferenc Laczó: "With greater temporal distance, it might … be easier to acknowledge that members of the Council made politically and morally problematic choices because there was no alternative; it was impossible for them to make good decisions."

My father could never forgive himself for leaving his mother behind when he escaped in 1944. *I should have done something to save her*, he would say. But what could he have done? Shortly after the Germans occupied Hungary, my grandmother was arrested on the far-fetched charge that she was a threat to the Reich. My father, aged sixteen, accompanied her to the Gestapo detention centre on Rökk Szilárd Street, carrying her brown leather valise. Assured by elder statesmen of the community that she would soon be released, my father would only later learn that she had been sent to Auschwitz and then forced into labour for the Nazis at a factory in Zschopau, Germany. She survived the ordeal, only to later commit suicide. Not surprisingly, my father empathized with his cousin Ernő's impossible dilemma.

In the years it has taken to bring this project to fruition, I've come to understand why my father adamantly insisted that Ernő Munkácsi's *How It Happened* be translated and made available to a wide audience. This is a book that illuminates the agony and moral weight of "choiceless choices." It's a book of history, certainly; yet it feels particularly vital right now as Jews everywhere anxiously confront a surge of antisemitism, as bigotry and hatred have again become embedded in our everyday discourse. The Holocaust is fading from memory. Among Americans, two-thirds of millennials and 41 percent of all adults do not know what Auschwitz was, according to a recent poll commissioned by the Conference on Jewish Material Claims Against Germany. It was Elie Wiesel, himself a survivor of Auschwitz and the Holocaust in Hungary, who most eloquently implored that we remember the horrors of the past. "For the survivor who chooses to testify, it is clear: his duty is to bear witness for the dead *and* for the living," he wrote in the preface to the new English translation of his memoir, *Night*. "To forget would be not only dangerous but offensive; to forget the dead would be akin to killing them a second time."[3]

Nina Munk

Notes

1   Randolph L. Braham, *The Politics of Genocide: The Holocaust in Hungary, Vol 1* (New York: Columbia University Press, 1981), 462.
2   Rudolf Vrba, "Preparations for the Holocaust in Hungary," in Randolph L. Braham and Scott Miller (eds.), *The Nazis' Last Victims: The Holocaust in Hungary* (Detroit: Wayne State University Press, 1998), 94.
3   Elie Wiesel, *Night* (New York: Hill and Wang, 2006), xv.

Acknowledgments

This book was a team effort. Doris L. Bergen, the Chancellor Rose and Ray Wolfe Chair in Holocaust Studies at the University of Toronto, was an early champion of the project, not only enthusiastically supporting the idea but offering invaluable advice at every stage. She also served as an early reader. As the Hungarian experts on the team, Ferenc Laczó and László Csősz were critical to the project's success; they have left their imprint on every part of this book.

We were blessed to have McGill-Queen's University Press as our publisher: especially notable among many who helped shepherd the book to press were our editor, Richard Ratzlaff, and copyeditor, Jane McWhinney. The cartographer Michael J. Fisher, formerly of the University of Alberta, integrated a great deal of complex historical data into three deceptively simple maps, with the gracious aid of Béla Nagy of the Hungarian Institute of Sciences, while Katalin Jalsovszky, former director of the archival photo department at the Hungarian National Museum, selected the powerful photographs that illuminate the text. Thank you, Rebecca Carter-Chand, for creating the index. Thanks too to the directors and archivists of the museums that house Ernő Munkácsi's archives, particularly Zsuzsanna Toronyi of the Hungarian Jewish Museum and Archives in Budapest, and Ron Lustig and Naomi Singer of the Memorial Museum of Hungarian Speaking Jewry in Safed, Israel. At the University of Toronto, Larry Alford, Jeffrey Kopstein, and Anna Shternshis were early supporters of this project. As was the late George Jonas.

Lara Santoro offered sage counsel from start to finish. My children, Lucas Munk Galarza and Sofia Munk Galarza, graciously endured countless breakfast, lunch, and dinner conversations about the Hungarian Holocaust. To Peter Soriano I owe more than I can express in words.

My deepest gratitude goes to my remarkable father, Peter Munk, who died on 28 March 2018, as this book was being prepared to go to press. Were it not for him, this book would not exist.

Nina Munk

Bergen-Belsen

Ravensbrück

Hanover

Sachsenhausen

Berlin

Mittelbau

German Reich

Buchenwald

Dresden

Gross Rose

Frankfurt

Theresienstadt

Prague

Flossenbürg

Nuremberg

Protectorate of Bohemia & Moravia

Dachau

Munich

Mauthausen

Strasshof

Vienna

Bratislava

Switzerland

Liechtenstein

Győr

Szombathely

Lake B

Between 1938 and 1941, as a result of its alliance with Nazi Germany, Hungary regained about 40 percent of the territory it lost in the Trianon Peace Treaty of 1920. In the First Vienna Award, Hungary re-annexed from Czechoslovakia the southern strip of Slovakia. Then it occupied Subcarpathia and a strip of Eastern Slovakia. Next, in the Second Vienna Award, Hungary took back Northern Transylvania from Romania. Finally, in joining the Nazi invasion of Yugoslavia, Hungary annexed the Délvidék territories (Southern Province).

4

Zagreb

Italy

Abbazia

Croatia

Adriatic Sea

Central Europe, 1944

□   major extermination camp

⊙   concentration camp

---   borders of annexed territories

    territories annexed by Hungary, 1938–41

0   100   200 kilometres

Chełmno
(Kulmhof) □

Treblinka □

Warsaw

Sobibór □

Lublin-Majdanek ⊙

Reichskommissariat
Ukraine

schwitz-
Birkenau □

Bełżec □

Generalgouvernement

Kraków-Płaszów ⊙

Tarnopol ○

Slovakia

Kamenets-Podolsk

Kassa

Ungvár
Munkács

2

Kőrösmező ○

Cernăuți ○

1

Miskolc ○

Budapest ○

Debrecen ○

Székesfehérvár ○

3

Kecskemét ○

Nagyvárad ○

Piatra Neamț ○

Kolozsvár ○

Marosvásárhely ○

Szeged ○

s

4

1   First Vienna Award, 1938
2   Subcarpathia, 1939
3   Second Vienna Award, 1940
4   Délvidék (Southern Province), 1941

Romania

Serbia

Michael J. Fisher, cartographer

In just fifty-six days, between 15 May and 9 July 1944, the Germans and their Hungarian collaborators worked together to transport approximately 437,000 Jewish men, women, and children from Hungary to Auschwitz-Birkenau, where the vast majority were murdered on arrival. To facilitate efficient transports, Hungary was divided into six zones, with the first of 147 trains leaving from Munkács in Zone I.

Generalgouvernement

Ungvár
Munkács
Ökörmező
Sátoraljaújhely
I
Huszt
Kőrösmező
Beregszász
Szeklence
Kisvárda
Száldobos
Nyíregyháza
Mátészalka
Nagyszőlős
Técső
Aknaszlatina
Nagykálló
Máramarossziget
Szatmárnémeti
Felsővisó
brecen
Nagybánya
Szilágysomlyó
Dés
II
Beszterce
Nagyvárad
Szamosújvar
Szászrégen
Kolozsvár
Marosvásárhely

Romania

Sepsiszentgyörgy

Deportations from Hungary, 1944

Number of people deported

30,000
20,000
10,000
5,000

▫ major ghetto or collection camp

⊙ concentration camp

II deportation zone

--- deportation zone border

▨ territories annexed, 1938–41

0   100   200 kilometres

Michael J. Fisher, cartographer

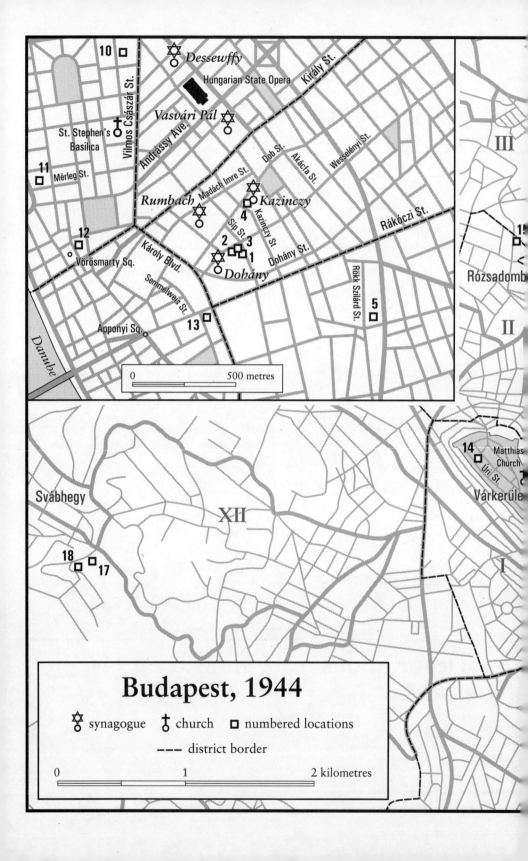

Budapest, 1944

✡ synagogue   ✝ church   □ numbered locations

--- district border

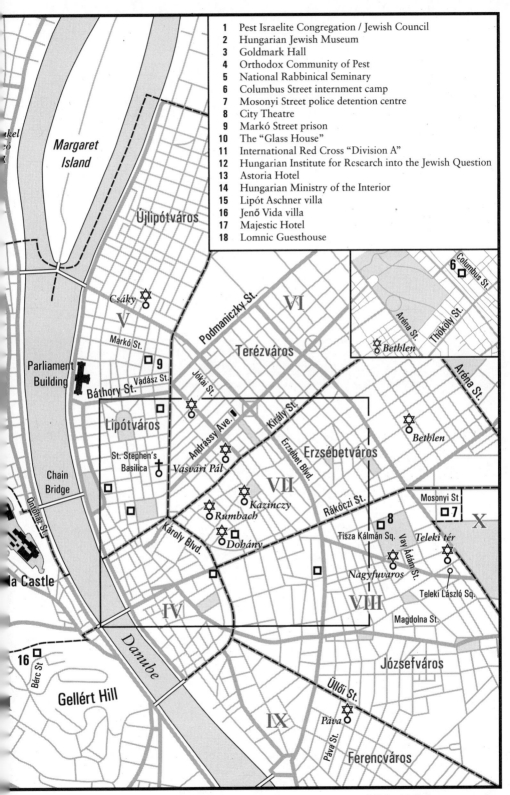

1. Pest Israelite Congregation / Jewish Council
2. Hungarian Jewish Museum
3. Goldmark Hall
4. Orthodox Community of Pest
5. National Rabbinical Seminary
6. Columbus Street internment camp
7. Mosonyi Street police detention centre
8. City Theatre
9. Markó Street prison
10. The "Glass House"
11. International Red Cross "Division A"
12. Hungarian Institute for Research into the Jewish Question
13. Astoria Hotel
14. Hungarian Ministry of the Interior
15. Lipót Aschner villa
16. Jenő Vida villa
17. Majestic Hotel
18. Lomnic Guesthouse

Margaret Island

Újlipótváros

Parliament Building

Csáky

V

Márkó St.

9

Vadász St.

Báthory St.

Podmaniczky St.

VI

Terézváros

Jókai St.

Lipótváros

Andrássy Ave.

Király St.

Erzsébet Blvd.

Erzsébetváros

Columbus St.

6

Aréna St.

Thököly St.

Bethlen

Aréna St.

Bethlen

St. Stephen's Basilica

Vasvári Pál

Chain Bridge

Ontótiaz St.

Károly Blvd.

VII

Kazinczy

Rumbach

Dohány

Rákóczi St.

Mosonyi St

7

X

Tisza Kálmán Sq.

8

Vay Ádám St.

Teleki tér

Nagyfuvaros

Teleki László Sq.

VIII

Magdolna St.

Józsefváros

la Castle

IV

Danube

16

Bérc St.

Gellért Hill

IX

Üllői St.

Páva

Páva St.

Ferencváros

Michael J. Fisher, cartographer

The Excruciating Dilemmas of Ernő Munkácsi

Ferenc Laczó

A Brief Opening in the Aftermath of Genocide

In recent decades, the Holocaust has often been understood as an event that acquired its wider cultural and political significance only several decades after the war when the widespread silence that supposedly surrounded it at first was finally broken. According to this influential but misleading interpretation, survivors in the immediate aftermath of the Holocaust were unable to express their all too traumatic recent experiences, and the full scope and coherence of the Nazi program of extermination could not yet be grasped.

In fact, Jewish survivors were anything but silent during the early postwar period. In Hungary particularly, despite being preoccupied with the immensely difficult tasks of reorganization, repatriation, and relief, survivors produced a vast quantity and variety of intellectual responses to the Holocaust. These diverse materials from the country amount to one of the most impressive such corpuses on the continent, directly comparable to those created in Poland and France, European countries widely viewed as having been at the forefront of Holocaust documentation and scholarship in the immediate postwar years. During the short few years between their liberation from Nazi German rule in 1945 and the Stalinization of their country in the late 1940s, Hungarian Jewish survivors recorded thousands of eyewitness accounts of the Nazi genocide, published dozens of detailed memoirs, and even managed to complete several precious works of contemporary history.[1] Adding to this vast library are hundreds of thousands of pages of transcripts from Hungary's so-called People's Courts, established in 1945 to try war criminals (*háborús és népellenes bűnök*).[2] Indeed, so great was the volume of early memoir literature by Jewish survivors that the Holocaust historian David Cesarani has insisted, in a supremely ironic manner, that "if anything, they succeeded too well, too soon," by which he alluded to the wider public's indifference to the topic.[3] Likewise, in her ground-breaking

2012 monograph, *Collect and Record!*, Laura Jockusch not only reveals the extent of early Holocaust documentation by survivors in postwar Europe but makes evident the degree to which these works have been ignored. Her goal, she writes, is to retrieve these chronicles and testimonies from oblivion and "establish their rightful place as the foundation stone for later historical writing on the Holocaust."[4]

Given this context, the appearance in English of one of the most valuable and intriguing publications belonging to the first wave of intellectual responses from Hungary is especially welcome. Seven decades after its original release in Hungarian, the English-language edition of Ernő Munkácsi's *Hogyan történt?* (*How It Happened*) finally enables wide international access to the excruciating dilemmas of interpretation that confronted the surviving chief secretary of the Hungarian Central Jewish Council upon liberation. How to continue identifying as a Hungarian Jew in the aftermath of a genocide co-perpetrated by agents of the Hungarian state? How to explain the murder of more than 400,000 Jews from wartime Hungary without censuring the nation's Jewish leaders during the war? How to rationalize the strategy adopted by the Jewish Council, or Judenrat, in 1944 without implying a connection between their choices and the devastating outcomes of the war years? While enabling profound insights into such painful dilemmas of a key witness, *How It Happened* also offers one of the earliest document-based, if far from uncontroversial, narratives on the history of the Holocaust in Hungary.

The Exceptional Drama of the Holocaust in Hungary

By 19 March 1944, when Nazi Germany invaded its ally Hungary, the Jewish community of Hungary had been persecuted for years. Already in 1920, the passage of the so-called *numerus clausus* law had sharply discriminated against Jews applying to Hungary's universities. Then, step by step beginning in 1938, Hungary annulled the legal equality of its Jewish citizens, pursued an official program of ever more severe socioeconomic exclusion, and, in 1941, adopted Nazi-style laws on "racial protection."[5] As early as 1941, agents of the Hungarian state helped implement the genocide against European Jewry by deporting nearly twenty thousand Jews from Hungary's recently annexed territory of Subcarpathia to the collection camp of Kőrösmező (now Yasinia, Ukraine) where, handed off to the Germans, most of them were murdered *en masse* in Kamenets-Podolsk before the end of the summer. Members of the Hungarian military were

Fig. 3   Taken in 1941, when Jews elsewhere in Europe were being rounded up, herded into ghettos, and deported, this photograph is notable for its ordinariness, reflecting the comparatively unperturbed life of most Jews in Hungary at the time. The girls, members of Budapest's Neolog Jewish high school gymnastics team, are carefully styled, their coiffed hair rolled and pinned. They gaze at a copy of *Magyar Iparművészet* (Hungarian Handicrafts) magazine. Although we don't know anything else about these girls, their names were noted on the back: Olga Klein, Klára Pfeifer, Eta Strasser, Éva Weisz, Edit Bartos, Lea Neumann, Gizella Bara, Éva Kaufmann, Éva Weisz, Klára Kós, Judit Bán.

involved as auxiliary forces on the Eastern Front where, on occasion, they participated in the mass shooting of Jews. There was the infamous massacre in the Hungarian-annexed parts of Vajdaság (now Vojvodina, Serbia) in early 1942, which was partly directed against Jews. Last but certainly not least, tens of thousands of Jewish men, forced by the Hungarian government into so-called labour service on the Eastern Front, perished between 1941 and early 1944 under the brutal conditions.[6]

Despite all this, the Jewish community of Hungary was still largely intact in early 1944. The Jewish community of Budapest, most of whom belonged to the Neolog branch of Hungarian Judaism, still numbered around 200,000, making it not only the single largest metropolitan Jewish community in the Nazi sphere of influence, but also the last still relatively free.[7] Another 500,000, mostly Orthodox Jews, were also living under Hungarian rule, the majority in territories such as Subcarpathia and the northern half of Transylvania, re-annexed by Hungary in 1939 and 1940, respectively.

By this time, members of the Hungarian Jewish community and intellectual elites, of whom Ernő Munkácsi was an eminent representative, were largely aware of the catastrophe that had befallen European Jewry, even if they remained unfamiliar with its precise details. In any case, members of these elite groups tended to be conscious of their own exceptional, and exceptionally precarious, situation. In the winter months of 1943–44, they were frightened of what the near future might bring but cherished reasonable hope that Nazi Germany would soon be defeated. However, upon Germany's invasion of Hungary on 19 March 1944, the approaching end of the war was to prove fatally distant.

The exact causes of the Holocaust in Hungary remain a bone of contention among historians.[8] What is agreed by all parties is that, as a result of the Nazis' accumulated expertise in genocide and the proactive collaboration of the Hungarian authorities under Regent Miklós Horthy and Prime Minister Döme Sztójay, this last major Jewish community under the aegis of the Nazis was mercilessly targeted.[9] In the very last year of the Second World War, between 15 May and 9 July 1944, Germans and their Hungarian collaborators deported approximately 437,000 Hungarian Jews from areas outside Budapest, most of whom were murdered at the death camp of Auschwitz-Birkenau.[10] Hungarian Jews were the single-largest group of victims at Auschwitz-Birkenau. Several hundreds of thousands of Hungarian Jews were murdered in a host of other locations.

The wartime experiences of Budapest Jews, including Ernő Munkácsi, significantly diverged from that of their fellow Jews elsewhere in the country. While Jews living outside Budapest were almost without exception deported in the months of May to July 1944, the Jews of Budapest, though forced to wear the yellow star, relinquish their livelihoods and liberties, and move into specially designated buildings (so-called Yellow-Star Houses), were spared deportation. Upon the Hungarian fascist Arrow Cross's takeover in mid-October 1944, however, the situation of Budapest Jewry drastically worsened. It was upon this takeover that Budapest Jews were concentrated in two overcrowded and undersupplied ghettos in the centre of Pest. Fascist thugs shot thousands of the city's Jewish men, women, and children, often in the icy Danube, deported tens of thousands of others to various Nazi camps, and forced still others on death marches. Around 100,000 people,

Fig. 4 Hungarian Jews were culturally and socially diverse. In the early twentieth century, most Jews in Budapest belonged to the Neolog branch of Judaism, which promoted modernization; many were acculturated or even secular. In the provinces, however, most Jewish communities were Orthodox. In Makó, a town in southeastern Hungary where this photo was taken in 1922, about two-thirds of the 2,800 Jews belonged to the Orthodox community. The style of this Orthodox woman and her eight children – her headscarf and modest dress, the boys' hats and side-locks – stands in sharp contrast to that of the Budapest girls' gymnastics team (Fig. 3, xxv). The photographer, Nándor Homonnai, who was Jewish, was renowned in Makó. His studio was active from 1904 to 1936.

approximately every second member of Budapest Jewry, were murdered in a matter of months. Yet the survival rate of Jews from the capital city remained notably higher than that of Jews from the rest of Hungary.

The experience of Budapest's Jews aside, it was the brutal, but also brutally efficient, campaign of murder against Jews from the Hungarian provinces in the spring and summer of 1944, at a time when the unprecedented crimes of the Nazis were already rather widely publicized, that significantly contributed to making the name Auschwitz a synonym of the Nazi genocide. However, this *pars pro toto* does not mean that Auschwitz has been widely identified as the capital of the Holocaust of Hungarian Jewry.[11] Nor did it make the Holocaust in Hungary into an international research priority for historians.

For several decades in the postwar period, the exact opposite was the case: the Holocaust in Hungary remained a rarely and superficially analyzed subject. Only in recent decades have international scholars started to discuss the immense drama and unprecedented tragedy of Hungarian Jews during the Second World War in more substantial ways.

On Responsibilities, Accusations, and Defences

In early postwar Hungary, the most controversial questions were directed at the Hungarian authorities who were in charge during the critical spring and summer months of 1944, when approximately 437,000 Jews were deported from Hungary. If the Hungarian authorities knew about the persecution of Jews by Nazi Germany but did not know of their annihilation, if they were ignorant of the terrible consequences of their deeds, as their apologists maintained, then they were not knowingly complicit in the mass murder of Hungary's Jews when organizing their deportations. However, if the Hungarian authorities had even a basic knowledge of the Nazi program of annihilation by 1944, and many of their representatives certainly had ample opportunities to gain such knowledge, then their actions in 1944 amounted to a conscious co-perpetration of genocide. In other words, assessing awareness and intention is essential in judging the Hungarian state's level of responsibility.

To judge the actions of the Hungarian Central Jewish Council in 1944 is something else altogether. Nevertheless, in attempting to assess their behaviour, the Council members' awareness at the time of the deportations and the choices they made emerge as key issues. In fact, few issues were more passionately contested among Hungarian Jewish survivors right after the war; few are more extensively discussed in Ernő Munkácsi's book. The fatal "choiceless choices" made by the Jewish Council during the Holocaust fuelled extreme bitterness among numerous survivors and led to accusations of an utter failure of leadership.[12]

In Hungary, during the spring and summer of 1944, the Nazis and their Hungarian allies established approximately 150 *Judenräte*, or Jewish councils. As in other countries occupied by the Nazis, these councils functioned essentially as administrative bodies responsible for the internal affairs of persecuted Jews. Any official contact between the Hungarian or German authorities and the country's Jews had to pass through the councils, whose job overwhelmingly involved the implementation and enforcement of ever-more restrictive measures against the Jewish population. Due to the swift

Fig. 5   Marking the opening of the Hungarian Jewish Museum's new building in Budapest in 1932, leaders of the Pest Israelite Congregation gather here in the state room of their headquarters at 12 Síp Street. Standing to the right of the speaker are Ernő Munkácsi, director of the museum; Samu Stern (1874–1947), president of the Pest Congregation; and Arnold Kiss (1869–1940), the celebrated chief rabbi of Buda and a poet. To the speaker's left is Simon Hevesi (1868–1943), noted scholar and chief rabbi of the Dohány Street Synagogue.

deportation of Jews (including members of the councils) from Hungary's provinces, the many Jewish councils outside Budapest typically ceased functioning within a few weeks. By contrast, the Budapest-based Hungarian Central Jewish Council – in theory, a national body, but one whose sphere of authority was in practice restricted to the capital city – continued to act for nine long months, from its formation on 20 March 1944, all the way until the liberation of the remaining Jews of Budapest in January 1945.

The Hungarian Central Jewish Council was founded on the order of Adolf Eichmann's special operations unit, Sondereinsatzkommando Eichmann, almost immediately after the Nazi Germans entered Budapest. The Eichmann commando did not appoint specific individuals to the Council; however, to give the administrative body a veneer of legitimacy, it insisted on the participation of community leaders, well-respected Jews drawn not only from the populous Neolog and Orthodox communities, but also Zionists and, later and to a lesser extent, Jewish converts to Christianity.[13] For the duration of the war, the Council went through various phases, operating under different names, adding new personnel, and shifting mandates, but always functioning more or less in accordance with its initial mandate.[14] Whereas certain members of the Council engaged in underground resistance activities, the chief strategy of the Council (as Munkácsi's book makes abundantly clear) consisted of compliance and petitioning.[15]

Viewed by some as little more than a government mouthpiece at the time of the genocide, members of the Budapest-based Council, nearly all of whom survived the war, were subsequently accused of having betrayed their own people.[16] The central charge was that by obeying orders from above instead of attempting to resist, they effectively served as accomplices of the *génocidaires*. A key point in the fierce accusation was that Council members failed to alert the Jewish masses to the gravest threats on the horizon and thereby "lulled them into submission."

On an emotional level, it may be relatively easy to comprehend these accusations and the desperate attempts that survivors – most of whom had just lost many of their closest relatives – made to scapegoat their own wartime leadership. With greater temporal distance, it might also be easier to acknowledge that members of the Council made politically and morally problematic choices because they had no alternatives; it was impossible for them to make good decisions. Historical research has also revealed that, no matter what choices were made by various Jewish councils across Europe, or even by different members of the same Council, those choices tended to make hardly any difference with respect to the devastating outcomes.[17]

As Susan Papp's biographical overview in this volume explains, Ernő Munkácsi (1896–1950), a son of the famed linguist and ethnographer Bernát Munkácsi, was a lawyer by profession and a highly reputed member of the Hungarian Jewish elite who, in the years leading up to the Second World War, served as chief secretary and chief legal counsel of the Israelite (Neolog) Congregation of Pest (numbering about 200,000 souls), and also as de facto director of the Hungarian Jewish Museum. In the spring of 1944, when the Germans entered Hungary, Munkácsi, along with other leaders of the Congregation of Pest, joined the Central Jewish Council as a senior officer, lending the appearance, as desired by the Nazis, of a continuous control of Jewish affairs by Hungary's Jewish elite. He carried on his work for the community as chief secretary, though now of the Jewish Council under radically changed circumstances – a role he was to exercise until the Arrow Cross takeover in mid-October 1944 when he was forced into hiding.

How It Happened covers precisely those decisive months of the Holocaust in Hungary which Munkácsi observed from his special vantage point and tried to shape, albeit marginally. Notably, Munkácsi also fulfilled important functions in the early postwar community of survivors at the time he was writing his book: having survived the last stages of the war hidden by a Gentile family just outside Budapest, he re-emerged as the executive director of the National Office of Hungarian Israelites, a position he held until his death in 1950.

Ernő Munkácsi was not among the Jewish Council's most important members, the strategy of the Council shaped, above all, by Chairman Samu Stern and his two deputies, Ernő Pető and Károly Wilhelm. Nor was he nearly as controversial as Béla Berend, the rabbi of Szigetvár, who would be accused of proactive collaboration with the *génocidaires*. Munkácsi nonetheless had to confront the various charges raised against members of the Council chiefly by their Zionist critics and also by Hungarian courts. In July 1945 the Hungarian Zionist Alliance, led by leftists long opposed to the Neolog Jewish leadership, organized a symbolic trial of the Council during which its former members were directly blamed not only for the lack of significant Hungarian Jewish resistance but even for the effective implementation of the Nazi policies. Specifically, the charges included collaboration with the occupier, betrayal of the masses, and unjust enrichment – harsh accusations that were rearticulated by Hannah Arendt in *Eichmann in Jerusalem*.[18] On the basis of these charges, Ernő Munkácsi was twice forced to defend his wartime activities before certification committees for lawyers. Several other members of the Central Jewish Council were even arrested and forced to defend themselves before the People's Courts. Even though the charges could not be legally substantiated, and were eventually dropped, the reputation of the Council was clearly damaged.

Like several other former members, Munkácsi must have felt an acute need to explicate and defend the Council's controversial choices and policies. In 1946 he decided to publish in the Jewish weekly *Új Élet* his account of several key events that took place between 19 March and 16 October 1944, which he then expanded into a book-length publication under the deceptively simple title *How It Happened: Documenting the Tragedy of Hungarian Jewry*. This account, published in 1947, did not purport to be a systematic history of the months of March to October 1944; nor did it aspire to formulate a final assessment of the various choices made during the Holocaust. *How It Happened* was intended rather as a first exploration of the Holocaust in

Fig. 6   From the salon in the villa of Jenő Vida (born Weil), one of Hungary's leading
industrialists and art collectors, the view over the Danube encompasses Buda Castle, the
Chain Bridge, and the central dome of Hungary's Parliament Building. Designed by the
architect Béla Málnai and completed in 1929–30, Vida's villa at 13–15 Bérc Street, in the
affluent residential area of Gellért Hill, was one of many private homes seized by the Nazis
in 1944, in this case for the personal use of SS-Obergruppenführer Otto Winkelmann,
head of the SS and police forces (*Höherer SS und Polizeiführer*) in Hungary. In addition to
running the Hungarian General Coal Mining Co., Vida (1872–1945) was a member of the
Upper House of Parliament, a leader of the Pest Israelite Congregation, and part of Regent
Horthy's inner circle. In 1936 Horthy awarded Vida the Hungarian Order of Merit for
his contributions to the nation. On 21 March 1944, two days after Nazi Germany invaded
Hungary, Vida and his family were arrested in their villa, imprisoned at Kistarcsa, then
deported to Auschwitz-Birkenau. Vida died in Auschwitz in 1945. His wife, Klára
(1878–1961), and their children survived the war, later emigrating to South America.

Hungary (*avant la lettre*) based on plentiful original documents. The book
was also clearly meant to depict the Hungarian Jewish leadership in an
apologetic manner and offer the definitive vindication of its author.

Munkácsi's book thus belongs among the key historical documents that
provide an insider's perspective on the operation of Jewish councils during
the Second World War. Arguably, the most famous of these sources is the diary
kept by Adam Czerniakow, head of the Warsaw Ghetto Jewish Council, for

nearly three years, until his suicide in 1942.[19] The devastating drama unfolding on the pages of Munkácsi's book is closely comparable to that of the Warsaw ghetto as observed by Czerniakow. Another major contemporaneous source on Jewish councils is the recently released collection of (unsent) letters written by the secretary of the Jewish Council in Amsterdam, Mirjam Bolle (then Mirjam Levie), to her fiancé in Eretz Israel during the deportation of Jews from the Netherlands.[20] Munkácsi's perspective might be usefully compared to that of Bolle, since they were in a similar position as intimate observers, as insiders without power. What distinguishes Munkácsi's *How It Happened* from such documents, however, is that he conveys a strong sense of immediacy even while offering a retrospective interpretation of events.

Whereas much of mainstream Holocaust history has focused primarily on exploring the organizations, motives, and actions of Nazi perpetrators, in *How It Happened* we may already discern the beginnings of the major alternative stream in history writing concerned primarily with the experiences and perspectives of the persecuted. Munkácsi eagerly asserts that "the true protagonist of the tragedy of 1944 is the Jewish people."[21] Accordingly, while *How It Happened* does portray practically all the key perpetrators of the Holocaust in Hungary, the book is based primarily on documents of Jewish provenance, mostly from the archives of the National Office of Hungarian Israelites and including the Council's key documents from 1944 (many of which Munkácsi helped write, but only some of which remained available to him).[22]

Ernő Munkácsi adds several insights from personal experience, though without discussing his own role in great depth. The author himself states that "The present work does not primarily draw on personal experience so much as on contemporaneous documents."[23] Munkácsi's choice to depersonalize his narrative clearly differs from those made by other former Council members who published their recollections, including the most important among them, that of former president Samu Stern.[24] *How It Happened* thus belongs to a somewhat unusual, mixed genre; supported by ample documentation and offering some personal recollections, it almost refuses to use the first-person singular.

As the reader will see, one of the few points in the text where Munkácsi highlights his own role relates to the preparation in June 1944 of an underground pamphlet titled "An Appeal to Christian Society." The case provides strong evidence that Munkácsi was not always deferential to the dominant and ultimately futile, if not downright counterproductive, strategy of the

Council. In his own assessment, if the pamphlet had been released and promoted by the Council, it would have led to a wider resistance movement. However, Samu Stern decided against issuing the pamphlet; instead, the Council submitted an appeal directly to Prime Minister Döme Sztójay, who, notably, was one of the key perpetrators of the very crimes from which the appeal sought protection. At considerable personal risk, Munkácsi and others working in various departments of the Council's Síp Street headquarters nonetheless clandestinely circulated the original pamphlet. As he pointedly notes, he was among those subsequently interrogated by the police about the attempted act of resistance, an investigation that fortunately had no severe personal consequences.

The various ways in which survivors aimed to create distance between themselves and their recent experiences constitute an important and intriguing subject. Some preferred to develop a seemingly fully detached account, which – despite their nominal intentions – often gave expression to their profound existential concern with the subject. Conversely, early postwar memoirs, which purported to recollect personal tribulations in a mostly subjective mode, almost regularly reverted to the third-person singular when referring to their author's most horrific experiences and also frequently employed other techniques of distancing painful experiences, such as irony and sarcasm.

Munkácsi has done something similarly ambivalent on the pages of *How It Happened.* He writes from the position of an insider, offering unparalleled access to key personalities and scenes of frightening drama, but with little explicit eyewitness account. Even more than some of the early Hungarian Jewish researchers of the Holocaust (some of whose key representatives will be introduced below), Munkácsi tries to view his subjective experiences from an objective perspective. There are strong personal reasons behind his choice in favour of objectivity: it would seem that Munkácsi essentially wanted to justify the Jewish Council's overall role, and thereby also his own behaviour, and believed that writing from a seemingly detached perspective would best achieve that goal.

The Interpretive Choices of a Key Witness

The explicit aim of *How It Happened* is to "commit to paper certain episodes" of the "most sinister crimes of universal history"[25] during what Munkácsi labels the time of "the German occupation" of Hungary.[26]

Munkácsi launches his narrative by enumerating the internal causes of Hungarian Jewry's eventual destruction, such as the nineteenth-century religious schism, the "naïve optimism" that its elite supposedly maintained even in the early 1940s, and also the detachment of this elite from the masses and their resulting impotence in the face of the genocidal onslaught.

While elaborating on the cunning methods employed by the already highly experienced German *génocidaires*, Munkácsi conveniently ascribes the controversial decisions the Jewish Council took in 1944 – the key decisions not to alert the Jewish masses of the grave threats and, more generally, not to attempt more courageous acts of resistance – to their ignorance, naïveté, and lack of foresight. Munkácsi also maintains that, even if the Council had acted differently, the outcome would not have been any different. Employing his formidable skills as a lawyer, Munkácsi thus carefully builds a case acknowledging poor judgment on the part of the Council members while categorically denying their guilt. In a shrewd but controversial manner, *How It Happened* undercuts the heaviest accusations raised against the Hungarian Jewish leadership, just as it paints a highly critical portrait of the Hungarian Jewish community as a whole: Munkácsi repeatedly implies that the paucity of resistance reveals how unhealthy the community had become.

To explicate the basic strategic choices of the Council and thereby clear its reputation, Munkácsi provides several additional arguments. Significant parts of *How It Happened* are in fact devoted to exposing how the Jewish Council tried to rescue the Jewish people through a defensive strategy combining compliance with petitioning. Munkácsi presents the Council's petitioning of the authorities as proof of its good intentions. He portrays compliance, which admittedly entailed "maintaining communications" with the Germans and taking pains "to minimize any friction,"[27] as a consistent choice of a lesser evil.

In this regard, the basic strategy of the Budapest-based Council might be compared with that employed by Chaim Rumkowski, the controversial head of the Jewish Council in the Litzmannstadt (now Łódź, Poland) ghetto. Rumkowski believed that compliance and productivity provided the keys to the survival of the largest possible segment of Jewry under Nazi occupation. Over the years, many aspects of Rumkowski's ruthless leadership have been harshly criticized; he has been decried by survivors and historians alike as a collaborator and even a traitor. Recently, however, scholars of the Holocaust have grown more sensitive to the fact that he lacked morally sound alternatives and was forced to make unacceptable bargains, but that

Fig. 7   One of the first Jewish ghettos in Hungary was established on 18 April 1944 in
the town of Munkács (today Mukačevo, Ukraine), where nearly half the population was
Jewish. Herded into the ghetto with less than a day's notice, the town's approximately
13,000 Jews endured horrific conditions, with food and drinking water in short supply and
sanitation non-existent. On their first Sabbath in the ghetto, known as "Black Saturday,"
Orthodox men and boys were forced by Hungarian gendarmes to tear apart the interior
of their synagogue and scrub the floor with their *tallitot* (prayer shawls), after which they
were beaten and in some cases shot. On May 14 the first deportation train left Munkács
for Auschwitz-Birkenau. The last deportation train left on May 24, marking the end of
Munkács's Jewish community. The bilingual sign at the entrance to the ghetto reads,
"Warning! Area populated by Jews."

his "choiceless choices" had their own rationale. Rumkowski's controversial
strategies allowed the Litzmannstadt ghetto to survive longer than any other
Jewish ghetto in Eastern Europe, but ultimately the ghetto and its inhabitants
were liquidated too. Upon his deportation to Auschwitz-Birkenau in August
1944, Rumkowski himself appears to have been murdered by fellow Jews in
retaliation for his choices and policies.[28]

If compliance and productivity formed the combination favoured by
Rumkowski in Litzmannstadt, compliance and petitioning became the key
strategy employed by the Central Jewish Council in Budapest. In Munkácsi's
depiction, however, this choice constituted only one of seven possible
strategies. There was also the path pursued by the Zionists who, according to
Munkácsi's retrospective valuation, had the most realistic assessment of the

Fig. 8 Sándor and Berta Guttman and their nine children in Budapest in 1944, with the yellow star sewn on their coats. Designed to visually stigmatize and separate Jews, Prime Minister's Decree No. 1240/1944 on the "distinguishing mark of the Jews" required all Jews over the age of six to wear "a canary-yellow, six-pointed star at least 10 × 10 centimetres in diameter ... affixed to an easily visible place over the left breast of their outer garments." The Guttman family survived the war in Budapest. They were originally from Ungvár (today Užhorod, Ukraine), a town whose entire Jewish population was deported to Auschwitz-Birkenau in May 1944. Thanks to the diplomat Raoul Wallenberg, they were issued a certificate of protection from the Swedish legation and sheltered in a building protected by the neutral diplomatic missions.

situation, had the best contacts abroad, and were the most daring; indeed, Hungarian Zionists, notably the de facto leader of the Aid and Rescue Committee, Rezső Kasztner (AKA Rudolf Kastner), were at the forefront of rescue missions. Three further options consisted of investing hope in the possibility that the Christian churches, the Hungarian Ministry of Defence, or one of the neutral foreign powers still represented in Budapest, primarily Switzerland and Sweden, would rescue Hungary's Jews. As Munkácsi does not fail to note, some controversial Jewish individuals, notably Council member Rabbi Béla Berend from Szigetvár, supported the collaborationist policy of "Jewish emigration." However, in the author's final assessment, the best means of saving Hungarian Jewry would have been a seventh option: mobilizing the Hungarian Left and the independent-minded members of the Christian middle classes to defy the persecution of Jews.

The book further explains that there were four main stages in the evolution of the Jewish Council's behaviour. Munkácsi argues that the first six weeks of the German occupation were characterized by a high degree of Jewish "inactivity," thereby partially accepting the charge of passivity. He insists, however, that regular interactions with the Hungarian authorities were pursued again during the months of May and June – which, though he fails to mention this, coincided with the main period of the deportations. According to *How It Happened*, this second period ended in early July and was followed by a phase lasting until the Arrow Cross takeover in mid-October 1944, a period shaped by the halting of the deportations just before the Jews of Budapest were scheduled to be herded onto the trains to Auschwitz. As Munkácsi argues, these months saw the gradual withering of the Jewish Council's authority; Jews desperate for help increasingly turned away from the Council's headquarters at 12 Síp Street and invested their flickering hopes in the embassies of neutral countries, in Carl Lutz's and Raoul Wallenberg's protective "Schutz-passes," and in the International Red Cross.[29]

As the reader will notice, a key point in the book's narrative is the arrival of the Auschwitz Protocols in Hungary.[30] Compiled in late April 1944 by Rudolf Vrba and Alfred Wetzler, prisoners who had escaped from Auschwitz earlier that month, the Protocols was a forty-page eyewitness account that exposed to a greater extent than ever before the full horrors of the Auschwitz-Birkenau camp complex. The report not only attempted to quantify the number of people imprisoned and murdered in Auschwitz but offered one of the earliest detailed descriptions of the gas chambers, explained exactly how prisoners were sent to their deaths, and included sketches marking the layout of the gas chambers and crematoria. After being translated from Slovak into German almost instantaneously by Oscar Krasniansky, a member of the Slovak Jewish Council, the Auschwitz Protocols was quickly smuggled to Budapest, translated into Hungarian by Mária Székely,[31] and circulated to a select few.

What remains highly contested even today is how quickly the Auschwitz Protocols made it to Hungary, and who received it on what date. It is widely acknowledged that the Protocols was translated into Hungarian before mid-May, when the mass deportations of Hungarian Jews began. It is also clear that in Hungary copies of the document were distributed in narrow circles during the first weeks of the deportations. On the side of the persecuted, there is evidence that Hungarian Zionist leaders, including Rezső Kasztner and Ottó Komoly, had early access to it. It also appears highly probable that, by mid-May, at least some members of the Jewish Council, including Fülöp Freudiger and Ernő Pető, either had received copies or had been briefed on its contents.

The morally and emotionally charged question is why those (and again, this probably includes several members of the Council) with access to the Auschwitz Protocols did not do more to publicize Vrba and Wetzler's eye-witness account of the atrocities. Of all the many excruciatingly difficult decisions made by the Hungarian Jewish Council, the decision to suppress or not broadcast the Auschwitz Protocols is widely considered the least comprehensible and least defensible. Arguably, however, this controversial decision fully conformed to a chief aim of the Council: to avoid mass panic. This fact might not make the decision more defensible – it was a misguided decision that proved fatal – but it makes it somewhat more comprehensible.

In *How It Happened*, Ernő Munkácsi audaciously argues that the Auschwitz Protocols belatedly dissolved the "ruinous, unfounded optimism" of Hungarian Jews: "Incredible as it may seem today, it is a telling fact of history that, before the second half of May 1944, Hungarian Jewry had had no idea of the horrors of the extermination camps or the details of the deportations."[32] *How It Happened* states that "Nobody had any inkling ... that this work of 'reorganization' ... would mean the ghettoization, deportation, and ultimate extermination of the Jews in the provinces."[33] Munkácsi thus defends the improbable thesis that, until the mass deportation of hundreds of thousands from Hungary from May to July 1944, even the members of the Central Council had been largely ignorant of the ongoing Nazi genocide.

It is true that in Hungary, as elsewhere, news of atrocities committed by the Germans against Jews was met with widespread disbelief. And yet, the

Fig. 9 On 15 June 1944, in the town of Dunaszerdahely (now Dunajská Streda, Slovakia), Jewish residents wearing threadbare coats and carrying bundles board a deportation train for Auschwitz-Birkenau. Designed to carry forty soldiers or six horses, cattle cars heading for Auschwitz were typically crammed with seventy or eighty people, many of whom were dead on arrival. Even before the Nazi occupation, the once-thriving Jewish community of Dunaszerdahely, located in territory annexed from Czechoslovakia under the First Vienna Award of 1938, was badly persecuted by the Hungarian state. Dunaszerdahely's Jewish men were conscripted into the labour service and forced to work under brutal conditions on the Eastern Front. In 1941 those with "unsettled citizenship" were expelled to Kamenets-Podolsk where, with few exceptions, they were murdered *en masse* by the SS. On the eve of the Second World War, Jews comprised more than 40 percent of Dunaszerdahely's population; after the war, only a handful returned.

Auschwitz Protocols of 1944 aside, there is little doubt that the Hungarian Jewish elites were largely aware of the ongoing mass murder almost as soon as it began in 1941. Even if we accept Munkácsi's timeline and allow that during the mass deportations of Jews from Hungary the Jewish Council knew little about Auschwitz and, more broadly, knew nothing about the Nazis' annihilation camps and gas chambers, they should still have suspected that the mass deportation would result in mass death. Munkácsi in fact revealingly remarks that in early 1944 Hungarian Jews were susceptible to "the kind of culpable optimism that made the Jews believe that, while all the Jews in Europe might perish, no harm could come to us in Hungary."[34]

"Culpable optimism" is indeed a fitting expression. However, it seems that the community elite, rather than the Jewish community as a whole, indulged in such optimism of the overly confident. It was the elite who knew significantly more about the devastation in the rest of Europe but continued to trust that they would survive if they remained loyal to the Hungarian authorities. By contrast, the occasional unfounded optimism of other community members could at most be called naïve.

The Ambiguities of Being a Hungarian Jew in the Aftermath of Genocide

Ernő Munkácsi's assessment of the causes and evolution of the Holocaust in Hungary is complex and nuanced, just as one would expect from a fine legal scholar, but in some respects it is profoundly ambivalent. *How It Happened* explicitly states that "the ghettoization in the provinces, the mushrooming of the ghettos, and the deportations proceeded at unprecedented breakneck speed" during the Holocaust in Hungary.[35] Munkácsi names as its central perpetrators "the proponents of German cultural supremacy," the Hungarian counter-revolutionaries, and "the right-wing Arrow Cross–ridden middle class of the Endre and Baky sort"[36] (referring to the high-ranking Hungarian antisemites László Endre and László Baky, undersecretaries of state for the Ministry of the Interior in 1944). Whereas it was widely maintained at the time of Adolf Eichmann's capture in Buenos Aires in 1960 that he was a Nazi *génocidaire* of "secondary significance," Munkácsi's book reveals that in Hungary Eichmann was immediately perceived as a key perpetrator. Specifically, the author argues that purging the countryside of Jews was the result of an agreement between Eichmann and Endre and their associates,[37] and that "the heinous crime of the extermination of the Hungarian Jewry in 1944 can be laid at the feet of four individuals: Adolf Eichmann, László Endre, László Baky, and the hands-on executioner László Ferenczy."[38]

How It Happened also raises the question as to whether the Germans could have executed the deportations without help from Hungarians. Munkácsi affirms in response that "there is plenty of conclusive evidence to prove that the deportation of Hungarian Jewry could not have been carried out except with the full cooperation of the Hungarian gendarmerie."[39] This assessment is in full accordance with historical scholarship, but remains to be more widely accepted in Hungarian society even after more than seven decades.

Fig. 10   In the town of Hajdúnánás, in Hungary's eastern plains, local residents are seen ransacking bed linens, kitchenware, tools, a spice chest, and whatever other few possessions remained in the ghetto after 17 June, when the town's entire Jewish population was transferred to a larger ghetto in the Serly brickyards outside Debrecen. A few days later, the Jews of Hajdúnánás were deported, most to the gas chambers of Auschwitz-Birkenau, but some to Strasshof, Austria, where they worked as slave labourers for Organisation Todt, the Nazi's military engineering consortium. Hajdúnánás's once-imposing synagogue, seen at the right, was destroyed in the 1960s.

How It Happened develops an alternative interpretation, however. Ernő Munkácsi wants to reassure his readers that the government's proclamation of 20 March 1944, in which the Jews were commanded to obey the Germans, "had to be seen as neither conclusive nor genuine, nor representative of the position of every Hungarian authority and every actor in public affairs."[40] Munkácsi thereby backs the counter-factual argument that if those who looked to "the mercy of the Germans for saving Hungarian Jewry" could have been brought to their senses, "the Hungarian authorities, bearing the support of the clear-headed part of Hungarian society, could have defied the deportations."[41]

Whereas Munkácsi is critical of the Jewish community while exonerating its leadership, he condemns the chief Hungarian *génocidaires* and depicts them as unrepresentative of Hungarians in general. Right after the war, anti-fascists condemned fascism and its unprecedented crimes, but also tended to trivialize the popular support that fascist movements and regimes had just enjoyed. According to the emerging consensus, the Hungarian masses were not to be held responsible for crimes committed against Jews because they had been innately opposed to the "reactionary" pre-1945 regimes led by Miklós Horthy and Ferenc Szálasi. Overlooking the broad participation of representatives of the Hungarian state and members of Hungarian society in the persecution of Hungarian Jews might thus be viewed as the price Munkácsi pays to accommodate postwar Hungary's programmatic but intellectually timid rejection of fascism. However, intent on maintaining his Hungarian Jewish identity in the aftermath of the Holocaust, Munkácsi appears to have been very much willing to pay this price.

While *How It Happened* acknowledges the Hungarian wartime leadership's share of political responsibility for the genocide, Munkácsi continues to insist on the "community of fate" (*sorsközösség*), the intertwined trajectory of the Jews of Hungary and their country. Indeed, the book depicts the last year of the Second World War as a shared tragedy; the downfall not only of Hungarian Jewry but of the country as a whole. As Munkácsi puts it, "In this way, the die – or rather a huge boulder – was cast, not only taking with it Hungarian Jewry, but precipitating Hungary itself to the brink of total annihilation."[42] Giving clear expression to the Hungarian part of his identity, Munkácsi at one point even presents the events of 1944 as a regrettable loss of reputation for Hungarians on the international stage.[43]

In a final twist of argument, the concluding page of *How It Happened* places the Holocaust into Jewish religious and national frames. Ernő Munkácsi quotes the dire prophesies of Jeremiah ("They shall die of grievous deaths; they shall not be lamented; neither shall they be buried," Jer. 16:4 KJV) and Theodor Herzl ("Destiny will catch up with the Hungarian Jews too, the more brutal and harsh, the longer it takes, the more influential they are, the further they will fall"), suggesting that "the blinded Jews of Hungary" (Munkácsi's words) were punished for their errors and sins.[44] *How It Happened* thus articulates a complex, seemingly contradictory position: on the one hand, its patriotic author reiterates the cherished ideals of assimilationists regarding a "community of fate" shared with Hungarians; on the other, he presents the Holocaust as proof that Herzl, the Hungarian-born "founding father" of Zionism, was essentially correct when he warned that without a state of their own, Jews were doomed.

When addressing the future of what he calls "the last vestiges of the once-grand Hungarian Jewish people," Munkácsi reiterates some of his favoured proposals from before 1944.[45] He admonishes the decimated Jewish community to be more religious, more Jewish than ever, while remaining dedicated Hungarians. Even in the face of irreparable human destruction and mass traumatization, Munkácsi remains hopeful that the much smaller Jewish community of postwar Hungary will prove "spiritually purer, morally more upright, and stronger in its convictions and adherence to the flock" than the community of recent years, whose members he saw as prone to abandon their identity and moral calling.[46]

The Tabooed Failure of *Realpolitik*

Even though the months of Ernő Munkácsi's involvement in the Jewish Council were meant to be the prime focus of *How It Happened*, it still seems perplexing that the author omits what happened prior to the spring of 1944. Instead of relating the history of the deportations to the anti-Jewish currents of Hungarian history, currents which escalated after 1938, Munkácsi places his emphasis on the German occupation of the country. What is more, his assertions concerning the ignorance of and belated response to information on Auschwitz make key arguments of *How It Happened* uncomfortably similar to those propagated by apologists of the Horthy regime in the early postwar period (and since): it appears that Munkácsi has a vested interest in denying how much he knew about the Holocaust by mid-1944, even at the price of appearing in the dubious company of Horthy apologists. As I shall argue next, he needed to deny wartime awareness to be able to defend the intentions of the Council in an accessible manner. A more truthful account of the war years would not only have been more painful to articulate, but would in all likelihood also have been less immediately convincing.

This is what such an account might have sounded like: by the years 1942–43, the antisemitic radicalization of Hungarian politics meant severe everyday discrimination against Hungarian Jews and constituted a frightening threat. At the same time, Hungarian ethnic nationalists, often staunchly antisemitic, offered the last hope to Jewish community leaders and intellectuals that the large majority of Hungarian Jews would survive the nearly continent-wide Nazi German onslaught. After all, ethnic nationalists in Hungary insisted on preserving Hungarian sovereignty and thus, despite their antisemitism, were generally keen to protect all Hungarian citizens from German imperialists, even those they had by then mostly deprived of their rights.

In the Jewish milieu of Hungary, more emphatically Jewish agendas largely replaced Hungarian national discourses when, in a matter of only a few years, between 1938 and 1941, Hungary passed ever-more-restrictive anti-Jewish laws. In those years, an increasing number of Jews in Hungary felt a need to get organized as Jews to defend themselves from a malevolent Hungarian state they used to consider theirs too. Ernő Munkácsi still expressed his continued trust in the Hungarian state in 1939 when contending that "the idea of legal equality was, at least in principle, not violated" by the anti-Jewish law of 1938.[47] By 1940, however, Munkácsi shared the grave concerns of Jews in Hungary, and Europe generally, reflecting that his generation was enduring "times which were almost unprecedented in the past two thousand years"[48] as they "passed, all at once, from legal equality and the possession of the full rights of citizens to a condition without them, even having to suffer under the imposition of specific restrictions."[49]

Shortly after the German attack on the Soviet Union in the summer of 1941, a transnational wave of extreme violence was unleashed against Jews. The first round of mass deportations from Hungary, or, more specifically, the recently re-annexed Subcarpathia of today's Ukraine, was also implemented right after the launching of Operation Barbarossa.[50] As the de facto director of the Jewish Museum, speaking at the museum's annual meeting on 21 September 1941, Ernő Munkácsi was uncharacteristically dramatic: "Many of us feel that the cup of our misfortune is close to being filled. In these horror-filled, apocalyptic times, Messianic, miraculous beliefs are spreading among the masses."[51]

Remarkably, it was precisely from 1941 onward that pro-Hungarian discourses and practices were gradually revived in some Jewish elite circles. As late as 1942, when the Nazi genocide was already being implemented just outside the borders of the country, László Bakonyi, a lawyer and secretary of the National Israelite Office, expressed his hopeful conviction in the pages of the yearbook *Ararát* that "the Hungarian soul enriched by Saint Stephenian ideas will reject racial hatred."[52] That same year, Fülöp Grünvald, a leading Hungarian Jewish historian, cited in *Libanon* (the official organ of the Jewish Museum under Ernő Munkácsi) the justified complaints of Hungarian Jews about their unfair discrimination during the revolution of 1848. Characteristically, Grünvald went on to emphasize, in an unmistakably patriotic fashion, that, despite this discrimination, Hungarian Jews nevertheless committed themselves to the defence of their endangered homeland. The lesson Grünvald thus offered in 1942 was that Jews would serve Hungary in spite of their negative experiences.[53] It might sound like a minor, almost insignificant example, but it is highly revealing that in 1942, Ernő Munkácsi explicitly criticized the Hungarian translation of Cecil Roth's history of Jews in the Middle Ages for lacking material specific to Hungary, which he maintained "could have provided light and consolation in the dark night."[54] Munkácsi thereby promoted the idea that Hungary had long been an exceptionally hospitable place for Jews – even shortly after the Holocaust had begun.

It thus appears that in the early 1940s, Hungarian Jews' loyalty to the ever-more radically antisemitic regime under Regent Horthy was strengthened *not in spite of*, but rather *because of* the implementation of the Nazi genocide. By 1942–43, Hungarian ethnic nationalists were persecuting the country's Jews in manifold ways, yet the Horthy regime now raised the last desperate hopes of Jewish survival; that Hungarians would still prove less full of murderous hatred toward Jews than their Nazi German, Slovak, Croatian, or Romanian neighbours. Whereas the strategy of compliance with the antisemitic Hungarian authorities may have appeared to be the only viable strategy of Jewish survival in 1942–43, the continuation of this strategy proved a fatal misjudgment under the radically changed circumstances of 1944.

This was the devastating story of the years of war and genocide that surviving members of the Hungarian Jewish elite, including Munkácsi, could not articulate in the immediate aftermath. Their story of adjustments and misjudgments was too complex to be immediately convincing to the broader public. What would have made recalling the twists and turns of this story worse is that they clearly exposed how morally ambiguous the Hungarian Jewish *realpolitik* of the early years of the Second World War was, and how the fatal choice of compliance in 1944 followed from this politically reasonable but morally ambiguous strategy of 1941–43.

The major concessions to the persecutors necessitated by the Council's strategy of compliance are not ignored in *How It Happened*, but the profound ambiguities involved in repeatedly trying to choose the lesser evil are not really dissected either. Neither did Ernő Munkácsi want to appear to be dodging the most uncomfortable questions, nor did he want to confront them directly. He therefore presents an ethics of intentions rather than outcomes; an ethics premised on the notion that actions should be evaluated by the intentions behind them rather than by their actual consequences. To this ethics of intentions, the book adds a heavy dose of doubt about how much contemporaries knew with certainty about the Nazi genocide. *How It Happened* thus amounts

Fig. 11   Taken by an SS officer in late May or early June 1944, this photo shows a trainload of Hungarian Jews having just arrived in Auschwitz. From here they would undergo the selection process to separate the few fit for slave labour from the majority relegated to the gas chambers. In the distance, at left and right, the smokestacks of Crematoria II and III are visible. Approximately one in every three victims of Auschwitz-Birkenau was a Jew from Hungary.

to a partially successful defence that manages to clear the Council of the harshest and crudest accusations levelled against it, but fails to tackle head-on the more nuanced criticisms targeting the consequences of the Council's "choiceless choices."

The Immediate Intellectual Context

Upon the release of *How It Happened* in 1947, early Holocaust researchers were eager to discuss Munkácsi's interpretation of events as well as some of his specific assertions. The reception of *How It Happened* took place at the highest level of incipient Holocaust scholarship, though it proved rather critical.

Next to Munkácsi's book, the most significant Hungarian Jewish monographs on the Holocaust published before the end of the 1940s were Jenő

Lévai's *Zsidósors Magyarországon* (*Jewish Fate in Hungary*) and Endre Sós's *Európai fasizmus és antiszemitizmus* (*European Fascism and Antisemitism*). Both these monographs addressed the key arguments made by Munkácsi in *How It Happened*. A journalist by profession, Jenő Lévai (1892–1983) proved the most prolific of Hungary's early survivor historians. His 1948 *Jewish Fate in Hungary*, published one year after *How It Happened*, was the major early overview of the Holocaust in Hungary and the most significant such study until the release of Randolph Braham's magisterial *The Politics of Genocide* more than three decades later. (In many ways, the work of the émigré author Braham, born in 1922, himself a survivor of the Holocaust in Hungary, was inspired by Jenő Lévai's comprehensive but polemical approach to the subject.) While giving expression to its author's anti-German sentiments, Lévai's massive work of contemporary history represents an unequivocal articulation of Hungarian responsibility, detailing and condemning, in a strikingly similar manner to Munkácsi, the Hungarian involvement in the genocide. It is on the role of the Jewish Council that Lévai takes a much different stance, remarking on the "unfathomable ignorance" displayed by the Jewish Council in 1944 and their apparent inability to grasp some of the clearest signs that a campaign of genocide had been launched against their people. Lévai's assessment of this ignorance was notably harsher than Munkácsi's, as he argued that the Council's naïveté led to "servile behaviour," "exaggerated benevolence aimed at fulfilling all demands and wishes," and even to "enthusiastic expert cooperation." Notwithstanding the differences between Munkácsi's agenda of vindication and Lévai's more critical spirit, and the fact that Munkácsi drew more heavily on traditional Jewish references, there was substantial common ground between them: both authors clearly belonged to the modern intellectual tradition of Hungarian Jews; both provided rich documentation to develop chiefly secular accounts of the Holocaust in Hungary.

In his *European Fascism and Antisemitism* of 1948, Endre Sós (1905–1969), who would later emerge as a controversial, pro-communist leader of the Jewish community after the suppression of the 1956 Hungarian Revolution, provided an impressive continent-wide panorama of the Holocaust. Among the early survivor historians from Hungary, Sós drew the most directly political conclusions from the genocide. According to a key argument of his 1948 book, the unprecedented Nazi crimes inevitably necessitated socialist revolutions. He also provided intriguing reflections on the most appropriate term to denote what had just been perpetrated against European

Jewry. Relating in a polemical fashion to Munkácsi's choice of naming the subject of his book "the tragedy of Hungarian Jewry," Sós argued that the term "catastrophe" was much more fitting than "tragedy" since Jews were, on the whole, "misfortunate victims" of the Nazis who could neither ethically nor aesthetically qualify as tragic heroes.

In short, by 1947–48, the Holocaust in Hungary had already been subjected to major book-length studies by a key figure of the Jewish wartime establishment (Munkácsi) and by a prolific journalist-researcher (Lévai), as well as explored from the perspective of an ideologically committed communist with a broad European outlook (Sós). The historiography created by these Hungarian Jewish survivors clearly belonged to an international wave of early research and writing on the Holocaust – a wave to which they made some of the most substantial contributions. Pride of place among the early historians of the Holocaust arguably belongs to Jews from Poland, especially Philip Friedman, Rachel Auerbach, and Szymon Datner.[55] Ground-breaking early works were also published in several languages other than Hungarian, Polish, and Yiddish notably by Matatias Carp in Romanian, Léon Poliakov in French, and Gerald Reitlinger in English[56] – all preceding Raul Hilberg's seminal *The Destruction of the European Jews* of 1961.[57]

The agendas of these early Holocaust historians were multilayered, but in several respects remarkably similar to each other. They all tended to understand their activities as having intellectual and commemorative functions, but also as being legally and politically relevant. They wanted to contribute, even if to different degrees, to historical documentation and explanation, to the symbolic burial of the unburied millions, to the ongoing trials, and to democratic political re-education. The valuable publications of these pioneering historians from different countries remain to be methodically compared. Having finally been translated into English, the contribution by Ernő Munkácsi will doubtlessly be among the subjects of future comparisons.

Major Later Trends in Coping with the Holocaust in Hungary

The publication of Ernő Munkácsi's *How It Happened* in 1947 marked a pivotal moment during the early wave of intellectual responses to the Holocaust. In Hungary, this early wave was abruptly followed by a period in which the Holocaust became an all-but-forbidden subject, as the Stalinist rulers effectively banned any discussion concerning the persecution and annihilation of the Jews. Remarkably, the prohibition of the subject under Stalinism in Eastern Europe by and large corresponded to Western European trends of the 1950s, where the first wave of responses was also followed by significantly diminished levels of engagement.

In later decades, communist-ruled Hungary to some extent participated in transnational waves of confronting and responding to the Holocaust. Not only did Hungarian survivors who made *aliyah* play eminent roles during the 1961 Eichmann trial in Jerusalem, but the trial rekindled debate in Hungary itself.[58] In parallel with Western trends, between the mid-1970s and 1989 there was another surge of interest in the extermination of Hungarian Jewry, epitomized, at least in retrospect, by the publication, in 1975, of *Fateless*, the autobiographical novel by the Hungarian Holocaust survivor (and later, Nobel laureate) Imre Kertész.[59]

Shortly after the lifting of the "Iron Curtain" in 1989, it appeared that, concurrently with ever-greater global critical scrutiny directed at the history of the Holocaust, decisive change would come to Hungary too. The key roles played by local perpetrators in the ghettoization and deportations of 1944 finally began to be openly acknowledged. However, such crucial steps in facing local responsibility coincided with nationalistic attempts at re-establishing a longstanding national historical tradition, a tradition supposedly interrupted only by the blip of consecutive occupations by the Germans and the Soviets. Ongoing public debates thus not only concern the level of Hungarian co-responsibility in the Holocaust, but also address larger questions regarding the place and function of Holocaust remembrance within a new national canon. In the early twenty-first century, Holocaust remembrance may appear well established; yet it has again become a politicized affair and continues to lack a clear place in the historical consciousness of Hungarian citizens.

The situation is similarly ambiguous internationally. It was arguably the postwar compartmentalization of European Jewish history into East and West, a scheme into which the history of Hungarian Jews could not be shoehorned, that resulted in the relative marginalization of the Hungarian Jewish catastrophe. Even now, the stories of Polish or German Jews in the age of genocide remain far more extensively studied and more widely known.

The English publication of Ernő Munkácsi's intriguing *How It Happened* ought to contribute to a long overdue rediscovery of the rich and varied responses by members of this major European Jewish community to persecution and extermination. It is also to be hoped that this publication fosters a new international appreciation of the excruciating dilemmas its surviving representatives had to confront during and right after the Holocaust.

Reading seminal original documents such as *How It Happened* allows us to perceive Jews not only as victims, but as human actors in an immense drama and unprecedented tragedy. As *How It Happened* shows, Ernő Munkácsi was a highly assimilated, self-aware Jew who struck a fine balance between modern methods of historical documentation, personal reflection, and traditional Jewish references. With all his excruciating dilemmas, Munkácsi serves as a prime example of the Hungarian Jewish synthesis that the Holocaust largely destroyed and the Cold War subsequently ignored. It is now our task to rediscover and critically appreciate this fine but devastated synthesis.

Notes

This essay draws on some of the key findings and reproduces some of the arguments of my monograph *Hungarian Jews in the Age of Genocide: An Intellectual History, 1929–1948* (Leiden: Brill, 2016).

1 For an annotated bibliography of such publications, see Arthúr Geyer, *A magyarországi fasizmus zsidóüldözésének bibliográfiája* [A Bibliography of the Fascist Persecution of Jews in Hungary] (Budapest: A Magyar Izraeliták Országos Képviseletének Kiadása, 1958).

2 For a sociohistorical analysis of the People's Tribunals, see Andrea Pető and Ildikó Barna, *Political Justice in Budapest after WWII* (Budapest: CEU Press, 2015).

3 David Cesarani, "Challenging the 'Myth of Silence': Postwar Responses to the Destruction of European Jewry," in David Cesarani and Eric J. Sundquist (eds.), *After the Holocaust: Challenging the Myth of Silence* (London: Routledge, 2012), 32.

4 Laura Jockusch, *Collect and Record! Jewish Holocaust Documentation in Early Postwar Europe* (Oxford: Oxford University Press, 2012), 17.

5 On the development of anti-Jewish policies of the times, see Nathaniel Katzburg, *Hungary and the Jews: Policy and Legislation, 1920–1943* (Ramat Gan: Bar Ilan University Press, 1981).

6 See the chapter "Discrimination, Radicalization and the First Mass Murders" in Zoltán Vági, László Csősz, and Gábor Kádár, *The Holocaust in Hungary: Evolution of a Genocide* (Lanham, MD: AltaMira Press, 2013). See also George Eisen and Tamás Stark, "The 1941 Galician Deportation and the Kamenets-Podolsk Massacre: A Prologue to the Hungarian Holocaust," *Holocaust and Genocide Studies* 2 (2013). On the Hungarian Army on the Eastern Front, see Krisztián

Ungváry, *Magyar megszálló csapatok a Szovjetunióban, 1941–1944* [The Hungarian Occupying Forces in the Soviet Union, 1941–1944] (Budapest: Osiris, 2015). On the institution of labour service, in English, see Robert Rozett, *Conscripted Slaves: Hungarian Jewish Forced Laborers on the Eastern Front during World War II* (Jerusalem: Yad Vashem Publications, 2014).

7 At the start of the Second World War in 1939, Warsaw's Jewish population was approximately 350,000, substantially larger than Budapest's. By early 1944, however, all but an estimated 20,000 of Warsaw's Jews had been murdered by the Nazis.

8 For a perceptive analysis of recent trends in history writing, see András Kovács, "Hungarian Intentionalism: New Directions in the Historiography of the Hungarian Holocaust," in Randolph L. Braham and András Kovács (eds.), *The Holocaust in Hungary: Seventy Years Later* (Budapest: CEU Press, 2016).

9 On the Holocaust in Hungary, see the major overview by Randolph L. Braham, *The Politics of Genocide: The Holocaust in Hungary* (Boulder, CO: East European Monographs, 2016). See also Zoltán Vági, László Csősz, and Gábor Kádár, *The Holocaust in Hungary: Evolution of a Genocide* (Lanham, MD: AltaMira Press, 2013).

10 Because the vast majority of the approximately 437,000 Jews deported from Hungary between May and July 1944 were immediately murdered on arrival at Auschwitz-Birkenau, without being registered, the precise number of victims is unknown. The estimated number of Hungarian Jewish victims of Auschwitz-Birkenau is based on subtracting from the overall number deported from Hungary (437,000) the far smaller number of those deported elsewhere (mostly to Strasshof concentration camp near Vienna), those transported from Auschwitz-Birkenau to other Nazi camps, as well as those registered at Auschwitz-Birkenau who survived. Such estimates reveal that approximately every third victim of the most infamous Nazi extermination and concentration camp was a Jew from Hungary.

11 On the early postwar treatment of the former camp, see Imke Hansen, *"Nie wieder Auschwitz!" Die Entstehung eines Symbols und der Alltag einer Gedenkstätte 1945–1955* ["Never Again Auschwitz!" The Emergence of a Symbol and the Everyday Life of a Memorial Site 1945–1955] (Göttingen: Wallstein, 2014). On the Nazi camps in Poland during early postwar period, more generally, see Zofia Wójcicka, *Arrested Mourning: Memory of the Nazi Camps in Poland, 1944–1950* (Frankfurt am Main: Peter Lang, 2013).

12 See Gábor Kádár and Zoltán Vági, "Compulsion of Bad Choices – Questions, Dilemmas, Decisions: The Activity of the Hungarian Central Jewish Council in 1944," in András Kovács and Michael Miller (eds.), *Jewish Studies at the Central European University. Vol. 5* (Budapest: Central European University Press, 2009).

13 See Vági, Csősz, and Kádár, *The Holocaust in Hungary: Evolution of a Genocide*, 255.

14 Scholars typically distinguish four phases of the Hungarian Jewish Council. The "First Council" begins with the formation of the Council in March 1944.

The second phase begins toward the end of April when the "Second Council" comes under the purview of Hungarian authorities, is renamed the Interim Executive Board of the Association of Jews in Hungary, and its personnel is slightly modified. Mid-July 1944 marks the third phase, when representatives of the Interim Executive Board of the Association of Christian Jews of Hungary, representing Jewish converts to Christianity, are added to the core Council. The final phase (the "Fourth Council") begins with the Arrow Cross party's rise to power in mid-October 1944.

15 The activities of the Jewish Council are studied in detail in Kádár and Vági, "Compulsion of Bad Choices – Questions, Dilemmas, Decisions." See also Judit Molnár, "The Foundation and Activities of the Hungarian Jewish Council, March 20 to July 7, 1944," in *Yad Vashem Studies* 30 (2002).

16 Counting all four iterations of the Hungarian Jewish Council (see note 14 above), there were twenty-five council members in total, of whom twenty-two survived the war.

17 The classic study on the highly sensitive and controversial topic of Jewish councils is Isaiah Trunk, *Judenrat: The Jewish Councils in Eastern Europe under Nazi Occupation* (Lincoln: University of Nebraska Press, 1972).

18 Hannah Arendt, *Eichmann in Jerusalem: A Report on the Banality of Evil* (New York: Viking Press, 1963).

19 Raul Hilberg, Stanislav Staron, and Josef Kermisz (eds.), *The Warsaw Diary of Adam Czerniakow: Prelude to Doom* (Chicago: Ivan R. Dee, 1999).

20 Mirjam Bolle, *Letters Never Sent: Amsterdam, Westerbork, Bergen-Belsen* (Jerusalem: Yad Vashem, 2014).

21 Munkácsi, *How It Happened*, 172.

22 Ibid., 5.

23 Ibid., 8.

24 The newest edition is Samu Stern, *Emlékirataim–Versenyfutás az idővel!* [My Memories: A Race with Time] (Budapest: Bábel, 2004). In English, see Samu Stern, "'A Race with Time': A Statement," *Hungarian Jewish Studies* 3 (1973).

25 Munkácsi, *How It Happened*, 7.

26 Ibid., 7. The term "occupation" is significant, since the German military intervention in Hungary was a curious instance of occupation by a more powerful ally. Even though the relationship between the two allies was clearly transformed upon 19 March 1944, Hungary preserved significant levels of autonomy and eagerly continued its alliance with Germany. By labelling the period "the German occupation," Munkácsi circumscribes Hungarian responsibility.

27 Ibid., 66.

28 On the Litzmannstadt ghetto and the city generally during the Second World War, see Gordon J. Horwitz, *Ghettostadt: Łódź and the Making of a Nazi City* (Cambridge, MA: Harvard University Press, 2010).

29 Ibid., 218.

30 See the critical edition, which also traces the reception of the document in Hungary: György Haraszti, *Auschwitzi jegyzőkönyv* [*The Auschwitz Protocols*] (Budapest: Múlt és Jövő, 2016).

31 Notably, Mária Székely's translation was first printed, in a slightly edited and abridged form, in the original 1947 edition of *Hogyan történt?* (*How It Happened*). As a matter of fact, Munkácsi's book remained the only Hungarian-language edition of the Protocols for nearly another half a century.

32 Munkácsi, *How It Happened*, 92.

33 Ibid., 77.

34 Ibid., 94.

35 Ibid., 133.

36 Ibid., 106.

37 Ibid., 218. The relationship between Eichmann and Endre is a key subject of Gábor Kádár and Zoltán Vági, *A végső döntés: Berlin, Budapest, Birkenau 1944* [The Final Decision: Berlin, Budapest, Birkenau 1944] (Budapest: Jaffa, 2013).

38 Ibid., 183.

39 Ibid., 250.

40 Ibid., 87.

41 Ibid., 88.

42 Ibid., 64.

43 He argues that if the Hungarians had shown more courage in opposing the Jewish tragedy, "we [i.e., Hungarians] would not have to stand alone bearing no one's sympathy before the People's Tribunals today" (173), referring, it seems, to Hungary's treatment at the Paris Peace Treaty of 1947, which was hotly debated at the time of his writing. Whereas many Hungarians had hoped the nation's "just" territorial expansions of 1938–41 would be upheld after the war, wholly or in part, the 1947 treaty rejected this ambition and essentially reaffirmed the earlier borders of the 1920 Treaty of Trianon.

44 Ibid., 284.

45 In 1943, Munkácsi published a collection of his writings that offers key insights into his stance during the years of persecution before the German invasion. See Ernő Munkácsi, *Küzdelmes évek ... Cikkek és tanulmányok a magyar zsidóság elmúlt évtizedéből* [Years of Struggle ... Articles and Studies from the Past Decade of Hungarian Jewry] (Budapest: Libanon, 1943).

46 Munkácsi, *How It Happened*, 284.

47 Ernő Munkácsi, "A magyar zsidóság és a zsidóvallású magyarok jogi helyzete" [The Legal Situation of Hungarian Jewry and of Hungarians of the Jewish Religion], *Ararát*, 1939, 19.

48 Ernő Munkácsi, "Az ókori zsidóság feliratos történeti forrásai (I. közlemény)" [The Inscriptions of Ancient Jewry as Historical Sources (First Installment)], *Libanon*, 1940, 68.

49　Ibid., 68. For the wider European Jewish response at the time, see Alexandra Garbarini with Emil Kerenji, Jan Lambertz, and Avinoam Patt (eds.), *Jewish Responses to Persecution, Volume II, 1938–1940* (Lanham, MD: AltaMira Press, 2011).

50　On the history of mass violence in Subcarpathia, see Raz Segal, *Genocide in the Carpathians: War, Social Breakdown, and Mass Violence, 1914–1945* (Palo Alto: Stanford University Press, 2016).

51　"Az Országos Magyar Zsidó Múzeum Közgyűlése" ["The Assembly of the Hungarian Jewish Museum"], *Libanon*, 1941, 56.

52　László Bakonyi, "Zsidó gondok és remények" ["Jewish Concerns and Hopes"], *Ararát*, 1942, 28.

53　Fülöp Grünvald, "Az Országos Magyar Zsidó Múzeum levéltárából" ["From the Archive of the Hungarian Jewish Museum"], *Libanon*, 1942, 121.

54　Ernő Munkácsi, "Cecil Roth. Zsidó középkor" ["Review of Cecil Roth: *Jewish Middle Ages*"], *Libanon*, 1942, 29.

55　Filip Friedman, *To jest Oświęcim* [This is Oświęcim] (Warsaw: Państwowe Wydanictwo Literatury Politycznej, 1945); Rachel Auerbach, *Oyf di felder fun Treblinke* [In the Fields of Treblinka] (Łódź: Centralna Żydowska Komisja Historyczna, 1947); Szymon Datner, *Walka i Zagłada białostockiego getta* [The Fight and Annihilation of the Białystok Ghetto] (Łódź: Centralna Żydowska Komisja Historyczna, 1946).

56　Matatias Carp, *Cartea Neagră. Suferințele evreilor din România 1940–1944*. Vols. 1–3 [The Black Book. The Suffering of the Jews from Romania 1940–1944]. (Bucharest: Socec, 1946–48); Léon Poliakov, *Bréviaire de la haine. Le IIIe Reich et les Juifs* (Paris: Calmann-Lévy, 1951) [*Harvest of Hate: The Nazi Program for the Destruction of the Jews of Europe* (New York: Schocken, 1979)]; Gerald Reitlinger, *The Final Solution: The Attempt to Exterminate the Jews of Europe, 1939–1945* (London: Vallentine Mitchell, 1953).

57　Raul Hilberg, *The Destruction of the European Jews* (New Haven: Yale University Press, 1961).

58　On this, see Hanna Yablonka, *The State of Israel vs. Adolf Eichmann* (New York: Schocken, 2004), 25 and 90. On the contemporary Hungarian reception of the trial, see Kata Bohus, "Not a Jewish Question? The Hungarian Holocaust in the Kádár Regime's Propaganda during Adolf Eichmann's Trial," *Hungarian Historical Review* 3, 4 (2015).

59　Other seminal publications of the mid-1970s include: Mária Ember, *Hajtűkanyar* [Hairpin Bend] (Budapest: Szépirodalmi, 1974) and György Száraz, *Egy előítélet nyomában* [Tracing a Prejudice] (Budapest: Magvető, 1976). For a recent reflection on the responses of the 1970s, see Gábor Gyáni, "Hungarian Memory of the Holocaust in Hungary," in Braham and Kovács (eds.), *The Holocaust in Hungary: Seventy Years Later.*

The Life and Times of Ernő Munkácsi

Susan M. Papp

Ernő Munkácsi was born on 7 August 1896 in Páncélcseh, a small village in the eastern part of the Kingdom of Hungary.[1] It was an era of peace and prosperity for the Jews of Hungary. Bit by bit, beginning around the middle of the nineteenth century, Hungarian Jewry had been granted full legal and economic emancipation. This relative freedom led to a surge of immigration from other parts of the Hapsburg Empire, mostly Moravia and Galicia. From a modest 83,000 (1 percent of the population) in 1787, the Jews of Hungary grew to nearly one million (5 percent) on the eve of the First World War,[2] just as Ernő Munkácsi was turning eighteen.

In many ways, Munkácsi's family perfectly illustrated the social and economic mobility made possible to many Hungarian Jews in those years. Munkácsi's great-grandfather Bernát (Be'er Dov) Munk (1800–1852) was an itinerant peddler in rural Nyitra County in northwestern Hungary (today Slovakia) where he and his wife, Chaile Felsenburg (1805–1842), lived a harsh hand-to-mouth existence. Only three of their eight children survived to adulthood, among them Ernő's grandfather Adolf (Méir Ávrahám) Munk (1830–1907). Adolf, a talented Talmud student, quickly climbed out of poverty; first working as a private tutor for Orthodox Jewish families and then later as a corn merchant in the thriving city of Nagyvárad (today Oradea, Romania). However, it is as an adherent of the Jewish Enlightenment, or Haskalah intellectual movement, and as a writer of poetry, short stories, and political essays that Adolf Munk made a name for himself; most notably as the author of *My Life's Histories*, his sweeping autobiography written in classical Hebrew in 1899 and published posthumously in Hungarian.[3]

The Munk family's move from Nyitra to Nagyvárad followed a common pattern of migration for Hungary's Jews in the nineteenth century, from rural backwater or *shtetl* to a cosmopolitan urban centre that, in this case, soon boasted the nation's second-largest Jewish population after Budapest. Around the time that Adolf Munk's eldest son (and Ernő Munkácsi's father) Bernát, was born in Nagyvárad in 1860, about 6 percent of the city's population

Fig. 12   Ernő Munkácsi's paternal grandparents, Adolf (Méir Ávráhám) Munk (1830–1907) and Sarah Stein (1839–1914), circa 1880. A corn merchant in Nagyvárad (today Oradea, Romania) and an adherent of the Jewish Enlightenment, Adolf Munk wrote poetry, short stories, and political essays. His best-known work is his 1899 autobiography written in classical Hebrew, a rare surviving account of traditional Jewish life in rural nineteenth-century Hungary. Adolf and Sarah had ten children, two of whom died in infancy. Their first-born was Ernő's father, Bernát Munkácsi (born Munk).

was Jewish. By 1910, that figure had surpassed 23 percent.[4] Almost inevitably, perhaps, the Munks, like many other Jews in Hungary at the time, became with each generation ever more loyal to and integrated into Hungarian culture. Whereas Adolf Munk and his wife, Sarah Stein (1839–1914), were devout Orthodox Jews who spoke German at home and initially sent their children to a *cheder* (a traditional Jewish primary school) to learn Hebrew and study the Torah, they eventually decided to enroll Bernát, and then his two younger brothers,[5] in the local Hungarian school, run by the Premonstratensians, a Catholic order, because it was the best *gymnasium* in Nagyvárad.[6]

There in the eighth grade, the precocious Bernát declared that he would dedicate his life to tracing the origins of the Hungarian language. Only a few years later, in 1881, after Bernát had moved to Budapest and was a student at the University of Pest, he officially changed his surname from the German "Munk" to the Hungarian "Munkácsi."[7] Among assimilated middle-class Jewish families, particularly in Budapest, the Magyarization of surnames was increasingly common; a way to demonstrate a fervent commitment to Hungary, facilitate upward social mobility, or avoid overt antisemitism. In fact, as Bernát later wrote, even as a teenager he had taken to using the Munkácsi name: "I was already using this name at the age of sixteen as a penname to sign my poems and writings in the school's literary circle."[8] At some point, like 40 percent of Jews in Hungary at the turn of the twentieth century, Bernát, who had been raised in an Orthodox household, embraced the more acculturated Neolog branch of Judaism.[9]

By the time Bernát's son Ernő Munkácsi was born in 1896, Bernát had built a respected career as a linguist and ethnologist. As a leading member of Hungary's "Orientalists," Bernát produced many scholarly publications, include a dictionary of the Udmurt language and a compilation and translation of the folk literature of the Mansi people of northwestern Siberia, thought to be the closest linguistic relatives of the Magyars. In 1890 Bernát was among the first Jewish scholars to be elected a corresponding member of the prestigious Hungarian Academy of Sciences; in 1910 he was named a full member.[10] In parallel with his scholarly career, Bernát worked as school inspector for the Jewish Community of Pest, representing Budapest's 200,000 Neolog Jews.

Adolf Munk's other children were also accomplished. Bernát's brother Gábor Munk (1865–1955) was a prosperous businessman in Budapest who acquired the regional sales rights to the Viennese-based Manner chocolate products (including the company's popular Neapolitan wafers), and then

Fig. 13 Ernő Munkácsi's father, Bernát Munkácsi (1860–1937), in Russia's historic Volga region in the spring of 1885 with his Votyak instructors Pjotr Vasziljev and Makszim Kirillov. Among the scholarly publications by Bernát, a linguist and ethnologist, is a dictionary of Votyak (AKA Udmurt), a Finno-Ugric language that resembles Hungarian. In 1890 Bernát was among the first Jewish scholars to be elected a corresponding member of the Hungarian Academy of Sciences; in 1910 he was named a full member. Like other assimilated Jews who wanted to demonstrate their patriotism to Hungary, Bernát changed his name from the Germanic "Munk" to the Hungarian "Munkácsi."

invested in residential rental properties. The youngest brother, Mór Munk (1873–1942), built a successful wholesale textile business in Nagyvárad.

Judging from his personal correspondence, Ernő Munkácsi and his siblings, Sándor and Noémi, were doted on by their parents, Bernát and Paula (née Jacobi).[11] Bernát was not rich, but he was a highly regarded member of the Jewish intellectual elite, committed to spending every spare korona on his children's education and determined to cement his family's newly acquired bourgeois credentials. At young Ernő's bar mitzvah in 1909, guests included not only sixty-four members of the extended Munk family, but also more than eighty members of the Jewish intelligentsia. They included: many notable rabbis and prominent scholars; Miksa Szabolcsi (1857–1915), editor of the largest Jewish weekly newspaper in Hungary; and Samu Stern (1874–1947), a prominent businessman and president of the Neolog Israelite Congregation of Pest, who would later, in 1944, become president of the Hungarian Central Jewish Council. The bar mitzvah gifts were meticulously recorded by Ernő's father: a trove of classical literature, including the works of Jules Verne, Heinrich Heine, Virgil, Napoleon, and Goethe; books of Judaica; leather-bound volumes by important Hungarian poets and writers; and various other hallmarks of the bourgeoisie, including a gold fountain pen and pencil set, a gold watch, opera glasses, a painting set, gold cufflinks, and a set of engraved calling cards.[12]

At the age of twenty-two, on 5 October 1918, Ernő graduated from the distinguished Budapest University (Budapesti Tudományegyetem) with a law degree,[13] joining numerous young Jews in Hungary who saw an opportunity to get ahead in the professions. In Budapest, where 20 percent of the population was Jewish in 1910, a disproportionate 62 percent of lawyers, 59 percent of physicians, and 33 percent of pharmacists were Jewish.[14] Soon after graduation, Ernő Munkácsi began his career as secretary of the Israelite Congregation of Pest, the largest Neolog congregation in Hungary, with 215,000 members.[15] By 1923 he was the congregation's legal counsel, and by 1930, chief legal counsel. He married a fellow member of Budapest's Jewish bourgeoisie, a graduate of the Hungarian Royal Academy of Music and a certified music teacher named Erzsébet Rózsa Mairovitz (1903–1994). They had two children, Paula Éva (1928–2012) and Mária Veronika (1930–2013). By all appearances, Munkácsi's life was unfolding precisely as might have been expected.

A pensive-looking man, Munkácsi had an extraordinary command of language, a quick mind, and a natural authority. As his reputation grew, he was elected to more community leadership positions. In 1935, in addition

Fig. 14 Ernő, age nineteen, with his parents, Bernát and Paula, and his younger sister Noémi (1903–1966) in Abbazia (now Opatija, Croatia), a fashionable seaside resort town on what was known as the Austrian Riviera. Absent from this 1915 family photo is Ernő's older brother, Sándor (1893–1965), who was interned in France as a prisoner of war from August 1914 to January 1917.

to his position at the Pest Jewish Community, he was named chief counsel of the National Office of Hungarian Jews (Magyar Izraeliták Országos Irodája). In 1937 he was also named co-president of the Hungarian Jewish Museum Association, acting as de facto director of the Hungarian Jewish Museum. And all the while, Munkácsi wrote prodigiously for a broad range of publications. He was a contributing editor to legal journals *Jogtudományi Közlöny* (*Journal of Jurisprudence*) and *Polgári Jog* (*Civil Rights*), and wrote regularly for Hungary's popular German-language newspaper, *Pester Lloyd*, as well as the Jewish newspapers *Egyenlőség* (*Equality*) and *Múlt és Jövő* (*The Past and Future*).

Munkácsi demonstrated a deep, scholarly interest in Judaica. During the 1930s he travelled to Padua, Livorno, Rome, Amsterdam, and Hamburg to research ghettos, Hebrew manuscripts, and archaeological remains. His many published books, written mostly in Hungarian but also in German

Fig. 15   Completed in 1930, the majestic synagogue of Gyöngyös, a small provincial town
in central Hungary, symbolized the wealth and optimism of modern Hungary's Jews. It
was designed by the renowned Hungarian-Jewish architect Lipót Baumhorn (1860–1932),
who took and then sent this photo to his friend Immánuel Löw (1854–1944), the great rabbi
of Szeged. After the Second World War, Gyöngyös's synagogue fell into disrepair. In 1959,
it became a furniture store. Plans are now underway to renovate and convert the building
into a cultural centre.

and English, include *Ancient and Medieval Synagogues in Representations of
the Fine Arts*,[16] *Miniatúraművészet Itália könyvtáraiban* (The Art of Miniatures
in Italy's Libraries: Hebrew Codices), and *Der Jude von Neapel* (The Jews of
Naples). Jewry should know more about its past, Munkácsi insisted, a past
"from which we can draw strength, become stronger and more steadfast."[17]

In 1939, in what Munkácsi hoped would be the first in a series of important
Hungarian Jewish genealogies, the Hungarian Jewish Museum published the
Munk/Munkácsi genealogy.[18] (Needless to say, perhaps, with the outbreak
of the Second World War that same year, the series was never continued.)
Compiled over many decades by Ernő Munkácsi's father, Bernát, then revised
and edited by Ernő, the genealogy even today stands as a remarkable document, detailing the births, deaths, occupations, and gravestone inscriptions of
a Hungarian Jewish family dating back to the sixteenth century.[19] Pointedly,
in a director's report for the Jewish Museum, Ernő Munkácsi called attention
to the value of Jewish genealogical research: "It is not only out of political
timeliness, but centuries-old traditions that live in the soul of the Jewish
community, that the preservation of the history of families is so important."[20]

As Europe edged ever closer to war, Ernő Munkácsi's speeches and articles became distinctly more politicized, reflecting the Jewish community's growing anxiety. Like most of the country's Jews, Munkácsi was distressed by the Hungarian government's anti-Jewish Law No. xv of 1938, which limited the proportion of Jews in the professions to no more than 20 percent. That law, however, was only a precursor to the draconian Second Jewish Law – Law No. iv of 1939 Concerning the Restriction of the Participation of Jews in Public and Economic Life – which, among other provisions, explicitly defined Jews as a race, prohibited them from obtaining citizenship by marriage or naturalization, and limited their proportion in the professions to no more than 6 percent.

In his role as chief legal counsel for the Pest Jewish Community, Munkácsi now spent much of his time protesting, writing about, and publicizing the devastating effects of these laws. In 1939, along with other leaders of the community, he submitted multiple memoranda to both chambers of the Hungarian Parliament, arguing that the Second Jewish Law violated the Hungarian Constitution and caused tens of thousands of Hungarian citizens to lose their jobs, citizens who happened to be Jewish. That same year, Munkácsi was instrumental in publishing a sixty-page illustrated booklet entitled *Ítéljetek!* (You Judge!), which outlined the illegality of the laws, provided a historical record of Jewry's long loyalty to Hungary, and included many photographs of artifacts from the Hungarian Jewish Museum.[21] Munkácsi referred to this campaign as a "press war."[22]

An anthology of Munkácsi's essays from 1928 to 1941 serves to chart his evolution from a proud and loyal "Magyar of the Israelite faith" to an increasingly outspoken critic of his nation. Munkácsi became noticeably more strident after the passage of Hungary's anti-Jewish laws. "A major legal action is in progress," begins the last article reprinted in the anthology. "The defendants on trial are the Jews of Hungary. Hardly has a verdict been reached in one case, the sentence passed, when the defendant is again indicted, further charges are levelled, and punishments are once again meted out."[23] Munkácsi suffered a heart attack in 1942 – in part no doubt due to the stress of his work – but he continued his relentless work of writing and publishing largely uninterrupted.

His book, *Könyvek és kövek* (Books and Stones), published just prior to the Nazi occupation of Hungary, is dedicated "to the Memory of my brothers in the labour service who never returned," a reference to the countless Jewish men who, like other "unreliables" deemed unfit for regular military service, were forced to work in Hungary's often-brutal auxiliary labour service on the Eastern Front.[24] No official record of Munkácsi's service appears to have survived,[25] but in his published writings he mentions that he "fulfilled his military service in the fall of 1940,"[26] suggesting that he served in the labour service, forced by the Hungarian army to dig ditches or build rail lines.

As life became increasingly difficult for the Jews of Hungary, Munkácsi extolled the virtues of remaining steadfast to his faith. In the Jewish Museum's annual report of 1940, he admonished converts for "disowning their ancient faith, their origins, denying the very essence of their being, rushing toward foreign lands, and, with fanatical elbowing, striving to forget about their Jewish past, trying to melt in among others."[27] He went on:

> Although all may be lost, established rights may be taken away, we
> may lose friends and become disillusioned with our co-religionists
> – our common past is with us, our forefathers are with us, the
> virtue of our ancestors, their lives, their ability to sacrifice, the entire
> thousand-year history of Hungary, which is proven by the stones of
> our museum, the faded documents, which declare that we have been
> here for one thousand years, we have lived and died here, just the same
> as other citizens of Hungary.[28]

Ernő Munkácsi's *How It Happened* opens on 19 March 1944, the day that Nazi Germany invaded Hungary. Poignantly, Munkácsi details the tumultuous days that followed, as Adolf Eichmann's special operations unit, Sondereinsatzkommando Eichmann, begins implementing the "final solution" in Hungary. Among the first steps, at a meeting held at the Jewish Community of Pest's headquarters on Síp Street, the Nazis ordered the creation of a Jewish Council (Judenrat), an administrative body composed of community leaders through which the Gestapo would communicate with and issue orders to Hungary's Jews. Munkácsi took on the role of secretary general for the Jewish Council, no doubt believing that his legal acumen and experience would serve as a bulwark against the persecution of Jews. He could not have anticipated just how powerless the Jewish Council would be.

In *How It Happened* Munkácsi describes the crush of more than a hundred decrees in a matter of months, issued by Sondereinsatzkommando Eichmann, by Eichmann himself, and by the Hungarian government, which severely limited the lives of the Jewish citizens of Hungary. Munkácsi details the seizure and looting of Jewish property under the euphemistic guise of

Fig. 16   Founded in 1909 as a small collection of Hungarian Judaica, and exhibited in a
private apartment in Budapest, the Hungarian Jewish Museum had collected more than
five thousand objects and documents by 1932 when it moved into its current location
behind the Dohány Street Synagogue. At this assembly for the Jewish Museum Association,
in one of the main exhibition halls, Ernő Munkácsi, the museum's de facto director from
1931 to 1945, is on the dais in the foreground, in profile at the far left.

"requisitions," noting that the requisitioning of Jewish homes in Budapest
was "the first sign of destiny waiting in the wings."[29] He recounts the Jewish
Council's desperate efforts to get help from their many contacts within the
Hungarian government, only to find that those contacts suddenly couldn't
be reached, wouldn't reply, had been arrested, or had gone into hiding. And
he explains how the Jewish Council soon learned that the gravest abuse was
being suffered by Jews in the provinces, where, between 15 May and 7 July
1944, in less than eight weeks, 437,402 men, women, and children were
rounded up, forced into ghettos, and deported by the wagonload to the
Auschwitz-Birkenau death camp.[30] The overwhelming question that hangs
over *How It Happened* is whether the Budapest-based Jewish Council could
have done more to save Hungarian Jewry.

    As related by Munkácsi, the Council was slow to understand or react to
what was happening in the provinces. As the weeks passed, more and more
clandestine reports of the atrocities filtered into Budapest, yet the Council's

response was "almost completely ineffectual."[31] Meanwhile, the Council faced mounting anger and resentment on the part of its constituents, many of whom had relatives deported from the countryside. On 10 June 1944, in his role as secretary general for the Jewish Council, Munkácsi recorded an explosive meeting between a delegation of Zionists, leftists, and other resistance-oriented Jews with the senior leaders of the Council.[32] The activists, led by spokesperson Imre Varga, accused the Council of cowardice: "How can we stand for this any longer? How can we content ourselves with mere petitions and servile supplications instead of revealing it all to Christian society? We must shout out to the whole world that they are murdering us! We must resist instead of slavishly obeying their orders!"[33]

Varga's speech and subsequent suicide appear to have been a turning point for Ernő Munkácsi. Immediately afterward, Munkácsi's work as scribe for the Jewish Council ended and he joined activists such as Lajos Gottesmann, Sándor Somló, Rabbi Fábián Herskovits, and Fülöp and Jenő Grünvald in writing and distributing an underground pamphlet informing Gentile Hungarians about the murder of Jewish Hungarians – and asking for their help.[34] Charged with drafting the secret pamphlet, Munkácsi aimed to write in such a way as to "move both the mind and the heart" of his fellow Hungarians:[35] "We did not raise our voices when we were robbed of our property and lost our human dignity and respect as citizens. We even desisted from this measure of last resort when we were torn away from our family hearths. But now it is our very existence that has come under threat."[36]

Although Council president Samu Stern would not support the underground pamphlet, Munkácsi and his fellow activists went ahead anyway, drafting, copying, and distributing two thousand copies at great personal risk.[37] Holocaust historian Randolph Braham has written that "the mimeographing and distribution of the appeal was the first overt act of defiance of any importance undertaken by members of the Council," although he also makes clear that "it is impossible to determine what if any impact the appeal had."[38]

The police arrested, interrogated, and tortured some of those involved in distributing the pamphlet.[39] Ernő Munkácsi was interrogated at the Council's offices, but managed to convince the police that any similarities between his writing style and the style of the pamphlet were coincidental: "'These are commonplaces used by everyone,' I answered by way of an explanation."[40] After being released, Munkácsi decided it was time to go into hiding. He and his wife and their two daughters were given refuge in the home of

Ferenc and Mária Fittler in Zsófialiget, a village near Budapest. (In addition to providing a safe hiding place for the Munkácsi family, the Fittlers saved the lives of eight other Jews.[41])

Ernő Munkácsi probably could have fled Hungary in 1944. After all, other leading members of the Jewish community, among them members of the Jewish Council, used their connections to escape. And in his own family, fourteen members – including his uncle Gábor Munk and three of Ernő's first cousins – escaped to Switzerland in June 1944 on the so-called Kasztner Train.[42] Moreover, in early October 1944, Munkácsi's brother Sándor, who had been living in Switzerland since 1917,[43] managed to secure for Ernő and his family a coveted entry permit to Switzerland, a deliverance that Ernő never used.[44] By then, Munkácsi, predicting like many others that the war was nearly over, might have decided it was easier to stay. But it would not be out of character if Ernő Munkácsi, proud "Magyar of the Israelite faith," deliberately chose to remain in Hungary to serve his community.

In January 1945, after five months in hiding, Munkácsi and his family returned to the severely damaged city of Budapest. Hungarian Jewry had been devastated; of the 760,000 citizens of Hungary classified as Jewish in 1944, only an estimated 250,000 survived.[45] Many members of Munkácsi's family, including an aunt and uncle and numerous cousins, were killed by the Nazis or the Arrow Cross. Munkácsi's beloved sister, Noémi, her husband, Ernő Winkler, chief rabbi of Nagykanizsa, and their two teenage children, Gábor and Sonja, had been deported to Auschwitz in 1944. Ernő Winkler and Gábor were murdered.[46] (Survivors Noémi and Sonja emigrated to Israel after the war.)

With the end of the war, Ernő Munkácsi returned to writing, now primarily for *Új Élet* (*New Life*), the postwar weekly newspaper of Hungarian Jewry. There was a new, uncompromising tone to his writings. He was relentless in demanding compensation and reparations for Hungarian Jews. He confronted and lambasted government bodies for not doing enough to help. In a 1946 article, "Speaking Openly," he wrote: "Why has this promise [of reparations], made by the interim government in Debrecen, taken not one month [as promised], but more than one year? … Jews cannot be asked to make more sacrifices and you cannot ask them to relinquish any more! This must be stated: the horrific murderous attack on Hungarian Jews must not remain an open wound on the body of the nation."[47]

In other ways too, Munkácsi resumed his role as a leader of the now much-diminished Jewish community in Budapest. He returned to his

Fig. 17   On 4 June 1935, with the Second World War nowhere in sight, Ernő Munkácsi's uncle Gábor Munk (1865–1955) hosted an elegant dinner at his Budapest home to celebrate the marriage of Munkácsi's cousin Éva Kahán to Miklós "Misi" Speter. Fourth from left, wearing glasses, is Gábor Munk, younger brother of Bernát Munkácsi and a prosperous businessman in interbellum Hungary. The bride's father, Niszon Kahán (1883–1949), second from right (marked "1") was a leading official in the Hungarian Zionist Alliance who, in 1944, would serve on the Jewish Council. A few years after this party, in June 1944, ten people at this table escaped Nazi-occupied Hungary on the so-called Kasztner Train, thanks to Kahán's Zionist connections and Munk's money. Kahán fled with his wife (and Gábor's daughter) Gizella Munk (marked "4"); his son Andor (Bandi) (marked "12"); his daughter the bride Éva; his son-in-law Misi; and his grandson (born in 1938). Munk fled with his wife Irma (third from left); his son Lajos (marked "3"); his daughter Ernesztina (marked "14"); his grandson Peter Munk (marked "13"); and four other family members not seen here.

position at the Hungarian Jewish Museum and was named to the executive bodies of the Jewish Hungarian Literary Society and the Hungarian Jewish Association for Palestine. Still, the question of what more the Hungarian Jewish Council could have done in 1944 to save Hungarian Jewry hung over Ernő Munkácsi. In 1945, with the post-war People's Courts and Certification Committees casting a wide net to capture and punish war criminals, Ernő Munkácsi was called to testify twice before the certification committee for lawyers, required to defend and justify his war-time activities. Records of his first appearance are lost or missing from the Budapest City Archives, but according to records of his second appearance, in June 1945, it was alleged that he "left his position at the most critical moment and went into hiding."[48]

Munkácsi rejected the findings. During the appeal, witnesses affirmed that he couldn't possibly have continued his work given that he was under suspicion for his involvement with the illegal pamphlets. On 11 October 1945, his appeal was upheld and he was provided with the appropriate "certification" to continue working as a lawyer.

Ferenc Laczó's essay in this volume details and places into historical context the conflicted role of the members of the Hungarian Central Jewish Council and the series of "choiceless choices" they faced. For the choices he made while he was secretary general of the Council, Munkácsi was personally attacked. In a widely distributed letter dated 22 October 1947, Henrik Fisch, a rabbi and Holocaust survivor, claimed that Munkácsi and other members of the Jewish Council had first-hand knowledge that Hungarian Jews were being deported to extermination camps, yet remained silent.[49] Stunned by the allegations, Munkácsi fought back vigorously, suing Henrik Fisch for defamation.[50] In a private letter to his friend and fellow Council member Lajos Stöckler,[51] Munkácsi insisted that he had done his utmost to help his fellow Jews: "When the truth came out about the deportations, I was the one who drafted illegal flyers to prevent further deportations." He added another, more personal detail: "Had I had any inkling of the deportations, then I certainly would have had the possibility to notify my sister and her family in Nagykanizsa, who were dragged away to Auschwitz. This fact alone says it all."[52]

The ordeals experienced by Munkácsi – the murder of family members, the destruction of the Jewish community, and the accusations made against him – seemed to strengthen his resolve to record his version of the events. Excerpts of *How It Happened* began appearing in the weekly Jewish newspaper *Új Élet* in 1946, drawing on documents Munkácsi could access, his notes, and his recollection of events. He wrote the book in an era of post-war retribution to offer his inside perspective on the tragic events of 1944, and also to justify his actions and defend his good name. In many ways, Munkácsi's *How It Happened*, published in Hungary in 1947, would be the capstone to his life's work.

Ernő Munkácsi died of heart failure on 1 September 1950, in the Hungarian resort town of Balatonfüred, where his family had often spent their summers. He was only fifty-four. Well-educated, cultured, and born into a hopeful era for Hungarian Jewry, Munkácsi's life had, right up to the eve the Second World War, followed a fairly predictable path of bourgeois privilege. For

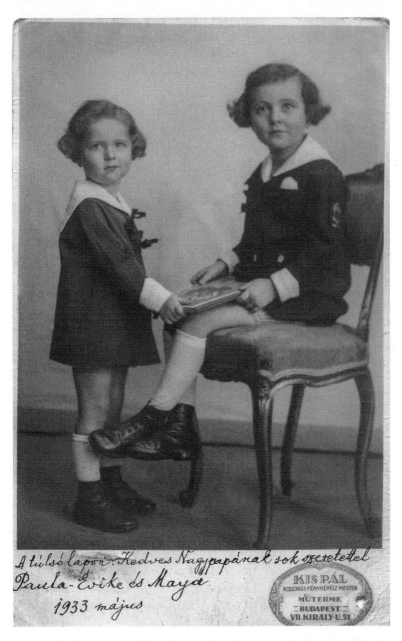

Fig. 18 Ernő Munkácsi and his wife, Erzsébet Rózsa Mairovitz (1903–1994), had two children, Paula Éva (1928–2012) and Mária Veronika (AKA Maya) (1930–2013), posing here in May 1933 for the well-known Hungarian photographer Pál Kis in his studio at 51 Király Street in Budapest. With their parents, Éva and Maya survived the last months of the war thanks to a Gentile couple, Ferenc and Mária Fittler, who allowed the Munkácsis and eight other Jews to hide in their home outside Budapest. The photographer Pál Kis and his wife, Ilona Klein, were deported from Budapest in December 1944 and murdered in the Buchenwald concentration camp.

Munkácsi, as for so many others, the Holocaust changed everything. In a wistful 1941 essay, "Utazás a múltba" (Journey into the Past), he wrote about a reverential feeling as he stood before the gravesite of his grandparents: "I felt that every suffering and struggle is transitory. The sun shines, the spirit lives, once in them, now in me, afterwards in my children." As if it were an epitaph, he added: "No one dies whose descendants remember them."[53]

Notes

1 Today, Panticeu, Romania.

2 Paul Lendvai, *The Hungarians: A Thousand Years of Victory in Defeat* (Princeton, NJ: Princeton University Press, 2003), 330.

3 Méir Ávrahám Munk, *Életem történetei* [My Life's Histories] (Budapest and Jerusalem: Múlt és Jövő, 2002). In the afterword, Michael K. Silber attests that Munk's autobiography remains a vital source for historians studying nineteenth-century Jewish life in rural Hungary. Although Ernő Munkácsi and his sister, Noémi Munkácsi, commissioned the Hungarian translation of the autobiography in 1942, it remained unpublished until 2002. The original Hebrew has been lost.

4 András Koerner, *How They Lived: The Everyday Lives of Hungarian Jews, 1867–1940* (Budapest: Central University Press, 2015), 135–6.

5 Adolf and Sarah Munk had five sons, but only three survived infancy.

6 István Kozmács, *The Life of Bernát Munkácsi* (Budapest: Hungarian National Organization of the World Congress of Finno-Ugric Peoples, 2010), 28–30.

7 *Századunk névváltoztatásai: Helytartósági és Miniszteri Engedéllyel, Megváltoztatott Nevek Gyüjteményei, 1800–1893* [Name Changes of Our Century: Collections of Name Changes Made with Governor and Ministerial Permission, 1800–1893] (Budapest: Hornyánszky Viktor, 1895), 164. Munkácsi literally means "from Munkács." Since the family did not originate from the city of Munkács, Bernát presumably selected the name because it so closely resembled his birth name.

8 Bernát Munkácsi, *Genealógiai Jegyzetek (A 80-as évektol kezdve) Származásunk és rokonságunk könyve I, Munk Alchönon ivadékai* [Genealogical Notes (starting in the 80s): The Book of Our Origins and Relatives, Book I, the Munk and Alchönon descendants]. Thanks to the late Peter Munk for giving me access to Volumes 1 and 2 of these notebooks, since donated to the Hungarian Jewish Museum and Archives in Budapest.

9 Kinga Frojimovics, *Szétszakadt történelem: Zsidó vallási irányzatok Magyarországon, 1868–1950* [History Torn Apart: Jewish Religious Directions in Hungary, 1868–1950] (Budapest: Balassi Kiadó, 2008), 14.

10 Between 1840 and 1917, twenty Jews (as well as twenty-one Jewish converts to Christianity) were elected to the Hungarian Academy of Sciences out of a total of 236 members. Raphael Patai, *The Jews of Hungary: History, Culture, Psychology* (Detroit: Wayne State University Press 1996), 389.

11 Correspondence of Ernő Munkácsi, xix-69, Hungarian Jewish Museum and Archives, Budapest.

12 "Ernő's Bar Mitzvah," Correspondence of Ernő Munkácsi, xix-69, Hungarian Jewish Museum and Archives, Budapest.

13 Hungarian Jewish Museum and Archives, Budapest. Thanks to Zsuzsanna Toronyi, who located the original diploma.

14 Victor Karády, "The Jewish Bourgeoisie of Budapest," *In the Land of Hagar: The Jews of Hungary, History, Society and Culture*, ed. Anna Szalai (Tel Aviv: Beth Hatefutsoth, the Nahum Goldmann Museum of Jewish Diaspora, Ministry of Defence Publishing House, 2002), 147.

15 Kinga Frojimovics, *Szétszakadt történelem: Zsidó vallási irányzatok Magyarországon, 1868–1950* [History Torn Apart: Jewish Religious Directions in Hungary, 1868–1950] (Budapest: Balassi Kiadó, 2008), 227.

16 This was a reprint of a Jubilee volume in honour of Prof. Bernhard Heller, published under the name Ernest Munkácsi, printed by József Kertész in Karcag, Hungary, no date.

17 Ernő Munkácsi, *Könyvek és kövek: történeti és müvészeti irások* [Books and Stones: Historical and Cultural Writings] (Budapest: Libanon, 1944), 7–8.

18 Bernát Munkácsi, összeállitotta [compiled by], *A nyitrai, nagyváradi és budapesti Munk-család valamint a nyitrai, nagytapolcsányi, balassagyarmati, nagykanizsai, szentesi és budapesti Felsenburg-család genealógiája, Ősök és ivadékok* [Genealogy of the Munk Family of Nyitra, Nagyvárad and Budapest, also of the Felsenburg Family of Nyitra, Nagytapolcsány, Balassagyarmat, Nagykanizsa, Szentes and Budapest, Ancestors and Descendants], Kiegészitette, átdolgozta és sajtó alá rendezte [Supplemented, revised, and edited by] Ernő Munkácsi, *Magyar Zsidó Családok Genealógiája, Elsö kötet* [Genealogy of Hungarian Jewish Families, Vol. 1] (Budapest: Országos Magyar Zsidó Múzeum [National Hungarian Jewish Museum], 1939).

19 The notebooks and sketchbooks comprising Bernát Munkácsi's genealogical research are at the Hungarian Jewish Museum and Archives in Budapest: *Genealógiai Jegyzetek (A 80-as évektol kezdve), Származásunk és rokonságunk könyve I, Munk Alchönon ivadékai* [Genealogical Notes (From the '80s on): Our Origins and relatives, Book I, Descendants of Munk and Alchönon]; *Genealógiai Jegyzetek, Származásunk és rokonságunk könyve II, Benét Gábriel, Felsenburg Mózes és Stein Gedelják anyai ágon való ősök leszármazottjai* [Genealogical Notes: Our origins and relatives, Book II, Maternal descendants of Gábriel Benét, Mózes Felsenburg, and Gedelják Stein].

20 Ernő Munkácsi, "Az Országos Magyar Zsidó Múzeum jelentése Előterjesztette
    az 1940 évi rendes közgyülésen Dr. Munkácsi Ernő ügyvezető igazgató" ["Report
    on the National Hungarian Jewish Museum presented on occasion of the
    1940 Annual General Meeting by Dr. Ernő Munkácsi, Director General"], in
    IMIT évkönyv *1940* [IMIT yearbook 1940] (Budapest: Izraelita Magyar Irodalmi
    Társulat [Israelite Hungarian Literary Society], 1940), 346.

21 Márton Vida, *Itéljetek! Néhány kiragadott lap a magyar-zsidó* életközösség
    könyvéből [You Judge! A Few Pages Torn from the Book on Magyar-Jewish
    Coexistence] (Budapest: [V. Márton], 1939).

22 Ernő Munkácsi, "Az Országos Magyar Zsidó Múzeum jelentése" ["Report on the
    National Hungarian Jewish Museum"], in IMIT évkönyv *1940*, 341.

23 Ernő Munkácsi, *Küzdelmes* évek ... *Cikkek és tanulmányok a magyar zsidóság elmúlt*
    évtizedéből [Years of Struggle ... Articles and Studies from the Past Decade of
    Hungarian Jewry] (Budapest: Libanon 1943), 141.

24 Ernő Munkácsi, *Könyvek és kövek: történeti és művészeti irások* [Books and Stones:
    Historical and Cultural Writings] (Budapest: Libanon, 1944). For more about
    the labour service, see Randolph Braham, *The Hungarian Labor Service System,*
    1939–1945 (Boulder, CO: *East European Quarterly*, 1977).

25 Thanks to the director of the Military History Archives in Budapest, Col.
    Dr Attila Bonhardt, who went out of his way to help me search for Munkácsi's
    war records. Large sections of military files were destroyed at the end of the war
    and during the siege of Budapest.

26 Ernő Munkácsi, "*Utazás a múltba*" [Journey into the Past], in IMIT évkönyv *1941*
    (Budapest: Izraelita Magyar Irodalmi Társulat [Israelite Hungarian Literary
    Society], 1941), 206.

27 Ernő Munkácsi, "Az Országos Magyar Zsidó Múzeum jelentése" ["Report on the
    National Hungarian Jewish Museum"], in IMIT évkönyv *1940*, 339.

28 Ibid., 341.

29 Ernő Munkácsi, *How It Happened*, 53.

30 Lendvai, *The Hungarians*, 422.

31 Munkácsi, *How It Happened*, 139.

32 Ibid., 139–40.

33 For full text of Varga's speech, see Randolph L. Braham, *The Politics of Genocide:*
    The Holocaust in Hungary, Vol. 1, Third Edition (Boulder, CO: Eastern European
    Monographs, 2016), 808.

34 For the complete pamphlet, see Zoltán Vági, László Csősz, and Gábor Kádár,
    The Holocaust in Hungary: Evolution of a Genocide (Lanham, MD: AltaMira Press,
    2013), 273–4.

35 Munkácsi, *How It Happened*, 141.

36 Ibid., 143.

37 Braham, *The Politics of Genocide, Vol. 2*, 1316.

38 Braham, *The Politics of Genocide, Vol. 1*, 809–12.

39 Munkácsi, *How It Happened*, 146.

40 Ibid., 147.

41 The Fittlers were awarded the Righteous Among the Nations honorific by the State of Israel in 2001.

42 See Anna Porter, *Kasztner's Train: The True Story of Rezső Kasztner, Unknown Hero of the Holocaust* (Vancouver: Douglas & McIntyre, 2008).

43 Correspondence of Sándor Munkácsi, 1914–1917, C.7414, H.460.10863, Memorial Museum of Hungarian Speaking Jewry, Safed, Israel.

44 Letter from Sándor Munkácsi to Gábor Munk, 7 October 1944, private collection of the estate of Peter Munk.

45 Vági, Csősz, and Kádár, *The Holocaust in Hungary: Evolution of a Genocide*, 330.

46 An updated English version of Bernát Munkácsi's genealogy of 1939, published privately in 1986, includes information about family members deported during the Second World War: *The Genealogy of the Munk Family from Hungary*, ed. Dr Arnold Ages, translated and updated by Dr Steven Nadasy, private collection of the estate of Peter Munk.

47 Ernő Munkácsi, "Nyíltan megmondjuk" [Speaking Openly], Új Élet: *A Magyar Zsidóság Lapja* [*New Life: The Newspaper of Hungarian Jewry*] 2, 18 (2 May 1946).

48 Nb.Ig.II 1099/1945/4.szám, Budapest Népbíróság Igazolófellebezési Tanács [Budapest People's Courts Certification Appeals Council], Budapest City Archives.

49 Letter from Henrik Fisch, 22 October 1947, Correspondence of Ernő Munkácsi, XIX–LI 74.172 D-5/3, Hungarian Jewish Museum and Archives, Budapest.

50 Declaration of the legal action, B.16.093/1947, Hungarian Jewish Museum and Archives, Budapest. The defamation suit against Fisch appears to have been settled or dropped, as no further relevant courts records could be located.

51 Lajos Stöckler (1897–1960), industrialist and member of the Jewish Council in Budapest from July 1944, served as de facto head of the Council during the regime of Ferenc Szálasi. After the war, he was president of the Pest Israelite Congregation and of the National Association of Hungarian Jews (*Magyar Izraeliták Országos Irodája*).

52 Letter to Lajos Stöckler, 29 October 1947, Correspondence of Ernő Munkácsi, XXIV-A-8C, Hungarian Jewish Museum and Archives, Budapest.

53 Ernő Munkácsi, "*Utazás a múltba*" [Journey into the Past], in IMIT évkönyv *1941* [IMIT yearbook 1941], 210.

HOW IT HAPPENED

Documenting the Tragedy of Hungarian Jewry

In memory of

DR ERNŐ WINKLER,

beloved brother-in-law and chief rabbi of Nagykanizsa,
who suffered martyrdom during the deportations.[1]

---

1 Born in Újpest in 1894, Dr Ernő Winkler served as chief rabbi of Nagykanizsa
from 1919 to 1944. He married Ernő's sister, Noémi Munkácsi, in the 1920s. In April
1944 Winkler was arrested by the Gestapo and later deported. He perished in the
Mauthausen concentration camp on 10 July 1944.

Preface

This book is not intended to provide an organized chronology of the tragedy of 1944. It will take a long time before the availability of sources can make such an undertaking possible. Instead, my main purpose here has been to publish the documents found in the archives of the National Office of Hungarian Israelites,[1] augmenting them as best I can by the authentic evidence of an eyewitness account. Formulating the task as such inevitably entails consequences. For instance, the tragic developments of 1944 may easily have included events, arguably even significant ones, which will go unmentioned in this book, as may certain individuals whose role I had no opportunity to directly observe. Being left out, however, does not detract one iota from the weight of the events in question any more than from the merits or, as the case may be, errors of the actors here passed over in silence. This is one reason why the book ends on October 16 – the date that, in any event, opened an altogether new chapter in the disastrous history of 1944.[2]

I wish to express my gratitude to the Chair of the Hungarian Joint Distribution Committee[3] for supporting the publication of this book.   *The Author*

1   The National Office of Hungarian Israelites (Magyarországi Izraeliták Országos Irodája, M101) was the central administrative body of the Neolog Jewish Communities in Hungary from the time of the great schism of the Jewish religious branches in Hungary in 1869 until 1950. In 1950 the organizations of the Jewish communities were united under the pressure of the communist state and in 1951 were renamed the National Representation of Hungarian Israelites (Magyar Izraeliták Országos Képviselete, M10K).

2   Following Regent Miklós Horthy's failed attempt to exit the war on 15 October 1944, he was forced by the Germans to resign and was replaced by Ferenc Szálasi, leader of the pro-Nazi Arrow Cross party. This opened a new chapter in the sufferings of the remaining Jews of Hungary.

3   The Hungarian branch of the American Jewish Joint Distribution Committee (Joint Magyarországi Bizottsága) was founded in March 1945 in Budapest under the chairmanship of Frigyes Görög (1890–1978). Görög held this office until February 1948 when, yielding to communist pressure, he resigned and emigrated from the country.

I

Introduction

How did it happen? This is the question posed by every Hungarian Jew and non-Jew who wants to be clear about the history of the tragedy that befell us in recent years.

It is in the natural order of things that momentous events of history are followed by mushrooming historical treatises, memoirs, and biographies. Undoubtedly, historiography will be concerned with the phenomenon of fascism for decades after its defeat, producing a swelling corpus of literature on Jewish history, including a string of works treating the catastrophe of Hungarian Jewry.

We have not yet reached the point where the demise of Hungarian Jewry could be chronicled with any valid claim to systematic completion. The political trials that shed light on the most sinister crimes of universal history have only recently concluded, and only in part.[1] In Hungary, some of those involved remain reluctant to come forward with the facts, while others are busy writing their memoirs. Furthermore, the vested interests of some of the actors in daily politics as we speak will certainly keep them from revealing the motives behind their past deeds.

Despite all these impediments, I feel a need – indeed an obligation – to commit to paper certain episodes of this critical phase of the tragedy, and to publish its documents. Public discourse today is rife with widely contradictory information about everything that happened to and around the Jews of Hungary during the German occupation.[2] The true driving force behind events is seldom recognized, and individual participants are often misidentified. It is thus vital to open the eyes of the public to allow a glimpse of historic reality.

---

1 In 1945, parallel to the International Military Tribunals, People's Courts were established in Hungary to prosecute war criminals. Of the approximately 60,000 people put on trial, 27,000 were convicted, 489 were sentenced to death, and 189 were eventually executed, mostly for crimes related to the Holocaust.
2 The German occupation of Hungary lasted from 19 March 1944 until 13 April 1945.

Any historian intent on fulfilling his mission faithfully will have no choice but to deny his friends and enemies alike. He cannot afford love or hate. He must remain cool and keep a marble face, subservient to none but the cause of truth – unconditionally, without regard to whether uncovering that truth is to the benefit of some and to the detriment of others.

This is certainly the fate awaiting the author of these lines. The present work does not draw primarily on personal experience so much as on contemporaneous documents. Regrettably, very few of the documents kept by the Jewish Council,[3] along with the meeting minutes and reports on talks between Hungarian and German authorities, survive. Although the impending Arrow Cross raids and searches forced the destruction of copies, one copy of every document was deposited for safekeeping in the basement of a villa on the Buda side of the city, owned by the university professor József Huszti.[4] Later on, the villa was hit by a bomb, and the thick bundles of documents are yet to be unearthed from under the ruins. Lacking this particular mass of evidence, I have had to rely on valuable alternative sources of my own, which I trust will in some way make up for the absence of the buried documents.

3   The Hungarian Central Jewish Council (Központi Zsidó Tanács), also known as
    the Judenrat, was founded by order of the Sondereinsatzkommando Eichmann on
    21 March 1944, right after the occupation of the country. As the administrative body
    responsible for the internal affairs of Jews in Hungary, the Council oversaw all official
    contact between the German or Hungarian authorities and the country's Jews,
    effectively acting to implement increasingly restrictive measures against the Jewish
    population. For more information, see the Glossary.
4   Professor József Huszti (1887–1954), literary scholar and member of the Hungarian
    Academy of Sciences. In 1944 his home in Buda's Farkasrét neighbourhood served as
    a place of refuge for colleagues and friends hiding from Nazis and the Arrow Cross,
    including historian Gyula Szekfű.

The Entrapment of Hungarian Jewry

Mistakes of the Jewish leadership – Jewish relations with the
Social Democratic and the Smallholders' Parties under the Kállay
cabinet – A general assembly on Occupation Day – Zionists against
official leaders – The Gestapo crops up in Síp Street – Formation
of the Jewish Council – The Hungarian government relinquishes
the Jews to the Germans – "Whatever the Germans want must be
given to them" – First measures of the Gestapo – The first Jewish
Council – The Gestapo entraps Hungarian Jewry – The identity of
SS Kommando staff responsible for liquidating Jews – Eichmann,
Krumey, Wisliceny – The great lies – The "education" of Jews in
the provinces – Envoys from around the country – Disorganization
of Hungarian Jewry in the service of the German "enterprise"

History rarely produces accidents; events usually occur in a concatenation of cause and effect. Whenever the random does seem to play a role, in reality its influence tends to be illusory or insignificant, leaving little doubt that the event in question would have transpired no matter what, at best with some delay or inconsequential variation.

Those familiar with the woes and problems of Hungarian Jewry should have been able to realize decades earlier that the tragedy would inevitably happen, and not just due to the pressure of external causes. The peril from the world outside could have been fended off, at least to some extent, by thorough internal organization and other purposeful measures. The ruin of Hungarian Jewry was for the most part rooted in a sense of inertia that prevailed despite the minority's considerable size, moral values, and economic achievements. In turn, this inertia came about as a direct consequence of

Fig. 19   In the state room of their headquarters at 12 Síp Street, the Pest Israelite
Congregation, representing Budapest's Neolog Jews, is gathered here for its general
assembly, circa 1937. On the wall at left is a portrait of the banker Mór Wahrmann
(1832–1892), the first Jew elected to the Hungarian Parliament (in 1869). At right hangs
the portrait of Wolf "Sáje" Schossberger, president of the Pest Israelite Congregation from
1869–71. The small man with white moustache on the dais next to the speaker is Samu
Stern, president of the Pest Israelite Congregation. Seated next to him is Ernő Munkácsi,
then chief counsel and secretary of the Pest Israelite Congregation. A few years later, when
Adolf Eichmann ordered the creation of a Hungarian Judenrat in March 1944, requiring
that it be run by men with authority in the community, Samu Stern became president and
Ernő Munkácsi secretary of the Jewish Council.

organizational divisions[1] and the aloofness of leaders from the Jewish masses,
whose problems and ideas they hardly knew – or, if they did, hardly shared
or represented. This gulf prevented the leadership in the most critical hours
from being able to exercise control over large masses of Jews, let alone
influence their actions in any meaningful way. The absence of democratic

1   The author is referring to the schism of the Jewish religious branches in Hungary
     in 1869–71, which led to the creation of three separate nationwide organizations or
     communities: Neolog, Orthodox, and Status Quo Ante.

voting rights and community institutions thwarted all talent, good intentions, and salutary initiatives. This ineptitude, indeed these blunders one might say, led to serious moral consequences. On the one hand, the well-heeled groups of the Jewish community failed, in the years of deepest crisis, to produce the means to provide adequate support for the impoverished Jewish masses, including clothing for the scores of thousands in labour service[2] who froze to the bone in the snowfields of Ukraine. On the other hand, many urban-dwelling Jews, the wealthy and the intellectuals chief among them, decided to get baptized *en masse*, denying their Jewish spiritual heritage. The resulting moral crisis made itself felt constantly not only among the Jews but within the fold of the Christian churches as well.

In February and March 1944, on the eve of the great tragedy, the creative energies of Hungarian Jews in high office were consumed by futile bickering. Specifically, the OMZSA[3] competed with the Veterans' Committee[4] for influence and assets to fund their activities.

The groups of progressive Jews[5] simply lived their red-tape-ridden lives from day to day – if you could call it a "life." They had been waiting seventy-five years for a renewal, but the miracle had always capsized on internal strife. The Pest Israelite Congregation[6] stood virtually alone as the only

---

2 In fact, the Jewish community made a considerable effort to improve the generally miserable conditions endured by those forced to serve in the labour service (*munkaszolgálat*, or *musz*) required of "political unreliables" and Jews after 1941. However, most of the goods sent to the front for (or taken along with) labour servicemen were confiscated by members of the German and Hungarian armies. It should also be noted that unarmed labour servicemen were officially members of the Hungarian Army; it would therefore have been the task of the state to provide them with clothing, food, and other necessities.

3 National Hungarian Association to Assist Jews (Országos Magyar Zsidó Segítő Akció, or OMZSA): aid agency founded in 1939 to support Jews drafted for labour service and their families.

4 Established as a department of the Pest Israelite Congregation in November 1939, the Veterans' Committee was soon turned into a joint body of the Neolog and Orthodox national offices (Országos Izraelita Irodák Hadviseltek Bizottsága). Its main task was to represent the Jewish veterans of the First World War and support the labour servicemen during the Second World War.

5 The author refers to the Neolog branch of Judaism.

6 The largest congregation or community of Jews in Hungary at that time, the Pest Israelite Congregation (Pesti Izraelita Hitközség), for which Ernő Munkácsi served as chief secretary, represented the approximately 200,000 Neolog Jews of Budapest. As established in the late eighteenth century, the Pest Israelite Congregation had

organization with a large constituency that undeniably managed, not without its own imperfections, to perform significant worship and cultural functions capable of reaching the entire Jewish population of the country. As destiny would have it, the overture to the cataclysm coincided with the session of the general assembly of the Pest Congregation, which in 1944 happened to fall on March 19, that fatal date.

Although the principals of Hungarian Jewry were caught off guard by the German invasion, it was hardly the kind of incident that could have escaped their attention as a looming threat. The fate of Germany's Jews had been more or less known, as had the Nazi practice of deporting Jews from any country they occupied. Most of this knowledge, however, was a matter of vague rumour rather than actual fact.

Just as the ex-regent,[7] his entourage, and Kállay[8] all hoped that the country would be spared the role of a theatre of military operations, the Jewish community elders, never averse to emulating the methods of national politics, entertained the illusion that Hungary would be the exception, a tiny foothold of an island in a sea of Jewish devastation.

It can be stated with objective certainty that the presidency of the National Office of Hungarian Israelites followed the Kállay cabinet's shift to the left[9] with keen interest, making a concerted effort to aid and take advantage of the thawing around the so-called Jewish issue, which set in at the end of 1943 and continued into the first few months of 1944. The National Office

---

represented all members of the Jewish community residing in what was then the city of Pest. However, after the 1869–71 schism in Hungarian Jewry, the Pest Israelite Congregation represented only the (dominant) Neolog Jews of Pest. Referred to variously in English as the Israelite Congregation of Pest, the Pest Jewish Congregation, and the Pest Jewish Community.

7 Regent Miklós Horthy (1868–1957), head of state of the Hungarian Kingdom between 1 March 1920 and 16 October 1944.

8 Miklós Kállay (1887–1967), landowner, politician, prime minister of Hungary between March 1942 and March 1944. After the German invasion of March 1944, he took refuge in the Turkish Embassy in Budapest until November 1944, when Arrow Cross authorities demanded that the embassy extradite him and he turned himself in. He was arrested and deported to Mauthausen, and later taken to Dachau. After the war, he lived in Italy before settling in the United States in 1951.

9 One of the principal aims of Kállay's cabinet was to cautiously distance Hungary from the Nazi orbit and re-establish relations with the Western Powers. This political ambition was reflected in internal policies: while continuing with crude antisemitic rhetoric and adopting another two anti-Jewish laws in 1942 (Laws xv and xvii), the Kállay government also made mitigating gestures toward the Jewish community of Hungary.

managed to bring home a few thousand labour servicemen from Ukraine.[10] Upon the request of the foreign ministry, they authored a memorandum,[11] to be disseminated in neutral territories abroad, which exposed the vicissitudes and sufferings of Hungarian Jews honestly, without any sentimental varnish. They maintained continuous contact with the Social Democratic and Smallholders' parties;[12] and, at Síp Street,[13] they passed from hand to hand a message to the regent from the Smallholders' Party calling for an immediate end to the war and revisions to the anti-Jewish laws.[14] Lawyers assigned by the Social Democratic and Smallholders' parties were met at Síp Street to discuss legislation drafted by the Jewish community designed to pave the way toward the systematic abolition of anti-Jewish provisions.

Meanwhile, the general climate remained tense, and the more reflective minds continued to suffer from gloomy premonitions. Everybody was aware that, due to pressure from Germany – and not least because of its own reluctance to deal with the Jewish question once and for all – the Kállay cabinet's position had been undermined. When on the afternoon of Saturday, March 18, word got around that the regent had been summoned by Hitler,[15] everybody felt we were on the brink of a cataclysm. The next day, on March 19, there was early morning news of expedited German troops having crossed the border and blazing their way toward Budapest.

10 As a result of the relatively moderate anti-Jewish policies of the Kállay government, several labour servicemen who were aged, sick, or had served longer than the required six months were relieved from duty in late 1942 and early 1943. At the same time, the government, wanting to appease the Axis, offered dozens of new, additional labour service units to the Germans. While it is true that the Jewish leadership made considerable efforts to ease the situation of the labour servicemen, it would be an exaggeration to attribute the positive developments exclusively to the activities of the National Office of Hungarian Israelites.

11 It is unclear which memorandum the author is referring to here.

12 Founded in 1930, the Party of Independent Smallholders, Agricultural Labourers and Citizens (Független Kisgazda-, Földmunkás és Polgári Párt), or Smallholders' Party, was an agrarian party of the centre-right with representation in parliament. It was abolished by a decree of the minister of the interior on 28 March 1944. Some of its former members subsequently played a role in resistance activities.

13 The headquarters of the Pest Israelite Congregation was located at 12 Síp Street in Budapest's 7th District.

14 On the anti-Jewish laws, see the Glossary.

15 The author is referring to the second meeting of Hitler and Horthy at Klessheim Castle in today's Austria on 18 March 1944, the last diplomatic step before the German military action against Hungary.

It was in this mood that elected representatives of the Pest Congregation began to gather at the Síp Street headquarters to hold their regular annual meeting. Even though these meetings had for quite some time been routinely orchestrated down to the minutest detail, they retained some of their importance as the only forum for many years – in the absence of any appreciable freedom of assembly and the press – where Jews could debate their issues, deliver speeches of nationwide import, and adopt resolutions that pointed the way forward for the community. Before the passage of the anti-Jewish laws,[16] these general meetings had been rife with clamorous episodes, courtesy of individuals often less than well-versed in public affairs but with a habit of stopping the words in the throats of certain opposition or Zionist speakers. In 1944, however, a pact was made with the Zionists[17] for the general congregation elections. Some of them were given a seat in the body of representatives, and even the leadership of the Pest Congregation now had a Zionist among its members. Since these concessions had been made, the Zionist speakers had reliably voted confidence in the incumbent Jewish leadership, albeit they never failed to emphasize their minority opinion in principle.

This was, then, the atmosphere engulfing Europe's largest Jewish community as it opened its general meeting on the day of the German invasion. The leaders hesitated until the very last minute about holding the assembly as planned, but finally they resolved to go ahead and run down the agenda in the space of half an hour.

Amid rumours that the regent had been detained,[18] the assembly adopted all the proposed resolutions in great haste, in a feverish few minutes, and approved the budget for 1944. The president[19] was about to adjourn when a

16 The first, second, and third anti-Jewish laws were passed in 1938, 1939, and 1941, respectively. See the Glossary.

17 It is unclear what pact the author is referring to here; however, the general reference is to the emergence of the Zionists as important partners of the dominant Neologs. Historically a small and stigmatized minority in Hungary, the Zionists became significantly more influential during the war thanks to their dedicated activism and international contacts.

18 Such rumours drew on the fact that Horthy was Hitler's "guest" at Klessheim Castle right before the German invasion and returned to Budapest only after the invasion had begun.

19 Samu Stern (1874–1947), businessman, president of the Pest Israelite Congregation (as of 1929) and of the National Office of Hungarian Israelites (as of 1932). Served as president of the Central Jewish Council (Központi Zsidó Tanács, Judenrat) from 21 March 1944 to the end of October 1944, when he went into hiding. Stern survived the Holocaust, returning to Budapest, where he died two years later.

Zionist rose to speak,[20] declared non-confidence on behalf of his party, and announced their refusal to authorize the budget. Surely this was a sign of the times. The first to realize the sheer magnitude of the historic juncture around the corner, the Zionists began to pursue what was essentially *realpolitik*. Barely two weeks later, the Zionist vanguard of the day – who, hot on the heels of a pact with the Gestapo, would set out for Palestine on June 30 but make it only to Bergen-Belsen and then to Switzerland, although most reside in Palestine today[21] – made themselves at home in the premises of the Jewish Council, particularly in the Information Office and the Provincial Division.[22] At about the same time, they began to nurture close ties with the council, mainly through the activities of Dr Rezső Kasztner,[23] a former journalist from Kolozsvár, whose role I will discuss later. To some degree, though, the Zionists continued to go their own way. The fact that contact with the ghettos around the provinces never completely broke off was due to the intrepid Zionist lads who travelled the country with forged papers, often wearing fake military uniforms, gathering news and delivering help where it was needed.

20 Probably Niszon Kahán, one of the leaders of the Hungarian Zionist Alliance. See 22.

21 A reference to the Kasztner Train, the result of secret negotiations between the Zionists' Relief and Rescue Committee of Budapest (known by its Hebrew name, *Va'ada*) and Adolf Eichmann, which carried a select group of 1,686 Jews out of Hungary on 30 June 1944 to eventual safety in Switzerland (after unexpectedly being detained at the Bergen-Belsen concentration camp). Passengers included a motley crew of Zionists (including Niszon Kahán, see 22), rabbis, artists, farmers, refugees, children, industrialists, Kasztner's own family and friends, and prominent community members, among them members of Ernő Munkácsi's extended family. See 68–71.

22 The Relief and Rescue Committee and other Zionist activists operated in secret from the ground floor of 12 Síp Street, headquarters of the Pest Israelite Congregation and later also of the Jewish Council.

23 Rezső Kasztner (1906–1957), lawyer, journalist, Zionist leader. Born and raised in Kolozsvár (today Cluj, Romania), he served as secretary-general of the parliamentary group of the Jewish Party in Romania and on the executive of the Palestine Office of the Jewish Agency. After the re-annexation of Transylvania in 1940, he moved to Budapest. As one of the leaders of the Relief and Rescue Committee (Va'ada), Kasztner played a central role in providing aid to Jewish refugees in Hungary and led the clandestine negotiations that resulted in the so-called Kasztner Train (see above). After the war, Kasztner moved to Israel, where, in an infamous libel suit of 1955, he was found guilty of collaboration – a charge overturned by the Supreme Court of Israel in 1958, but not before Kasztner had been shot dead in the street by a Jewish nationalist. Known in the West and in Israel as Rudolf (Israel) Kastner, he is referred to throughout this book as Rezső, the name he used in Hungary.

Following the meeting, the participants rushed home – not a minute too soon. Outside, the rumble of German tanks and vehicles advancing down the boulevards could barely drown cries of "Heil Hitler" from the scum of the city.

As soon as I got back to my office, I received a phone call from someone in the secret police telling me their offices had been occupied and that there were rumours that the Gestapo would be looking for prominent Jews. Shortly afterward, Dr M.B., then a senior congregation official, now a representative of the National Assembly,[24] availed himself of the phone in my office to call his family in the city of Győr; his wife told him about the occupation there. This same colleague of mine was arrested by the Gestapo the next day. Having survived Auschwitz, he returned to Hungary only recently after being away for a year and a half.

The headquarters at Síp Street suddenly abandoned, the always-noisy halls succumbed to a frightening, silent emptiness. By the afternoon, only a handful of clerks, paid by the hour, remained in the building, working in the tax office on the first floor.

Around half past four that day, the phone in my apartment rang again. It was the anxious voice of Mrs Á.Cs., the supervisor of hourly paid scribes.[25] She said she needed to come to my place immediately because of events she did not want to discuss over the phone. She showed up on my doorstep in fifteen minutes. She told me about cream-coloured German cars pulling up in front of the headquarters. Two officers seemingly of high rank disembarked and entered the premises,[26] demanding to know where the prefecture was.

24   Probably Mihály Borsa (1906–1986), born Glück, journalist and lawyer employed by the Pest Israelite Congregation in 1943–44. Immediately after the German invasion, Borsa was arrested and interned in Kistarcsa. In late April 1944, he was deported first to Auschwitz and later to other camps. He was liberated in Dachau. After the war, he became a public servant and served as an MP of the Independent Smallholders' Party between 1945 and 1948. He was the chairman of the Hungarian branch of the American Jewish Joint Distribution Committee from 1957 until his death.

25   Mrs Á.Cs. could not be identified.

26   The two officials who appeared at Síp Street that day were Hermann Krumey and Dieter Wisliceny. Hermann Alois Krumey (1905–1981), SS-Obersturmbannführer, deputy head of Adolf Eichmann's special operations unit (Sondereinsatzkommando Eichmann). In July 1944, he was appointed head of the Vienna branch of the SiPo (Security Police), where he was given responsibility for the supervision of Hungarian Jewish slave labourers in Austria and the Kasztner operation (see 68–71). Arrested but then released by the Allies right after the war, it was not until the arrest of his former boss Adolf Eichmann in 1960 that Krumey, along with his former colleague Otto Hunsche, was put on trial in Germany and, in 1969, eventually sentenced to life

She explained to them there were no office hours on Sunday afternoons and that no senior officials were around. "Don't be scared," said the officers, who must have seen how frightened she was. "I am not scared," the head clerk answered with a smile. "Wir sind Kameraden [we are comrades]," she added quickly, as befits the wife of a decorated lieutenant. (This single sentence condensed the infinite naïveté and ruinous, unfounded optimism of the Jews of Budapest, and perhaps of the whole country.) Finally, the Gestapo officers ordered the clerk to make sure that all senior officials and the entire college of rabbis were present at the headquarters at half past nine the following morning, including "Liberalen und Orthodoxen [Reformed and Orthodox]," and that an envoy would be waiting at the door to lead the officers upstairs. "We want everybody to come," they added. "We are not going to detain anyone." These words already reflected the devilish cunning and unscrupulous hypocrisy of the Gestapo. The idea was to lure the Jews into a trap slowly, step by step, treating them kindly at first, then stepping up the cruelty until they reached the gas chambers of Auschwitz. One of the "affable" Gestapo officers was none other than Baron von Wisliceny, Himmler's brother-in-law, who would make a name for himself as the hangman responsible for deporting the Hungarian Jews.

No sooner had I finished my conversation with the lady clerk than I received another call, this time from Hugó Csergő,[27] who told me that László Bánóczi, then director of the OMIKE theatre,[28] had just had a similar exchange with Gestapo officers. We agreed to meet at six in the evening in Csergő's apartment and ask the presidents of the Pest Congregation to join us. When

---

imprisonment, a sentence upheld on appeal in 1973. Dieter Wisliceny (1911–1948), SS-Hauptsturmführer. As a member of Sondereinsatzkommando Eichmann, he was responsible for the deportation and murder of Jews in Greece, Slovakia, and Hungary. After the war, he was tried as a war criminal in Czechoslovakia, sentenced to death, and executed. Despite Munkácsi's reference to him as "Baron von Wisliceny" further down the page, there is no available evidence that he was a baron or that he was related to Heinrich Himmler.

27 Hugó Csergő (1877–1944/45), journalist, writer, leading official of the Pest Israelite Congregation and personal secretary of its President Samu Stern (see 14). After March 1944, Csergő served as adviser to the Jewish Council. Arrested by the Arrow Cross in October 1944, he was deported to the Sachsenhausen concentration camp, where he perished.

28 László Bánóczi (1884–1945), theatre director and dramaturg. Between 1940 and 1944, he headed the National Hungarian Jewish Cultural Association (Országos Magyar Izraelita Közművelődési Egyesület, OMIKE), which provided employment opportunities to Jewish artists who lost their jobs due to the anti-Jewish laws.

I got there, I found vice presidents Dr Ernő Boda and Dr Ernő Pető,[29] along with Béla Fábián[30] and two clerks, already waiting. The clerks had been put in charge of the logistics of gathering the participants on such short notice.

As we began to talk, what occurred to me instinctively was something that I would come to consciously recognize a few days later as the only way to save Hungarian Jewry – an assumption that the ensuing events would bear out to a tee. This was the recognition that, in their menacing isolation, Hungarian Jews had no one to look to for help but the Hungarians themselves. It was inconceivable that the Hungarian state would betray its loyal citizens who had resided here for a thousand years;[31] that it would settle for aiding and abetting Hitlerian barbarism by watching idly as the Jews fought for sheer survival. I thus proposed that we turn to the Hungarian authorities before entering into any talks with the Germans: "After all, we represent Hungarian citizens!"[32] Those present having conceded my argument, we began to make calls. First we dialled the Ministry of Culture,[33] where the drowsy voice of the secretary on duty informed us, "The minister is out." At the Ministry of the Interior we were told, "The minister is in a council session at Sándor Palace."[34] (As it turned out, this claim was patently false. Now we know that the Gestapo had arrested Keresztes-Fischer[35] on the afternoon of March 19.)

29 Ernő Pető (1882–196?), lawyer, deputy president of the Pest Jewish Congregation, and a member of the Central Jewish Council in 1944. After the war he emigrated to Sao Paulo, Brazil.

30 Béla Fábián (1889–1966), lawyer, publicist, liberal party MP between 1922 and 1939, and president of the Jewish Veterans' Committee (see page oonooo) during the war. Deported to concentration camp, he survived and, in 1948, emigrated to the United States.

31 Jewish communities are indeed known to have existed in Hungary since the first centuries BCE. However, due to repeated expulsions and other historical cataclysms, the Jews living in modern-day Hungary are the descendants of immigrants who arrived in the eighteenth and nineteenth centuries.

32 Ernő Munkácsi is repeating a conviction held by many Hungarian Jews that their long roots in and demonstrated loyalty to the nation made them every bit as Hungarian as any other citizen.

33 Officially the Ministry of Religion and Education, headed by Jenő Szinyei Merse (1888–1957) from July 1942 to March 1944. Szinyei Merse was ousted from his post right after the German occupation.

34 The official residence of the prime minister during the Horthy era. (Today the official residence of the president of Hungary.)

35 Ferenc Keresztes-Fischer (1881–1948), lawyer, conservative politician, minister of the interior from 1931 to 1935 and 1938 to 1944. Arrested by the Gestapo right after the

"Try the Prime Minister's Office," the secretary said. Then we called and were finally able to contact Undersecretary Thuránszky,[36] who asked us to call back in half an hour. When we did, we only reached a deputy. To our question as to whether we should sit down and talk with the Germans, the undersecretary's message was that the answer would be given by the police chief the following morning. This was a bad omen. We had to hurry to send out the telegrams convening the participants.

When we turned to the office of the police chief on Monday morning, we got a peremptory answer: "Whatever the Germans want must be given to them."

This reply decided the policy of the Jewish Council for months to come and, for all intents and purposes, settled the fate of Hungarian Jewry. The Hungarian government of the day let go of the hands of its Jewish citizens, leaving them at the mercy of their enemies. Yet even if the official ranks of Hungary defaulted on their duty, we should not have despaired of shaking up the entire administrative and social machinery from their torpor, resorting to underground propaganda if necessary, to explain to people that the German occupation would lead to the ruin not only of the Jews but of everyone else as well. But the Jewish branch was disorganized, with many of the younger generations toiling away in forced labour, and most of the elderly and others who stayed at home reluctant in their inert optimism to diverge from the "path of law." Under the circumstances, an underground ploy seemed out of the question.

When members of the prefecture began to gather on the morning of March 20, several of them – apparently fearing the worst – brought their wives with them and carried small handbags containing bare necessities. "What if the Germans go back on their word and we are taken straight to the internment camp from Síp Street?" Everyone from the Pest prefecture and the rabbinical body was there without exception, although the Orthodox side was only represented by Fülöp Freudiger,[37] president of the congregation.

German invasion on 19 March 1944, Keresztes-Fischer was deported to Mauthausen and then to the Flossenburg concentration camp. Liberated by US troops, he died in Austria three years later.

36 László Thuránszky (1892–1955), undersecretary in the Prime Minister's Office from 1939 to 8 April 1944, when he was dismissed from his post.

37 Fülöp Freudiger (1900–1976), businessman, factory owner, president of the Orthodox Israelite Congregation in Budapest between 1939 and 1944, and a member of a prominent family of Orthodox leaders. One of the founders in 1943 of the Relief and

Minutes passed amid anxious expectation. At quarter past nine I asked congregation lawyer Dr János Gábor[38] to walk down to the entrance door and wait there for the Germans. When they arrived he duly ushered them to the prefecture room on the third floor. Introductions were made, and talks between Gábor and the Gestapo commanders began. With his candid style of negotiation, Gábor immediately gained the trust of the Gestapo and quickly became one of the most influential Jews of the country as the "head of the government contact group." A good-hearted man, Gábor went on to help a great many people.

We stood in the corridor, basking in the light of the March sun; the rabbis and the leaders awaited the fatal visit in the council chamber. At exactly nine thirty-two in the morning, Gestapo officers in leather coats showed up, carrying sub-machine guns, followed by a civilian with a bad leg and a repulsive face, wearing a black bowler hat – obviously a professional informant or spy.[39] "Gut' Morgen," the Germans said, raising their hands to their caps, the Jewish leaders saluting them by rising from their seats.

When everyone sat down, Hitler's hatchet men asked for a German stenographer and set about "organizing things" with their proverbial German thoroughness. In essence, this consisted of dictating commands. They started by stating for the record that, from that moment onward, all Jewish affairs in Hungary belonged to their discretionary powers and competence. Nobody was allowed to leave his city of residence; those attempting to do so would

---

Rescue Committee (Va'ada) (about which see 15). Also, a first cousin once removed of Ernő Munkácsi's (Freudiger's paternal grandmother, Charlotte Lindenbaum, was a sister of Munkácsi's aunt by marriage). In early August 1944, Freudiger escaped to Romania with his family. He survived the Holocaust and later settled in Israel. His testimony as a witness for the prosecution in the Eichmann trial served as a lightning rod for Holocaust survivors who accused him and his fellow Jewish Council members of not warning them to flee. He was also known as Philipp von Freudiger, and Pinhas or Pinchas Freudiger.

38 János Gábor, lawyer of the Pest Israelite Congregation and one of Ernő Munkácsi's close associates. Thanks to his excellent command of German, he served as liaison between the Jewish Council and Eichmann's Sondereinsatzkommando. Gábor also headed the Jewish Council's working group responsible for relations with the German and Hungarian authorities. In April 1944, he was appointed a member of the "Second" Jewish Council (see Glossary entry on Jewish Councils), a post he held until early August when he was arrested by the Germans, deported, and murdered.

39 It is unclear whom Munkácsi is referring to here. Other contemporary sources do not mention the presence of an informant or spy at the meeting.

be detained. A National Jewish Council (Judenrat) was to be set up by noon the next day as the sole organ through which the SS would communicate with the Jews. All individuals qualifying as Jews were subject to the authority of the Jewish Council, to which they owed unconditional obedience. The Jewish newspaper,[40] and in general any publication of Jewish origin, had to go through censorship by the Gestapo before being published. The Jewish Council, as soon as it had been formed, was to immediately establish its administrative organization, for which they expected to receive a proposal. They stressed that no harm would be done to anyone on account of his Jewish origin. They would be issuing identity documents so that the Council and its administrators could do their jobs. (These were the infamous Gestapo identity cards.) Finally, they ordered the leaders of all Jewish institutions in the city to be convened by five the following afternoon; as well, a comprehensive register was to be made, by the same deadline, of Jewish institutions, associations, and the like, indicating the names of their leaders. They emphatically warned against any attempt to mislead them, saying they were deeply familiar with Jewish affairs and had been the ones to "deal with them" all over Europe.

When they left the building within an hour, a handful of SS privates armed with machine guns were waiting for them at the gate.

One of the congregation elders came into my room and called his wife on the phone. "Everything is all right here," he said. "The Germans still want to help us." This turn of mind was only too typical.

The chairman of the National Office[41] left the chamber with a finished plan for the composition of the Jewish Council as follows:[42] himself; the two vice presidents of the Pest Congregation;[43] prefect Dr Károly Wilhelm;[44] on behalf

---

40 After the occupation, the Germans shut down all but one Jewish newspaper, *Magyar Zsidók Lapja* (*Journal of Hungarian Jews*), which became the official journal of the Jewish Council. As of 27 April 1944, its name was changed to *Magyarországi Zsidók Lapja* (*Journal of Jews in Hungary*).

41 Samu Stern. See 14.

42 It should to be noted that, although he does not mention his own role here, Ernő Munkácsi acted as chief secretary of the Jewish Council.

43 Ernő Pető, see 18, and Ernő Boda (1887–1967), lawyer, deputy president of the Pest Israelite Congregation and a member of the Jewish Council.

44 Károly Wilhelm (1886–1951), lawyer, one of the most influential leaders of the Pest Israelite Congregation and a member of President Samu Stern's inner circle. A member of the Central Jewish Council until the Arrow Cross coup on 15 October 1944, Wilhelm survived the Holocaust in the Budapest ghetto and emigrated to Switzerland in 1948.

of the Zionists, Dr Niszon Kahán;[45] as well, Samu Csobádi,[46] president of the Buda Congregation; and, representing the Orthodox community, national president Samu Kahán-Frankl[47] and Pest president Fülöp Freudiger.[48] The next day, the Germans approved this list without any changes, so it was in this form that the first Jewish Council convened.[49]

In most cases, it takes a certain distance of time to gain the perspective from which one can recognize and properly assess the significance of historical events. If your angle of vision is too narrow, you will get a false picture. If you live in the moment, it is like standing directly in front of the façade of a building; you will not be able to take in the whole.

This is precisely what happened in the hours and days directly following the German occupation. Amid the rampant uncertainty, nobody could be sure about the true nature and breadth of the occupation and, most importantly, whether the Germans had gained comprehensive and permanent discretion over the fate of Hungarian Jewry. Information gleaned from the political trials that have been completed to date lend credence to assumptions at the time that certain German groups had planned the occupation to last for a limited period only, and made it contingent upon the formation of a government to their liking. Today, we are aware of the rather limited number

45   Niszon Kahán (1883–1949), one of the leaders of the Hungarian Zionist Alliance, head of the National Hungarian Association to Assist Jews (Országos Magyar Zsidó Segítő Akció or OMZSA), and a relative of Ernő Munkácsi's (Kahán's wife, Gizella Munk, was Munkácsi's first cousin). A member of the Central Jewish Council from 21 March to 8 May 1944, Kahán escaped Hungary in June 1944 on the Kasztner Train (see 68–71), taking refuge in Switzerland before making *aliyah*, or emigrating to Mandatory Palestine, in 1945.

46   Samu Csobádi (1879–19?), an attorney and the president of the Neolog Israelite Congregation of Buda.

47   Samu Kahán-Frankl (1890–1970), rabbi, president of the Central Office of the Orthodox Israelite Congregation of Hungary. He was a member of the Jewish Council from 21 March to June 1944, when he left his post and went into hiding in Budapest. After the war, between 1945 and 1950, Kahán-Frankl again led the Orthodox community in Hungary. He emigrated first to Israel in 1950, then to the United States.

48   On Freudiger, see 19.

49   Scholars typically distinguish four phases of the Hungarian Central Jewish Council. The first begins with its formation in March 1944. The second begins toward the end of April when the Council comes under the purview of Hungarian authorities. Mid-July 1944 marks the third phase, when representatives of converts to Christianity are added to the Council. The fourth and final Council begins with the Arrow Cross Party's rise to power in mid-October 1944. For more about the Central Jewish Council, see the Glossary.

of Gestapo stationed in the country, how frequently they had to resort to bluffing, and that they could not initially have foretold what degree of resistance they would encounter.

These circumstances go a long way toward explaining why Eichmann's chiefs of staff[50] set about "working" the Jewry with kid gloves. After all, they were dealing with a mass of nearly a million people[51] scattered across hundreds of settlements throughout the country. It was not an easy task to stigmatize, arraign, mobilize, enslave, and destroy so many people, especially as they wanted to accomplish all this while shrouding the ultimate objective in secrecy in an attempt to prevent humane sentiment from welling up in the Hungarians who, for all intents and purposes, had thrown in their lot with their Jewish neighbours despite all the antisemitic propaganda. Yet the Jews of Hungary, lacking foresight and especially organization in their blind torpor, obeyed without any resistance the commands of their executioners, who, unlike their victims, paved the way toward their envisioned future with cold calculation. They had experience and knew how to spare their work energies. They went by the maxim favoured by all dictators through the ages: "*divide et impera.*" As they used Jews in most camps to beat other Jews and even to carry the corpses of their brethren to the crematorium, they enlisted the same tried-and-true method in the service of exterminating Hungarian Jewry. They had Jews organize the ranks of the Jewry, vesting the leaders with apparently broad powers and, just to be on the safe side, set up an extensive network of informants. This enabled them to minimize the use of German resources in their march toward their final goal: the wholesale extermination of Hungarian Jews. Later on, I will address the question of whether the Gestapo was certain from the outset that in Hungary it would follow the model that had worked so well in Germany, Italy, the Netherlands, etc., or whether it had better act as it had in Romania.[52]

---

50 Krumey and Wisliceny. See 16.

51 In fact, the number of people considered Jewish in Hungary on the eve of the occupation was somewhere between 760,000 and 780,000, including converts and recent refugees.

52 It is not clear what Munkácsi is alluding to here. He might be referring to the activities of Eichmann aide and "adviser on Jewish affairs" Gustav Richter (1913–1982) in Romania, who closely cooperated with pro-Nazi local authorities in the murder of hundreds of thousands of Jews. Richter also reached an agreement with Romanian leader Ion Antonescu to organize the deportation of the remaining Jews of Romania to Nazi camps (an agreement which fell through).

The Gestapo forces dispatched to Budapest were divided into several Kommandos. Today we know that one group was dedicated to the task of dealing with left-wing politicians, while other units were in charge of keeping suspicious Hungarian military officers under surveillance. The "liquidation" of Jews was assigned to a third Kommando under the simple soldierly cover name of "Einsatzkommando der Sicherheitspolizei und des SS."[53]

The commander of this last unit was none other than Obersturmbann-führer Eichmann, who claimed to have been born in Palestine, to speak Hebrew, and to be well versed in Jewish studies. These claims were hardly substantiated when Eichmann, bent on showing off his Hebrew, did not use the living Hebrew tongue but quoted the first few words of the Holy Scripture, which any non-Jewish novice of theology will know by heart. It is more likely that he simply picked up a few words from a German-Hebrew language book.

On his single appearance at Síp Street, one early afternoon, Eichmann burst out in a Hitlerian fit of rage upon finding a few offices from the old Pest Congregation remaining where he expected everyone in the newly established bureaucratic mechanism to work. "Sie wissen noch nicht, wer ich bin. Ich bin der Bluthund. Hinaus mit der Kultusgemeinde [You don't yet know who I am. I am the bloodhound. Out with the Jewish community]," he roared, beside himself with fury.

Following Eichmann in rank was Obersturmbannführer Krumey, who was – as he himself revealed once – a merchant from Berlin. He had the kind of demeanour in which it was not impossible to detect signs of humanity every once in a while. Of all the officers, he was the most amenable to being influenced by János Gábor.[54] He did not take part in the deportations from the provinces, and disappeared just before the deportations from Budapest began – either recalled, as rumours had it, or simply departed. Later, he

53 A paramilitary force under the command of the Nazis' security police and security service, the Einsatzkommando der Sicherheitspolizei und des SD was responsible for rounding up and exterminating Jews and other "undesirables" in captured territories. In Hungary, the Einsatzkommando arrived in the wake of the Wehrmacht armed forces on the morning of 19 March 1944, led by SS-Standartenführer Hans Geschke (1907–1945) and consisting of approximately 500–600 members, including Adolf Eichmann's Sondereinsatzkommando. In a matter of days, they largely eliminated Hungary's rather small anti-Nazi opposition by detaining hundreds of key left-wing and conservative politicians, administrative and economic leaders, military and law enforcement officers, journalists, intellectuals, and others perceived to be a threat.

54 See 20.

returned to the scene with a mission to clear up the situation of the Bergen-Belsen group.[55] In December 1944 he accompanied the 1,300 people[56] from the camp in Hanover to the Swiss border, delivering the group to Dr Rezső Kasztner. Uncommonly among the senior SS officers, he was always known as a soft-spoken but deliberate man of few words.[57]

The biggest con man of all was "the honourable" Baron von Wisliceny, whose plump, Göringesque, almost jovial figure concealed a mass murderer responsible for the death of Hungarian Jewry in the provinces. He was "The Orator" often seen around the nightclubs, who loved women, booze, and money. Before his "venture" in Hungary, he had been a regular patron of the Carlton Hotel in Bratislava, where he earned a reputation for being an "approachable man"[58] among the Jews of that city, who hastened to alert their Orthodox brethren in Budapest to this. (Indeed, this became the starting point of the special action orchestrated by Fülöp Freudiger,[59] who with seventy compatriots managed in early August to steal their way through the Nazi ring via the village of Kelebia, equipped with Romanian passports.)

Of this illustrious company, only Krumey and Wisliceny were present at the "meeting" of March 20 in the principal hall of the Pest Congregation, duly attended by the leaders of Jewish institutions in Budapest as ordered on the first day. The room was crammed full, and I felt a flush of excitement. The podium – where the proposed resolution for the reception of Hungarian Jewry[60] had once been announced and which had been graced by so many distinguished statesmen, priests, writers, and poets for half a century – was now expansively occupied by these two notables of the Gestapo. (To me, the scene emblematized the tragedy of Hungarian Jewry, reminiscent as it was of the destruction of Jerusalem, the echo of Jeremiah.) The meeting itself was

55 A reference to the Kasztner Train passengers detained in Bergen-Belsen. See 68–71. Krumey at various points acted as a liaison with the group.

56 The Kasztner Train's 1,686 passengers were divided into two groups for the final leg of the journey from the Bergen-Belsen to Switzerland. The first 318 passengers arrived in Switzerland in August 1944, with the balance arriving in December 1944.

57 It is not clear why Munkácsi depicts Hermann Krumey sympathetically; certainly, his statements about him here are highly misleading. Krumey was one of the chief perpetrators of the Holocaust, directly responsible for the deportations from Hungary.

58 "Approachable" meaning here that Wisliceny could be easily bribed.

59 See 19.

60 A reference to Hungary's Law of Emancipation (Act XVII of 1867), which made Jews equal as individual citizens. It was followed by the Law of Reception (XLII of 1895), which made Judaism a state-endorsed religion in Hungary, formally equal to Christianity.

conducted with due deference to form, with Samu Stern, president of the National Office, seated next to the officers. He was addressed as "Herr Hofrat [Mr Court Councillor]" with great refinement and decorum. Wisliceny spoke, presenting the most egregious lies nonchalantly, cigarette in hand. "Make no mistake, there is no occupation here," he said. "The Germans expect calm discipline from the local Jewry ... Do your best to prevent panic ... Do not rush to the banks to withdraw your deposits ... Nobody will be harmed just because he happens to be Jewish." Yet the Germans must have felt the need to come up with some explanation for the arrests already in progress, for they added that some individuals had indeed been detained on charges of violating regulations or because of their former political activities. In any event, "One needs hostages in times of war."

No sooner had the Hauptsturmbannführer finished his talk than the podium was surrounded by the attendees, who began to shower question after question upon the Germans as if they were invited speakers at a conference hosted by an open university.

This miserable spectacle was repeated a week later, on March 28, at an event intended to "wisen up" Jews from the provinces. The telegram and invitation sent out by the National Office read as follows:

> This telegram is to notify you of a nationwide meeting of the utmost importance, to be held at eleven o'clock on Tuesday, the 28th of this month, at No. 12 Síp Street, where your attendance is most emphatically expected. Your travel permit will be mailed to you. Should you be unable to attend, you will need to report to us by telegram, naming your proxy ... As background to the invitation, we inform you that, since the 20th of this month, we have been in constant negotiations with the authorities of the German military, who set great store by ensuring that the Israelite population of the country may continue to pursue their private lives, religious engagements, as well as social and cultural activities undisturbed, in a panic-free mood. To this end, we have formed and vested with nationwide authority the Central Council of Hungarian Jews, which will proceed to establish a National Committee as the administrative organization next in rank below it.[61] This is why the meeting noted above is necessary. We kindly ask you to honour the event with

61   See the Glossary entry on the Jewish Councils.

your presence by all means. In these days of hardship, appropriate organization and the maintenance of a panic-free atmosphere form the crucial interest of the entire Jewish community. Attached please find a travel document made out by the German authorities strictly in your name only; this document is not transferable. In the event of your incapacitation, no deputy will be allowed to travel and attend on your behalf; the text of our telegram is thus modified accordingly. It goes without saying that resolutions adopted by those present will be binding for absentees. Dated Budapest, 24 March 1944. With brotherly regards, the President of the Central Council of Hungarian Jews.

Although the Germans did issue special one-time travel permits for the occasion, only a few Jews undertook the trip to Budapest from around the country. Those attending included the following local presidents: Dr József Greiner from Pécs; Imre Wesel from Szombathely; Dr Ákos Kolos from Kassa; Dr Gyula Unger from Győr; Dr Miklós Szegő from Székesfehérvár; Dr Samu Meer from Nagyvárad; Dr Sándor Mandel from Szolnok; Dr József Fischer from Kolozsvár; Dr Róbert Pap from Szeged; Dr Mór Feldmann from Miskolc; Sándor Leitner on behalf of the Orthodox community in Nagyvárad; and Jenő Ungár from Debrecen. Today, these names seem to beckon to us from the mists of history. Did any of them have an inkling that, barring a handful of exceptions, they were headed toward annihilation and martyrdom?

On behalf of the occupiers, the meeting was attended by Krumey, who spoke little, as was his wont, waiting instead for the others to ask questions. The "gentlemen of the country" rose to speak in broken German in great humility. This was the last nationwide meeting of a Jewry with a long historic tradition. Dr Imre Reiner,[62] legal counsel for the Orthodox Central Office, protested against the detentions the Germans carried out on the first day of the occupation at railway stations, customs borders, and other checkpoints in Budapest. He argued that the three thousand Jews interned at Kistarcsa[63] during the first few days had not been aware of the travel ban and were

---

62   Imre Reiner (1885–1963), rabbi and lawyer, legal adviser of the Autonomous Orthodox Congregation in Budapest.

63   See the Glossary entry on the Kistarcsa internment camp, which, because of its proximity to Budapest, served as a detention centre for many thousands of Jews arrested immediately after the German invasion.

therefore innocent of any disobedience. These people had been arrested on their way home to or from Budapest. Reiner emphatically called for their immediate release.

Krumey, in his hallmark soft voice, muttered something that could have been assent, sounding almost apologetic as he mentioned that he had already addressed the issue, "aber ich bin noch nicht durchgekommen [but I haven't yet succeeded]." Guesswork continued for days as to what he really meant by that. Those privy to the intricacies of the German language favoured the interpretation that he had been trying his best, but to no avail so far. This smooth-talking executioner was the most consummate master of mystification.

Incidentally, what talks there were to mention were soon derailed when the Budapest Kommando[64] pledged to vest the Central Jewish Council in Budapest with discretion over all Jewish affairs around the country. Contrary to these promises, local Jewish councils with autonomous powers were soon set up in certain cities.[65] With the concurrence of Krumey, the meeting resolved to have a single nationwide organization. I am not sure if Krumey's passivity was not the result of his knowing full well that any and all actions taken would merely have served to camouflage the inevitable; that for Hungarian Jews, the only path ahead led to Auschwitz.

64 Munkácsi seems to be referring here to the Sondereinsatzkommando Eichmann.
65 In addition to the Budapest-based Central Jewish Council, a nominally nationwide body whose sphere of authority was in practice largely restricted to the capital city, another approximately 150 local Jewish councils were established in other parts of Hungary by the Nazis and their Hungarian allies. However, as a result of the swift deportation of Hungary's Jews, including members of the councils, the councils outside Budapest typically ceased functioning within weeks. By contrast, the Central Jewish Council was active from 20 March 1944 until the liberation of the remaining Jews of Budapest in January 1945. See the Glossary for more details.

3

From Yellow Star to Ghetto

*Busybodies around the Jewish Council – The Gestapo takes up
position and embarks on blackmail and robbery – "Volunteers"
take over Síp Street – SS corps visit the Congregation –
Obersturmbannführer Eichmann's program – The introduction
of the yellow star – The first Jewish Council under German
occupation – Jewish unity on command – The Jewish Council's
rescue attempts – Travel ban – Release applications by the Jewish
Council – Jewish flats seized – Atrocities begin – László Koltay
(Kundics) enters the scene – Koltay's threats – The first demand:
500 Jewish flats – Why did the Council "yield"? – Flat requisitions
by the Jewish Council – Shock and despair – Demands up for
1,500 flats – Two new requisition commands – The downhill of
no return – What would have happened if ...? – Trends in the
policy of the Jewish Council – The "Kasztner line" – 1,600 set
out for Palestine – The "Hungarian line" – Dr Berend, chief
rabbi of Szigetvár – A strange interrogation – First news of
ghettoization – From Nyíregyháza to Máramarossziget – The
demise of Heves-County Jews – The "compaction" in Csepel
– Formation of the Jewish Association and related negotiations –
The political significance of the Jewish Association – Talks with
county clerk Chief Notary Blaskovich and Zoltán Bosnyák – The
foundation of the Alliance of Hungarian Jews – The ignorance
of Hungarian Jewry – Eichmann, Endre, and Ferenczy prepare
for the deportations – A pleading letter from the Újpest
Congregation – An attempt to save the Jews of Kassa – First word
of deportation – László Ferenczy – Preparations for deportation –
Why the Jews of Pozsony? – Appalling news – A submission
by the Ladies' Club of Kassa – Atrocities in the provinces*

Fig. 20   Immediately after the Nazi invasion on 19 March 1944, the Gestapo and the
Hungarian police used a converted factory in the village of Kistarcsa, in the outskirts
of Budapest, to imprison thousands of Jews considered hostile to the Reich, including
prominent industrialists, journalists, scholars, and political figures. The Jews detained
here at Kistarcsa were the first victims of deportations from Hungary; on 28 April 1944,
1,800 inmates were deported to Auschwitz-Birkenau. This photo appeared in the 20 May
1944 edition of the antisemitic *Harc* (*Struggle*), published by the Hungarian Institute
for Research into the Jewish Question, with the headline: "The whole notorious gang is
together now!"

The news of the formation of the Jewish Council – and especially reports
that the Gestapo had released a few Jewish leaders from custody – triggered
a veritable mass migration toward the Síp Street headquarters. Since Jewish
public servants had been sacked from their offices and Jewish lives had
been ruined in great numbers in the wake of the anti-Jewish laws, many
Jews sought and received shelter within the folds of Jewish organizations,
swelling the staff of congregational administrations. In the days following
the German occupation, the migration escalated, with some of the most
distinguished lawyers, industrialists, and bankers joining the ranks of those

applying for, and more than happy to accept, volunteer positions in the Council administration. A celebrated opera singer and a dramatist famous since the Franz Joseph era served duty as ushers in front of the entrance to the presidential rooms on the third floor. By the time the housing office was set up a few weeks later, the staff employed in the Síp Street headquarters and the ancillary buildings numbered several thousand.[1]

The bustle in the building was aggravated by a throng of people looking for family members, bringing food for the interned, applying for travel passes, protesting housing-related violations, and, last but not least, seeking to convert to Christianity. The courtyards and corridors resembled a swarming oriental bazaar, the hubbub amplified to the frantic ecstasy of a macabre dance in the ominous heat of those summer days. Taking in the sight, a Gestapo officer remarked that it had been the same scene in Lemberg[2] and Warsaw, and that all this "commotion" would invariably be followed by the eerie silence of doom.

The enlisted volunteers lent a special character to each agency. As mentioned before, the Zionists set up camp mainly in the Information Office and the Provincial Division, while the lawyers gathered in the government relations and housing administrations. The Orthodox volunteers favoured food-provision units and warehouses, where they rendered indispensable services by organizing food supplies, without which the crowded camps would have endured the most severe famine. (Steeped in Kosher regulations, the Orthodox had substantial know-how of Jewish soup kitchens, experience that would serve them well in the ghetto era.)

The senior officials of the Council departments were recruited mostly from the new volunteer force – a heterogeneous group that defies uniform assessment. Some of them were courageous, well-intentioned people who fought tooth and nail to save the Jews, while others worked away in quiet indifference. And, as in any formation that springs up overnight, there were go-getters ready to trample anything and anyone under foot if their own interests so demanded. These individuals assumed dictatorial airs and claimed to have free and open access to everyone from the Gestapo

---

1   There is no indication that the number of people employed was anywhere near that size. Munkácsi may be referring to the very many people who hung around the Síp Street headquarters trying to prove themselves useful.
2   Today Lviv, Ukraine.

to Colonel Winckelmann[3] to the anti-communist hound Péter Hain.[4] The Jewish public, already high-strung under all the adversity, had no stomach left to tolerate the mien and machinations of these eager beavers, and blamed the Council for taking them on.

Many eyed the operations of the Council with suspicion for other reasons as well. A prominent Jewish businessman, who had a hand in every boom cycle and walked about without wearing a star, was spotted daily in Síp Street. In the Majestic Hotel[5] in Svábhegy, the seat of the Gestapo, this man went by the name of "Dr Kovács" and was recognized as a quasi-official person. He had up-to-date information on just about everything. (Ultimately, though, he was unable to escape his fate: toward the end of the Arrow Cross period he was shot to death by the Germans. Evidently, he knew too much![6]) There were also women who, lacking an appropriate sense of "self-criticism," maintained intimate relations with the Gestapo.

Proper voting sessions were held by the Council only exceptionally: once when it was founded; then, when orders were first issued for the requisitioning of apartments; then, upon the establishment of the Executive Board of the Council[7] and the adoption of the statutes of the Jewish Association;[8] and

3 Otto Winkelmann (1894–1977), SS-Obergruppenführer. At the end of March 1944, he was appointed head of the SS and police forces (*Höherer SS- und Polizeiführer*) in Hungary, a post he held until 5 December 1944.

4 Péter Hain (1895–1946), chief inspector at the Budapest headquarters of the Royal Hungarian Police in the interbellum years, specialist in investigations conducted against the political left. On 28 March 1944, he was appointed head of the newly created State Security Police (Állambiztonsági Rendészet), colloquially known as the "Hungarian Gestapo," notorious for its brutal interrogation methods. Hain was discharged from duty in June due to his abuse of power and personal conflicts. Following the Arrow Cross takeover in mid-October 1944, he was appointed head of the political surveillance department of the Budapest Police. After the war, the People's Court sentenced Hain to death for war crimes and he was executed.

5 The Majestic Hotel in Svábhegy (Swabian Hill), an upper-class neighbourhood on the Buda side of the city, served as headquarters for Eichmann, among other senior Nazis. Numerous other luxury hotels, inns, and private villas were requisitioned from Jews and used as offices and residences by German security forces and their Hungarian associates.

6 "Dr Kovács" could not be identified.

7 A reference to the second phase of the Council, when it was renamed Interim Executive Board of the Association of Jews in Hungary. See the Glossary entry on the Jewish Councils.

8 Confusingly, "Executive Board of the Council" and "Jewish Association" both seem to refer to the Central Jewish Council, albeit the "Second Jewish Council." See the Glossary.

finally when the main point on the agenda was whether leaflets should be issued to advise Christian society about the deportations. The urgency of the new tasks that sprang up almost every minute necessarily led to a mechanism whereby the so-called presidency[9] brought measures on behalf of the Council. As I said, regular "meetings" concluding with the formal adoption of a "resolution" were infrequent, although the Council never tired of "consultations." Council members, senior officials, and others would gather in the president's room in the morning, and quite often in the afternoon as well, some seated and others standing, feverishly debating the latest bad news, woes, and action plans. As conditions gradually worsened, these conferences became increasingly irregular, although Council members continued to be briefed in writing of the more important events. These reports spelled history.

The very first time they showed up at Síp Street, the Gestapo ordered a telephone hotline to be maintained twenty-four hours a day. A few days later technical troopers came by to study the telephone exchange of the headquarters building, and proceeded to mount equipment that enabled them to tap every call. Also at the first "meeting," the Gestapo expressed the need for the Council to set up a dedicated "technical department."[10] The true significance of this was only revealed later, when the Germans began to demand delivery of various goods. In fact, the extortions had started from day one of the occupation. Initially, the Germans only wanted a few hundred blankets and mattresses, which the congregation supplied from warehouse inventories collected for those in labour service, and from hospital resources.

SS units arrived in Budapest one after the other, and almost every one of them made their first stop at the offices of the Jewish congregations, following a routine rehearsed to perfection elsewhere in Europe. In fact, similar visits in other capitals of the continent must have been even more successful, considering the smaller Jewish communities there and the immediate access in congregation buildings to the list of Jewish merchants and tradesmen that such smaller numbers entailed.

---

9 The Council's "presidency," or senior leadership team, consisted of President Samu Stern and his closest associates, mainly Ernő Pető and Károly Wilhelm.

10 The Economic and Technical Department of the Jewish Council was set up in early April, under the leadership of Miksa Domonkos (1890–1953), a renowned engineer and decorated veteran of the First World War. In late 1944, under Arrow Cross rule, Domonkos became one of the leaders of the Jewish Council (the last and so-called Fourth Jewish Council).

The Orthodox Congregation of Budapest was not spared, either. On March 21, SS soldiers armed to the teeth stormed the headquarters on Dob Street, along with the adjacent temple and school.[11] Schoolmaster Dr Deutsch[12] was ousted from his home and, along with the entire faculty, herded into the synagogue on Kazinczy Street, where they were lined up face against the wall at gunpoint. Amid the cruellest verbal abuse and threats of summary execution, they had no choice but to be "persuaded" that any procrastination in delivering the demanded goods would be pointless.

A similar incident took place at Síp Street a couple of hours later. A young SS officer, who seemed to be a sergeant, burst into the president's room and, revolver in hand, roared peremptory demands for a large inventory of cleaning supplies within an hour.

And this was only the beginning. Periodic, large-scale requisitions followed later. This was in addition to the constant looting of Jewish shops, warehouses, and apartments under an evacuation order. The acquisition of supplies, however, was invariably executed through the agency of the Jewish Council, which was why the Germans insisted on having a separate technical division at their disposal. In the Orthodox school building on Dob Street, they established a manufacturing operation employing hundreds of workers paid by the Jewish Council. Before long, the Germans had the Council organize special labour crews that were put to work around the Gestapo's haunts in Svábhegy on jobs such as building roads and excavating air raid shelter pits.

Until the middle of summer of 1944, the costs of deliveries to the Gestapo were almost exclusively paid for by the Pest Congregation. It was only a few months before the congregation had depleted the savings it had accumulated for decades and had to resort to putting its securities up for sale. This marked the beginning of the congregation's financial downturn, which continues to make itself felt today.

---

11   The centre of Budapest's Orthodox Jewish community at the corner of Kazinczy and Dob streets in the 7th District, the complex, built in the 1910s, consists of a synagogue (in the Art Nouveau style), an office building, and a school surrounding a central courtyard.

12   Adolf (later Avraham) Deutsch (1889–1953), director of the educational institutions of the Pest Orthodox Congregation from 1920. Deutsch escaped on the Kasztner Train and made *aliyah*, or emigrated to Mandatory Palestine, in 1950. From 1951 until his death, he was a member of the Israeli Parliament, representing the orthodox party Agudat Yisrael.

As a typical symptom of the looting, each SS Kommando was prone to defend its own milking cow against the others. This was evidently the case when, upon the request of the Council, Krumey issued an order prohibiting German military personnel from entering the Síp Street building except with his express permission. An enlarged copy of this document was posted on the gate. Later on, similar "letters of protection" were affixed to the buildings of the hospital on Szabolcs Street, the boys' orphanage, and other institutions. (We will see shortly just how much these measures were worth.)

Eichmann's Sondereinsatzkommando set up its first headquarters in the Astoria Hotel.[13] At first, this was where they locked up their prisoners in the cellar. Already on the second day, the Gestapo went on to sequester the Rabbinical Seminary on Rökk Szilárd Street. The building, ostensibly dubbed an "auxiliary detention house," was quickly transformed into a prison, and the rabbinical students were forced to perform servant duties around it.[14]

Ultimately, the Gestapo picked the Síp Street building to serve as its permanent headquarters. Floor plans had been requested and planning begun on how to furnish the premises. At this point, Krumey was advised that having the Jewish Council and all its offices move out would paralyze the Council's operations for months to come, preventing it from performing any of the duties it was expected to carry out. This worked!

For a few days, the Germans moved into the ironworkers' building on Magdolna Street[15] (this was also where Koltay, the infamous detective-inspector,[16] was first spotted) but they remained dissatisfied with the location.

---

13 Elegant hotel in downtown Budapest where Eichmann first stayed on his arrival in Budapest. Soon afterward, he moved to 13 Apostol Street, a villa expropriated from the Jewish industrialist Lipót Aschner, who was deported to Mauthausen. Eichmann maintained his offices at the Majestic Hotel in Svábhegy.

14 Since it was established in 1877 on Rökk Szilárd Street, in Budapest's 8th District, the Rabbinical Seminary has operated from the same building almost uninterrupted, with one major exception when, on 20 March 1944, the building was seized by the Gestapo. Under the command of SS-Hauptsturmführer Dieter Wisliceny, the building was turned into a detention facility for arrested Jews. The site was guarded by a Hungarian police detachment led by police officer Pál Ubrizsi. Detainees were regularly taken from there to other internment camps, including the ones on Csepel Island. The site also served as a transit centre for deportations, notably a transport of some 1,800 prisoners to Auschwitz in late April 1944. The Germans closed the detention facility in September, but it was re-opened by the Arrow Cross regime in October.

15 Headquarters of the Central Alliance of Iron and Metal Workers in Hungary, in Budapest's 8th District.

16 László Koltay (1902–1946), police inspector, was head of the Jewish Affairs

The officers – sentimental monsters that they were – constantly enquired after a place where one could see "a spot of green" in the summer and "indulge in a little singing." (One of them even ordered a piano to be delivered and, from the moment it arrived, never ceased to play Chopin on it.) Driven by fantasies of summer heat in the freezing month of March, they finally settled in Svábhegy, where they stormed the holiday homes and threw out their tenants in a matter of minutes. (From the accounts of the cleaning staff from the Jewish Hospital who happened to be put in charge of furnishings, the Germans looted the villas with no trace of scruple or remorse.) The Jewish patients of the sanatorium were trucked directly to the transit camp on Rökk Szilárd Street.

Shortly after the Germans had moved in, Eichmann summoned the Council leaders and gave them a "program." The report on the meeting reads as follows:

Pro memoria of the meeting of 31 March 1944, held from 8:30 to 9:45 in the morning at the Majestic Hotel in Svábhegy.

Present are: On behalf of the German authorities, Obersturmbann-führers Eichmann and Krumey, Hauptsturmbannführer Wisliceny, and one other officer. On behalf of the Council: Samu Stern, president; Dr Ernő Boda and Dr Ernő Pető, vice presidents; Dr János Gábor, legal counsel.

President Samu Stern submits current petitions as incorporated in separate memoranda. Obersturmbannführer Eichmann takes over and focuses on the yellow star, stating his wish that the stars be issued by the Central Council. To the objection that the task could not possibly be carried out by April 5, he answers that a provisional badge must in that case be issued by April 5 and then replaced later by the official version issued by the Council. He adds that all individuals subject to the requirement of wearing a star shall be under the authority of the Central Council irrespective of their actual religion. He advised us to make contact with a factory urgently, given the approximately three million stars that need to be manufactured. He wants the star to be

---

Sub-department (No. IV. 4.) of the State Security Police (Állambiztonsági Rendészet) between 28 March and 10 June 1944. Koltay's group consisted of about thirty detectives and closely cooperated with Eichmann's unit. After the Arrow Cross takeover, he was appointed the head of the Jewish Department (No. V.) of the political surveillance department of the Budapest Police. In 1946 he was tried by the People's Court, sentenced to death, and hanged.

of uniform shape, size, and colour throughout the country, and wants each piece to be trimmed to shape at the factory. We should solicit the Ministry of Public Supply[17] to issue the required quantity of fabric. If encountering any difficulty, we should contact Undersecretary of State László Endre,[18] who is in charge of all such affairs. Mr Eichmann believes that 70,000 metres of fabric will be required. He further advises the Central Council to charge a nominal fee, say 3 pengős, for each badge.[19] To the objection that many poor families could not afford such a sum, Mr Eichmann replies that, in that case, the wealthy should assume the burden from the poor, although he thinks the Central Council should be able to sell enough stars to cover the manufacturing costs for the entire country.

Obersturmbannführer Eichmann continued by considering each of the petitions submitted by President Samu Stern as follows:

In the matter of travel, he is not going to address the issue of long-distance travel for the time being (he has, in the meantime, approved numerous such petitions by permitting travel). As for officials and workers employed in the city who need to commute short distances to and from work, he asks how many they could be. Told that such commuters number in the thousands, he pledges to consider the matter and supply an answer in writing.

17 Béla Jurcsek (1893–1945), landowner, politician, and MP of the Party of Hungarian Life between 1935 and 1945. From 22 March to 16 October 1944, he served as minister of agriculture and was also the minister temporarily responsible for public supply. Under the Arrow Cross, Jurcsek was minister of public supply from 16 October 1944 until 28 March 1945. After the war, he escaped to Austria, where he committed suicide shortly before the arrival of Soviet troops in April 1945.

18 László Endre (1895–1946), extreme right-wing politician, civil servant, administrative expert, and one of the most influential antisemitic public figures in the Horthy era. Between 1938 and 1944, as the sub-prefect of the largest county in Hungary, Pest-Pilis-Solt-Kiskun, he introduced antisemitic measures that were even more stringent than the existing anti-Jewish laws and decrees. After the Nazi invasion in 1944, he was appointed undersecretary of state in the Ministry of the Interior under the Sztójay government. In close cooperation with Eichmann, Endre orchestrated the mass deportation of Hungarian Jews in the spring and summer of 1944. After the war, he was arrested by US troops in Austria and extradited to Hungary, where he was sentenced to death as a war criminal and executed.

19 The *pengő* was the Hungarian currency from 1927 until 1946.

Moving on to housing matters, he suggests that people displaced from their homes who have not had the time to look for another apartment may join a friend or relative. In that case, the change of address must be reported to the Central Council for approval. If someone wants to move on his own accord, however, he will have to apply to the Central Council for a prior permit.

Regarding German supply orders, he agrees that we should only satisfy requests that are submitted in writing and have their explicit approval. In other words, we need to send upstairs to them each order written in German for signing and stamping. This document will then serve as a proof of approval if needed.

He is going to look into the matter of the Kistarcsa internment camp.[20] He is not saying when, but the better the conduct of the people kept there, the sooner something will happen. He will come back to the issue. In the meantime, we should feel free to submit a list of detainees. He is willing to release officials, but we had better be sure nobody schemes to double-cross him.

Of the deliveries completed to date, we may submit invoices to Obersturmbannführer Eichmann.

We mention our plans to request a hearing from the government. He acknowledges our plan.

In general terms, he considers it his principal mission to boost industrial and war production. To that end, he is going to set up labour squads, comprising mostly Jewish workers. If the Jews bear themselves appropriately, no harm will come to them, but they will share in everything in proportion to the work performed by them, just as any other worker. It is conceivable they might be allowed to go home for the night. We ask him if the labour camp detainees will remain in Hungarian territory. He cannot give us a definite answer to that for now. We refer to the fact that male Jews up to the age of 42 are being held in labour camps. He says the Germans have no plans to relocate these camps, but they will be happy to accept men aged 45 to 56. They are asking for 300 or 400 men for now. He would prefer them to volunteer, because if we are unable to produce that number of our own accord he will have no choice but to use force. These people will be treated and paid well, just like any other

20   See the Glossary entry on Kistarcsa.

worker. We interject that we would need an authorization for such recruitment. He retorts that we had better give up our liberal habits and learn to issue orders instead of requests.

Financially, he wants to centralize the entire Hungarian Jewry, meaning that everyone subject to the requirement of wearing the star, including those converted to Christianity, will be under the authority of the Central Council. The converts are the wealthiest; why don't we collect larger sums from them? This measure will be authorized by a regulation now being drafted. Also, the Council must be structured in a hierarchy that has a tangible function for everything. For instance, it should have a department that is familiar with the ins and outs of Jewish schooling in Hungary, knows where the schools are located, how many students are enrolled in which building, etc. There should be a department for statistics and another one for technical support to respond quickly when supplies are needed. Obersturmbannführer Eichmann adds that, personally, he is deeply fascinated by relics of Jewish history and the library. He has been active in Jewish affairs since 1934, and his command of Hebrew is in fact superior to ours. We tell him about the libraries and the museum where we keep old relics. He will probably pay a visit as early as Wednesday and asks us to appoint someone to take charge of these institutions.

He brings up the Orthodox group who appealed to him to approve the publication of their own Orthodox newspaper, but he will not allow it. What he wants instead is to have the *Magyar Zsidók Lapja* as the only Jewish daily, in which we could perhaps reserve a page or two for purposes of the Orthodox. Every Jewish family in the country must be mandated to subscribe to the *Magyar Zsidók Lapja*, providing much-needed income for the congregation.[21]

In the next point, we remonstrate that it is very embarrassing and difficult for us to designate a shop every time they need something.

In reply he explains that they always take a meticulous inventory so that they can return or pay for all items according to the record. Nevertheless, we remain the ones in charge of sourcing the supplies they require.

Regarding organization, they require us to draw up a map indicating the location of Jewish institutions in each city, with

21 See 20.

an *Anlage* [appendix] explaining the name and type of each institution. In terms of organization, each congregation will remain a congregation; otherwise, all institutions belonging to a congregation will be moved under the authority of the Central Council. But if someone has endowed a foundation, for instance to ensure prayers for his salvation in the Talmud Torah Society, would it not make sense to preserve such a foundation? No, the money should be put to better use, and all foundations should come under the authority of the Central Council as well.

He emphasizes that all these things will last only as long as the war goes on. When the war is over, the Jews will be free to do whatever they want. Whatever is now happening in Jewish affairs is really only for the duration of the war. Come peace, the Germans will revert to their old *gutmütig*[22] selves and will condone everything as they have before.

He declares himself not to be a friend of violence in general, and wishes that things could be taken care of peacefully, for the word *Personal*[23] in German is spelled with a capital "P." They need all capable men to work, and cannot afford to assign a guard to everyone. In his experience, no violence or executions have ever occurred except where the Jews turned to resistance. If the Hungarian Jews chose to join the Ruthenian partisans[24] or Tito's pack,[25] as they did in Greece, he will show no mercy and slay them all, because it's a war and in times of war you cannot afford to do otherwise. On the other hand, if the Jews comprehend that all he expects from them is order and discipline, and to work honestly in the trade to which they are assigned, be it saddlery, forestry, or work at home, such as glove-making, then he

---

22　German for "good-natured."

23　German for "personnel" or "staff."

24　A reference to the anti-Axis resistance movement in Subcarpathia (today in Ukraine), which began after the territory was annexed by Hungary in March 1939. The partisans, supported by the Soviets, were composed of Ruthenians and Ukrainians as well as Hungarians (mostly Hungarian Jews who deserted labour service units on the Eastern front). Partisan activities directed from Moscow peaked in the summer of 1944 and lasted until September–October of that same year when the Red Army occupied the area.

25　A reference to the communist-led Yugoslav Partisans, the anti-Axis resistance movement commanded by Josip Broz Tito.

will not only keep them from harm but extend to them the same treatment and pay them as he pays other workers. Because he deems it very important that this thought be communicated to the broadest masses of the Jewry, the decree to be issued will make it mandatory for all Jewish households to subscribe to the *Magyar Zsidók Lapja*. He recommends that we set the subscription price so as to ensure adequate revenues for the Jewish Council.

It is only natural in such a large Jewish population that certain individuals will commit acts for which the entire community cannot be held responsible. He himself takes this for granted and will be able to deliberate each case accordingly. He reiterates his wish to protect the Jews from all individually initiated atrocities, even by German troops. He wants all such incidents reported to him immediately so that he may take appropriately harsh countermeasures. Likewise, he will mete out the most severe punishment to those who attempt to get rich on Jewish assets.

The organization of the Jewry should be uniform and standardized. We may raise the congregational tax if need be. Everyone is obliged to abide by the measures of the Jewish Council. He will personally see to it that the measures are enforced.

As a self-professed proponent of straight talk, he wants us to tell him about everything frankly and openly, and he will always give us a sincere answer. He has accumulated so much experience dealing with Jewish affairs that we should never for a moment entertain the idea that anyone could fool him. Those who try will be in trouble with him.

Finally, a poignant scene ensues. Dr János Gábor stands up and voices his dismay over the introduction of the yellow star. His late father served as major and court martial assessor in the world war, and his grandfather had been a patriot private in 1848.[26] He is concerned that the yellow star will incite the mobs to assault and humiliate Jews in the streets. Eichmann promises not to tolerate any abuse on

---

26   The Hungarian Revolution of 1848 marked the beginning of Hungary's war of independence against the Habsburg Empire. Thousands of Jewish volunteers fought as members of the revolutionary Hungarian army (*honvédség*), which became an important touchstone for patriotic Hungarian Jews determined to prove their allegiance to the nation.

account of a yellow star. If something like this happens, he wants to hear about it immediately so that he can deal with the perpetrators as they deserve.

Obersturmbannführer Eichmann's bluffing reassurances made it into the newspapers, and the public, particularly the deeply assimilated middle class of Hungarian Jewry, took these statements at face value for a long time. The SS had accomplished its purpose: Instead of scattering far and wide, the country's one million Jews stayed put, snug in the hope that they would escape their fate if they obeyed orders. (Naturally, the same attitude was widespread among the Christian population, who remained averse to being persuaded of the harsh realities and horrors of the deportations even when these operations were in full swing.)

The most important part of Eichmann's "exposé" concerned the yellow star – a measure that the examples seen in other countries had left no doubt would be introduced shortly. Typical of the public sentiments of the day, most Jews – and, again, I mean the highly assimilated groups in the first place – regarded the yellow star as a tool of humiliation rather than the first stage of the deportation process.

It was only later that the true significance of the yellow star became apparent, explaining the ruthless rigour with which the Nazis and their Hungarian helpers monitored compliance and punished evaders. (Almost always, this punishment equalled internment, which in turn led directly to deportation in most cases.) The smokescreen was so effective that a Council member, otherwise famous for his keen intellect, once told me he was proud of his Jewish identity and wore his yellow star with his head held high.

Obeying Eichmann's order, the Council set about obtaining the quantity of fabric necessary for fabricating the stars. A number of large companies brought their canary-yellow samples. However, upon learning that the Jewish Council intended to claim a monopoly on distributing the stars as instructed by the Germans, the Hungarian government refused to authorize the purchase order. "Why should we let the Jews pocket all that money when it could go into the treasury?" asked the Arrow Cross civil servants,[27] who entertained plans to sell the stars through tobacco shops as a state

27 Given that the Arrow Cross party did not come into power until October 1944, the author seems to use the term here to refer generally to pro-Nazi civil servants.

monopoly. While the case remained entangled in red tape in the labyrinth of state bureaucracy, Eichmann pressed László Endre to come out with the yellow star regulation. The decree was promulgated with the effective date of April 5,[28] but it failed to identify an appointed manufacturer or the manner of commercial release.

As I mentioned before, the SS Sondereinsatzkommando demanded that the Council enact its own organizational statutes that would provide for the establishment of various divisions. (This goes to show that, in Hungary, the Germans relied on experiences from countries where the Germans qualified as occupiers not only in effect but officially as well. To wit: In Hungary, ostensibly at least, state administration remained in charge of the internal affairs of the country; *de facto* measures brought by the Germans were legitimized *de jure* retroactively, at the end of April, through a decree providing for the Association of Jews in Hungary.[29])

In the first days of April, following lengthy debate, the Jewish Council adopted a charter that, by and large, continued to define its organizational framework until October 15.[30] After seventy-five years, this document consolidated the Jewry of Hungary under a single administrative organization on the order of the Germans, redeeming the long-held promise of unification or, rather, enacted a mockery thereof, as if in imitation of the "gift of the Danaides."[31]

To form an opinion of certain ensuing circumstances and factors, it is instructive to take a closer look at this new organization, unveiled on April 4 to Eichmann and company, to their satisfaction:

---

28 Prime Minister's Decree No. 1240/1944 on the distinguishing mark of the Jews, published in the official bulletin *Budapesti Közlöny* on 31 March 1944, p. 3. The document is available in English in Vági, Csősz, and Kádár, *The Holocaust in Hungary: Evolution of a Genocide* (Lanham: AltaMira Press, 2013), 72–4.

29 Whereas the Jewish Council was established on German orders on 20 March, it was officially recognized only on 22 April when the Sztójay government *ex post facto* legalized the Council as the "Interim Executive Board of the Association of Jews in Hungary." Prime Minister's Decree No. 1520/1944 on the self-government and representation of the Jews, *Budapesti Közlöny*, 22 April 1944, pp. 1–2.

30 It is unclear what charter the author is referring to here.

31 The author might have intended to cite the "gift of Danaos" here instead, a reference to Virgil's famous phrase from *Aeneid*, "Quidquid id est, Timeo Danaos et dona ferentes" ("Beware of Greeks bearing gifts").

I. Budapest Central and National Organization

The affairs of Hungarian Jewry are administered by the eight-member Central Council as the sole representative body of Hungarian Jewry, exclusively empowered to negotiate with the authorities. In matters of purport, the Central Council shall consult the opinion of the Budapest Grand Council and, if the matter is of concern for the Jewry of the entire country, also the opinion of the National Grand Council, without being bound by resolutions of the same. The Budapest Grand Council comprises 25–27 members.[32] The composition of the National Grand Council is arrived at by complementing the Budapest Grand Council by ten district presidents, the presidents of ten major Orthodox congregations, and the presidents of two Status Quo congregations. The proper administration of the Jewish population is ensured by dividing the country into ten administrative districts. The presidents of the Congressional,[33] Orthodox, and Status Quo congregations established in the seat of their respective districts shall receive instructions from the Central Council and forward them to the congregations in their jurisdiction. The Central Council shall communicate with the Budapest congregations via their presidents, of whom the presidents of the Pest and Buda congregations and the Orthodox congregation serve on the Central Council, while the presidents of Kőbánya and Óbuda[34] serve on the Budapest Grand Council.

II. Congregational Societies

As per the instructions, congregational-type societies and institutions managing foundations shall lose their autonomy and merge under the congregation itself in the case of local societies such as ladies' clubs, girls' societies, *chevra kadisha*,[35] etc. If the society or institution is a nationwide one, such as MIKÉFE, OMIKE, IMIT, and MIPI,[36] it shall fall

32 See the Glossary entry on the Jewish Councils.
33 "Congressional" was the official term for what is colloquially known as the Neolog branch of Judaism.
34 Kőbánya and Óbuda were large Orthodox communities in Budapest's 10th and 3rd Districts.
35 Jewish burial society, tasked with performing the rituals necessary to prepare the bodies of the deceased for a traditional burial.
36 MIKÉFE: Hungarian Israelite Handicrafts and Agricultural Society (*Magyar Izraelita*

under the administrative powers of the Central Council. The National Offices shall survive without the power to act in cases belonging to the competence of the Central Council.

III. The Administration of the Central Council
From the point of view of management, the Central Council shall be divided into the following departments: 1. Presidential; 2. Finance; 3. Welfare; 4. Economic and technical; 5. Education and culture; 6. Foreign Affairs (including statistics and demography); 7. Worship; 8. Housing and Travel; 9. Convert Affairs.

Presidential branch: In charge of implementing resolutions and measures brought by the Central Council and instructions incumbent upon the Central Council. To facilitate these tasks, the following divisions shall be established within the Presidential Branch: a) communications with Hungarian and German authorities; b) translation agency; c) communications with country districts and congregations; d) press releases; e) statistical and demographic records; f) personnel, including the administration of legal aid.

Finances: In charge of managing the central taxation of Hungarian Jewry.

Welfare: Tasks within the powers of the Support Office of Hungarian Israelites (MIPI), to the effect that the MIPI shall in the future continue as the welfare division of the Central Council. Chief target areas include camps, internment affairs, nationwide welfare, training, cross-training, apprentice homes, soup kitchens, and other welfare responsibilities.

Economic: Overseeing the economic and technical affairs of all institutions under the Central Council, as well as supplies and deliveries ordered from Hungarian Jewry. To this latter end, subcommittees shall be established for each important trade.

Kézmű- és Földművelési Egyesület), established in 1842, its main task was to promote physical labour among the Hungarian Jews; OMIKE: see 17; IMIT: Israelite Hungarian Literary Society (Izraelita Magyar Irodalmi Társulat), established by the Pest Israelite Congregation in 1894 to publish and promote religious and scholarly literature; MIPI: Support Office of Hungarian Israelites (Magyar Izraeliták Pártfogó Irodája), a joint welfare organization of the main Hungarian Jewish congregations created in 1938 to support people who lost their jobs due to the anti-Jewish laws.

The instructions envisioned splitting the branch responsible for education and cultural affairs into subdivisions handling the affairs of Neolog and Orthodox Jewish schools, respectively.

The foreign affairs branch was assigned to deal with issues of emigration, Zionist organizations, and the Palestine Office.[37]

As per German order, converts remained under the authority of the Jewish Council. Their affairs were to be managed by a separate administrative branch within the Jewish Council.

After the Gestapo consented to the new organization, on April 6 the Council addressed a circular to each congregation in Hungary, which read as follows:

Dear Mr President,

The Central Council of Hungarian Jews has received instructions from superior authorities to organize the country's Jewry by delegating instructions from the Central Council, seated in Budapest, to the president of the congregation in each county,[38] or to both presidents if the county has two congregations. The presidents will then be accountable for implementing the instructions. The interests of the Jews in each county shall be represented by the congregation in the county seat and the congregation president. Please note, once again, that the Central Council of Hungarian Jews in Budapest obeys instructions from superior authorities, and every one of its members is personally and maximally responsible, under pain of extreme sanctions, for having those instructions carried out promptly and with precision. The same accountability and sanctions apply to individuals who fail to execute instructions from the Central Council, risking fatal consequences for the entire Jewish community in Hungary. We will be sending further instructions for organization to Your Excellency shortly. We would appreciate confirmation of receipt of this letter by return post.

Budapest, 6 April 1944.

Yours sincerely,

The Central Council of Hungarian Jews.

37 About the Palestine Office, see note on Miklós Kraus, 216.
38 Israelite congregations were organized by territorial districts (községkerület), which were not always the same as counties.

Attached to this circular was a questionnaire requesting various congregation data in eighteen points.[39]

Contact with the Gestapo enabled the Jewish Council to intervene on behalf of distressed individuals or the entire community. The possible breadth of its influence fluctuated practically day by day depending on several circumstances, including the mood of Gestapo officers (which was highly volatile and varied with news from the front) and even sheer chance. The Germans wasted no time in warning, in no uncertain terms, that interventions by the Council would only be considered if they fell within its actual mandate and would only prove beneficial if they concerned those who maintained close ties with the congregation and, in general, with Jewish organizations. The Germans opposed attempts by the Council to help individuals detained on account of their political actions or their distinguished social and financial positions. All the same, the Germans desired to maintain at least a semblance of good faith during the first few days, and released a considerable number of detainees on two occasions.

Although the first official announcement of a travel ban imposed on Jews was made between 9:30 and 11:00 in the morning of March 20 at Síp Street, the Germans had the day before rounded up large groups of Jews around the railway stations. In the days to come, simply waiting for a tram at a stop near the station was reason enough to be detained. The arrested were taken to the detention house on Mosonyi Street, from where about 150 people – women, children, and students – were released after being screened during the first few days.[40] The rest were transported to the ill-famed internment camp at Kistarcsa. The Council intervened on their behalf as well, with partial success. On March 24, Dr József Vági,[41] accompanied by two officials from the Support Office, reported to the command of the Kistarcsa camp with the request to take over and return to Budapest some 160 detainees, including elderly people, pregnant women, and children. When the envoys from the Jewish Council entered the camp office, they found Obersturmbannführer Wisliceny in the company of a few Gestapo officers and chief inspector

39 The required eighteen points of data included: the congregation's name; branches (if any); number of taxpayers; real estate, personal property, and funds of the community; names of local Jewish social and religious organizations; and names of rabbis, chairmen, and other leading officials.

40 Detention house of the Royal Hungarian Police on Mosonyi Street in Budapest's 8th District.

41 József Vági (1892–1957), a lawyer and legal adviser on cases concerning Jewish congregations.

Vasdényei,[42] the Hungarian commander of the camp. As they were about to leave – the Germans had departed earlier – Vasdényei turned to Vági and told him, in an almost imploring voice, "Doctor, please don't send us any more clients."

The first to have been released from Rökk Szilárd Street[43] on the intervention of the Council was an aged, venerable patriarch. He had apparently been detained by the Gestapo because he had served as the chief executive officer of a major bank some fifteen years earlier.

On March 26 the Council handed over an application for the release from Kistarcsa of Jenő Lázár, vice president of the Szombathely district and a noted collector of archaeological objects.[44] (Lázár had travelled to Budapest to attend the funeral of his brother-in-law, and was detained at the railway tracks on his way back home.) The Council's multiple attempts at intercession produced no results. Lázár was taken to Auschwitz, from where he eventually returned, as if by divine intervention. He was more fortunate than the president of his district, Imre Wesel, who enjoyed a reputation for his zealous dedication to Jewish affairs and had first written to the National Office on behalf of Lázár. Shortly after the capture of Lázár, Wesel was taken into custody and never returned from deportation.[45]

In another petition, dated April 5, the Council requested the release from Kistarcsa of Ervin Gergely and Dr Mihály Glück (later Borsa), senior officials from MIPI and the Pest congregation,[46] respectively, on the grounds that both were indispensable to the technical division owing to their "excellence and substantial experience in the field of logistics." On April 13, the Council acted

42 Chief Inspector of Police István Vasdényei, commander-in-chief of the Kistarcsa internment camp, tended to treat the detainees rather leniently, permitting them to receive letters and packages, and allowing the release of children under fourteen. Vasdényei even tried to thwart German plans to deport camp inmates in July 1944. He was awarded the Righteous Among the Nations honorific by the State of Israel in 1969.

43 About the Rökk Szilárd detention centre, see 35.

44 Jenő Lázár (1903–1964), mechanical engineer and vice chairman of the Szombathely Jewish Congregation. Detained at the Kistarcsa internment camp, he was then deported to Auschwitz.

45 Imre Wesel (1903–1944), chairman of the Szombathely Jewish Congregation and head of that city's Jewish Council from 23 March until early May when he was arrested by the Gestapo. Wesel was deported and perished in Auschwitz-Birkenau.

46 No personal information could be found on Ervin Gergely. About Mihály Borsa, see 16.

on behalf of Lajos Vajda of Kecskemét and György Benedek of Nagykőrös,[47] arguing that the work of organizing Jews in the countryside would be inconceivable without the contribution of these two presidents, "both of whom have decades of experience and practice in the field." The petition dated May 2 makes it clear that the German military command had arrested Szombathely district president Imre Wesel ten days previously, and was keeping him in custody in the local prison. His release was now requested by the Council, citing his "indispensable work and energy." On May 9 it was time to put in a word for the release of Székesfehérvár district president Dr Miklós Szegő,[48] a long-time stalwart champion of Jewish affairs. The petition points out that Dr Szegő was present as the representative for Fejér and Veszprém counties at the nationwide meeting of March 28, where the Germans made their solemn promises. Despite that, Dr Szegő was arrested and incarcerated in a detention house in Budapest. In its petition, the Council emphasized that "his qualifications and tireless work habits make his continued engagement a vital national interest," adding that "the Central Council is ready to assume full responsibility for his person." A petition voiced in a similar tone urged the release of Samu Meer, president of the Jewish Congregation of Nagyvárad, a distinguished and conscientious physician, who had been hauled to a ghetto and tortured despite having recently undergone an operation and suffered severe pneumonia. (The Council pleaded with the Germans to let him be taken care of in his home at least until he recovered – all in vain!) Similar requests were filed on behalf of Gyula Weisz, the Kolozsvár member of the Orthodox National Committee, and Sándor Német, Orthodox president of Nyíregyháza. The Orthodox Central Office sent out special invitations in an attempt to usher the members of its Rabbinical Council[49] to Budapest on the pretext of an important meeting. Such invitations were mailed to, among others, the highly esteemed rabbis Joel Teitelbaum in Szatmárnémeti[50] and Lezer Solem Halberstam in Újfehértó.

---

47 Lajos Vajda, head of the Kecskemét branch of the Hungarian General Savings Bank, and György Benedek, a merchant, were the presidents of their towns' respective Israelite (Neolog) congregations.

48 Miklós Szegő was vice president and, as of 1939, president of the Székesfehérvár Israelite (Neolog) Congregation. He was member of the so-called Fourth Jewish Council, formed in late 1944. On 15 January 1945, he was murdered by Arrow Cross militiamen in Budapest.

49 The rabbis of the Orthodox communities.

50 Joel Teitelbaum (1887–1979), the founder and first grand rebbe of the Satmar Hasidic dynasty, was a key personality in the renaissance of a strictly anti-modern Hasidism. He escaped Hungary in June 1944 on the Kasztner Train (see 68–71), eventually emigrating to Brooklyn, New York.

On May 12, yet another submission was addressed to Interior Minister Jaross,[51] asking for the release of Dr József Fischer, president of Kolozsvár.[52] "We have received word that Dr József Fischer, president of the Congressional Israelite Congregation of Kolozsvár and Kolozs County commissioner of the Central Council of Hungarian Jews, was taken into custody on the 12th of this month. Simultaneously, the congregation's cash assets of P 500,000 were seized," the petition read. "As far as we know, the action was justified by allegations that Dr Fischer had neglected to report the congregation's assets as required under Decree No. 1600/1944." (Later, in the course of the Zionist campaign, which I will discuss in detail, Dr Fischer made it to the Columbus Street camp[53] in Budapest, from where he went on to Bergen-Belsen and then to Switzerland.) On May 20, when the deportations from around the country were well underway, the leaders of the Status Quo community of Debrecen sent a telegram on behalf of Nyíregyháza Chief Rabbi Dr Béla Bernstein.[54] The message was seconded two days later by the Council in a submission asking to stop the deportation of this eminent gentleman, the author of a historic treatise documenting the role of Hungarian Jews in the country's war of independence a century before. Again, all in vain! On June 5, another petition was addressed to the Gestapo on behalf of Miklós Szegő. We know from this document that Szegő had been released in May, but remained under police surveillance. Subsequently, he was taken into custody again and, at the time of the submission, was lying in the prisoners' hospital on Mosonyi Street.[55] A few days later, the Council intervened on behalf of Szeged Chief Rabbi Immanuel Lőw, asking for his relocation to Budapest. On June 15 release requests were filed on behalf of the chief rabbi and other

---

51   On Andor Jaross, see 105.

52   József Fischer was a lawyer and journalist, president of the Transylvanian Jewish
     National Alliance and member of the Romanian Parliament. He was also the father-
     in-law of Rezső Kasztner (see 15). In 1944 he served as president of the local Jewish
     Council for the city of Kolozsvár (now Cluj, Romania) until escaping on the Kasztner
     Train in June of that year.

53   Special SS detention facility (Sonderlager) erected on the grounds of the Wechselmann
     Institute for the Deaf and Dumb on Columbus Street, in Budapest's 14th District. In
     June 1944, the camp served as a transit camp for the future passengers of the Kasztner
     Train. Later, during the Arrow Cross rule, the Columbus Street camp was under the
     protection of the International Red Cross and offered asylum to thousands of Jews.

54   Béla Bernstein (1868–1944), rabbi of Szombathely and, between 1909 and 1944, chief
     rabbi of the Nyíregyháza Jewish community. He was deported and perished in
     Auschwitz in June 1944.

55   See 47.

leaders of the community in Losonc,[56] as well as for Dr Samu Szemere and his wife.[57] The above list may be extensive but it is far from complete, confined as it is to cases that can still be traced in the archives as of this writing. Complete or not, the list certainly gives an idea of the petitioning process and of the gradual perishing of Jews from the provinces. Contemplating these events, one could do worse than cite the prophet Jeremiah: "The crown is fallen from our head."

The submissions dating from the early days of the German occupation were more generic in scope. To cite one example, the Council appealed to the Gestapo to release eighteen members of the congregation of Mezőberény – each individually named – who had been arrested by the local Gendarmerie on April 3 and transported to the capital.

A very interesting report from the same day describes the situation in the city of Székesfehérvár.

Apart from quite a few, evidently isolated incidents involving the seizure of valuables from shops and private residences, about fifty individuals have been arrested recently ... The occupying authorities collected the extortionate tribute of P 100,000 from the congregation for allegedly enabling local Hungarian authorities to be informed about cases which they had no right to know. The occupiers strictly prohibit the congregation from telling the Hungarian authorities anything, no exceptions granted. The latest demand has been for an alphabetized list of all the Jewish residents of Székesfehérvár, again subject to the strict stipulation that nobody may know about it.

On April 12 reports were received complaining about the dissolution of several congregations in Transdanubia.[58] In any event, the Transdanubian situation clashed with Eichmann's program, which envisioned the entire Hungarian Jewry subsumed under the authority of the Central Council seated in Budapest. As the first step, as soon as they reached the city of Győr in their march toward Budapest, the Germans had conferred with the office of *Ältestenrat* [council of elders] upon János Biringer[59] and consolidated the

56 Today Lučenec, Slovakia.
57 Samu Szemere (1881–1978), philosopher, teacher and aesthete, director of the National Israelite Teacher Training Seminary between 1927 and 1942. After the war, he served as director of the Israelite Hungarian Literary Society (IMIT); see 45.
58 The area of Hungary west of the Danube.
59 János Biringer (1890–1945), a lumber merchant from Győr. Biringer was deported,

whole Jewish population of the western counties under his powers.[60] The Jewish Council of Budapest protested, to no avail; the Germans insisted on keeping Biringer in office, who, obeying instructions from the Gestapo, in early April sent a letter to the congregations of Zala, Vas, Veszprém, Sopron, Moson, Győr, Komárom, Nyitra, Bars, and Hont counties, informing them of their dissolution. A few days later, he did the same with the congregations of Fejér County. The Central Jewish Council remonstrated with the Gestapo against these measures as follows:

> Furthermore, we permit ourselves to point out that the intent of the guidelines communicated to us is that the religious communities under the supervision of the Central Council should be allowed to survive. Nevertheless, many religious communities have already been liquidated. We request therefore that our mandate extend across the entire country, that the religious communities continue to exist also into the future, and that their current leadership remain in office. Without such a mandate, it will be impossible for us to complete the country-wide organizing we have already begun.

The same day, the Council asked the Gestapo to uphold the freedom of movement and self-determination of the congregations of Nagyvárad. The submission complains about demands of the local Gestapo there which the congregations were unable to satisfy.[61]

~ ~ ~

survived the selections at Auschwitz, and was forced to work as a slave labourer for Mettenheim I, a sub-camp of Mühldorf (part of the satellite system of the Dachau concentration camp), where he died on 11 February 1945.

60 In the provinces, local Jewish councils were generally appointed and organized by the local congregations. However, in western Hungary, where the city Győr and other congregations named in this paragraph are located, the Nazi police ordered the creation of a territorial Jewish council, temporarily consolidating ten counties under the leadership of Biringer – thus undermining the authority of the Central Jewish Council, as Munkácsi goes on to suggest.

61 The "demands" made on Jews in Nagyvárad (today Oradea, Romania), as in every other major Hungarian city and town, included requisitioning community property, including the hospital and private apartments, seizing valuables, and demanding exorbitant ransoms for the release of members of the Jewish elite taken hostage by the Nazis.

While the Council was bogged down by teething troubles, administrative hindrances, and attempts to save individuals as well as groups of Jews, Eichmann and his team struck a deal with Endre that ultimately entailed the liquidation of Hungarian Jewry. The first sign of destiny waiting in the wings consisted of *the requisitioning of apartments and homes in Budapest.*

In the days following March 19, Svábhegy became a scene busy with bustling movers as this sought-after district of the Hungarian metropolis was speedily "de-Judaized"[62] and transformed into a veritable Bastille of the armed mobocracy. On the Hungarian side, the commander was Péter Hain, the scourge of leftist freedom-fighters for decades, as well as Regent Horthy's bodyguard and a traitor.[63]

One morning following the takeover, "Royal Hungarian Councillor" Hain summoned his most reliable detectives to the sanatorium building in Svábhegy at eight o'clock. Among them was detective-inspector László Koltay (Kundics),[64] an obscure figure who had previously worked in document forgery investigations on cases such as the baptismal certificate forged by the Calvinist pastor of Kispest. From the sanatorium everyone went over to the Lomnic guesthouse,[65] where Hain delivered a program speech, appointing Dr Koltay to head the iv/4 department of the Royal Hungarian State Security Police. His powers were to include the implementation of anti-Jewish measures.

Koltay accepted the position despite the fact that his wife was Jewish.[66] A few days later, Krumey summoned Jewish Council leaders to the Ironworkers' building[67] and told them they would all be working together with the Hungarian police under Dr László Koltay, whom he duly introduced. The next few days brought a temporary lull, giving the Jewish leaders time to mull over what the Germans would do next. (On the occasion of Koltay's

---

62 The word Munkácsi uses here is *zsidótlanítás*, the Hungarian version of the Nazi neologism *Entjudung*, literally "de-Jewification" or "de-Judaization," or, to use another Nazi term, Aryanization (*Arisierung*). Rather than use Nazi German neologisms, the literal English translation is employed throughout this book in quotation marks.

63 Hain, head of the newly created State Security Police (Állambiztonsági Rendészet), was responsible for the safety of Miklós Horthy and prominent international guests – at the same time, as alluded to by Munkácsi, he was a paid agent of the Gestapo. See 32.

64 See 35.

65 Lomnic *panzió*, or guesthouse, on Evetke Street was one of the numerous hotels and homes in Svábhegy taken over by the Nazis. See 56.

66 Historians have not found evidence that Koltay's wife was Jewish.

67 See 35.

introduction, a German officer had cracked jokes about the Gestapo actually being an arm of the "Königliche ungarische Staatspolizei [Royal Hungarian National Police]".) As it turned out, Koltay did not have to wait long for an opportunity to reveal his true cruel nature and earn a name for himself.

It was April 4, the day before the yellow-star decree came into force. Jews worked away at home, quietly cutting and sewing the yellow stars, in a petrified expectation of upheaval. The same day, Budapest suffered a bomb raid[68] that damaged or destroyed a great many apartment buildings, mainly along Soroksári Street and in the Ferencváros district. In the early afternoon hours, Councillor Dr József Szentmiklóssy[69] dispatched a confidential private letter to Dr I.K., who had headed the so-called public-interest housing initiative, asking I.K. to visit him in City Hall immediately.[70] At this meeting, which took place immediately thereafter, Councillor Szentmiklóssy shared the confidential information that the same afternoon the Council would be instructed by László Endre to vacate five hundred Jewish apartments and hand them over to the city housing office – to provide accommodation for those who had lost their homes in the attack, and also in retribution for the bombing itself. All equipment and amenities – such as bed linens, cookware, cutlery, and so on – had to be left behind in the apartments for the bomb victims. Dr Szentmiklóssy related how he immediately objected to the measure proposed by the plenipotentiary secretary of the Ministry of the Interior. However, Endre remained intractable and insisted on his instructions being carried out by the Jewish Council to a tee, or else he would act himself with the utmost severity and have the flats vacated by his own men. No sooner had this news been relayed to the Council leaders than inspector Koltay materialized, with a mission from the state police stationed in Svábhegy to deliver the same news in the form of actual instructions: the keys to five hundred flats had to be delivered to the housing office of the city by four in the afternoon the following day, April 5. He also ordered that inventories be taken, by the same deadline, of all household goods and chattels in the

68   The first major Allied air raid hit Budapest on 3 and 4 April. The main targets were the classification yard at the Ferencváros freight railway station in Budapest's 9th District, neighbouring industrial sites, and an aircraft factory.

69   City Councillor József Szentmiklóssy, head of the Department of Social Policy for the City of Budapest.

70   István Kurzweil (1897–1958), a leading official in the Jewish Council's housing department and, formerly, employee of the Pest Israelite Congregation's Public-Interest Housing Office.

abandoned apartments. Koltay further informed the Council that smaller apartments were especially preferred, as most of the apartments damaged or destroyed in the raid had been of this type. This bloodhound of a sleuth rejected all protestation out of hand, and warned the Council that missing the twenty-four-hour deadline would entail the most severe consequences. Dr Imre Reiner,[71] one of the eyewitnesses, describes as follows the actual manner in which the requisitioning instruction was issued:

> The Council members went home for their lunch break. The custom was to have a Council member and a senior official on duty in the afternoon hours. That day, it was the turn of Samu Kahán-Frankl[72] and Dr László Bakonyi, head secretary of the Neolog National Office.[73] I myself checked back in regularly every afternoon. Around three o'clock, who turned up but detective Ödön Martinidesz,[74] the second-in-command below László Koltay reporting to Péter Hain? This evil, antisemite assassin, who was responsible for the transport of Hungarian Jews to the first large-scale massacre in Kamenets-Podolsk while he headed the investigative unit of the KEOKH, had been known to me for quite some time.[75] I asked him what he wanted. He was there to see the Council president. I answered that he was in hospital with a fever. Martinidesz gave me to understand, in a sinister manner,

71 See 55.
72 See 22.
73 László Bakonyi (1891–?), lawyer, writer, executive secretary of the National Office of Hungarian Israelites (MIOI) between 1927 and 1944. After the German occupation, he served as legal adviser to the Jewish Council.
74 Ödön Martinidesz (1899–1945), police inspector, detective of the National Central Authority for Controlling Aliens (Külföldieket Ellenőrző Országos Központi Hatóság, KEOKH), the main agency responsible for refugee policy, operating out of the Department of Public Security of the Ministry of the Interior. Taken captive by Soviet troops at the end of the war, Martinidesz died in the Focsani POW camp in Romania on 18 November 1945.
75 The expulsion from Hungary to the occupied Soviet territories of some 20,000 refugees and Hungarian Jews in July–August 1941 resulted in the first five-digit mass murder of the Holocaust, committed by the SS and Ukrainian auxiliaries on August 27–29 at Kamenets-Podolsk, Ukraine. While Martinidesz, in his capacity as head of KEOKH, oversaw the arbitrary deportations that led to the Kamenets-Podolsk massacre, it is an exaggeration to present him as the main perpetrator. The massacre was initiated by the leadership of the Hungarian army and carried out with the support of the government, the local administration, and the leaders of KEOKH.

that the bombings in the morning had left crowds of people without a roof over their heads, and that the Germans issued instructions for the prompt accommodation of the homeless. Overcome by apprehension, I tried and managed to get in contact with the president, who sent the message that the congregation was happy to offer the gymnasium of the school on Wesselényi Street as shelter for the homeless.

When Martinidesz realized he would have to make do without Samu Stern and learned that we had Kahán-Frankl and Dr Bakonyi on duty, he decided to take them with him to the Gestapo in Svábhegy. And probably because he wanted to pay me back for the many complaints I had raised against him with his superiors over his machinations within the KEOKH, he added that I should come along as well. His four-seater car was waiting for us downstairs. With the driver, there were the five of us. We had President Kahán-Frankl sit in the front, while Martinidesz, Bakonyi, and I squeezed into the rear seat.

I really wanted him not to bring President Kahán-Frankl with us, and I asked him so. I explained jokingly that the four of us would be much more comfortable in the car.

"No. The president stays," he said.

Then I asked him to let Bakonyi get out. But Bakonyi said he would save some of the way home if he came with us, as he lived in Zugliget. He did not realize that we had practically been taken into custody. Martinidesz grinned at him, stopped the car that had barely pulled away from the curb, and motioned Bakonyi to get out on Wesselényi Street.

On the way to our destination, I made an effort to elicit details about what they planned to do with us.

"They thirst to avenge today's bombing upon the Jews," he said in his hushed, insidious voice.

"That is perfectly understandable," I replied sarcastically. "The whole bombing was obviously orchestrated by the Jews."

"Whatever," he said wryly. "This is the official standpoint."

In Svábhegy, he dropped us off at the Lomnic guesthouse into the custody of a detective.

We had to wait a long time. At long last, a dozen men burst into the room with a tall and thin officer in the lead who addressed us in the rudest tone. This was the first time I had set eyes on him – it was Eichmann, widely reputed to be the meanest bloodhound of them all.

The week before, we had heard about his threats to line up a thousand Jews from Pest against the wall and teach them how to carry out his instructions if they didn't have the good sense to toe the line on their own accord.

He now demanded to see the president of the Council.

We told him the president was lying in hospital ill with a fever. He grew red in the face and began to yell about teaching the Council a lesson.

"Ich werde mit euch Schlitten fahren!" ["I'll rake you over the coals!"], he threatened.

Then came the seething command for the Jewish Council to make available, within twenty-four hours, five hundred apartments for the ordinary Christian citizens who had lost their homes in the bombing. As the victims were common workers, he only wanted small flats with one or two rooms from the nearby 9th and 8th Districts. So we were supposed to evacuate five hundred Jews in this area, relocate them somehow to the 6th and 7th Districts, and issue the vacated apartments to the bombed-out citizens.

We did our best to explain to him why it was impossible to carry out his order. Stomping his feet, he reiterated his threats of retribution and said he would have the Jews and their baggage thrown out into the street himself if the Council was incapable of vacating the flats on its own. At this point, the civilians present entered the fray. We realized that Péter Hain, László Koltay, and Councillor Szentmiklóssy were among them.

When I brought up the idea of the gym as a solution, Koltay threw a tantrum.

"This is not about your Jewish tricks," he roared. "It's not a gym that we need, but five hundred apartments. If you can't vacate the apartments by the deadline, we will empty them for you, Jews and all."

A lengthy debate ensued, with Eichmann and Koltay trying to outdo one another in bullying us into submission. Szentmiklóssy advised that it was in the best interest of Jews if the apartments were vacated by the Council, since otherwise, as we had heard, the Germans would toss out the inhabitants and their belongings.

This, then, was the first great trial that set off an avalanche. The Council was at a loss as to what to do. They called a meeting for eight o'clock in the evening, which continued into the wee hours in shelter No. I on Síp Street after being interrupted by another air-raid alarm. Finally, having weighed all possible options, the Council resolved to try the impossible because nothing could be worse than having Endre deploy his own men to vacate the homes. The Council was divided on the issue. Dr Samu Csobádi[76] voiced grave concern, but nobody was willing to assume responsibility for disobedience. (Later, I will address the factors and options considered by the Council, and why what happened had to inevitably happen.) Before the night was out, the Council had drafted sample forms and appointed Rezső Müller[77] to organize and implement the job of requisitioning.

The yellow stars first lit up in the streets of Budapest on April 5. People flooded the main hall of the Síp Street building where volunteers and officials from the congregation, the *chevra kadisha*, and the support office gathered to be briefed on the details of the apartment requisitioning. Threats were issued to warn those who would fail to achieve the necessary tangible results. In the morning hours, employees, teachers, and schoolteachers from the congregation went to the housing department of City Hall, where a policeman and a city teacher were assigned to each requisitioning team to be dispatched. The Christian teachers were put in charge of checking the inventories of goods and chattels left behind by Jewish tenants, and of sealing the vacated apartments.

The head of the Budapest housing office knew only too well that the action was completely unlawful, and worded his instruction very carefully, making sure to name the Jewish Council as the entity actually in charge of implementing the requisitioning, and relegating the police officers and teachers to the role of helpers and inspectors. Of historic significance no doubt, this instruction contained the following material provisions:

619.926/1944. XVII.

Instructions for the teaching faculty appointed to the official task of inspecting the process of requisitioning apartments for families rendered homeless by the bombing raid.

For purposes of providing accommodation for families rendered homeless by the bombing raid, in accordance with Decrees 1200/1943

76 See 46.
77 Rezső Müller (1894–?), banker and, in 1944, head of the housing department of the Jewish Council. Among other tasks, he directed the relocation of Budapest Jews to yellow-star houses in June 1944 (about which, see 154–5). In early June 1944, while Ernő Munkácsi was recovering from an illness, he temporarily assumed the role of executive secretary of the Jewish Council. He survived the Holocaust in Budapest.

M.E. and 1280/1943 B.M.,[78] the Royal Hungarian Ministry of the Interior has ordered the requisitioning of five hundred flats complete with furnishings and equipment, provided that the apartments to be requisitioned shall be designated by the Central Jewish Council.

The designation is to be carried out by calling on the tenants to hand over their apartments, complete with the necessary furnishings and equipment and accompanied by an inventory, by four o'clock in the afternoon of this day.

The mayor of the capital city[79] engages members of the teaching faculty as proxy of the authority to take the inventories.

The requisitioning team calling at each flat shall comprise one faculty member, one police officer, and two emissaries of the Central Jewish Council. The inventory of the apartment shall be drafted under the supervision of the faculty member.

The contribution of faculty members to the operation shall consist of the following tasks:

1) They shall determine the scope of furnishings, equipment, and necessities to be left behind in the apartments – such as beds with linen, wardrobes, tables, chairs, lamps, outerwear clothing, kitchen- and tableware, including plates, cutlery, cookware etc. – in sufficient quantity to enable families who have lost their homes and belongings to continue their lives with living amenities necessary for the long term. Therefore, the furnishings and equipment to be left in the apartments shall be determined and inventoried with this requirement in mind.

2) During the moving-out, the faculty members shall, in the presence of the concierge, check that the inventoried objects have indeed been left behind by the tenants. Furthermore, they shall take down the electricity and gas meter readings and record those readings at the bottom of the inventory list, make

---

78 Prime Minister's Decree No. 1200 of 1943 on solving the consequences of air raids and settling related legal issues (*légitámadások következményeinek elhárításáról és az ezzel kapcsolatos jogviszonyok rendezéséről*), Rendeletek Tára (Collection of Decrees), 1943, 174–204. The other key decree related to requisitioning was Prime Minister's Decree No. 100 of 1943 on regulating certain issues of renting apartments (*lakásbérletekkel kapcsolatos egyes kérdések újabb szabályozásáról*), Rendeletek Tára 1943, 7–15. Minister of the Interior's Decree No. 1280/1943 could not be found in the official bulletins.

79 Ákos Farkas (1894–1955), mayor of Budapest from 19 March 1944 until the end of the war.

sure that the fire in the stove has been put out and all faucets
turned off, and check whether the furnishings, equipment,
and the apartment itself are in proper working condition.
Thereupon they shall proceed to carefully lock and seal the
entrance door with a signed sealing label certified by a stamp
or other suitable means.

The tenant moving out shall deliver the sealed envelope to
the Central Jewish Council.

3) Subsequently, the apartment shall be allocated and the
envelopes handed over by the competent district aldermen.
Upon separate notice, the members of the faculty, accompanied
by the new designated tenant, shall go to the apartment and
make sure, in the presence of the concierge, that the seal has
been undisturbed, the inventory objects are all there as they
left them, and that the meter readings are the same as indicated
on the inventory list. If everything about the apartment is
found in order, they shall have the tenant sign a receipt of
the apartment in such condition, and shall deliver the receipt
to the office of the competent district officials. Executed
on 4 April 1944, on behalf of the mayor; signed Dr József
Szentmiklóssy, Councillor.

Around noon, sixty or seventy requisitioning committees set out to call
at the apartments of unsuspecting Jews to tell them they had to leave their
tenements by four o'clock that afternoon, without taking any furnishings
or equipment with them. I am at a loss for words to describe the shock and
despair into which the requisitioning mission plunged the unwary Jews,
who had hardly recouped from the confusion and lethargy wreaked by the
yellow-star edict. As the work of the requisitioning parties took longer than
expected, while the four-o'clock deadline remained unchanged, the Jewish
tenants often only had a few minutes to pack and leave.

The parties were quite "successful" in performing their duty, and the
pile of keys at City Hall grew at a reassuring pace. (In the meantime, Koltay
raised the number of flats required from 500 to 1,500 in the wake of another
bombing raid on April 4, without changing the time frame allotted for
the requisitioning.)

The taking of keys and inventories obviously took time. The four-o'clock
deadline passed, and by half past four only a thousand keys had been delivered.

Inspector Koltay showed up at Síp Street and, upon finding that the Jewish Council had failed to produce all 1,500 keys by the deadline, picked two officials on duty, namely Orthodox office president Samu Kahán-Frankl and Dr Károly Wilhelm, and drove them to his lair in Svábhegy. Council member Dr Pető arrived at the gate on Síp Street as Koltay was hustling the two councilmen into his car. Pető began to protest, but Koltay ignored him, other than to say he would be happy to give a ride to Pető as well if he went on resisting. In vain did the Council members point out that the keys were on the way and that every one of the 1,500 keys demanded would be in City Hall shortly. Koltay simply glanced at his watch and asked them:

"What time is it now?"

"Four thirty."

"And what time did I tell you I wanted all the keys?"

"By four o'clock."

"See, you did not carry out the order."

When told that all the keys would be delivered to City Hall within an hour, Koltay answered with a shrug, "I'm afraid that will be too late and won't do any good to the members of the Council." As they got out of the car, Kahán-Frankl clearly heard Koltay tell one of the detectives in his escort to "give him a good shove or two with your blackjack." The detective, however, was of a more benign disposition and, as they walked on, whispered to Kahán-Frankl that he had no mind to hurt him.

News of the appalling arrest was promptly reported to Councillor Szentmiklóssy, who called László Endre, or rather his secretary. Eager to apologize for the delay on the part of the Council, he explained that engaging the Christian faculty and the police turned out to be a lengthy procedure, so the Council was not to blame for the delay. Following this conversation, Endre allegedly gave the parties a two-hour extension on the original deadline. Probably owing to the same intercession, the two Council members were released from custody in Svábhegy the following morning, after being forced to stay up all night sitting on a stool and facing a blank wall. By six thirty in the evening, all 1,500 keys and inventories had been collected at City Hall.

Needless to say, such speedy requisitioning, often performed in a few minutes, could not have been fair and equitable in absolute terms, nor often by comparison between one requisition and another. The Council envoys had to make hasty and therefore often ill-advised decisions as to whether to take or leave an apartment. To make things worse, these decisions often had to be made in the absence of the tenant, who happened to be out shopping or on some other errand. Moreover, the attitude of the emissaries themselves varied greatly, some of them filled with solidarity and compassion for the Jewish community, others – especially the so-called volunteers – going about their work impassively. Not all congregation employees participated in this horrendous mission, either because their special position kept them from being assigned, or because they otherwise managed to stay out of the action. In many cases, the tenants had to vacate their flats in such haste, sometimes within minutes, that they forgot to take with them necessities they were not required to leave behind, such as ration cards, identification documents, food, and underwear. Where this happened, the Council did its best to retrieve the key for the time it took the tenants to recover their eligible personal belongings. Many odd incidents occurred on account of the inexperience of the Council emissaries, or because they simply misunderstood their mission. In one case, they evacuated a Jewish tenant who had moved into his crowded kitchen and sublet his main room to a Christian person. As the room occupied by the Christian tenant was untouchable anyway, requisitioning the whole apartment was clearly out of the question.

A similar apartment requisitioning order was issued on two more occasions. Already after the first campaign, Endre warned the Council via inspector Koltay that requisitioning would continue in retribution if the city was bombed again, as many times as the number of raids, and extended to ever-larger numbers of apartments. In addition, local evacuation orders were issued daily. For instance, all the Jews had to be removed from houses where senior party or government officials or SS officers resided. This was the case in the upper section of the Castle District and on many streets in Pasarét.[80] Furthermore, the Council was advised to keep an adequate number of keys handy in order to be able to make evacuated apartments available on command, within a few hours.

The tempestuous experiences of the first few days convinced the Council to set up a separate housing department. Most of the unit occupied Goldmark Hall,[81] but it spilled over into many other premises as well. Split into numerous subdivisions, including "Commands" and "Defence," the department soon

---

80 A middle-class neighbourhood with villas and detached houses in Budapest's
     2nd District.
81 Named after the Jewish composer Károly Goldmark (1830–1915), Goldmark Hall was
     a grand performance and cultural-events venue on the third floor of the Cultural
     Centre, a building belonging to the Israelite Congregation of Pest at 7 Wesselényi
     Street, just behind the Dohány Street Synagogue in Budapest's 7th District. Today,
     part of the Hungarian Jewish Museum and Archives.

turned into the most distinctive administrative outfit of the entire Council. It handled an enormous turnover of cases, employed countless clerks, and its combined powers bordered on the unimaginable.

This office became lord over life and death, and not just in affairs confined to apartment requisitioning. The Jews evacuated from their apartments had to be accommodated somewhere, especially if they had no friends or relatives in the city where they could be put up. The requisitioning process continued to cause interminable complications, as new Jewish tenants had to be forcefully relocated to occupied apartments spared by the wave of requisitioning. To address the most grievous errors, the Council organized so-called Objection Hearings, in which a great number of attorneys were employed (despite the fact that one of the most powerful Council administrators of housing affairs point-blank declared that he "hated to work with lawyers").

Ultimately, this set-up produced unfathomable chaos and endemic legal uncertainty, which prepared the ground for the most radical, final solution of the Jewish question: the wholesale liquidation of Jews. The story corroborated the vision of this author who, upon the implementation of the first requisitioning order, foresaw and predicted the consequences: a downhill progression beyond a point of no return. Once again, the truth of the English legal proverb, "My house is my castle," stood proven. The evacuated Jews not only lost their homes but were deprived of the nourishing soil of their lives, ceased to be counted as human beings, and took a long stride toward being reduced in the camps to sheer numerical sequences without a name or documents to identify them.

The question that must inevitably be asked is whether the Council had it in its power to act differently than it did, and if it had, what consequences that would have entailed. Disobeying orders would have indisputably led to the internment of its members and the appointment of a new Jewish Council. Those in power would have attempted to carry out the requisitioning all the same, either via a new Jewish Council or by using their own forces. In those days, however – remember, we are talking about April 1944 – the Germans could hardly have afforded to implement the requisitioning program using their own corps if that implementation were accompanied by bloody atrocities. As I explained earlier in this book, the Gestapo at the time was still reluctant to resort to violence in public, not to mention their shortage of personnel and their distrust of the Budapest police. (The latter circumstance explains their decision to bring in gendarmes to Budapest from around the country in the second half of June and early July, to help with the deportations.[82]) As we have seen, in the requisitioning missions carried out by the Jewish Council, the Gestapo chose to assign municipal teachers and police officers to secondary ancillary duties rather than vesting them with genuine executive powers. This much is evident from the mayor's instruction reprinted in the foregoing, if from nothing else. In those days, it was not yet possible to have such people expel thousands of their Jewish fellow citizens from their homes – certainly not without arousing a hostile mood against the occupiers, which the Germans and their Hungarian hacks wanted to avoid by all means. It is much more likely that Eichmann et al. would have easily found a second and third suite of Council staff to carry out their orders without hesitation. As I have suggested before, one of the main reasons behind the tragedy of Hungarian Jewry consisted of its lack of organization. The absence of solidarity – not to mention the presence of madmen and carpetbaggers – would have produced a new Jewish Council instantly, delivering themselves as tools in the hands of Eichmann, Endre, and company. The only way to escape would have been through mobilizing the left-wing and the Christian Hungarian middle class of independent thought and spirit. Hungarian Jewry, still numbering a million souls[83] at the time, could not realistically have found anyone else to rely on. But just as the Hungarian Jewish leadership had been unable to organize its own ranks in a systematic fashion, they had a deficit of communication with these Christian classes. (Speaking of communication, it took the deportation of hundreds of thousands of Jews from the provinces to Auschwitz before the Christian crowds realized that the country had drifted so close to defeat and ruin.) In this way, the die – or rather a huge boulder – was cast, not only taking with it Hungarian Jewry, but precipitating Hungary itself to the brink of

82   According to the plan of Eichmann and his Hungarian accomplices, the deportation of the Jews from Budapest was to have taken place in early July 1944, with the participation of Hungarian gendarme units transferred from the provinces under the pretext of a flag consecration ceremony. The gendarmes arrived as planned. However, Regent Horthy thwarted the plan by ordering the gendarmes out of Budapest and ultimately halting the deportations. Horthy's decision was partly due to international pressure, but also a response to his fear that pro-Nazi extremists in the government, including László Baky, undersecretary of state in the Ministry of the Interior responsible for overseeing the Hungarian Gendarmerie, would attempt a coup d'état.

83   The figure is inflated. In 1944, Hungary's Jewish population was between 760,000 and 780,000.

total annihilation. Amid the crisis, the Jewish Council continued its policy of salvaging what it could by fumbling in all directions.

~ ~ ~

Gazing at the chronological sequence of events, it only makes sense that one look into the past – this is what one calls history. Or one may cast his gaze forward – this is what one calls politics. In other words, the politician must bring unerring logic to the task of deliberating and weighing the potential consequences of various events, and choose to allocate the resources available to him accordingly. This is what one must bear in mind when, thinking of the greatest cataclysm in Jewish history, one examines the policy followed by the Jewish leadership of those days.

This is still a difficult and delicate subject to talk about, for several reasons, not least because we have not yet unearthed all the details of those events of history. One day, when we have all the pertinent documents in our hands and can read the memoirs of the agents of those events, who are the real makers of history, and when we have gained the necessary historic perspective over time – only then shall we be able to draw up the final balance of accounts.

The details I make public in this book are simply intended to propose certain currently available documents for scrutiny and to record impartial observations to preserve them for the genuine historiographers of the future. Yet I need some kind of cementing material that makes the diverse events and documents cohere to form an organic whole. Otherwise I would have my reader merely stare at the discrete pieces of a puzzle instead of viewing a coherent picture. This is why it is crucial to talk about the Jewish Council's policy, which guided the manoeuvres of one of two opposing parties. Without being familiar with that policy, the events of the time cannot be comprehended.

The Jewry of Hungary has never been a homogenous, undivided unit. It was split into various congregations and social classes; it numbered in its ranks capitalists and proletarians, Zionists and assimilationists, Israelites, and Christians. I have mentioned before that the so-called Jewish leadership did not depend on the broad popular masses as its base. It was by dint of an abrupt turn of history that the members of the Jewish Council found themselves in the role they did, facing tasks that undoubtedly called for the greatest human stamina. They found themselves in a predicament in which the obtainment of even partly favourable results would have presupposed direct communication with broad masses of the Jewish people. But this is precisely what was lacking. The internal divisions within the Council faithfully reflected the heterogeneity of the Jewry itself. It is hardly surprising, then, that its policy unfolded in several concurrent directions. We may thus state for the record that the Jewish Council pursued a rather motley policy. (Not that this in itself would have been harmful – on the contrary ...) Let us now look at the main threads of this policy.

First and foremost, the Council took pains to minimize any friction with the Germans, maintaining communications with them in an attempt to achieve the little that could be achieved. The inception of this line of policy can be located in the official announcement by the Budapest police headquarters of March 20 that "the commands of the Germans must be obeyed." For a long time, the Hungarian authorities were reluctant to even talk to the Jewish Council (I will come back to this later), while sidelined and/or leftist politicians had not moved to action with any success before May 1944. Communication with the Germans was conducted via members of the Council or officials of the so-called Group in Contact with the Authorities. This policy, favoured by the Council, had its benefits and disadvantages. On the positive side, it allowed the Council to buy time (albeit only with respect to the Jewry of Budapest), continue food supply deliveries to the internment camps, release detainees on a few occasions, relieve some of the German pressure in general, and even to procure a limited amount of political intelligence. On the downside, this policy almost completely pulled the rug from under any illegal resistance activity, and kept the Jewish masses from the truth, in a state of total stupor. The ghastly consequences of this ignorance only really materialized later, in the horrors of deportations from the provinces. The Jews of the provinces – nearly two-thirds of the total Hungarian Jewish population – entered the ghettos, brickyards, and then the cattle cars in a profound daze. The Council had no choice but to follow German instructions, and supply most of the goods and labour that the Gestapo demanded. Even though the Sondereinsatzkommando did give the Council a certain number of *Immunitäts Ausweis* [certificates of immunity], it would be a delusion to believe that this privilege was reserved for the Council itself. The pass recipients included other private individuals, particularly if they had the right connections and pockets deep enough to pay.

This, then, was one thread of the Council's policy.

Another led to the line associated with the name of Kasztner, commonly referred to as the Zionist line, although it remains doubtful whether it truly represented a Zionist policy. This marked one of the most fascinating and perhaps least understood chapters of the story. I have already discussed the official Jewish leadership in relation to the Zionists at the historic turning point of March 19. Prior to the German occupation, there were general signs that the Zionist movement in Hungary had grown long in the tooth and come to a standstill due to its wartime isolation. The Zionists contented themselves with the single seat they had in the leadership of the Pest Congregation, and if some of them rose to speak at the meetings once or twice a year to express their unique perspective, they ultimately always toed the line of official Jewish policy. It was the deportations from Slovakia[84] and the re-annexation of Transylvanian territories to Hungary[85] that breathed new life into the Zionist idea. Most of the thousands who fled to Hungary from Slovakia[86] were embraced by Zionist organizations (and some by the support offices[87]), who kept the refugees in hiding or helped conceal their illegal status. The young Zionists arriving from Slovakia and Subcarpathia injected fresh blood into the movement, as did the re-annexation of territories from Northern Transylvania. There, the Jewry and the Zionist leaders differed greatly from their counterparts in the heartland, characterized as they were by a deep immersion in Zionist ideology, political maturity, and substantial experience in the service of the state. Many of them were members of Romania's Jewish party with seats in parliament, so they were accustomed to having their interests enforced in the political arena and by political means – something that was all but unheard of in Hungary. More than once, they would come up with proposals that simply amazed the old guard as notions entirely alien and unimaginable to the *ancien régime* of Hungarian Jewry. The newcomers knew from experience that it was possible to represent Jewish interests through international political

84 Between March and October 1942, some 58,000 Jews were deported from the Slovak Republic to Auschwitz-Birkenau, where most of them were murdered.

85 On 30 August 1940, as a result of the Second Vienna Award arbitrated by Germany and Italy, Hungary re-annexed Northern Transylvania from Romania. See the Glossary entry on Border Revisions.

86 Following the dismemberment of Czechoslovakia in 1939, thousands of Jews were expelled or escaped from the newly created Slovak state. Another wave of refugees arrived after the deportations from Slovakia began in 1942.

87 Presumably referring to the Support Office of Hungarian Israelites (Magyar Izraeliták Pártfogó Irodája or MIPI).

channels and tended to look at all Jewish affairs from this perspective. This Jewish political faction from Transylvania counted among its members one Dr Rezső Kasztner, a fine journalist and excellent speaker.[88] We did not know much more about him, other than he was the son-in-law of the head of the Neolog congregation in Kolozsvár, Dr József Fischer – himself a renowned attorney, popular figure, and member of the Romanian Parliament. The fact that Dr Kasztner was introduced to the leaders of the Jewish Council by Ottó Komoly[89] guaranteed the newcomer's reliability.

Ottó Komoly was not a long-time member of the Zionist leadership; he had recently acceded to the post of president, replacing Dr Gyula Miklós, who had died unexpectedly during the war. Taciturn, deeply contemplative, unsentimental, and calculating, he was above all a man of action. He really came into his own when the deportations from the provinces ended in early July 1944. Then he began to act in full swing. When the independent Jewish line collapsed, Komoly became one of the few who held the fate of the remaining Jewry in his hands, owing to his good relations with foreign embassies as an agent of the International Red Cross. However, he had a long and arduous path ahead of him before he attained that position.

On March 19 the Zionist leaders voted non-confidence in the leadership of the Pest Congregation. Yet a few days later Komoly and Kasztner entered the cushioned room of the Council president, and secretive talks ensued. Despite the utter discretion, information soon leaked that the Germans were willing to allow a certain number of Jews, possibly the entire Hungarian Jewry, to leave the country for a neutral foreign territory in exchange for a specific amount of American supplies. These clandestine negotiations with the Council leaders continued almost on a daily basis, transforming Kasztner into a mythical figure in the dizzy centre of obscure and ineffably portentous happenings. We seemed to detect a resemblance between him

88 See 15.

89 Ottó Komoly (1892–1945, born Natan Kohn), engineer, decorated veteran of the First World War, president of the Hungarian Zionist Alliance from 1941 onward. Beginning in 1943, Komoly headed the Zionists' Relief and Rescue Committee (Va'ada) (about which see 15) with Kasztner as his deputy. Later, under the Arrow Cross rule, he was appointed a member of the Jewish Council. As a senior representative of the International Red Cross, Komoly oversaw the so-called Section A division, with a focus on organizing safe houses and rescue operations for children. In retaliation for his rescue efforts, Arrow Cross militiamen arrested and murdered him on 1 January 1945.

and the fantastic adventurers of Jewish history – David Reubeni, Sabbataj Cewi, Frank, and others come to mind – who appeared as miraculous comets over the unfathomable sea of Jewish suffering.[90] Kasztner did not wear a yellow star, yet the doors of the Gestapo's Sondereinsatzkommando were flung wide open to him, just as David Reubeni had had free access to the audience rooms of the Pope and the princes. The Jewish masses looked up to Kasztner with veneration much as David was once admired by those who barely eked out a living in the abject alleys of the ghetto.

In the wake of the surreptitious talks, word got around that a certain number of Jews would be allowed to leave for Palestine and the Spanish-French border after spending a few weeks in German lagers. One thing is certain: One day in late May the infamous Frau Eva of the Sondereinsatzkommando in Svábhegy[91] announced the receipt of permission from Berlin: "Brand fährt morgen [Brand departs tomorrow.]" (Brand was a member of Zionist vanguard.[92]) In the outcome of this deal, the Germans picked out several hundred Jews just before the deportations from the provinces began and brought them to Budapest, where they were taken to the lager in the synagogue on Aréna Street[93] and the barracks at the Institute for the Blind on Columbus Street.[94]

In the final episode of this plan, on June 30 – when the deportation of Jews from the outskirts of Budapest had started and the "rooster-feathers" (as the Gendarmerie was known[95]) had surrounded the city and even appeared on the streets of Kőbánya[96] and the tree-lined avenue of Zugliget within the capital's city limits – some 1,600 people set out for a destination that was ultimately supposed to be Palestine. After being detained briefly in

---

90 David Reubeni (1490–1541?), Sabbataj Cewi (or Sabbatai Sevi) (1626–1676), and Jacob Frank (1726–1791) were self-proclaimed messianic leaders of the Jews in Portugal, the Ottoman Empire, and Poland, respectively.

91 "Frau Eva" could not be identified.

92 Joel (Jenő) Brand (1906–1964), Zionist leader, member of the Budapest Relief and Rescue Committee. Thanks in part to his excellent command of German, he played a key role in the negotiations between the local Zionists and the SS, particularly with regard to the Kasztner Train (see 15). Brand emigrated to Israel after the war.

93 Now called Dózsa György Street in Budapest's 13th District.

94 See 50.

95 A reference to the plume of rooster feathers that adorned the hats worn by the Hungarian Gendarmerie (Csendőrség).

96 A neighbourhood in Budapest's 10th District, just east of the city centre.

Mosonmagyaróvár, they made it to the *Sonderlager* in Bergen-Belsen.[97] From there, some three hundred managed to continue on to Switzerland after eight weeks; the rest only followed in December 1944. The operation, which stirred up and still occupies the thoughts of the entire Jewry despite involving only 1,600 Jews reminded me of an illustration gracing a medieval German Haggadah,[98] painted at a time of great uncertainty, when the Jews did not know what tomorrow would bring – whether they would be expelled and killed or allowed to stay in their homes. On the eve of freedom, the dreamy Jewish artist envisioned the arrival of the Messiah, riding a mule in fine tradition, preceded by a herald sounding his *shofar*. And the gates of the narrow Jewish alleyways open, releasing an outpouring of the stigmatized, these martyrs of anguish, who begin to follow the Messiah toward delivery and redemption in the ancient homeland. With pain mingling with hope on their faces, some of them grab the tail of the mule to have themselves hauled out of captivity.

Judging from this sequence of events, some details of which remain unclear, Kasztner must have been in contact with the Gestapo during the days following the occupation. His negotiations were aimed at striking a deal whereby the Germans would allow some Jews to flee abroad in return for supplies from neutral foreign countries, or for some other unspecified consideration. In a letter sent to Budapest in the summer of 1945, Kasztner relates how he proposed the resettlement of the entire Hungarian Jewry, although he admits to having said, "We will try to help the whole community, but will not push for 'All or nothing.'" While Kasztner was still negotiating, Eichmann's gang and Endre began deporting Jews from the country.[99] At that point, Kasztner suggested that the Germans should fly Brand to Istanbul to serve as liaison with the Allies. (The Gestapo wanted trucks, textiles, machinery, and military supplies in exchange for the Hungarian Jews.) The Germans granted him permission and Brand flew to Istanbul, where he entered negotiations that remain steeped in obscurity. What we do know is that the Allies refused Germany's blackmail offer; the official reply from

---

97   A "special detention camp" at Bergen-Belsen, in this case the so-called *Ungarnlager* or "Hungarian camp," where the passengers of the Kasztner Train were detained during negotiations for their release.

98   Recounting the liberation of the Jewish people from slavery in Egypt, as described in the book of Exodus, the Haggadah is a liturgical text read during the Seder service on the festival of Passover.

99   Mass deportations from Hungary began on 15 May 1944.

London was soon aired by the BBC.[100] Those close to the fire were aware of these developments and witnessed the infernal tantrums and frothing curses of Eichmann and his cohorts in reaction. Yet, just when this approach had seemed to collapse for good, a deal was unexpectedly made with the Gestapo, this time involving payment in gold and precious stones for Jewish lives. The Germans promised to allow 1,200 Jews to emigrate from Europe via Spain, provided they possessed certificates and other foreign passports or visas. Kasztner proceeded to draft a list. Several veteran Zionists made it onto the list on account of their sheer merit, without having to offer any remuneration, while many rich Jews paid for their place in gold and other valuables they had stashed away. Ultimately, 1,684 people left the city on 30 June 1944. (Among them were some who went to the Józsefváros railway station, ostensibly to wave good-bye to friends and relatives, but ended up on the train.)

Along with Rezső Kasztner's *aliyah*,[101] the large majority of the great old Zionist leaders who had spearheaded the movement left Hungary for good. Ottó Komoly drew his own conclusions, sent off his only child, and stayed home with his wife to organize future transports to the Holy Land. His stature kept rising in veneration and importance in the tumult of events. He wielded his sword on several fronts until his own fall and martyrdom. (Kasztner's report submitted to the Congress in Basel was published after the manuscript for this book had been finalized. The data of this one-sided report demand scrutiny before their credibility can be established.[102])

I will skip a few events now to discuss another policy direction taken by the Council. This is the Hungarian line. Here, four phases can be distinguished in the chronology: (1) March 20 to about May 1; (2) from the formation of the Jewish Association[103] to about July 7, the scheduled date of the first deportation from Budapest; (3) July 7 to October 15; (4) the period after that.

---

100 Shortly after Brand's arrival in Istanbul on 19 May 1944, he was expelled by the Turkish authorities. Agreeing to go to Aleppo, Syria, he was arrested there on his arrival on 7 June by the British, who promptly leaked details of Eichmann's blackmail attempt to the media.

101 The immigration (literally, in Hebrew, "ascent") of Jews to "Eretz Israel" or what was then Mandatory Palestine.

102 Originally published in German in 1946, available in English as *The Kasztner Report: The Report of the Budapest Jewish Rescue Committee, 1942–1945*, eds. László Karsai and Judit Molnár (Jerusalem: Yad Vashem, 2013).

103 A reference to the second phase of the Council, when it was renamed Interim Executive Board of the Association of Jews in Hungary. See the Glossary.

The first six weeks were characterized by a general lack of activity. It appeared that Christian Hungary would permanently and completely expose its Jewish citizens to the mercy of the Germans. As we will see shortly, the Council made attempts to enlist the help of Jaross, Endre, and Baky[104] – to no avail. Following the formation of the Jewish Association, official relations were established between the Council and the sub-department for associations of the Ministry of the Interior. (This agency exercised supervisory powers over the Association and employed Zoltán Bosnyák,[105] head of the Institute for Research into the Jewish Question.)

Concurrently, secretary Zsigmond Székely-Molnár[106] and councillor Perlaky[107] from the law enforcement department of the ministry initiated negotiations with the Council and its envoys. Later on, the Budapest police also claimed a hand in the events on a separate front. The period from July 7 to October 15 was marked by the pro-Jewish involvement of the churches and certain groups of the Christian middle classes (to be discussed later), which was in part responsible for the halt of deportations from Budapest, originally slated for July 7, then postponed to August 27. Unfortunately, this

---

104 It is worth noting that, as recounted by Munkácsi throughout this book, the Jewish Council attempted "to enlist the help of" the very men who directly oversaw the persecution of Jews; attempts that were utterly futile. The three men named here were primarily responsible for overseeing the looting and deportation of Hungarian Jews, and all were sentenced to death after the war and executed. Andor Jaross (1896–1946), politician, formerly a leading member of the Hungarian Party in Czechoslovakia, joined the pro-Nazi Party of Hungarian Renewal in 1939, and was appointed minister of the interior after the German invasion, a post he held until August 1944. On László Endre, see 37. László Baky (1898–1946), a major in the Gendarmerie until 1938 and pro-Nazi MP, served as state secretary in Jaross's Ministry of the Interior between late March and late August 1944.

105 Zoltán Bosnyák (1905–1952), journalist, antisemitic ideologue, one of Hungary's most notorious authors of antisemitic articles and books. As a close associate of László Endre, Bosnyák established the semi-official Hungarian Institute for Research into the Jewish Question in 1943, which acquired official status during the German occupation. In 1944 he started the rabidly antisemitic newspaper Harc (Hungarian for "struggle") which was modelled after the Nazis' Der Stürmer. He was put on trial in 1952, found guilty, and executed.

106 Zsigmond Székely-Molnár, deputy state secretary of the Ministry of the Interior, head of special sub-department xxi/b. responsible for "Jewish matters" between late March and late May 1944.

107 Gyula Perlaky was head of the public security sub-department (xxi/a) of the Ministry of the Interior.

line of policy failed to produce meaningful results in deepening relations with the resistance and the Hungarian left – a shortfall I will come back to later as well.

The Jewish Council also maintained certain less significant lines of communication, including one with Minister of Finance Reményi-Schneller[108] and another with politicians of the underground left. A third contact was the far-right politician Rajniss,[109] whom the Council tried to win over to the cause of using Jewish labour in Hungary rather than across the border.

Yet another strategy consisted of rallying behind the Christian churches. Orchestrated not so much by the Jewish Council as by one of its members and, later, by the Alliance of Christian Jews,[110] the movement resulted in a flood of conversions using forms distributed at Síp Street. Masses of Jews reported to shelters with applications to break with Judaism.

Via the Veterans' Committee, the Council maintained close relations with the Ministry of Defence, as a result of which thousands of draft calls for labour service (*musz*)[111] were sent out – some of the recipients managed to evade deportation.[112]

108 Lajos Reményi-Schneller (1892–1946), Hungarian minister of finance between March 1938 and April 1945, who also served as the so-called economic super-minister (*csúcsminiszter*) in the governments of Teleki, Bárdossy, and Kállay between 1939 and 1944. He was sentenced to death and executed as a war criminal in 1946.

109 Ferenc Rajniss (1893–1946), journalist, economist, extreme-right politician. An MP between 1935 and 1944, he edited the far-right *New Hungariandom* (*Új Magyarság*) and the *Hungarian Courier* (*Magyar Futár*), which were among the most influential antisemitic and pro-Nazi newspapers of the era. He served as minister of religion and education in the Arrow Cross government between 16 October 1944 and April 1945. After the war he was sentenced to death as a war criminal and executed.

110 In its third phase, beginning mid-July 1944, the Jewish Council added members from the Interim Executive Board of the Alliance of Christian Jews of Hungary (who represented converts to Christianity). See Glossary entry on the Jewish Councils.

111 Beginning in 1939, Hungarian Jewish men (and other "political unreliables") were drafted into the country's forced labour service (*munkaszolgálat* or *musz*), which, for them, gradually replaced regular military service (in fact, by 1941, Jews were prohibited from carrying arms). See II.

112 The Ministry of Defence, headed by Horthy loyalist General Lajos Csatay, sent out numerous draft summonses right before the mass deportations began, with the goal of saving the lives of Jewish men by deploying them as labour servicemen (while also responding to the country's manpower shortage). So late in the process did this occur that these summonses were delivered to men already in ghettos and collection camps; nonetheless, they permitted several thousand able-bodied men to escape deportation at the very last minute.

Finally, mention must be made of the activities of Dr Béla Berend,[113] former chief rabbi of Szigetvár. Berend later came under various accusations, but the National Council of People's Tribunals, the supreme judicial forum, acquitted him of every one of the charges in a final and non-appealable verdict. Berend proclaimed ardently that Jews had no business in Hungary and must emigrate. His approach had a certain revolutionary air about it, defying the old capitalist Jewish elite. It is also a fact of history that Berend, a member of the Council, was seen daily in the building of the Ministry of the Interior. In fact, it was he who obtained entry permits for Council members when Endre had banned from the ministry everyone with a yellow star in an attempt to prevent the Hungarian authorities from being "contaminated" and influenced by them. It can be demonstrated that Berend managed to influence certain public servants in a positive way and that they were malleable to his influence. This is how the chief rabbi of Szigetvár rose to prominence in those apocalyptic times; he is also remembered for the eloquent sermons he delivered to large crowds from the pulpit of the Dohány Street Synagogue.

These political trends were supplemented by certain foreign policy missions best described as the Swedish line, of which I shall speak when I discuss the events of the summer of 1944.

~ ~ ~

The decree on designating places of residence for the Jews came out on April 28.[114] This was practically the only government decree that the usurpers of power were able to formally invoke as a "source of law" justifying

113 Béla Berend (1911–1987), chief rabbi of Szigetvár, member of the Jewish Council between May 1944 and January 1945, and a highly controversial figure. Berend acted bravely during the ghettoization in Budapest, offering support and aid to the persecuted. At the same time, he nursed relations with notorious antisemitic politicians, including Zoltán Bosnyák and László Endre. After the war, he was charged with collaboration and sentenced to ten years in prison, then acquitted on appeal. In 1947 he emigrated to New York where, despite changing his name to Albert Bruce Belton, he continued to be criticized for his wartime activities. In 1973, he launched a libel suit against the Holocaust scholar Randolph L. Braham (the case was dismissed) and for many years after, until his death, continued to sue his detractors.

114 Prime Minister's Decree No. 1610/1944 on the "Regulation of Certain Questions Concerning the Accommodation and Place of Residence for the Jews." *Budapesti Közlöny*, 28 April 1944, 2–3. For an English translation of key parts of the decree, see Vági, Csősz, and Kádár, *The Holocaust in Hungary*, 80–2.

ghettoization and the marking of designated buildings with a yellow star. However, the SS thugs and their Hungarian friends did not wait for such a trifling formality to act. They launched the ghettoization campaign ten days before the promulgation of the decree, driving hundreds of people out of their homes, herding them into facilities unfit for animals, or simply rounding them up under the open sky. First on the list were the towns of Nagykanizsa and Munkács. They were soon followed by the northern and northeastern regions, and then the entire country.[115]

The onset of ghettoization was preceded by a peculiar audience, obviously designed to divert attention from the events that threatened the Jewry. It was around April 20. A telephone call came from Eichmann's base in Svábhegy, ordering representatives of the Jewish Council to come to Rökk Szilárd Street[116] at three o'clock in the afternoon. Everybody summoned showed up on time and waited anxiously to see what would happen next. Half an hour later Wisliceny, Novak,[117] and another Gestapo officer appeared. The venue of the hearing consisted of the faculty room and the schoolmaster's room on the ground floor of the Rabbinical Seminary. The Germans were seated while the Jews listened to their instructions standing up. Wisliceny issued sharp commands and expressed his frustration over the delay in the drafting of the large map that was supposed to display the sociographic situation of the entire Hungarian Jewry.[118] He wanted the number of Jewish residents and institutions to be indicated for each settlement. Then he mentioned that a new organization representing Hungarian Jewry had to be set up, with the reckoning that Jews were not permitted to maintain

115 Based on the Ministry of the Interior's Confidential Decree No. 6163/1944 desig-
     nating residences for Jews, issued on 7 April, Hungarian public administration and
     law enforcement agencies started the ghettoization in the northeastern part of the
     country, including Munkács (today Mukacheve, Ukraine), on 16 April 1944. In the
     southwestern border region, including Nagykanizsa, the campaign began on 26 April.
     It appears that Munkácsi was not aware of the confidential 7 April decree, which pre-
     ceded the 28 April decree he cites at the beginning of the paragraph. See Vági, Csősz,
     and Kádár, *The Holocaust in Hungary*, 76–83.
116 About the Rökk Szilárd detention centre, see 35.
117 Franz Novak (1913–1983), SS-Hauptsturmführer and member of Eichmann's
     Sondereinsatzkommando. Known as the "station master of death," he was the trans-
     port specialist responsible for mass deportations throughout Europe, including the
     deportation of the Hungarian Jews in 1944. After the war, he went into hiding until
     1961 when he was charged with war crimes. Following repeated trials, he was found
     guilty and sentenced to a seven-year prison term.
118 This refers to data that the Jewish Council was earlier ordered to solicit from each
     congregation in Hungary. See 47.

residence in settlements with a population of fewer than ten thousand souls (this instantly sounded quite suspicious). When told that the Jews had hitherto been organized under so-called settlement districts, he said that a county-level administration was a much better idea, and that the supervision of each county district should be entrusted to the president of the local congregation. "If local Jews have any grievance or petition, they will be able to turn to the local prefect directly, so this new structure will be much more convenient for the Jews themselves," Wisliceny explained. He criticized the generally sluggish administration of the Central Council and urged the appointment of a managing officer whom they could be in touch with twenty-four hours a day. He quickly cited the example of Vienna's Lőwenherz[119] (originally vice president, later *Amtsdirektor* of the Viennese congregation) of whom he evidently approved, although he had to prompt the other Gestapo officer for the name of the office manager in Berlin. Of the latter, Wisliceny remarked in passing that "he was being difficult at first, so he had to be dispatched to Dachau for a few months. From the moment he came back from there, everything went beautifully with him." (Under the influence of this conversation, the Council quickly looked for a managing director. There were a number of candidates. Finally, the post was given to Dr Zoltán Kohn[120] on a provisional basis, until such time as the Council president recovered from the illness with which he had been hospitalized, and a permanent appointment could be made. Although this temporary assignment was tacitly extended later, the actual administrative powers of the Council remained concentrated in the hands of Rezső Müller,[121] particularly as of June 1944.) The meeting with Wisliceny devoted such painstaking attention to the issue of incitement in Jewish communities that one could have been forgiven for thinking that the Gestapo had an

---

119   Josef Löwenherz (1884–1960), lawyer, Zionist leader, head of Vienna's Jewish community during the Holocaust, first as deputy chairman (from 1929) and then as director (from 1936). After the Nazi Anschluss of Austria, he was arrested but soon released to reorganize the community according to the orders of Adolf Eichmann. After the war, he was charged with collaboration, but never tried. He emigrated to New York, where he died in 1960.

120   Zoltán Kohn (1902–1944), teacher at Budapest's Neolog Jewish high school (Pesti Izraelita Hitközség Gimnáziuma), editor of the literary journal *Libanon* between 1936 and 1941, co-editor of the yearbooks of the National Hungarian Association to Assist Jews (Országos Magyar Zsidó Segítő Akció, or OMZSA).

121   See 58.

interest in perpetuating the status quo, when all of this was nothing more than yet another instance of Nazi bluffing and duplicity.

The audience was nearing its end when Wisliceny casually mentioned that he would be leaving for a week or two to "reorganize the provincial Jewry." No one had any inkling – remember, the ghettoization decree had not yet been issued – that this work of "reorganization," for help with which Wisliceny wished to be accompanied by a Jewish expert familiar with the conditions in the provinces, would mean the ghettoization, deportation, and ultimate extermination of the Jews in the provinces. At this point, Wisliceny stood up to signal that the meeting was over and motioned the Council members to leave.

Barely a few days passed before the most disturbing reports from the provinces were received in Budapest. The Council leaders made an appointment with László Endre in the Ministry of the Interior, but when they got there Endre only had a few words with them and, gloves in hand, said he had to leave. The envoys then turned to Endre's secretary Takács for information, but he denied the terrifying news. Prompted by these circumstances, on April 26 the Council sent a telegram to Interior Minister Jaross, alerting him to the atrocities and followed up by mailing a two-page submission the following day. The telegram read as follows:

To the Right Honourable Vitéz Andor Jaross[122]
Hun. Roy. Minister of the Interior
Budapest

According to reports received by the Central Council of Hungarian Jews, Jewish residents in the northeastern region of the country,[123] in the counties of Ung, Ugocsa, Bereg, Máramaros, Abaúj-Torna, Zemplén, and Szabolcs, were rounded up and transported, without regard to age or gender, to the seats of the above-mentioned counties,

---

122 "Vitéz" refers to the Order of Vitéz, an honorary state title awarded to qualifying ex-servicemen in interbellum Hungary. The staunch antisemitism of the era precluded Jews from receiving the honour.

123 Ghettoization in Hungary began on 16 April 1944 in the northeastern 8th Gendarmerie District of Kassa. Deportation began there on 15 May. Between May and July 1944, Hungary's ten Gendarmerie districts were converted into six deportation zones, with the 8th District falling into deportation Zone I. For details, see the map "Deportation from Hungary, 1944" (xviii–xix).

where some of them are being held under the open sky locked away
from the outer world without any food, shelter, or sanitary services,
and thus exposed to the most severe of dangers. In the name of
humane compassion, we respectfully ask Your Excellency to remedy
this grave situation, which threatens hundreds of thousands of people
in their very existence, if only with regard to the impending possibility
of an epidemic.
Respectfully yours,

CENTRAL COUNCIL OF HUNGARIAN JEWS
Transmitted by telephone on 26 April 1944

The full text of the submission is as follows:

Central Council of Hungarian Jews
Budapest, District VII, Síp Street 12
No. 2378/1944

Re: Situation of the Jewry in the Northeast
The Right Honourable Hun. Roy. Minister of Interior

Your Excellency,
On behalf of the Central Council of Hungarian Jews, with the
deepest respect, we wish to outline to Your Excellency an extremely
sombre and critical situation into which the Jewish residents of
the northeastern parts of the country have been plunged under
instructions implemented by the authorities.

According to reports received by us, Jewish residents in the
northeastern region of the country, specifically in the counties of Ung,
Ugocsa, Bereg, Máramaros, Abaúj-Torna, Zemplén and Szabolcs, were
in recent days rounded up and transported, without regard to age
or gender, to the seats of the above mentioned counties and certain
major district seats, where some are being held under the open sky,
others in the outskirts of the towns, in very tight quarters and locked
away from the outside world.

The pertinent communications we have received include the
following, among others:

(1) Ung County: On the 16th, Jews from around the county were transported to Ungvár[124] and stationed in a brickyard and a lumberyard. The Jews from Ungvár were also brought here from the city on the 21st, 22nd, and 23rd of this month. The Jews from both the county and the county seat were allowed to bring with them only the sum of 30 pengős per capita plus food provisions for fourteen days, one change of underwear, the clothes they were wearing, and bed linens. They had to leave all other belongings back in their homes. The detainees, crowded together in the mentioned brickyard and lumberyard, exposed to the inclemency of weather under the open sky, currently number approximately twenty thousand. Their daily food allotment is a meager 100 ml of soup. No food is allowed to be brought in, and there is a shortage of water.

Needless to say, conditions such as these rule out adequate boarding and health services.

(2) Szabolcs County: There is a similar situation in Szabolcs County, where the Jews were rounded up in the city of Nyíregyháza from around the county. As far as we know, these people were only allowed to bring with them foodstuff to last for two days, the sum of 30 pengős, and 50 kilos of baggage a head.

The people transported to Nyíregyháza were quartered in private homes, in such great numbers that far exceed the capacity of these buildings. As in Ung, sustenance and care for the sick are practically impossible.

(3) Abaúj-Torna County: The Jewry from around the county and most of the Jewish population of the city of Kassa[125] have been squeezed into a brickyard outside the city without any water utility, where the most basic necessaries of life are absent.

(4) Bereg County: A similar procedure was inflicted upon the Jews in this county, where the evicted were stripped of all their valuables, including wedding rings and any money over the amount of one pengő.

(5) Máramaros County: The Jews of this county were crammed together in the town of Máramarossziget[126] and certain larger villages.

---

124 Today Uzhhorod, Ukraine.
125 Today Košice, Slovakia.
126 Today Sighetu Marmaţiei, Romania.

In the town, a significant part of the Jewish intelligentsia, about
140 individuals, were lodged in a small prayer house where they have
been without food and water for days.

From these reports one can conclude that, in the northeastern
parts, large masses of Jews – several hundred thousand people – have
found themselves in the most austere predicament through no fault of
their own. Due precisely to the large number of individuals involved
and the short time frame available, no provisions could have been
made for adequate lodging, healthcare amenities, food supplies,
medical services, and medicine.

Under the circumstances, in the absence of food, proper quarters,
or medical care, there are well-founded reasons to fear impending
famine and epidemics that will claim many lives, particularly among
pregnant women, babies, children, the sick, and the elderly.

With the deepest respect, therefore, we ask that Your Excellency
be kind enough to make arrangements for the proper boarding and
lodging of the relocated masses.

Furthermore, we respectfully request Your Excellency to authorize
us to dispatch representatives to these locations to assist with the
implementation of the necessary measures in consultation with the
authorities and local Jewish leaders.

Given the grave import and pressing nature of this matter, may we
respectfully ask for prompt action on the part of Your Excellency.

Please accept our most sincere respect and appreciation,

Dated Budapest, 27 April 1944
CENTRAL COUNCIL OF HUNGARIAN JEWS

To the Right Honourable Vitéz Andor Jaross of Nemes-Mitics
Hun. Roy. Privy Councillor and Minister of the Interior

This, then, was the situation in the provinces as reports of sinister events kept
coming in almost by the hour. The ghettoization of the Jewry of Ungvár and
its environs was recorded in the following minutes thus:

Minutes taken by School Commissioner Dr Zoltán Kohn at three
thirty in the afternoon of 25 April 1944. Appearing in the premises was
a gentleman from the area who currently stays in Budapest and wishes

to remain anonymous. Based on the first-hand report of a credible eyewitness, he gives the following account of the events:

The transportation of Jews from around Ungvár to the Moskovitz Brickyard on Minai Street in the city began last Sunday. They were each allowed to bring with them 30 pengős, food for 14 days, one change of underwear, the clothes they were wearing, and bed linens for one. The Jewish residents of Ungvár itself were informed Thursday morning by notices posted around the city, ordering them to stay in their homes and wait for further instructions. Further conditions as stated above. The city's resident Jews were taken to the same industrial facility on Friday, Saturday, and Sunday. The eyewitness who spent some three hours in the camp estimates the number of people gathered there at about 25,000. This huge crowd is completely helpless and exposed to the vicissitudes of weather under the open sky. During the first days, the residents of Ungvár were not yet massed together and there was a soup kitchen in the camp cooking for a thousand people or so. Since there are no more Jews left in town, it is doubtful if this kitchen is still up and running. It is permitted to enter the camp and to bring packages to family members. Labour servicemen are also allowed to enter and to bring food. The inmates are guarded by the camp's gendarmes, who demarcated the area of free movement with small flags; it is strictly forbidden for inmates to cross this line. The eyewitness relates the following incident he heard about: "A small child while playing crossed the line. The distraught mother ran after the child to fetch him, and crossed the line herself. Both were shot dead on the spot by the gendarmes."

On May 3, the Council addressed a German-language petition "An das Einsatzkommando der Sicherheitspolizei des S.D. [to the Operations Unit of the Security Police of the Security Service]" as follows:

Further to our personal meeting with Obersturmbannführer Krumey on the 2nd of this month, we hereby act on his suggestion and submit the urgent request for the authorities to permit the Jewish Council to dispatch representatives to the territories allocated for the Jewry in the northeastern and southern parts of the country. This request is based on serious complaints received from most of the concentration centres regarding lodging conditions, provisions, and health services.

The dispatched representatives would be assigned to the task of determining, with the approval of local authorities and in cooperation with local Jewry, any material deficiency as may be encountered in the camps, and to submit to the Central Council in Budapest a proposal regarding the same. Please help advance the success of this mission by allowing our representatives freedom to travel and interact with local authorities and Jews.

The submission goes on to describe the specific situation in each location, which makes it an invaluable source of history:

(1) Nyíregyháza: 4,120 city residents and 6,600 residents, a total of 10,759 people were brought into this ghetto. They were put up in 123 houses with a total surface area of 9,165 m², including kitchens and hallways. Under these circumstances, the living area comes to less than one square metre per person. To make things worse, there is no running water or sewerage, so sanitary conditions are unsafe. According to the general instructions, each inmate was allowed to bring food for fourteen days, except that the Jews were evicted from the villages on such a short notice that it was impossible for them to gather the allowed quantity of food. The Jews of Nyíregyháza thus soon ran out of food, and the local Jewish Council was unable to replenish provisions for the ghetto.

(2) Kisvárda: Here, the biggest problem was finding a place for the Jews from around the area. For the time being, they were corralled in the courtyard of a Jewish temple. They have run out of food; the entire situation is desperate.

(3) Ungvár: The majority of the Jewry herded together are without a roof.

(4) Kassa: The Jews were rounded up in the drying rooms of the local brickyard that have no walls, making conditions miserable for the 11,500 people kept there.

(5) Munkács: Most of the 18,000 Jews concentrated here were set up in the brickyard building. Those who did not fit had to stay outdoors.

(6) From Máramarossziget we got the following report: "Armed soldiers call on each house and take what there is to be taken. The ghetto is being readied; all the Jews will have to move there between the 20th and the 30th of this month. The Jews rousted from the villages have suffered all kinds of atrocities. Women are being bullied.

Young girls are body-searched by midwives to make sure they have no jewelry hidden."

Permission for representatives of the Jewish Council to make field trips was requested by Dr Imre Reiner to Eichmann himself, so that they could ascertain grievances on location with a view to proposing remedies. At first even Eichmann, this notoriously intimidating raging lunatic, feigned acquiescence, saying that over time he might allow a few Council representatives to visit the camps – but for now, everything was in flux in the provinces.

"Erst muss ich den Dreck, den Judendreck zusammenkehren [first I have to sweep up the dirt, the Jewish dirt]," he said later in an honest outburst of hatred and iniquity.

On May 12, the Jewish Council sent a petition to Minister of the Interior Jaross which documents the tragedy of the Heves-County Jews as follows:

The Jews of Heves were taken, on the 9th of this month, to an abandoned mining facility named Bagólyuk (Egercsehi) some 80 kilometres from the municipality of Heves. The same day, a representative from the undersigned Central Council had an exchange over the telephone with Chief Constable Dr Takáts,[127] who told him that Your Excellency had stopped the transport of Jews to the camps under instructions cabled to the prefects. Upon receiving this information, we called the Heves district chief constable telling him about Your Excellency's instruction and asking him to cease the transports accordingly. The chief constable informed us that the transport was on its way already, but that he would be requesting instructions from the prefect. The transport arrived in Eger on the morning of the 10th and stayed there until one o'clock in the afternoon before continuing its way to the destination. May we take the liberty to point out that, on the evidence of the certificate made out by municipal officials and delivered in the original to the secretary of Your Excellency Mr Zsigmond Székely-Molnár, the population of the municipality of Heves stood at 10,597 at the time of the 1941 census. Therefore, pursuant to the decree issued by Your Excellency in the matter of the concentration of Jews, the Jewish residents of this town would not have been eligible for relocation in the first place.

127   Albert Takáts, chief constable, personal secretary to László Endre.

According to reports we have received from Bagólyuk, the quartering
there is insufficient inasmuch as the abandoned buildings are missing
their doors and windows and there is so little room that only the
elderly have roofs over their heads and all personal belongings have
had to be left outdoors. The number of people kept at the facility
is reported to be around two thousand. In light of the fact that the
population of the municipality of Heves exceeds ten thousand,
and further in view of Your Excellency's radio message to suspend
the transport of Jews to camps, and finally, considering the current
disastrous situation of the Jews of Heves, may we request with the
utmost respect that Your Excellency order that the Jews of Heves
be transported back to their place of residence. We take the liberty
to mention that the Jews of Heves have signalled their readiness to
build barracks for their accommodation at their own cost outside the
administrative limits of the town, in a location completely segregated
from other residents.

In its attempts to save the Jews of Heves, the Jewish Council also contacted
Secretary Zsigmond Székely-Molnár[128] and submitted a report to the
Gestapo itself.

On May 12, the president of the Csepel[129] congregation made the following
report in writing:

This is to respectfully report that, on the 10th of this month, the
council of the municipality of Csepel notified me as the president of
the local Jewish congregation of having been verbally instructed by
the prefect of Pest County to concentrate the local resident Jews in a
single location where they were to be put up in barracks. According
to the municipal authorities, the bicycle storage barracks adjacent to
the Manfred Weiss factory would be suitable for this function. Let me
respectfully submit to you my view that this accommodation would
be the worst possible solution, as it would mean crowding together
some 1,200 souls in so-called barracks, where eight people would share
a floor space of two square metres, and where there are no sanitary

128 On Zsigmond Székely-Molnár, see 72.
129 A large island on the Danube River just south of Budapest, now officially part of the
     capital city.

facilities whatsoever, ruling out even a remote chance for hygiene. As there are no water closets, the most elementary human needs could only be served by latrines. However, in view of the approaching warm weather and the situation of the barracks in a densely populated section of the settlement, the latrine solution would only amplify the threat of spreading contagious diseases. It is a vital interest of national defence that the local military-industry work force, amounting to about 80 percent of the Jewish residents of Csepel, be enabled to work at full capacity without impediment. This would be impossible under the present lodging conditions which are not suited to allow them any rest. It is another important military interest to preserve the original intended function of the bicycle storage buildings in view of the fact that most of the workers commute from a radius of more than 60 kilometres mostly by bicycle and need to park their bicycles near the factory but outside its grounds. Let me also take the liberty to state that, on April 15, Dr László Koltay, head of the IV/4 division of State Security Police, and SS-Obersturmbannführer Krumey instructed me in no ambiguous terms to move the Jews of Csepel to a location designated by them. I complied fully with this instruction with the assistance of the Csepel municipal authorities, so I am at a loss to understand why this first instruction, issued by the secretary of the interior, has been overruled. I respectfully ask for your intervention to the effect of preventing this grievous and inhumane measure from being implemented and to keep the Jews of Csepel in the living quarters specified by the two gentlemen mentioned above.

On the basis of this report, the Central Council lodged a petition with the minister of the interior asking him to "take into consideration the above-mentioned interests of humane treatment, public health, and national defence, and issue an order for keeping the Jews of Csepel in the location originally designated by the State Security Police."

~ ~ ~

The date of 27 April 1944 was important in the history of Hungarian Jewry under German occupation as the date on which the ministry's Decree

No. 1520/1944 "on the self-government and federation of Jews" was issued.[130] The decree applied to everyone subject to wearing a yellow star, whether Israelite or Christian by religion, and consolidated all these subjects into a forced association called the "Association of Jews in Hungary." The decree provided that this association "shall perform self-government functions supervising the conduct of Jews within its purview, and may in this regard adopt measures that shall be binding for them." (It was these "binding measures" that the Jewish Council routinely invoked in acting to the detriment of the Jews, for instance by implementing requisitioning orders or issuing summonses to Rökk Szilárd Street.) The decree also empowered the association to "represent the common interests of Jews in its purview" while dissolving every other Jewish society, including the *chevras*,[131] and declared in principle that the property and assets thereof shall devolve to the Association. (It goes without saying that, in practice, this worked out very differently: Most of these societies were simply looted or their assets otherwise turned over to fascist organizations, leaving but morsels for the Association, which was nominally in charge of liquidating the societies.) Preparations for forming the Association were assigned to a nine-member temporary implementation committee appointed by Minister of the Interior Jaross, to the task, as per the decree, of administering urgent affairs until such time as the Association was properly formed with its own statutes. Given that the Association was never founded on a permanent basis, the temporary committee remained in charge of Jewish affairs and often lorded over life and death at the most crucial junctures. (This was the so-called second Jewish Council; I will return to the circumstances of its formation later on.) It was most probably while the decree was being reviewed by the Ministry of Justice that a provision (Section 5, paragraph 4) slipped into the text, exempting from the liquidation order "the organizations and institutions of the Israelite Congregation." This provision was instrumental in ensuring the legal survival of the national offices and the congregations in Budapest. However, during Szálasi's reign of terror, and even before it, these congregational institutions really only existed on paper.

130 Actually, the decree was issued on 19 April and came into force on 22 April. Regardless, the reference is to the Sztójay government's decree that established the "second" Jewish Council under the name the "Interim Executive Board of the Association of Jews in Hungary." See the Glossary.
131 *Chevra kadisha* burial societies. See 44.

As nobody could have foreseen the decree, it came as the greatest surprise. The foundation of the Association was an event of the utmost political importance, in part because it corroborated the view of those – including the author of this book – that the "Hungarian line" should have been pursued more forcefully, and that the seminal proclamation of March 20 (i.e., that Hungarian Jews had to obey whatever the Germans said) had to be seen as neither conclusive nor genuine, nor representative of the position of every Hungarian authority and every actor in public affairs. During the five weeks since the Germans had occupied the country, practically everything happened with the awareness that Hungary had turned over its Jewish citizens to the Germans and legally abandoned them to their mercy – "Let the Germans do with them as they please." The true motives behind the foundation of the Association remain unknown, but they must have been numerous. In any case, Eichmann's Sondereinsatzkommando was surely not happy with this development, and must have seen it as a sign of willingness on the part of the Hungarian authorities to infringe upon the occupier's powers. (The other occupied countries, including Italy, France, and Yugoslavia, never adopted even remotely similar provisions.) The reasons for issuing the decree could be surmised as follows: (a) Sheer greed: the fascist Hungarian authorities saw how the Germans robbed the Jews, and they simply wanted a slice of the pie; (b) The gaining ground of legal formalism (as suggested by the fact that ministry departmental councillor Argalás[132] drafted the decree): the Hungarian authorities needed provisions to formally legitimize the violations and future actions committed against the Jewry; (c) The infringement upon Hungarian national sovereignty: the authorities perhaps realized that "if they begin with the Jews, they will do the same to the others, so we had better restore legal continuity in Jewish affairs by placing the Jewish Council under the authority of the Hungarian ministry rather than of the SS Sondereinsatzkommando."

Whatever the motive, the decree could have been expected to bring to their senses those who looked to the mercy of the Germans for saving Hungarian Jewry. Only then would it have been possible to find a common ground where "disobedience could gain a foothold," and from where the Hungarian

---

132　Lajos Argalás (1904–?), ministerial department councillor, deputy head of the Legislative Department of the Ministry of the Interior and a close associate of Undersecretary of State László Endre. After the war, the People's Court found him guilty of war crimes and he was imprisoned.

authorities, bearing the support of the clear-headed part of Hungarian society, could have defied the deportations. Unfortunately, Hungarian Jewry was far too disorganized, ignorant, and feeble to enable this to happen.

The release of the decree provided a good excuse for establishing communications with the Hungarian authorities. The very next day, the Council called Constable Takács, secretary to László Endre, asking him to name the party to negotiate with in the matter of the foundation of the association. "Get in contact with Councillor Argalás or Director Bosnyák," he suggested. (At the time, none of the Council members knew who that "Director Bosnyák" at the Ministry of the Interior was.[133]) A few minutes later they got through to Argalás, who promised to receive representatives of the Council at noon. Since the occupation, this was the first time that the Ministry of the Interior had entered into official talks with Jewish representatives. It was a different story at the Ministry of the Culture and the Ministry of Justice. As I informed them confidentially of the events since March 19, the officials of both ministries listened in utter disbelief and assured me of their assistance and support. (I will provide a detailed account of these talks when I discuss the events of the summer of 1944.) At noon that day, Ernő Pető, Niszon Kahán, and myself were received by Argalás – a man who later turned out to have masterminded all the anti-Jewish regulations of the Sztójay cabinet,[134] for which the People's Tribunal would sentence him to several years of imprisonment.

Argalás told us that he had been personally in charge of drafting the decree, which was intended to retroactively legalize the anti-Jewish measures implemented since the occupation, provide the Jews with a forum for representing their interests, and bring the body administering Jewish affairs – termed *Zentral Judenrat* by the Germans and "Executive Board" in the language of the decree – within the purview of Hungarian authorities. However, when I asked point-blank whether the entry into force of the decree divested the Germans of their powers of authority, Argalás did not offer a straightforward answer. He also told us that he had acted on behalf of the legislation-drafting division and that his mission had practically ended with the final wording of the decree; the actual creation and supervision of

133   About Zoltán Bosnyák, see 72.
134   About Döme Sztójay, prime minister of Hungary from 22 March to 29 August 1944, see 168.

the Association were the responsibility of the department of associations of the ministry, headed by county notary Lajos Blaskovich,[135] a cadre from Endre's team. Argalás instructed us to contact Blaskovich in matters pertaining to the drafting of the Association's statutes and the appointment of the temporary committee. In its later phase, the meeting inevitably turned into a poignant speech as we briefed Argalás on the atrocities in Budapest and the ongoing ghettoization in the provinces, soliciting his help as a Hungarian official and legal expert. Argalás remained silent throughout our narrative. Evidently, nothing we said was really news to him. At last he said that acting in these matters fell outside the scope of his powers; he would forward our concerns in a report to his superior Endre. This, then, was the inception of our regular communications with the Ministry of the Interior during the occupation. The Hungarian Jews – once equal citizens in the eyes of the law – became the subjects of law enforcement, and their affairs were transferred from the Ministry of Culture to the Ministry of the Interior.

A few days later, on May 1, county notary Blaskovich summoned me to the Ministry of the Interior. It was not a very pleasant visit. László Endre, the true overlord of the ministry, had issued instructions to keep yellow stars out of the building to prevent the "contamination" of the officials working there. I was only able to get inside by being accompanied by a police officer, who presented me to the department head as "the Jewish lawyer."

Blaskovich was a man of far lower than average intelligence, the model of a puny public servant. Even though he refused to acknowledge the horrors of the ghettoization and the subsequent abominations as being real, I at least managed to "neutralize" this subservient chief notary, who always followed László Endre's orders blindly. My communication with him was facilitated further when, with the help of Ernő Bródy,[136] we managed to exert greater influence on him through the mediation of one of his relatives. Present at this first meeting with the notary were Argalás, head of the legislation-

135 Lajos Blaskovich (1892–19?), civil servant, notorious antisemite, chief notary of Pest-Pilis-Solt-Kiskun County between 1938 and 1944, and, as such, one of the close associates of sub-prefect László Endre. In 1944 Blaskovich was appointed head of the sub-department responsible for social associations (No. vii.b.) at the public security department of the Ministry of the Interior, a sub-department charged, among others, with supervising the Jewish Council and other Jewish organizations.

136 Ernő Bródy (1875–1961), lawyer, publicist, liberal politician, MP in 1906–18, 1920–44 and 1944–49, and a leading official of the Pest Israelite Congregation.

drafting department, and Dr István Vassányi,[137] the rapporteur for the Jewish Association, who had formerly served under Councillor Dr Páskándy[138] and inherited his superior's goodwill toward the Jewry.

We had just begun to talk when we were interrupted by the entry of an albino man who never looked anyone in the eye and was visibly reluctant to shake hands with me. I realized he was the real "boss" and when the others addressed him as "Mr Director," I immediately knew he was none other than the notorious Zoltán Bosnyák, head of the Institute for Research into the Jewish Question, which had been up and running for some time by then.[139]

My notes describe the proceedings of the meeting as follows:

We discussed the creation of the interim executive board. The chief notary asked questions about the details of the creation of the Jewish Council and about the personal background of its members. He said that one of the new nine members to be appointed to the new committee must be a converted Jew. He nominated Dr Cavallier[140] for the post, but when it turned out that his candidate was born a Christian, Bosnyák went on to recommend the journalist Sándor Török.[141] Blaskovich took his assignment so seriously that he made it mandatory for the central executive board in Budapest to appoint a local temporary committee in each settlement with a population of at least ten thousand in each case with one convert among the members. The notary gave us to understand that, in the future, the assets of every Jewish-affiliated society would devolve to the Association, and

137 István Vassányi, civil servant, secretary of the sub-department responsible for social associations (No. vii.b.) at the Ministry of the Interior.

138 János Páskándy, head of the sub-department responsible for social associations (No. vii.b.) at the Ministry of the Interior until 1944.

139 See 72.

140 József Cavallier (1891–1970), journalist, editor, and Christian socialist activist. In 1939, Cavallier took the office of the executive chairman and later president of the Hungarian Holy Cross Society (Magyar Szent Kereszt Egyesület), a Catholic organization established under the patronage of Bishop Vilmos Apor, to support and offer legal advice to Catholics of Jewish origin. In 1944, at great risk to himself, Cavallier played a leading role in the rescue and support of Jews in Budapest. In November, an Arrow Cross gang abused and arrested him, but he survived the ordeal.

141 Sándor Török (1904–1985), writer, journalist, deputy chairman of the Interim Executive Board of the Alliance of Christian Jews, and member of the Jewish Council representing Christian converts. After the Arrow Cross takeover, he went into hiding and survived the war in Budapest.

expressed special interest in the *chevras*. (By then, all the societies with substantial assets had been dissolved and their assets transferred to fascist organizations.) Even though I pointed out that the sacred societies had intimate ties to the congregations and were religious in nature, Blaskovich insisted on his plan to dissolve every *chevra*. When I drew his attention to the fact that the decree guaranteed the survival of the organizations and institutions of the Israelite Congregation, he retorted that this did not prevent him from shutting down these societies or apply other types of sanctions if they engaged in activities against the state. He ended the meeting by saying he would submit to Endre the list of members to be appointed to the new Jewish Council for approval, and that their appointment would be published in the government's official journal.

Indeed, the Ministry of the Interior came out with the decree a few days later under the number 176.774/1944, listing the members of the executive board as follows: Samu Stern, Dr Károly Wilhelm, Dr Ernő Pető, Samu Kahán-Frankl, Fülöp Freudiger (all these men had served on the former Jewish Council), as well as new appointees Dr János Gábor, the lawyer of the Pest Congregation, Dr József Nagy, a head surgeon, Dr Béla Berend, chief rabbi of Szigetvár, and Sándor Török, a journalist.[142]

The appointed executive board held its inaugural session on May 15. Illness prevented Samu Stern from attending, Dr Berend was away on a trip to the country, and Török was still in detention in an internment camp in Csepel.[143] The session was chaired by Kahán-Frankl, president of the Orthodox Office; the committee accepted his recommendation of Samu Stern for the post of board president. The board then resolved to invite former members left off the board to participate with consultative status and to assign them to the same tasks that they had performed to date, on the grounds that "they have rendered such vital services as members of the Central Council that their contribution cannot be spared in the future." The board elected Dr Niszon Kahán as its notary, and concluded the session by dispatching a team to draft the statutes of the association.

142 See the Glossary entry on the Jewish Councils.
143 Csepel Island was the location of a cluster of internment and labour camps set up in factories, including the Duna aircraft factory (Horthyliget), the Tsuk fur factory, and the Mauthner grain-processing plant.

The statutes were drafted within a couple of days and adopted by vote of the board following a discussion on May 22. While these statutes are obsolete today and are of little interest other than to legal historians, it is symptomatic of the general naïveté in those days that they included within the purview of the Association "tasks in education and cultural affairs," and empowered the Association to "solicit and use work and financial contributions from the Israelite congregations and their national and other organizations that continue to perform religious and cultural functions under effective statutory provisions."

The statutes were speedily submitted to the Ministry of the Interior, which refused to approve them after a series of protracted meetings. The process was thwarted by Zoltán Bosnyák, chief advisor to László Endre, with whom Béla Berend communicated regularly. As I have mentioned in the foregoing, the Council pursued several strategies simultaneously, and Berend was frequently asked to intercede with Bosnyák. In any event, Berend was a daily visitor to the ministry, the best-known member of the Jewish Council there.

~ ~ ~

Incredible as it may seem today, it is a telling fact of history that, before the second half of May 1944, Hungarian Jewry had had no idea of the horrors of the extermination camps or the details of the deportations. In those days, hundreds of thousands of Jews were being deported to death camps in Poland just a few hundred kilometres from the Hungarian border, from neighbouring countries such as Germany, Austria, Poland itself, the Moldova and Bucovina territories of Romania, and then from more distant countries including France, Belgium, the Netherlands, and finally from Italy and Greece – yet the Hungarian Jews did not awaken to the facts. The only information known to the masses was that German Jews had been deported to Poland and "accommodated" around Lublin, where they were put to "work" in abysmal conditions – but the true extent and reality of the horror remained enveloped in darkness. We knew certain details about the deportations, the "concentration" of our brethren from Vienna; at first that they were relocated to designated streets and houses, then that they were taken from there to somewhere else, but we had no way of keeping track of them – it was as if they had disappeared into the mist. During the war, a few pieces of specific news surfaced, about naturalized French Jews being put to work, or the transportation of Dutch Jews to Poland, but all these events seemed so distant that they flew under the radar of Hungary's Jews. At the beginning of January 1944, word got out that a train of wagons crammed full of Italian Jews was standing in one of the outlying railway stations of Budapest, and that our misfortunate brethren, locked in the cars, were wailing for a drink of water. Steps were immediately taken to find out the truth and extend help, but Sombor-Schweinitzer,[144] who headed the political department of the police, said, "All of this is nothing but fabrication." (The "Auschwitz Protocols" I shall talk about later will prove that it was stark reality!) The little that we did know was about the events in Slovakia. It was known, for example, that hundreds of Jewish girls had been taken to Germany and Poland for dishonourable purposes, and that labour camps for Jews had been established in several locations where the evicted Jews were rounded up, and that thousands of Slovakian Jews had been transported by the Hlinka Guard[145] militia to "work" in Poland. At the same time, we thought we knew that Jews remained in some of the cities, even in Pozsony.[146] And we did know about the demise of Jews of Hungarian extraction in Kamenets-Podolsk. These were non-Hungarian citizens whom the KEOKH drove across the border and who were later massacred by the SS in Galicia.[147] This was about all that we knew of the deportations, and nothing more.

Looking for the roots of this sinful ignorance, one may identify several contributing factors. As always in times of war, intelligence in the sense of obtaining news became extremely difficult. As the fascist champions of terror punished "alarmists" with cruel torture, many people simply feared to relay information that they had learned of by sheer chance. The death camp in Auschwitz/Oświęcim had been in operation and several millions of Jews had

144 József Sombor-Schweinitzer (1895–1953), detective, deputy superintendent of police, head of the political department of the Budapest police headquarters between 1938 and 1944. Sombor-Schweinitzer was renowned for conducting political investigation against left-wing and extreme right-wing parties and movements. In March 1944, the Gestapo arrested and deported him to Mauthausen and later to the Flossenburg concentration camp. Sombor-Schweinitzer was eventually liberated in Augsburg. In 1945–48, he worked for the US intelligence services (OSS, CIC) in Germany and Austria. Around 1950 he emigrated to the United States.

145 Hlinková Garda, a uniformed paramilitary wing of Hlinka's Slovak People's Party, a pro-Nazi organization that played a leading role in actions against Jews and other minorities. About the deportations from Slovakia, see 67.

146 Today Bratislava, Slovakia.

147 See 55.

been murdered there since 1942,[148] and still Hungarian Jewry had not even heard the name.[149] The horrors of the extermination camps could not have been leaked out to the public simply because no Jew had ever escaped from them. (The first to succeed in that unlikely feat were a couple of Slovakian Jews who got out in 1944 and fled to Switzerland. The notes taken of the interview with these escapees were eventually smuggled to Budapest and came to be known as the "Auschwitz Protocols." It was this document that finally opened the eyes of Hungarian Jewry.)[150] As it is known from depositions made at the Nuremberg Trials, the SS members assigned to these camps were required to take an oath of utter secrecy, and the Nazis – acculturated as they were to slavish discipline – did take these oaths very seriously. Compounding these circumstances was the fact that Hungary's Jews had been trained for decades not to concern themselves with foreign relations because it was not worth the trouble. As a result, the Jews buried their heads in the sand, convincing themselves that whatever they could not see did not exist. This artificially induced fog proved to be a hotbed for the kind of culpable optimism that made the Jews believe that, while all the Jews of Europe might perish, no harm could come to us in Hungary. The few who had foresight were accused of defeatism. In their gullible ignorance, even in the first months of 1944, everyone else kept telling themselves, "We will get away with it." Nor were they willing to believe the impending danger that the German occupation meant, and even with the first deportations underway, the Jews of each city and each region in the country looked on themselves as the exception that would be saved. At first there was talk about merely "clearing" routes for military supplies and logistics, and when all the Jews from the provinces, and even from Újpest on the outskirts of Budapest, had been taken away, the Jews still thought the deportations would stop at the borders of the capital. When the Jews from the immediate vicinity of Budapest began to disappear, the Jews of Budapest made believe that what happened around the country could not

148 Between 1940 and 1945, approximately 1.1 million people were murdered in the Auschwitz-Birkenau camp complex, with Jews from Hungary constituting the single-largest group of victims.

149 It is true that the name "Auschwitz" meant nothing to the overwhelming majority of Hungarian Jews facing deportation in 1944. Many, however, received pieces of information about the mass murder taking place in Hitler's Europe from various sources, such as refugees, labour servicemen who witnessed executions on the Eastern front, and Allied radio broadcasts. Still, few seem to have given credence to such horrific news stories and fewer still believed that similar events could engulf a "civilized" country like Hungary.

150 On the Auschwitz Protocols, see the Glossary.

possibly repeat itself in Budapest proper. The same myopic vision saw the yellow star as nothing more than a means of humiliation, and ghettoization as merely an inhumane measure, at a time when Slovakian refugees, who had come to Budapest in large numbers, tried to warn everyone not to believe a word of the Germans. The Slovakians knew that in every country where the Nazis gained a foothold they started by using the same gentle language as they did in Hungary, and ended up orchestrating their bloody deportations. During the weeks following the occupation, János Gábor, who was in charge of authority relations on behalf of the Jewish Council, began to feel increasingly apprehensive. One time, tormented by unspeakable doubts, he asked Eichmann if there was any reason to fear deportations. "As long as the Jews do not join the Ruthenian partisans or Tito's troops," Eichmann reassured Gábor, "such drastic measures will not be needed." This conversation quickly took wind, and the people believed Eichmann. Now we know that in the first week of April 1944 Eichmann et al. and Endre conferred in the Ministry of the Interior and decided on the deportation of Hungarian Jewry.[151]

The first reports of deportation came in almost simultaneously from Nagykanizsa and Munkács, between April 27 and 30.[152] While it was theoretically conceivable that the deportations from Munkács had to do with military operations and clearing the area for supplies, this explanation was untenable in the case of Nagykanizsa.[153] (True enough, here the Gestapo used the threat of incursions by Tito's troops as an excuse.) In Nagykanizsa, on April 27, the Germans brought in police from the nearby city of Szombathely who, with the collaboration of local authorities,[154] herded the Jews of the city in the most brutal manner into the ancient temple where Lipót Löw once

---

151 Munkácsi refers to the confidential 4 April 1944 administrative meeting organized by Eichmann and Endre on the concentration of the Hungarian Jews. See 75. According to our current knowledge, the formal decision to deport all Hungarian Jews to Auschwitz-Birkenau was made a few weeks later, probably on 22 April 1944. See Vági, Csősz, and Kádár, *The Holocaust in Hungary*, li–liii.

152 Given that the deportation began on 16 April, this suggests the relay of this information was substantially delayed, by more than ten days, or the author has his dates wrong.

153 On 19 April 1944, as a way to support and camouflage the impending genocide, the southwestern part of Hungary, including the region of Nagykanizsa, was declared a military-operation zone.

154 The ghettoization began on 26 April and was completed on 28 April with the participation of a Hungarian gendarme battalion and police cadet troops under orders from the Ministry of the Interior. The ghettoized Jews were deported from Nagykanizsa in two waves, on 28–29 April and 17–18 May.

delivered his sermons.[155] (At dawn they burst into Jewish residences yelling, "Get up, stinking Jew!" and drove them out of their houses.) This was how destiny caught up with one of the most assimilated Jewish communities in Hungary. The next day, able-bodied Jews from the younger generations were rounded up and taken ostensibly to Gödöllő near Budapest for labour duty. In fact, the train was bound for Auschwitz.[156] At the time, around April 30, nobody among the Hungarian Jewry knew this. It really seemed it was only about sourcing labour for some kind of project, given that only the young and able-bodied were chosen. But by then the deportation of Hungarian Jews had been decided conclusively, and a Hungarian liaison officer had been named directly in charge of the execution of the plan: gendarme lieutenant colonel László Ferenczy.[157]

Ferenczy must be counted among the most despicable mass murderers of universal history. This gendarme officer, who was forty-six years old in that woeful year, sullied the millennium-long history of the Hungarian nation with the filthiest iniquity. Even though he claimed his father was a chief constable, that his mother also came from a family of judges, and that he had no Swabians[158] in his lineage, he was of an entirely different disposition than

155 Lipót Lőw (1811–1875), rabbi of Nagykanizsa, Pápa, and Szeged, was one of the most influential Jewish spiritual leaders in nineteenth-century Hungary and a champion of Jewish emancipation and integration.

156 On 28 April 1944, the German Sicherheitsdienst deported about 800 people from the Nagykanizsa internment camp to Auschwitz. Altogether, approximately 2,700 Jews from Nagykanizsa, about 90 percent of the city's Jewish population, were murdered in the Holocaust.

157 László Ferenczy (1898–1946), lieutenant colonel of the Hungarian Gendarmerie. In the spring and summer of 1944, Ferenczy served as liaison officer between the Hungarian Ministry of the Interior and Eichmann's Sondereinsatzkommando, playing a crucial role in the mass deportation of Hungarian Jews. After the halting of the deportations, he manoeuvred to try to foster relations with the Jewish leadership. After the Arrow Cross takeover came another *volte-face*, when he took a position at the Ministry of the Interior as an expert on "Jewish matters." Ferenczy was found guilty and executed in 1946 as a war criminal.

158 "Swabians" is used here as an umbrella term to refer to ethnic Germans living in Hungary. (Originally, and correctly, the term denoted ethnic Germans from or with ancestral roots in the region of Swabia, an area in today's Baden-Württenberg and Bavaria.) By suggesting that ethnic German Hungarians shared the Nazis' characteristic traits, and that they were of "an entirely different disposition than Hungarians," Munkácsi employs a racialist argument here.

Hungarians in general. He was ruthless, sneaky, duplicitous, and flippant. He flaunted his spotless insignia without remorse and professed himself to be a staunch supporter of Regent Horthy while not only aiding the Germans but enthusiastically carrying out their instructions. Although he had not become visible to the Jews of Budapest until the end of May, in reality he had had a hand in everything from the outset.

From the trial documents before the People's Tribunal we now know that the decision in principle on the deportations was made at a meeting with Baky in the Ministry of the Interior on April 6.[159] Baky had summoned senior officers from the police and the Gendarmerie as well as the heads of civil administration and issued to them written instructions concerning the deportations, saying that László Endre would be in charge of administering the project. The starting dates were set by Eichmann, who dispatched Ferenczy to Munkács on his first mission. Here, the job was carried out by gendarme colonel Győző Tölgyessy[160] under the supervision and in the general spirit of Ferenczy. A meeting convened in Munkács on April 26 was chaired by Endre himself,[161] but the detailed instructions were specified by Ferenczy, who issued the command to deport exempted Jewish persons, half-blood Jews, and the intermarried as well. "The local residents slated for deportation must be squeezed into the wagons, irrespective of the trains' holding capacity."[162] Ferenczy procured the padlocks and chains for locking the

159 The meeting actually took place on 4 April 1944. As a result, on 7 April Baky issued Confidential Decree 6163/1944 (which had been drafted by László Endre). About the decree, see 75.

160 Győző Tölgyessy (1890–1954), gendarme colonel, commander of the 8th Gendarme District of Kassa between 1940 and 28 October 1944. During the Arrow Cross rule, he served as the deputy superintendent of the Gendarmerie and was promoted to major general. After the war he escaped punishment, living first in Germany and later in Canada, where he died in 1954.

161 The author has the details wrong. The first meeting of the administrative and law enforcement leaders of Deportation Zone I (which included Northeastern Hungary, Subcarpathia, and Northern Transylvania), chaired by László Endre, took place on April 26 in Szatmárnémeti; whereas the Munkács meeting, chaired by Ferenczy, was held on 12 May.

162 According to the minutes of the Munkács meeting, this quote (or something very similar) was said not by Ferenczy, but by Captain László Lulay. See: Historical Archives of the State Security, Records of State Security Investigations of Hungarian War Criminals, V-116.292. Regardless, the trains were overpacked and undersupplied – thousands of men, women, and children died en route, even before they reached

wagons himself. He ruthlessly ordered hospital patients and children from state-run orphanages to be taken as well. The atrocious measure of having women body-searched by midwives was also his idea, albeit in his testimony he made an effort to pin this on Endre. In the first days of May, Ferenczy reappeared in Munkács to confer with gendarme captain Leó Lulay[163] and gendarme officer Zöldy,[164] who had recently been promoted to the rank of SS captain, to settle details of the deportation from Kassa. This "meeting," which criminal law prefers to term "conspiracy for murder," is described by Ferenczy as follows in his testimony:

> We established that 110 trains would be used for the deportations from the station of Kassa. Exemption was to be given to Jews of foreign citizenship. These were to be removed from the camps to cells at the police station to keep them from seeing the deportation of the others. The trains were to be marked "D.A. Umsiedler,[165] German labour-force resettlement." Each train would consist of 45 "G" cars and carry three thousand souls, with seventy individuals plus luggage per car. Seriously sick Jews and their relatives would be in the last transport designated for the location. There would be a medical train with a physician and a nurse on board, for Jewish Council members and Jews of questionable citizenship. Labour service physicians assigned to air raid precautions and pharmacists would come along as well. The wagons would be locked. In case the lineup included German wagons,

---

the border town of Kassa (today Košice, Slovakia). Trains designed to transport forty people carried at least seventy, and often far more.

163 Leó László Lulay (1898–196?), Gendarmerie captain, adjutant and German-Hungarian interpreter for Lieutenant Colonel László Ferenczy from the end of April 1944. The People's Court found him guilty of war crimes and sentenced him to life in prison in 1950.

164 Márton Zöldi (1912–1946), also spelled Zöldy, Hungarian Gendarmerie captain, one of the main perpetrators of the mass murder of Serbians and Jews committed by the Hungarian Army and law enforcement agencies in Hungary's Southern Province (today Vojvodina Serbia) in January 1942. A court-martial was initiated against him and other high-ranking officers in 1943, but he escaped trial by fleeing to Germany, where he joined the SS. After the German invasion of Hungary, he returned to Hungary to take an active role in the deportation of Hungarian Jews. Following the war, he was captured, and extradited to Yugoslavia, where he was found guilty of war crimes and executed.

165 Probably an abbreviation for "Deutsche Arbeitkräfte Umsiedler," literally, as translated by the author, "German labour-force resettlement."

which cannot be locked with a padlock directly, these would be fitted with a 30cm length of chain with links held together by a padlock.[166]

As part of the preparations, Ferenczy, Endre, and Eichmann went on an "inspection" tour around May 10 to discuss the details of deportations from the provinces. Eichmann expressed the wish to have the Gendarmerie placed at his disposal, and Endre was happy to comply.[167]

Ferenczy's testimony offers a clue as to why – as we will see shortly – the Jews of Pozsony,[168] of all places, were the first to become aware of the impending deportations from Hungary and their timetable. Given that the Kassa-Auschwitz railway line crosses Slovakia, it was from this country that the Germans deployed railway cars to Kassa and performed railway logistics in general. Ferenczy provided the following details:

I was approached during Endre's tour, as I have mentioned, and again a few days later by Hauptsturmführer Wisliceny, who communicated to me the wish of Eichmann to have an officer appointed from Department xx of the Ministry of the Interior to serve on a joint German-Slovakian-Hungarian committee responsible for negotiating the details of the transports with the railway authorities in Pozsony and Vienna. I relayed this request of the Germans the next day and recommended the appointment of the lieutenant commander of the Kassa Gendarmerie District, who I knew had a perfect command of the German language. When I got back to my office, Captain Dr Leó Lulay reported that the issue was no longer relevant, as Eichmann had just appointed Lulay himself and another Hauptsturmführer to this committee.

All of this went unnoticed by the Hungarian Jewry. The Council's department of "provincial affairs," under József Goldschmied,[169] maintained communications with the ghettos in the provinces via devoted young Zionists

---

166 This citation originates in the minutes from the meeting in Munkács on the deportation of the Jews, 12 May 1944.
167 Historians have not found supporting evidence for this statement.
168 Today Bratislava, Slovakia.
169 József Goldschmied, Zionist leader who headed the Central Jewish Council's department of provincial affairs, but about whom no further personal information could be found.

who used forged documents and disguised themselves wearing military or railwayman uniforms as they attempted to approach and infiltrate the camps in the provinces to bring news. Many of them perished during these heroic exploits. In all certainty, we have principally these young Zionists to thank for the reports that reached Budapest. There were hardly any non-Jews who would have undertaken such missions.

The incoming news appalled everyone and suddenly shed light on the naked truth: the clear and present danger of annihilation, and the fact that the Gestapo, aided and abetted by the Gendarmerie and the Hungarian authorities, had decided on the wholesale deportation of Hungarian Jewry.

In those days, the building on Síp Street became a stage for narratives more stirring and blood-curdling than anything we had heard to date. We had constant visits by relatives of families forced into ghettos in the provinces, who read stories of horror from letters smuggled out. Then there were those exhausted, bedraggled women, almost insane with anguish, who had escaped to Budapest from ghettos in the provinces and sought shelter at Síp Street, huddling up in the premises of the central office or in secluded nooks of the temple. They were so distraught and paralyzed under the influence of what they had had to endure that weeks went by before they could utter a composed, intelligible sentence.

~ ~ ~

Upon the request of the Council, the head of the Kassa Ladies' Club lodged the following petition with the wife of the ex-regent:[170]

> As Your Lady Excellency will be aware, about four weeks ago the Jews of Kassa and the County of Abaúj-Torna were transported to the brickyard in Kassa. The deportation to Germany of the Jewry rounded up here commenced on the evening of the 15th of this month. They were prohibited from bringing with them anything except a most scant provision of clothes, food, and medicine. Nor do the authorities in charge take age into consideration; they consign all Jews for deportation, babies included.
>
> When we made inquiries, we were told that the mentioned individuals were being taken to Germany to work, but the inclusion

170 Magdolna Purgly (1881–1959), wife of Regent Miklós Horthy.

of the elderly, the sick, and infants gives us cause for the gravest concern regarding the fate of the deported.

Your Lady Excellency!

I the undersigned, Mrs Sámuel Gotterer, president of the Ladies' Club and founder of the girls' orphanage in Kassa, exempt on account of my veteran husband with a 75 percent disability, on the 16th of this month filed a petition for a personal hearing. If Your Excellency were to be so kind as to receive us, we would be putting forward a twofold request as follows:

1. We would ask Your Excellency to intercede for the complete halting of the deportations from Kassa;

2. Were this not possible, be so kind as to intervene to ensure the exemption at least of children of either sex under the age of 18, men over 60, women over 50, the sick, and mothers of children of either sex under the age of 18, as these individuals would be unfit to perform any useful work outside the country anyway.

We are aware of our option to submit this request to other authorities, but we know full well we would never find anyone else with the compassionate heart of Your Excellency.

Hopeful and confident that Your Excellency will be generous enough to give us an opportunity to deliver our arguments in person, we remain faithfully yours on behalf of the Israelite Ladies' Clubs of Kassa,

[signed]

Budapest, May 17, 1944.

By mid-May, the direct threat of ghettoization had reached the capital, as evidenced by this letter from the Jews of Újpest:[171]

This is to respectfully report that the mayor of Újpest has designated the areas and individual houses where the Jewish residents are to be accommodated. On this day, the city has lodged a proposal with the Minister of the Interior, requesting *inter alia* a ban prohibiting Jewish residents from leaving their homes from six in the evening to eleven in the morning. Exceptions would only be granted to officials and workers in the military industries.

171   A city north of Budapest. Today the capital's 4th District.

In view of the large number of enterprises in Újpest outside the military sector, where many Jewish individuals are in employment as of this writing, and because in general everyone has the right and duty to earn a living by work, we intend to file an objection with the mayor against this measure. Given that Budapest and Újpest form a single police jurisdiction, it is likewise inconceivable that two disparate measures could be implemented in this matter in these two respective locations.

Újpest has a Jewish population of about 14,000 souls who would be dealt a lethal blow by the contemplated curfew order. For the aforementioned reasons we respectfully request that you take steps in the Ministry of the Interior with the utmost urgency, meaning within the next few hours, to persuade Secretary Zsigmond Székely-Molnár, special rapporteur assigned to these affairs, to keep the ministry from instructing the police headquarters as petitioned by the city. We further request that in Újpest, a borough merged with Budapest geographically, no measures ever be brought that would not be applied equally to the capital as the case may be.

Most respectfully yours,
Relocation Committee of the Israelite Congregation of Újpest.

The terrible brutality of the atrocities in the provinces is described vividly in this report from the municipality of Salgótarján:

Report as of four o'clock in the afternoon on 7 June 1944:
In the municipality of Salgótarján, during the night of May 1 this year, several well-to-do Jews were herded into the building of the local state civil school, where they were interrogated by the most horrendously cruel methods.

The fifty gendarmes dispatched from other villages grilled both men and women, breaking bones in their bodies, having them take off their shoes, and beating and sticking dressmaking pins in the naked soles of their feet to extort confessions about any valuables they might have hidden in the homes of Christian citizens. We have no confirmed information about how long the torture sessions lasted or how many victims were involved. A local Jewish attorney, who could not take the beating any more, offered the confession that he had buried valuables in a garden in the village of Bárna a few kilometres away. This was untrue; he only resorted to this lie to escape further beating at least on the way to that village. When they got there, no valuables of any kind were found. We do not know what happened to the attorney on the way back.

A local dentist suffered similar atrocities. He was taken to the second floor of the building, beaten until he was half dead, and thrown out of the window into the back yard in this unconscious state. A handful of Christian women splashed water on the body in an attempt to resuscitate him. The brutality created a great commotion, but the gendarmes scattered the Christian crowd with their batons. The gendarmes tried to make it appear that their victim committed suicide, even though he had been nearly dead when they threw him out the window. Needless to say, the dentist died of his injuries shortly thereafter.

This report is supplemented by the following details:

Dr Ödön Szalvendy: (a) He was beaten until he signed a deposition admitting that he kept and operated an illegal radio transmitter stashed away in his chimney; (b) Mrs Lenke Grünwald, née Steiner, was beaten until she signed a deposition confessing that she kept handy 300 kilograms of poisoned lemon drops which she planned to distribute in town; (c) Four pregnant women were beaten until they went into labour; (d) The score is sixteen dead in a few days. One or two relatives per each victim were permitted to wheelbarrow the corpses to the cemetery, where they had to bury the bodies themselves, without any clerical assistance, in graves dug by labour servicemen.

4

The Auschwitz Protocols and Their Fallout

*Fülöp Freudiger receives a letter – The Auschwitz Protocols –
The "tattoo" – "Work makes you free" – Escape attempts punished
by hanging – A collecting point for the moribund – "Selection" –
Gassing – The first transports – Gassing off the record – Brothers
of Thorez and Leon Blum among the gassed – Gas day and
night – Financial and barter transactions with the SS – Systematic
extermination in Polish ghettos – New crematorium and gas
chamber in Birkenau – Everybody dead in three minutes – Murder
by injections – Ceaseless transports – Family transports – Czech
Jews – The block supervisor (Blockältester) – The block scribe
(Blockschreiber) – The nurse and the block servants – The second
Auschwitz Protocol – The tragic death of a rabbi – Eruptive
typhoid epidemic – Fallout of the Auschwitz Protocols*

The first ringing bell directly warning us of the annihilation of Hungarian
Jewry was a letter sent to Fülöp Freudiger[1] from Pozsony. It must have been
the second half of May. A heat wave had set in, as if to intensify the sizzling
emotions radiating from the swelling crowds at Síp Street. It was sometime
in the afternoon, one of those interminable afternoons that offered a measure
of respite after the ever-mounting afflictions and orders from both German
and Hungarian authorities had come in for the day. The devastating news
we normally received during the morning hours left no room for thought;
the tension relaxed somewhat by the early evening.

Fülöp Freudiger, the head of the Orthodox Israelite Congregation – who
had a vision so keen he often glimpsed things before anyone else – produced

---

[1] About Fülöp Freudiger, see 19.

Fig. 21   Women and children line up after arriving in Auschwitz-Birkenau on one of the first trains from Hungary in May 1944. The letters "DR" on the train stand for Deutsche Reichsbahn (German State Railway). This image is part of the "Auschwitz Album," a rare and horrifying collection of photographs taken by SS officers that documents Hungarian Jews as they disembark, proceed through the selection process, and are deloused and shaved in preparation for work or sent to their death in the gas chambers.

a letter in Hebrew from Pozsony and proceeded to translate it on the spot. The letter warned that, according to a reliable source, the Germans had completed all necessary preparations for the deportation of Hungarian Jewry, concentrating a huge number of train wagons in Slovakia to be forwarded to Jewish transit camps in Hungary, including those in Kassa, Munkács, Ungvár, Máramarossziget, Nyíregyháza, and Szatmárnémeti. The author of the letter added that the deportation transports were bound for Oświęcim/ Auschwitz, where the delivery of Jews from Slovakia had been going on for two years. The letter ended by hinting at future updates. Freudiger's disclosure had the impact of a bombshell. Although there remained a few whose naïve or simply thick-headed optimism made them take the news for some distasteful fairy tale, the rest of us knew that time was up and that the death knells had tolled for Hungarian Jewry.

We only had to wait a few more days for even more dreadful news to come.

Via the Swiss embassy, the Protocols in German were disclosed of testimony dictated by two Slovakian Jews, plus a woman and another man, who managed to escape from the German death camp to neutral territories. They were the first Jews to have fled from Auschwitz and survived. Since the liberation, many accounts of Auschwitz have been published, but none command a historical significance comparable to these first reports. The authors – these Slovakian Jews – had been among the first to be taken there directly after the camp had been set up, and thus had the opportunity from the start to observe its operation, master plan, and gruesome equipment.[2] Since 1942 they had witnessed the extermination of Jews from Poland, France, Belgium, the Netherlands, and, finally, from Greece and Italy. When they escaped, in April 1944, there followed a few weeks' lull in the operation of the "machinery," only to resume with redoubled force at the end of May, when large numbers of Hungarian Jews arrived and had to be gassed. Because Hungary's Jews were chronologically the last among the transports, the accounts provided by our Hungarian brethren survivors must be regarded as a continuation or sequel to the Auschwitz Protocols.

Now I turn the "proceedings" over to the Protocols themselves. I apologize to my readers if these records cause them sleepless nights or nightmares, but I want all to know what the proponents of German cultural supremacy contrived against us, how deep in misery Hungarian Jews were plunged by the counter-revolution and the right-wing Arrow Cross–ridden middle class of the Endre and Baky sort – in short, I want to familiarize all with the vortex that swallowed the historic Jewry of Hungary.

On 13 April 1942, a thousand of us – all men – in the assembly camp in Szered[3] were loaded into freight wagons. The wagons were locked from the outside, so we were unable to determine the direction we were headed. When, after a long journey, the doors were opened, we were surprised to find that we had crossed the Slovakian border and

2   The authors of the first eye-witness account were Walter Rosenberg (later Rudolf Vrba) and Alfred Wetzler, Jewish prisoners who escaped from Auschwitz in early April 1944. See Glossary entry on the Auschwitz Protocols.

3   Today Sered; Slovakia, where a labour camp for Jews was established in 1941. The camp served as transit centre during the first deportation of Jews from Slovakia to Auschwitz in 1942. Later, after the Slovak National Uprising in late August 1944, the SS turned the site into a concentration camp.

were standing at the station in Zwardon, Poland. The guards recruited
from the Hlinka Guard had been replaced by Waffen-SS crew. After
a few cars were decoupled from our train, we moved on. We came to
the Auschwitz station at night and stopped on sidetracks. Apparently,
the disconnected cars had been left behind due to lack of room in
Auschwitz. In any case, those left behind followed us a few days later.
When we arrived, we were lined up in rows of five, then counted.
We were 640. After marching for some twenty minutes carrying our
heavy baggage (we had left Slovakia well equipped) we arrived at the
Auschwitz camp.

Once in Auschwitz, we were directly led into a large barrack. To one
side, we had to hand over our baggage; on the opposite side, they made
us undress. We had to relinquish our clothes and valuables as well. We
were then walked over to another barrack next door where they shaved
our heads as well as our whole bodies and disinfected us with Lysol.
Upon leaving this barrack, each one of us was given a number. The
numbers started with 28,600 and continued in an unbroken sequence.
We were then herded into a third barrack with numbers in hand, where
the actual admission procedure took place. This consisted of tattooing
on our left chest the number we got in the second barrack, which they
performed with extreme brutality. Many of us fainted at this point.
This was also where our personal data were taken for the record. From
here, we were ushered, in groups of a hundred, to a cellar and then to
a barrack where we were given striped inmate uniforms and wooden
clogs. Later in the day they took these uniforms away from us and
gave us old Russian military uniforms (more like rags) instead. Once
outfitted in this manner, we were led to Birkenau.

Essentially, Auschwitz is a concentration camp designed
for political prisoners – so-called protective custody prisoners
(*Schutzhäftlinge*). At the time of my admission, that is, in April 1942,
some fifteen thousand prisoners, mostly Poles, Reich Germans, and
"civilian Russians," were concentrated here. A smaller number of the
prisoners consisted of criminals and shirkers.[4]

Also subordinated to the Auschwitz camp command were the
Birkenau labour camp and a small agricultural farm (Harmansee). All
admitted prisoners are first taken to Auschwitz, where they are given a

4   AKA "dodgers," "vagrants," or others who avoid work.

number, then they are either kept there or sent to Birkenau or, in very small numbers, to Harmansee. The numbers are issued consecutively, in the order of arrival. Each number is used only once, so that the last number always shows the total number of prisoners registered up to that point. At the time of our escape from the Birkenau camp, in early April (1944), this number stood at approximately 180,000. Initially, the numbers were tattooed on the left chest of prisoners; later, when it was found out that the numbers had smudged, on the left arm just above the wrist.

Each category of prisoners was handled in an identical manner, without regard to nationality, except that, to facilitate keeping count, the prisoners were marked by triangles of different colours painted on the left side of the upper uniform under the number itself. The nationality of the prisoner was indicated by the appropriate initial painted inside the triangle, such as P for "Polen" for the Poles. The colours referred to the following categories:

red triangle = political protective custody prisoner
green triangle = professional criminal
black triangle = shirker (mainly Russians)
pink triangle = homosexual
purple = Bible student sect member[5]

Jewish prisoners were merely distinguished by supplementing the appropriate triangle (which, in the majority of cases, is red) by yellow points (to make a star of David).

The grounds of the Auschwitz camp were home to various factories and workshops, including, among others, plants each of DAW (Deutsche Ausrüstungswerke), Krupp, and Siemens. In addition, an industrial complex several kilometres in length called "BUNA" was being built outside the grounds of the camp proper. The prisoners worked in these plants.

The living quarters, meaning the camp itself in the narrow sense of the word, occupies an area roughly 500 by 300 metres in size. This area is surrounded by two parallel rows of concrete posts curved inward at the top. The posts in each row are connected by high voltage barbed wire stretched on the inner and outer sides of the posts. Between the

5   A literal translation of the German *Bibelforscher*, which at the time referred to Jehovah's Witnesses, who were badly persecuted by the Nazis.

two rows there are 5-metre-tall watchtowers at intervals of 150 metres, equipped with machine guns and floodlights. A short distance inward of the inner electrified fence row is an ordinary wire fence. If anyone even approached this innermost fence, the guards in the towers fired at him. The camp itself consists of three rows of houses. The camp road leads down between the first and second rows of buildings. Between the second and third rows, there used to be a wall. The houses behind the wall were used as accommodation for Slovakian Jewish girls deported in March and April 1942. They numbered around seven thousand. When these girls had been taken to Birkenau, this wall was torn down. A sign with large letters over the entrance to the camp reads *Arbeit macht frei* ("Work makes you free").

The entire broader camp has a surface area of about 2,000 m² and is surrounded by watchtowers for each section at intervals of 150 metres. The security system described before is called *Kleine Postenkette* or "inner security belt," while this latter system forms the *Grosse Postenkette* or "outer security belt." The various industrial plants and workshops are situated between these two security belts. The towers of the inner security belt are only occupied during the night; this is only when the electricity in the wire is switched on. The guards of the inner security belt leave in the morning and are replaced by guards occupying the towers of the outer security belt. Escape through both security belts is virtually impossible. At night, it is impossible to get through the inner belt, and the towers of the outer belt are spaced so close together (at intervals of 150 metres, so that one tower looks over a radius of 75 metres) as to make it impossible to approach them undetected. If someone approaches, the guards will fire without warning. The guard of the outer belt is not relieved of duty at night until roll call inside the inner belt has been taken to make sure that all the prisoners are inside. If the roll call determines an absence, they sound the alarm sirens. When this happens, the guards of the great belt remain in the towers while the guards of the small belt reassume their position in the towers. Then the search of the area between the two belts begins with a few hundred SS men and bloodhounds. As the alarm sirens can be heard at a distance from the camp, any fugitive who miraculously manages to break through the belts will in all probability be caught by one of the frequent patrols of the German police and the SS. A potential fugitive is greatly hampered by his shaven head, marked clothing, striped convict uniform or rags doused in red paint, as well as the attitude of nearby residents, which is one of passivity at best, owing to their intimidation. Helping fugitives in any way, let alone the failure to report to the authorities immediately, carries the death penalty. If the fugitive is not caught within three days, the guards of the outer belt leave the towers, because by then it will be assumed that the fugitive has somehow managed to break through the twin belt. The fugitive captured alive is hanged in the presence of the entire camp. If his dead body is found anywhere, it is brought back to the camp and placed at the entrance with a sign pressed into his hands that says, *Hier bin ich* ("Here I am").

During our two years in captivity, there were many escape attempts. With two or three exceptions, the fugitives were invariably brought back in, dead or alive. We don't know if the fugitives not brought back to camp ever really made it. Yet we can state with certainty that, among the Jews transported from Slovakia to Auschwitz or Birkenau, we are the only ones to have managed to escape so far.[6]

Until the middle of May 1942, a total of four transports of Jewish men arrived in Birkenau from Slovakia, who were handled the same way.

From the first and second transport, 120 men including us were picked and taken to Auschwitz on the orders of the camp commandant, who wanted physicians, dentists, college graduates, and professional clerks. The group consisted of 90 Slovakian and 30 French Jews. Following a week's stay in Auschwitz, 18 doctors and nurses and three clerks were chosen from among the 180 white collar workers. The doctors were employed at the hospital in Auschwitz while the three clerks, including myself, were sent back to Birkenau. My two mates, László Braun from Nagyszombat[7] and Grosz from Verbó,[8] both of whom are now dead, were assigned to the Slovakian block,

6   There are numerous differences between Munkácsi's Hungarian version of the Protocols and the "official" English-language version, which was translated from German by the US War Refugee Board in November 1944. Many of those differences are minor. At this point in the document, however, it is worth noting that Munkácsi's version omits a long section (approximately 1,200 words) that appears in the US War Refugee Board version.

7   Today Trnava, Slovakia.

8   Today Vrbové, Slovakia.

while I joined the French group, where I was assigned to record-keeping duties. The remaining 99 men were sent to the gravel pits of Auschwitz for labour duty, where they shortly perished.

Soon afterward, a so-called "hospital" (*Krankenbau*) was furnished in one of the barracks. This was the infamous Block No. 7. At first I worked here as head male nurse, and later as supervisor. The head of the hospital was Viktor Mordarki, Polish political prisoner No. 3550. The hospital was nothing more than a collection point for the moribund. All incapacitated prisoners were referred to this place. Naturally, medical care and nursing were out of the question. We counted about 150 dead daily. The corpses were taken to the crematorium in Auschwitz on a daily basis.

At about the same time the so-called selections began. Twice a week, on Monday and Thursday, the camp doctor determined the number of prisoners to be killed by gassing and their bodies burnt. The selected were loaded onto a truck and driven to the birch grove. Those who got there still alive were gassed in a large barrack built for this purpose next to the cremation pit, and then burnt. From Block No. 7, approximately 2,000 perished each week in this way; some 1,200 died from "natural causes" and 800 from "selection." Of those who died of "natural causes," death certificates were made out and sent to the camp command in Oranienburg. The data of the "selected" were entered in a book marked "SB" for *Sonderbehandlung* or "Special Handling." Until 15 January 1943, while I worked as supervisor of Block No. 7 and thus had the opportunity to directly witness the events that transpired there, about 50,000 prisoners died, from "natural causes" or by "selection."

Since all prisoners were numbered, as I have mentioned, I was in the position to establish the sequence and fate of the incoming transports with considerable accuracy.

The first transport consisted of 1,320 naturalized French Jews, numbered approx. 27,400–28,600.

Approx. 28,600–29,000 were issued to the first transport of Jews from Slovakia arrived in April 1942 (this was my transport).

Approx. 29,600–29,700: 100 men (Aryans) from various transit camps.

Approx. 29,700–32,700: another transport of Slovakian Jews (3,000 men).

Approx. 32,700–33,100: 100 common-law criminals (Aryans) from the penitentiary in Warsaw.

Approx. 33,100–35,000: about 2,000 Jews from Krakow.

Approx. 35,000–36,000: 1,000 Polish (Aryan) political protective custody prisoners.

Approx. 36,000–37,000: (in May 1942) 1,330 Slovakian Jews from Lublin-Majdanek.

Approx. 37,300–37,900: 600 Poles (Aryans) from Rador, including a few Jews.

Approx. 37,900–38,000: 100 Poles (Aryans) from the Dachau concentration camp.

Approx. 38,000–38,400: 400 French naturalized Jews, who arrived with their families. The total transport numbered about 1,600 souls, of which only about 400 men and 200 women were admitted to the camp in the manner already described, while the remaining 1,000 (women, older men, and children) were brought from the side-tracks, without taking records of any kind, straight to the birch grove where they were gassed and burnt. From this point onward, every incoming transport of Jews received this same treatment.

Polish Jews had been treated like this for quite some time. For months and months, there was no end of truckloads of Jews from various ghettos in Poland, arriving directly at the birch grove, where they were gassed and burnt by the thousands.

Approx. 38,400–39,200: 800 naturalized French Jews. Most of the transport were gassed as already described.

Approx. 39,200–40,000: 800 Polish (Aryan) political protective custody prisoners.

Approx. 40,000–40,150: 150 Slovakian Jews; most of the transport were gassed in the birch grove.

Approx. 40,150–43,800: about 4,000 French naturalized Jews, mostly intellectuals. From the incoming transports, 1,000 women went to the women's camp; the remaining 3,000 people were gassed in the birch grove.

Approx. 43,800–44,200: 400 Slovakian Jews from the camp in Lublin. This transport arrived on 30 June 1942.

Approx. 44,200–45,000: About 200 Jews from Slovakia. The transport consisted of about 1,000 souls. A few women were assigned to the women's camp, the others went to the birch grove.

Approx. 45,000–47,000: 2,000 French (Aryan) persons, communists, and other political prisoners, among them Thorez and the brothers of Leon Blum. The latter were tortured with uncommon cruelty before being gassed and burnt.

Approx. 47,000–47,500: 500 Dutch Jews, many of them German émigrés. The better part of the transport, some 2,500 souls, met their fate in the birch grove.

Approx. 47,500–47,800: about 300 Russian civilians.

Approx. 48,300–48,600: 320 Jews from Slovakia. From this transport, about 70 women went to the women's camp, the remaining 650 people to the birch grove. This transport also contained the 30 individuals whom the Hungarian police transferred to Szered.

Approx. 49,000–64,800: 15,000 naturalized Jews from France, Belgium, and the Netherlands. This number barely represents 10 percent of the head count of the incoming transports from June 1 to September 15; most were taken directly to the birch grove.

The "Sonderkommando" that performed the gassing and cremation duties worked in two teams day and night. In those days, Jews were being gassed and burnt by the hundreds of thousands.

Approx. 64,800–65,000: about 500 Slovakian Jews. From this transport, some 100 women were sent to the women's camp; the rest went to the birch grove.

Approx. 65,000–68,000: naturalized Jews from France, Belgium, and the Netherlands. From the incoming transports, some 1,000 women were sent to the women's camp and at least 30,000 people were gassed.[9]

Approx. 68,000–70,500: 2,500 German Jews, from the Sachsenhausen concentration camp.

Approx. 71,000–80,000: naturalized Jews from France, Belgium, and the Netherlands. The number of those admitted to the camp hardly amounted to 10 percent of the transports. I would conservatively estimate the number of those from these transports who were gassed at 65,000 to 70,000.

On 17 December 1942, two hundred young Slovakian men, all members of the Sonderkommando employed at gassing and

9   The figure "30,000" is surely a typo, intended to be "3,000" in accordance with the figures "65,000–68,000."

cremation jobs, were executed in Birkenau on charges of mutiny
and attempted escape after someone blew the whistle on their plans.
Their team was replaced by two hundred Polish Jews just arrived
from Makow.

These changes in the Sonderkommando deprived us of our direct
contact with this "workplace," impairing our ability to source supplies.
Even though they had to leave their baggage in Auschwitz, prisoners
in the transports that ended up in the birch grove had brought along
large amounts of money in foreign currency, particularly dollars in
banknotes and gold coins, as well as tremendous quantities of gold,
precious stones, and food. While the valuables obviously had to be
turned in, some of the valuable objects – mainly gold dollar coins
– inevitably ended up on the hands and in the pockets of the lads
when they searched the clothes of the gassed. In this way, considerable
financial assets and even food entered the camp. Of course, officially
you could not buy anything for money in the camp, but it was possible
to make deals with some of the SS staff and civilian workers assigned
to various specialized jobs within the camp perimeters, who had the
opportunity to smuggle in small quantities of foodstuff and cigarettes.
Naturally, the prices were extremely high for the circumstances; a few
hundred cigarettes would be paid for with a twenty-dollar gold coin.
Barter trade also flourished. In any case, expense was not an issue,
we had all the money we wanted. We even obtained clothes through
the Sonderkommando. Over time, we replaced our rags by the fine
clothes of the gassed. For example, the coat I am wearing now used to
belong to a Dutch Jew. The label in the lining indicates a tailor shop
in Amsterdam.

The quarters of the Sonderkommando were isolated from the
rest. We could not have personal contact with them, if only because
of the hideous stench they exuded. They were always filthy and had
turned totally wild, brutal, and violent. In some cases – not that
this was unheard of among the other prisoners – one would simply
bludgeon another to death. Beating a fellow prisoner to death was
not considered an offence. The administration simply registered the
death of the prisoner entering his number; the cause of death was
entirely beside the point. One time I witnessed a young Polish Jew
named Jossel explaining the technique of "workmanlike killing" to an

SS operative. He demonstrated the technique by killing a Jew on the spot with his bare hands, without using any weapon.

The systematic extermination of Jews from the Polish ghettos started with prisoner number 80,000 approximately.

Approx. 80,000–85,000: About 5,000 Jews from various ghettos in Poland, including in Mława, Łomża, Maków, Grodno, Zichonow, and Białystok. Transports kept coming in over a period of thirty days. Only 5,000 people were consigned to the camp; the others were gassed. The Sonderkommando worked feverishly in two shifts twenty-four hours a day, hardly able to keep up with the work of gassing and burning. It can be assumed, without any exaggeration, that those gassed from these transports numbered around 80,000 to 90,000. These transports brought with them unusually large amounts of money, foreign currency, and precious stones.

Approx. 85,000–92,000: 6,000 Jews from Grodno, Białystok, and Kraków, plus 1,000 Aryan Poles. The overwhelming majority of the Jewish transports went straight to the birch grove. On average, 4,000 Jews were herded into the gas chambers each day. In the middle of January 1943, we received three transports of 2,000 souls each from Theresienstadt.[10] The meaning of the markings on these transports, "cu" "cr," "r," was unknown to us. Of these 6,000 people, only 600 men and 300 women were sent to the camp; all the others were gassed.

Approx. 99,000–100,000: Large transports of Jews from the Netherlands and France arrived in late January 1943. Only a fraction of them were consigned to the camp.

Approx. 100,000–102,000: In February 1943, 2,000 Aryan Poles, mainly intellectuals, arrived.

Approx. 102,000–103,000: 700 Aryan Czechs. Those who remained alive from this transport were later transferred to Buchenwald.

Approx. 103,000–108,000: 3,000 French and Dutch Jews plus 2,000 Aryan Poles. In February 1943, a daily average of two transports came in carrying Jews from Poland, France, and the Netherlands, most of whom were gassed without ever seeing the camp. The number of those gassed during this month can be estimated at around 90,000.

10   Today Terezín, Czech Republic.

The newly built crematorium and gas chamber in Birkenau opened in February 1943. At this point, gassing and burning in the birch grove were stopped, and continued in the new purpose-built crematorium exclusively. The huge trench in the birch grove was filled in and earth was spread evenly on top. As had been the practice before, the ashes were utilized as fertilizer at the Harmansee farm, so that it is unlikely that any trace of the mass murders remains there today.

At the present time there are four crematoria in operation at Birkenau, two larger ones (models I and II) and two smaller ones (models III and IV). The model I and II crematoria consist of three parts:

a) furnaces;

b) hall;

c) gas chambers.

Protruding from among the furnaces is a tall smokestack. Around it nine furnaces were built, each with four muffles. Each muffle holds three average-sized bodies and burns them to ashes within an hour and a half. This adds up to a total capacity of processing 2,000 corpses per day. Next door is an enormous undressing hall designed to create the impression of being part of the baths. This hall has a capacity of 2,000 persons, and has a waiting room of the same dimensions underneath it. From here, the way leads through a door down a few steps to a rather long and narrow gas chamber. False showers are fitted on the walls to create the illusion of a common shower room. The flat roof of the chamber has three windows that can be hermetically sealed by means of valves. A track runs from the gas chamber to the incineration room through the halls. The procedure of gassing begins by leading the victims to the hall and telling them they are being taken to the baths. To reinforce the impression, when they undress they are each given a towel and a bar of soap by two men wearing white smocks. Then they are squeezed into the gas chamber. The 2,000 people barely fit in the chamber, so everyone must stand up straight. The SS often shoot into the crowd to force those in front further inward. When all are inside, the door is locked shut from the outside. There is a short pause, probably to allow the temperature inside to reach a certain degree. Then the SS, wearing gas masks, go onto the roof, open the valves, and sprinkle the Jews with a dust-like preparation emptied from tin cans. The label on the tins reads "Zyklon zur Schädlingsbekämpfung"[11] and bears the trademark of a factory in Hamburg.

Obviously, the cans contain some form of cyanide, which gasifies at a certain temperature. In three minutes, everyone in the chamber is dead. To date, not a single victim is known to have given a sign of life after the chamber door was opened – something that was not uncommon with the former primitive process employed in the birch grove. When the door has been opened, the chamber is ventilated, and the Sonderkommando hauls the bodies on flat trolleys to the furnaces where they are burnt. The other two crematoria operate on roughly the same principle, although their capacity is only half as great. All in all, the four crematoria together can handle the gassing and burning of 6,000 people a day.

Theoretically, only Jews are killed by gassing. Aryans are gassed on rare occasions only; they are normally shot. Before the crematoria were commissioned, this used to be done in the birch grove, where the corpses were subsequently burnt in the pit. Later, many were shot in the back of the neck in the crematorium hall, equipped specifically for this purpose.

The formal opening of the first crematoria early in March 1943, when 8,000 Jews from Krakow were gassed and burnt, took place in the presence of several "dignitaries," both senior officers and civilians, invited from Berlin for the occasion. The guests were more than satisfied with the performance of the crematorium, and frequently availed themselves of a glimpse through the spy hole in the door of the gas chamber. They only had words of praise for the new "industrial operation."

In early March 1943, 45,000 Jews arrived from Thessaloniki. Some 10,000 men and a smaller number of women were consigned to the camp, while the rest – at least 30,000 people – went to the crematorium. Almost all of the 10,000 in the camp died shortly thereafter. Most perished from a disease similar to malaria. Many

11 Zyklon-B, aka Cyclone-B, was the trade name for the cyanide-based pesticide (*Schädlingsbekämpfung* means "pest control") used in Auschwitz and other Nazi death camps. It was manufactured by the German firm Degesch (Deutsche Gesellschaft für Schädlingsbekämpfung mbH).

fell victim to the eruptive typhoid that raised its head and began to spread; some simply could not take the overall harsh conditions at the camp.

Since mortality rates rose sharply due to the malaria, which claimed a particularly heavy toll among the Greek Jews, and the eruptive typhoid, which killed many in general, the "selections" were temporarily suspended. The sick Greek Jews were called on to report for treatment. Despite being warned by others, many of them volunteered anyway. All of them were then killed by intracardiac phenol injection. The injections were administered by a low-ranking health officer, while the doctors tried to help the poor souls as best they could, if nothing else by easing their suffering.

The approximately 1,000 people who survived from the Greek transport, plus another 500 Jews, were soon dispatched to Warsaw to work on a fortification construction site. Some weeks later, hundreds of them returned in a hopeless condition; many of them were gassed right away. When the administration of phenol injections was discontinued, 400 malaria-patient Greek Jews were sent to Lublin, ostensibly for "further treatment." We received word that they had indeed arrived in Lublin, but we know nothing about what became of them there. One thing is certain: Not one of the 10,000 Greek Jews remains in the camp today.

Concurrently with the suspension of selections, murdering fellow prisoners was banned as well. The most notorious, repeat murderers, were caned and forced to sign a statement on having killed a certain number of their fellow inmates.

Sometime in early 1943, the political division in Auschwitz received 500,000 blank release forms. We were overjoyed by the news, hoping that at least a few of us would be set free. However, the forms were filled in with the data of the gassed victims and filed in the archive.

110,000–120,000: Aryan Poles from the Pawiak penitentiary in Warsaw.

120,000–123,000: 3,000 Greek Jews, some of whom were sent to Warsaw to make up for their fellow countrymen who had perished there. Those left in the camp died soon afterward.

Approx. 123,000–124,000: 1,000 Aryans from Radow and Tarnów.

Approx. 124,000–126,000: 2,000 individuals from various Aryan transports.

Meanwhile, there was a constant influx of transports of Poles, as well as of French and Belgian Jews, all of whom were gassed without a single person being consigned to the camp. At the end of July 1943, the succession of transports came to a sudden halt and a brief intermission set in. The crematoria were cleaned thoroughly, refurbished, and readied for further operation. Then, on August 3, business as usual was resumed as we witnessed the arrival of the first transports carrying Jews from Brenzburg and Sosnowiec. These were followed by a steady stream of further transports through the month of August. The Jews from Brenzburg and Sosnowiec were assigned numbers from about 132,000 to 136,000. Only 3,000 men and a few women made it to the camp; more than 35,000 were taken directly to the crematorium. The majority of the 4,000 men consigned to the camp died in the so-called quarantine camp due to inhumane treatment, starvation, various diseases, and murders among them. Responsibility for the outrage heaped upon these Jews goes mainly to a man named Tyn, a Reich-German common-law criminal transferred from the concentration camp in Sachsenhausen, and one Mieczislaw Katerzinski, a Polish prisoner.

Selections were resumed at about this time, with particular emphasis on the women's camp. The camp doctor – an SS Sturmführer and the son or nephew of the Berlin police chief – acted with a brutality that seemed conspicuous even by the camp's standards. From that day, the technique of "selection" continued to be practised without relief until the day of our escape.

Approx. 137,000–138,000: At the end of August, 1,000 Aryan Poles were brought to the camp from the Pawiak penitentiary, along with some 80 Greek Jews.

Approx. 138,000–141,000: 3,000 men from different Aryan transports.

Approx. 142,000–145,000: In early 1943, 3,000 Jews from various labour camps in Poland, plus a group of Russian prisoners of war.

Approx. 148,000–152,000: In the week following September 7, family transports arrived from Theresienstadt. We were at a complete loss to grasp why, but these transports enjoyed very privileged treatment. The families stayed together, none of them were gassed, or even shaven. They were put up as they were, family by family, in a separate section of the camp. They were even allowed to keep their personal belongings. The men did not go to work, the children were permitted to attend a special school headed by Fredy Hirsch, and correspondence with relatives was also allowed. The only thing they had to endure was the sadistic harassments of a "camp capo" named Arno Böhm, a Reich German common-law criminal and one of the most contemptible villains of the camp. Our bewilderment only grew when we had a chance to glance at the official roll of these transports. The list of names bore the unusual heading "SB – Transport, teschecische Juden mit 6 monatlicher Quarantain" ("Special handling – Transport, Czech Jews with six months of quarantine"). We knew only too well what "SB" meant, but we could not find an explanation for the privileged treatment and the six-month quarantine – an unusually long period. In our experience to date, such quarantines lasted three months at best. We became suspicious. The closer we got to the end of the six months, the more we were convinced that these Jews would end their lives in the gas chamber like the others. We found an opportunity to contact the leaders of the group. We explained their situation to them and left no doubt in their minds about the fate awaiting them. Some of them, notably Fredy Hirsch, the former youth leader of the Prague Maccabi[12] who apparently enjoyed the unqualified trust of his peers, told us they would put up resistance if our misgivings came true. The men of the "Sonderkommando" pledged to join the Czech Jews instantly if they decided to fight. Many entertained hopes that it would be possible to organize a wholesale uprising in the camp. On 8 March 1944, we learned that the crematoria were at the ready for the Czech Jews. I rushed to Fredy Hirsch to tell him they had no time to lose and urged him to take immediate action. "I know what I must do," he answered. Just before sunset I sneaked up to the Czech camp again, only to be told that Fredy Hirsch was dying. He had poisoned himself with Luminol.[13] The next day, on March 7, while he was still in a trance, he was trucked to the crematorium and gassed along with the other 3,791 Czechs with whom he had arrived in Birkenau after 7 September 1943. The young went to their deaths singing. We were bitterly disappointed.

12   A Zionist youth movement that aims to promote sport and exercise among Jews. Established in the Czech Republic, it remains active today in Israel.

13   The brand name for phenobarbital, a barbiturate or sedative commonly used to control seizures and treat insomnia.

The plans for resistance had fallen through; the determined men of the "Sonderkommando" had waited in vain. Some five hundred older people had died during the six months of the quarantine. Now only eleven pairs of twins were spared, only to be taken to Auschwitz for biological experiments. These children were alive when we left Birkenau. One week before they were gassed, on March 1, they were coerced to send word to their relatives telling them they were fine. The letters had to be dated March 23 or 25. The children were told to ask their foreign relatives to send packages.

Approx. 153,000–154,000: 1,000 Aryan Poles from the Pawiak penitentiary in Warsaw.

Approx. 155,000–159,000: In October and November 1943, we had transports of 4,000 men from various penitentiaries, Jews from around Brenzburg who had been caught in hiding, as well as a group of Russians. At the same time, Russian prisoners of war were brought in and given numbers from 1 to 12,000.

Approx. 160,000–165,000: In December 1943, we had around 1,000 men in transports consisting mainly of Jews from the Netherlands, France, Belgium and, for the first time, Italy. These were Jews from Fiume,[14] Trieste, and Rome. Of these transports, at least 3,000 people were taken to the gas chambers directly. The death rate was particularly high among those consigned to the camp. In addition, the technique of "selection" claimed even more lives than usual. The application of this method reached its peak between 10 and 24 January 1944, when even strong, healthy, able-bodied Jews were selected without regard to job description and occupation; only the doctors were spared. For the selection, the prisoners would be lined up for a rigorous inspection to make sure everyone was present. The actual selection was performed by the camp doctor (the son or nephew of the Berlin police chief) and SS Untersturmführer Schwarzenburg,[15] the camp commandant of Birkenau. The Jews transferred from Barrack 7 to a "hospital" (Krankenbau) that had been moved to a different section of the camp were gassed without exception. During this period, another 2,500 men and 6,000 women ended up in the gas chamber through selection.

14 Today Rijeka, Croatia.
15 Johann Schwarzhuber (1904–1947), commander of Birkenau, promoted to Obersturmführer in 1944. He was sentenced after the war and executed.

Approx. 165,000–168,000: On 20 December 1943, another 3,000
Jews came from Theresienstadt. The roster bore the same title as the
transport back in September: "sb – Transport, tschechische Juden mit
6 monatlicher Quarantain." Upon arrival, each family was put up with
those who had come in September and enjoyed the same benefits as
they had. Just twenty-four hours before the first group was gassed, they
were taken to a section of the camp that happened to be vacant, as a
means of separating the two groups. They remain accommodated in
those quarters today. As the gassing of the first group left no doubt
whatsoever about the fate awaiting them, they are now preparing for
resistance. The resistance effort is organized by Laufer Ruzenko from
Prague and Hugo Lengsfeld, also from Prague. They are collecting
flammable materials so they can set fire to the blocks in their section
if the opportunity arises. Their quarantine time will be up on
20 June 1944.

169,000–170,000: 1,000 people in smaller groups, including Poles,
Jews, and Russians.

170,000–171,000: 1,000 Poles and Russians (Aryans) as well as a
smaller number of Yugoslavians.

171,000–174,000: In late February and early March 1944,
3,000 Dutch, Belgian and native (not naturalized) French Jews came.
The French Jews had been brought from the unoccupied territories of
France. Most of these transports were gassed promptly upon arrival.

In the middle of March, a smaller group came in, consisting of
Jews from Brenzburg who had been caught in hiding. From them we
learned that some Polish Jews had fled to Hungary via Slovakia.

Following the gassing of the Jews from Theresienstadt, no
more transports arrived at the camp until March 15. As a result, the
headcount in the camp dwindled quickly, explaining why all men
who arrived with subsequent transports, especially Dutch Jews, were
consigned to the camp. We escaped from the camp on 7 April 1944,
just after hearing about the arrival of large trainloads of Greek Jews.

The internal administration of the Birkenau camp is performed by
prisoners appointed to this task. The prisoners are grouped in blocks
by their work assignment or Kommando, rather than by nationality.
Each block has five functionaries: one block elder (*Blockältester*), one
block scribe (*Blockschreiber*), one male nurse, two block attendants.

The block elder (*Blockältester*) wears a white band on his left arm indicating the number of his block. He is, for all intents and purposes, lord of life and death, and responsible for the overall order of the block. Until February 1944, nearly half of all block elders were Jews. Later, instructions were received from Berlin prohibiting Jews from filling this position, so they were replaced. Despite the ban, three Jews from Slovakia continue in this post.

The block scribe (*Blockschreiber*) serves as the administrative arm of the block leader. He takes care of all paperwork, keeps track of the headcount, and keeps files. The position of the scribe is one of great responsibility. He must keep track of the prevailing headcount with painstaking thoroughness. Prisoners are kept on the record not by name but by number, which increases the likelihood of an error slipping in. An error like this can easily lead to fatal consequences, however. If the scribe has reported one fewer than the actual number of prisoners by mistake – which can and does happen, given the higher than normal mortality rates – the SS rectifies the error by executing one prisoner. Once forwarded, reports cannot be corrected retroactively, but the reported headcount must always tally with the actual number precisely. The scribe is vested with considerable powers over the block. Unfortunately, there are frequent abuses of this position.

The nurse and the block attendants perform physical work around the block. The actual nursing of the sick is obviously out of the question.

The entire camp is overseen by the *Lagerältester* or camp elder, also recruited from among the prisoners. The post of camp elder in Birkenau is currently filled by one Franz Danisch, political prisoner No. 11182, from the Upper Silesian town of Königshütte.[16] The camp elder has virtually unlimited powers over the camp. He has the right to appoint or relieve block elders and scribes, issue work assignments, etc. Danisch acts evenhandedly even with Jews; he is impartial and incorruptible.

Assigned as an aide to the camp elder is the camp scribe, who possesses the most extensive powers over the camp. Alone among the prisoners, he has direct communications with the camp command; he

16   Today Chorzów, Poland.

is the one who receives orders from the command and delivers reports from the camp. In this capacity, he has a certain degree of influence over the camp command. The block scribes are subordinated and report directly to him. At present, the camp scribe of Birkenau is Gork Kazimir, Polish political prisoner No. 30029, formerly a bank clerk in Warsaw. Despite his antisemitic views, Gork does not hurt the Jews.

The blocks are ultimately overseen by six to eight SS block supervisors. They are in charge of conducting roll calls in the evenings, reporting the results to the *Lagerführer*, Untersturmführer Schwarzhuber, who is from Tirol. Schwarzhuber is a drunk and a sadist. Above the Lagerführer is the camp commandant, who is also in command of the Auschwitz camp. The concentration camp of Auschwitz has its own camp commandant subordinated to the joint commandant of Auschwitz and Birkenau. The name of the current Auschwitz commandant is Höss.

Each labour detail (*Arbeitskommando*) is under the ultimate command of a so-called capo, who has unlimited powers of discretion over the prisoners in his detail during work hours. It is not unheard of for a capo to beat a prisoner on labour duty to death.

Larger labour details have several capos assigned to them under the supervision of a "head capo." It used to be common for a Jew to be appointed to the position of capo, but the regulation from Berlin already mentioned put an end to this practice.

At the highest level, the work is supervised by German professionals.

This concludes the first Auschwitz Protocol.

~ ~ ~

The second Auschwitz Protocol:

On 14 July 1942, we left Nováky, passed Zsolna, and arrived in Zwarnon at five o'clock. Here we un-boarded the train and were counted. The transport was taken over by SS men. One of them expressed loud indignation over the fact that we had had no water for the journey. "These barbaric Slovakians didn't even give them water." We moved on, and arrived in Lublin two days later. As soon as the train pulled to a halt, we heard someone give the following command:

"Those aged fifteen to fifty who are fit to work get out. Children and old people stay in the wagons." We got out. The station was surrounded by Lithuanian SS men armed with machine guns. The wagons in which the incapacitated, children and the elderly stayed behind were locked and the train moved on. Where it went or what happened to those on board we do not know.

At the station, command was taken over by an SS squad leader who said we had a longer march ahead of us. Those who thought they could carry their luggage with them were allowed to keep it; the others had to put it on a truck that had been waiting. They reassured us that this truck would arrive at the destination. Some decided to take their luggage with them, others loaded it on the truck. Immediately behind the town we saw a factory with a sign that said "Bekleidungswerke." Some thousand people wearing dirty striped prisoner garb were standing lined up in the factory yard, obviously waiting for lunch. The spectacle – as we recognized all of them to be Jews – was hardly promising. As we came to a high point in terrain, a rather extensive camp of barracks came into view, surrounded by a three-metre-tall wire fence. As soon as I entered the camp gate, I caught sight of Max Winkler from Nagyszombat, who warned that all my clothes and luggage would be taken away from me. We were surrounded by Slovakian Jews who had come with earlier transports. They wore badly tattered prisoner's uniform and had their heads shaven. Some wore wooden clogs, others were standing around barefoot. Many had badly swollen legs and feet. They begged us for food and other small articles. We handed out our belongings among them as best we could, for we knew we would not be allowed to keep anything on us. We were led to the warehouse where indeed we had to turn in everything we had. From here, we were marched in double-time to another barrack where they made us undress, shaved our heads, made us stand under a shower, then gave us prisoner's clothes, underwear, a cap, and wooden clogs.

I was assigned to what they called labour division II. The entire camp consisted of three such labour divisions, each separated by a wire fence. Slovak and Czech Jews were assigned to division II. For two days, we did nothing other than drills learning how to raise our caps in salutation upon seeing a German. They also made us practise how to fall in line for endless hours in the pouring rain.

The barracks were furnished in a rather original way. The only furniture consisted of three very long tables stacked one on top of another. Prisoners would lie under the table on the floor, as well as on top of each table.

For breakfast we had soup that was so thick we had to eat it with our hands. At noon they gave us soup much the same as before, and in the evening something they called "tea" with 300 grams of inedible bread. We also got 20 or 30 grams of fruit jam or oleomargarine, of course of the most loathsome quality.

In the first days, they placed the emphasis on the flawless singing of the camp anthem. We would stand there for hours on end, practising the song:

To Work We Go[17]

From the whole of Europe came
We Jews to Lublin
Much work is to be done
And this is the beginning

To fulfill this duty
Forget all about the past
For in fulfillment of duty
There is community.

Therefore, on to work with vigour
Let everyone play his part
Together we want to work
At the same pace and rhythm.

17   The German lyrics, as published in the original Hungarian edition of *How It Happened*: Wir Juden nach Lublin / Viel Arbeit gibt zu leisten / Und dies ist der Beginn. / Um diese Pflicht zu leisten / Vergiss Vergangenheit, / Denn in der Pflichterfüllung / Liegt die Gemeinsamkeit. / Drum rüstig an die Arbeit / Ein jeder halte mit / Gemeinsam wollen wir schaffen / Im gleichen Arbeitsschritt. / Nicht alle wollen begreifen / Wozu in Reihen wir stehen / Die müssen wir dann zwingen / Dies alles zu verstehen. / Die neue Zeit muss alle / Uns alle stets belehren, / Dass wir schon nur der Arbeit, / Der Arbeit angehören. / Drum rüstig an die Arbeit / Ein jeder halte mit, / Gemeinsam wollen wir schaffen / In gleichen Arbeitsschritt.

Not all will comprehend
Why we stand here in rows
Those must we soon force
To understand its meaning.

New times must teach us
Over and over again
That it is to work And only to work we belong.

Therefore, on to work with vigour
Let everyone play his part
Together we want to work
At the same pace and rhythm.

In labour division I, there were Slovakian Jews; in labour division II, Slovakian and Czech Jews; and in labour division III, partisans. The partisans assigned to division III were locked up in their barracks. They were not allowed to work or leave their barracks. The guards did not dare to get close to them. They would die in heaps in the overcrowded barracks, and the guards would fire at them whenever they had a chance.

The capos were all Reich Germans and Czechs. The former treated the prisoners brutally, while the Czechs helped every way they could. The *Lagerführer* was a Gypsy from Holics[18] named Galbavy, his deputy a Jew from Szered named Mittley. Obviously, Mittley had his cruelty to thank for his appointment. He used his position of power to inflict even more pain on the already tormented Jews. He never passed up an opportunity for torture.

While the evening list of commands was being read, we had to endure much abuse from the SS. We stood there for hours after a hard day's work and had to sing the anthem. Our choir was conducted by an old Jewish conductor from the rooftop of a nearby house. This elicited frequent laughs from the SS men, while they did not stop making frequent use of their whips and canes.

18 Today Holíč, Slovakia.

Rabbi Eckstein of Szered reached a tragic end. One time he came a little late to the reading of commands as he had been in the outhouse with an upset stomach. The squad leader simply grabbed him by the ankles and, holding his body upside down, dipped him twice in the contents of the lavatory, then dumped a bucket of cold water on his head, and shot him dead with a revolver.

The crematorium stood between labour divisions I and II. This was where the corpses were burnt. Initially, the death rate was about 30 per each division per day, at a total head count of 6,000–8,000. This number soon increased five- or sixfold. Later it became quite common for eleven or twelve sick people to be taken from the infirmary to the crematorium, from which they never returned. The crematorium ran on electricity and was operated by Russian prisoners.

The poor nutrition and the generally unbearable conditions caused various diseases to spread among us. In addition to very frequent and severe gastrointestinal ailments, most victims were claimed by the incurable inflammation of the legs and feet. People would have their legs so swollen they could not move. More and more of these people ended up in the crematorium, where they were murdered by a method unknown to me. When the number of the misfortunate souls reached seventy, on 27 June 1942, I decided to use an opportunity that had presented itself, and volunteered to be transferred to Auschwitz.

On 27 June 1942, they made me turn in my prisoner's garb, gave me civilian clothes, and put me on a transport bound for Auschwitz. We journeyed for forty-eight hours in locked freight cars, without food or water, before finally arriving in Auschwitz half-dead. Upon entering the camp, we were greeted by a sign over the gate that read *Arbeit macht frei* ("Work makes you free"). The grounds were clean and neat, with the brick buildings and the well-kept lawn creating a positive impression in contrast to the rudimentary, filthy barracks of Lublin. We thought we had made a good deal. Upon arrival, we were led to a cellar where we were given some tea and bread. The next day they made us hand over our civilian clothes, shaved us, tattooed our prisoner number on the lower arm just above the wrist, and issued us prisoner's garb like the ones we had had in Lublin. Finally, our personal data were registered and we became regular "political prisoners" of the Auschwitz concentration camp.

For living quarters we were assigned to Barrack 17, where we slept on the floor. The row of buildings next to us, from which we were separated by a wall, was occupied by Slovakian girls deported here from Slovakia in March and April 1942. Because our place of work fell outside the greater, outer "security belt" – we worked at the construction site of the Buna factory compound – the work area was divided into squares 10 by 10 metres in size. Each square was guarded by a separate SS man. Whoever overstepped the boundary of the square during work was shot without warning as a "prisoner in flight." SS guards would frequently order their prisoner to fetch an object from across the square perimeter. If the prisoner obeyed and crossed the boundary, the guard would shoot him.

After a few weeks of agonizing labour, a terrifying typhoid epidemic raised its head in the camp. The weak prisoners perished by the hundreds. The camp was closed and the Buna construction halted. At the end of July 1942, those who had survived were taken to work in a gravel pit. Work here was even harder, if that is possible. So this is where I was working when I learned about some vacancies in the *Aufräumungskommando*. I applied and got the transfer. The Aufräumungskommando employed a hundred prisoners, all of them Jews. We worked in a completely segregated section of the camp, surrounded by heaps of rucksacks, suitcases, and other luggage. The work consisted of opening the pieces of luggage, sorting the articles they contained, and putting them in suitcases by type or in a separate warehouse. In this way, we had suitcases of combs, suitcases of mirrors, of canned food, chocolate, medicine, and so on. Suitcases packed with bed linen were stored away by type. We brought all clothes and underwear to a large barrack where they were sorted and packed by Jewish girls from Slovakia, then all these textile goods were shipped away by train. Useless pieces of clothing were sent to a textile factory in Memel, while serviceable ones were sent to a charity in Berlin. Valuables, money, gold, foreign currency, and precious stones had to be surrendered to the political department.

Most of these valuables, however, were stolen by the SS supervisors or the prisoners working here. The sorting work was headed by Albert Davidovics from Igló,[19] an authority in the field, who continues to fill

---

19 Today Spišská Nová Ves, Slovakia.

this position today. The detachment was under the command of SS Sturmführer Wikleff, a brutally cruel man who often beat up even the girls. The girls came over from Birkenau to work every day. They told us unimaginable things about the conditions there. They were always tortured and beaten. They had a higher death rate among them than did the men. Selection was held twice a week. Every day, new girls would come to work in place of those who had fallen victim to selection or died in some other way.

I soon lost my relatively comfortable position in the Aufräumungskommando and was transferred as a punishment to Birkenau, where I spent a year and a half. On 7 April 1944, I managed to escape with my friend.

This concludes the Auschwitz Protocols.

~ ~ ~

History knows decisive turns, which describe a graph line rising and falling, suddenly forcing the train of events in a new direction. This phenomenon is replicated in the structure of drama, the poetic form of history, in which momentous dramatic turns highlight the propelling force of progress as it blazes a new path. In the tragedy of Hungarian Jewry, such a turn came about with the disclosure of the Auschwitz Protocols, which dispelled the gullible and culpable optimism that had dulled the minds of the vast majority of Jews on the one hand and, on the other hand, stirred up the conscience of certain Christian leaders and revealed where their policies had led. All of a sudden it became obvious that the fate of Hungarian Jewry – one of extermination – was inseparable from the demise of the Hungarian nation. By then, and especially after the Western landings,[20] everybody with a little common sense had no doubt that the war had been lost. The events bore out the prophecy the Jews of Hungary had expressed in their remonstrations against the anti-Jewish laws to the National Assembly: "Our ruin is tantamount to the downfall of the entire country!" For the first time, the Auschwitz Protocols revealed to the clerical and lay elite of the country that hundreds of thousands of Jews, all of them Hungarian citizens, were being driven straight into annihilation. People had to wake up with a start and

20   The Normandy Landings on 6 June 1944, widely known as D-Day.

realize that everything would soon have to be answered for. Those who then took action to halt the deportations did not do so to save the Jews, but to save themselves, their own positions of power, and the country entrusted to their leadership. Alas, it was all too late for the Jews in the provinces.

Copies of the Auschwitz Protocols began to be made at Síp Street in the greatest secrecy. At first, the document was handled "confidentially" in an effort "to prevent panic," but it quickly reached wider audiences. It was translated into several languages for the embassies, including into Italian for the papal nuncio.[21] Several people volunteered to deliver the Protocols to influential clergymen and lay figures, including Prince Primate Cardinal Serédi,[22] Bishop Ravasz[23] and, via two channels, Regent Horthy, who received copies through Miklós Horthy Jr and the would-be minister of justice of the Lakatos cabinet.[24] The news elicited utter horror among the Jews and shocked all righteous Christians. Both groups realized that there was no other option, that the time for procrastination was over, and the historic moment had come to intervene. Neither side, however, had the strength to act. It was with the utmost trepidation that one understood how little, if anything, could be done in this terminal phase of the disease. Never before had we glimpsed the true depth of the abyss, to the brink of which we had

21 Angelo Rotta, Msgr (1872–1965), papal nuncio, envoy of the Vatican to Budapest, 1930–45. Rotta was one of the key actors in the international rescue activities in Budapest. He relentlessly protested the deportations and issued thousands of protective documents to persecuted Jews. Upon Soviet demand, the Allied Advisory Commission expelled him from Hungary in April 1945. Posthumously, in 1997, he was awarded the honorific Righteous Among the Nations by the State of Israel.

22 Jusztinián Serédi (1884–1945), Archbishop of Esztergom and the Prince Primate of Hungary, head of the Hungarian Catholic Church from 1927 until his death. Serédi supported the first and second anti-Jewish laws in the late 1930s, but rejected the Nazi-style Law XV of 1941 (see the Glossary). While he protested the persecution of Jews in 1944, he did not make his stance public, refrained from confronting the government, and acted mostly on behalf of Jewish converts.

23 László Ravasz (1882–1975), Calvinist bishop, journalist, writer. As the senior bishop of the Hungarian Calvinist Church, Ravasz had a formative influence on the intellectual climate of the era, including its antisemitism. He actively promoted and voted in favour of the first and second anti-Jewish laws. However, he strictly opposed Nazi-style persecution. In 1944 Ravasz became actively involved in the rescue efforts of his church, albeit mostly in favour of Jews who had converted to Christianity.

24 Gábor Vladár (1881–1972), lawyer, civil servant, head of the Legislative Department of the Ministry of Justice from 1929, and minister of justice in the Lakatos government from 29 August to 16 October 1944.

been pushed by twenty-five years of antisemitism, the plague spread by the anti-Jewish laws, a shackled press, and everything that every Hungarian government from Gömbös to Sztójay stood for.[25] Most of the country had fallen for the fascist propaganda, and could hardly wait for the next anti-Jewish measure to be issued. They were eager to witness the progress of deportations from the provinces and, more important, eager to finally lay their hands on what mattered to them the most: their share of the spoils.

By the time the Auschwitz Protocols became known to the elders of the Jewish community in Pest, the deportations had begun in earnest and were in full swing. Any notion of German "goodwill" gleaned from the Gestapo's cunning lies during the first few weeks, which so many had courted in the antechambers of the SS lairs in Svábhegy, had vanished into thin air. Not aggressively pursuing the "Hungarian line" of policy[26] entailed disastrous consequences by pre-empting a genuine Hungarian resistance movement that could have come to the rescue of the Jewry in the provinces. The events since then have confirmed the opinion that Hungarian resistance should have been encouraged and buttressed by all available means from the start, and that the failure to do so was the gravest oversight in the nation's history. The testimony of Veesenmayer[27] and General Winkelmann[28] revealed that the Gestapo had been so massively understaffed in Hungary that they simply would not have been able to carry out the deportations from the provinces without the assistance of the Hungarian Gendarmerie.

25 The author is referring to the years between 1932 and 1944.
26 Presumably a reference to the Council's policy, mentioned earlier by the author (see 71–3), of trying to "enlist the help of" such Hungarian authorities as Andor Jaross, László Endre, and László Baky, as well as senior members of the church and others in positions of power.
27 Edmund Veesenmayer (1904–1977), German diplomat, member of the Nazi Party from 1932 and of the SS from 1934. In May 1941 he helped organize the collaborationist Ustasha government in Croatia. From 19 March 1944, he was Reich plenipotentiary in Hungary and promoted to SS-Brigadeführer. He cooperated closely with Adolf Eichmann in organizing the deportation of Hungarian Jews. Sentenced in Nuremberg to twenty years of imprisonment on 2 April 1949, he was released in December 1951 through the general amnesty granted by American High Commissioner John J. McCloy.
28 About SS-Obergruppenführer Otto Winkelmann, see 32.

5

Deportations from the Provinces/
Star-Marked Buildings in Budapest

News of torture in the ghettos – The first deportation statistics –
Ghettoization in the provinces – Internal commotion against
the Jewish Council – An illegal pamphlet to Christians –
The consequences of the pamphlets – Council petition for halting
the deportations – The concentration of the Jewry of Budapest
– László Endre's scheme – The designation of houses – The last
day of the concentration – The Gendarmerie enters the scene

The ghettoization in the provinces, the mushrooming of the ghettos, and the deportations proceeded at unprecedented breakneck speed. The Gestapo seemed to have realized – or at least sensed – the need to finish its job before the Jews woke from their torpor and the decent part of Christian society began to stir. By the day and by the hour, fresh news would come in of the horrors in the provincial ghettos, and the regional divisions of the Jewish Council began to compile statistics of the deportations. A report received at the end of May describes the atrocities in the town of Salgótarján, which I have already discussed, then goes on to provide the following account:

In Miskolc, the Jews were taken to the grounds of a textile factory lying between the city and the steel works of Diósgyőr, amid much cruel abuse. Retired Supreme Court judge Márk Tyrnhauer, off-duty captain Sándor Klein, and a merchant named Hofbauer died of their injuries from the beating.

In the ghetto in Losonc,[1] a Gendarmerie detachment assumed command from the police and began to search for hidden valuables.

---

1 Today Lučenec, Slovakia.

Fig. 22   In the town of Kőszeg, on 18 June 1944, two Hungarian gendarmes lead a group of Jews from the ghetto to the train station. Carrying leather valises, umbrellas, and wicker baskets, the group is evidently unaware that after being transported to a collection camp in the nearby city of Szombathely, they would be deported to Auschwitz-Birkenau two weeks later, on 4 July.

The interrogations were accompanied by physical abuse that left many seriously injured.

On June 6, all the Jews of Párkány[2] were transported to Léva.[3] Before being taken away, the Jews – those from Párkány proper and those who had been previously moved there from Esztergom – were subjected to interrogation under torture to elicit confessions specifying the whereabouts of allegedly hidden valuables.

In Székesfehérvár, the Gendarmerie took over from the police at five in the morning on June 5. They relocated some 2,900 people to a dilapidated brickyard next to the railway station, where no more than a hundred could comfortably fit. Before taking the Jews away, the

2   Today Štúrovo, Slovakia.
3   Today Levice, Slovakia.

gendarmes interrogated them to find out where they had hidden their possessions, beating both men and women on the naked soles of their feet with their batons.

On May 30, the congregation of the Salgótarján sent the following cable to the Jewish Council:

This is to humbly report that the Jews of Salgótarján and neighbouring municipalities, numbering 3,200 souls in total, have been ordered to move, by June 5, into provisional quarters designated in the horse stables of the local mining company. The individuals subject to the relocation are aged fifty to eighty, many of them sick, as well as pregnant women and babies; the men have all been conscripted. Figuring a bare minimum of 50 centimetres of width a head, there is only room for 800 or 900 people to lie down. The stables are dark and the ground is soaking wet with dung water. The heat is unbearable in the heavily infected lofts, and free movement is impossible. On the occasion of an inspection, the sub-prefect had found everything in order about the former accommodation arrangement, but we are willing to accept any further restriction of the current ghetto as the authorities may see fit. With reference to the aforementioned statements of the government and in the name of Christian love, we appeal for mercy and clemency to save the lives of thousands. – The Israelite Congregation of Salgótarján.

Around June 10, the Jewish Council addressed a memorandum to certain members of the government. The document reads as follows:

We have knowledge that over 300,000 of our brothers and sisters have been deported abroad so far, where they must not only endure the pains of hard physical labour but have come under the threat of disastrous annihilation. According to data aggregated on June 6, the number of the deported at that date stood at 303,000. As the deportation campaign continues, this number can be estimated at 320,000 as of today, and is expected to rise further.

Equally appalling are the circumstances surrounding the concentration of the Jews in ghettos and their subsequent relocation and deportation. We do not wish to go into details about the specific

phases of this grievous process, other than to record our utter
shock upon finding that the Jews gathered in ghettos around the
country have been thrust into unspeakably close quarters and the
most primitive living conditions. (Nyírség, Subcarpathia, Northern
Province, Transylvania, Tiszahát, and Southern Province.)[4]

In some places, the Jews were accommodated in brickyard sheds
outside the towns with no walls and a loose, flapping roof at best
(where they have been exposed to wind and rain and generally the
inclemency of weather), as well as in mills, warehouses, factories, and
barrack camps, all of them without water and water closets (towns
of Győr, Székesfehérvár, Komárom, Bicske, Miskolc). Camped under
a mere semblance of a roof or directly under the open sky, they have
fallen prey to rats, mice, insects, and other vermin.

In some of the ghettos, gendarmes have questioned the wealthier
Jews and those otherwise surmised to have hidden valuables. These
people, including the elderly and the sick, were bullied and hurt so
severely that some of them died from the abuse.

After these preliminaries, having been stripped of all their
possession, the Jews were loaded into freight cars, seventy or eighty
a car, without regard to gender, age, or health, and without such bare
necessities as spare clothes, blankets, and food. A bucket of water and
an empty bucket were placed in each wagon. The transports were
usually moved out of the stations during the night, amid the most
dismal conditions. Several Jews died during the trip in the terribly
overcrowded wagons, so that when the sealed wagon doors were
finally opened, corpses fell out.

It is to be emphasized that the deportation of Jews from the
ghettos was far from confined to healthy individuals fit to work.
This marked a departure from the selection practice followed in
the Kistarcsa camp, whereby only persons aged sixteen to fifty were
chosen for deportation while the sick and people in other age
groups were spared. This circumstance gave the anxious families a
certain measure of hope that these people were really being moved
abroad for work. The deportations from other locations bypassed
this phase of selection. Not only did the masses loaded into the

4 Nyírség and Tiszahát are historic micro-regions in present-day northeastern Hungary.
   Regarding Subcarpathia, Northern Province, Transylvania, and Southern Province, see
   the Glossary entry on Border Revisions and the map on xvi–xvii.

wagons include octogenarians, but in one town – specifically in Beregszász,[5] as far as we know – old Jews roused from the nursing home were the first to be trucked to the railway station. Babies and infants were also taken away. The fact that these deportation transports comprised Jews without any regard for age, gender, health, and thus suitability for work, has filled with trepidation any family members left behind as well as the entire Hungarian Jewry, nearly driving them over the edge of utter despair.

~ ~ ~

By early June, the sentiments against the Jewish Council had intensified to the point of outburst. The Zionists had been natural opponents of the Council from the start, if only on account of the decade-long tension between them and the assimilationist elite.[6] At this critical juncture, however, the Zionists, who had always represented the most independent-minded group within the Jewry, set aside their differences in a most disciplined manner and resisted the temptation to instigate a revolution. A number of their leaders and party members worked in the Council offices, and witnessed everything they needed to assess the constantly changing situation. They had trust in the negotiations conducted by Komoly[7] and Kasztner,[8] not least because a separatist Zionist *aliyah*[9] was rapidly becoming a distinct possibility. For all intents and purposes, they remained single-handedly in control of the underground rescue movement. They employed methods mastered in Slovakia to keep in touch with the ghettos around the provinces through undercover agents. Had it not been for the heroic efforts of these young Zionist men, most of the Jewry in the

---

5 Today Beregovo, Ukraine.
6 The "assimilationist elite" refers mostly to the (Neolog) Jews of Budapest who tended to view Zionism as delusionary and dangerous, and Zionists as traitors to their homeland (Hungary). Until the Second World War proved otherwise, the assimilationist elite insisted that the Jews of Hungary were simply Hungarians who happened to be Jewish. Meanwhile, Zionists, who sought to build a Jewish national consciousness, accused the assimilationist elite of being undemocratic and blinded by privilege. From their perspective, assimilationists were pursuing a path that would result in the end of the Jews.
7 About Komoly, see 68.
8 About Kasztner, see 15.
9 A reference to the Kasztner Train, which was originally intended to deliver its passengers to Mandatory Palestine. See 69–71.

capital would hardly have been alerted to the events transpiring in the ghettos and the brickyards.

At the same time, ever larger masses of Jews in Budapest began to condemn the role undertaken by the Jewish Council. The anomalies of the flat requisitioning, the tactless attitude of some of the agents in the field, and the rude, petulant tone of the clerks sitting in the office embittered the people against the Síp Street headquarters, which had never been particularly popular to begin with. Of course, this was just one side of the coin. On the flip side, everybody who had connections exploited them to the best of his abilities to get a job at the Council, and cemented his own personal safety by means of the pink identity document issued to Council employees. Those who tried to obtain such a pass in vain grew jealous of the "happy card holders." The anti-Council sentiment escalated further in the wake of summons to Rökk Szilárd Street. The Council – or, to be more precise, the Interim Executive Board of the Association of Jews in Hungary – cited orders issued "at the pain of the most severe consequences," which they allegedly only carried out to enable the poor souls they called in to catch their breaths, rather than allow them to be dragged out of their homes by SS thugs.

The situation was aggravated by the mounting anxiety with which the Jews of Budapest followed the events in the provinces, to the extent that they even knew what was happening. Needless to say, the daily papers did not cover the events. Fateful as it was, the deportation of the entire Jewry of the provinces may have been an event of great historic importance, but in Budapest one could learn of it only by way of vague hints by certain right-wing politicians, such as in the memorable speech delivered by Lajos Szász[10] in Nyíregyháza.[11] The official Jewish press confined itself to spoon-feeding

10 Lajos Szász (1888–1946), lawyer, politician, university professor, and MP of the right-
    wing Party of Hungarian Life from 1939 to 1945. He served as minister without
    portfolio responsible for public supply in 1942–44, minister of trade from 22 March
    to 29 August 1944, and minister of commerce and transport from 7 to 29 August 1944,
    and again from 16 October 1944 to 28 March 1945. He was president of the National
    Alliance of Legislators, the quasi-parliament of the Arrow Cross era in 1944–45. After
    the war, Szász was found guilty of war crimes, the People's Court sentenced him to
    death, and he was executed.
11 Munkácsi refers here to a speech of 23 May 1944 in which the minister of trade
    cited the "final and radical solution of the Jewish question," adding that "after the
    Jews, we have to get rid of those as well who are hiding them." Aware perhaps that
    the Hungarian public was only willing to go so far when it came to dealing with

reassuring news. However, certain Jews in Budapest with families in the provinces wisened up to the events from letters smuggled out of the ghettos and began to bombard the Council with demands for action and tangible results. The Council's efforts with the Germans remained almost completely ineffectual, as did their pleas to the Ministry of the Interior. The people did not know about the Council's shots in the dark; all they saw was the relentless speed with which the ghettos in the provinces were being liquidated, one after another, and their parents, siblings, and children hurried off into the unknown – and that all the while the walls of the Síp Street building were still standing. Nothing had collapsed, after all; one could still go on pretending that nothing had really happened.

The mood against the Jewish Council in those days is exemplified perfectly by a joke imported from the Netherlands. A Jew is woken up in the middle of the night by a banging on his door. "Who's there?" he calls out. "The Gestapo," comes the answer. "Thank God," says the Jew, with obvious relief. "I thought it was the Jewish Council!" The voices of discontent were seconded by a few elders of the Pest Congregation who, not being members of the Jewish Council, had been following its conduct of affairs from the outside, with great dissatisfaction. They made no secret of their grudge, nor of their readiness to come out in the open in the event of an internal show of force.

After much bickering, around June 10 an opportunity presented itself for the two camps to face each other. The disgruntled Jews sent a message to the president of the Council saying they wanted to speak with him to voice their concerns. Around five in the afternoon, Samu Stern received a large delegation led by Dr Imre Varga, a young physician from Pest.[12] Among the members of the delegation were some Zionists of the younger generation and, making a first appearance at Síp Street, left-wing Jews hardened by forced-labour service and not shy about active resistance. Two members of the Pest prefecture and the chief secretary of the Support Office were also present. This was the first time that the detractors, who had been grumbling for months, were given

---

"the Jewish question," Szász aimed to assuage his audience with the assurance that "nobody intends to exterminate, extirpate, or mortify the Jews." The censored Hungarian press was banned from writing about the deportations; however, Szász's speech was reported in the far-right-wing *Új Magyarság* (*New Hungariandom*), 24 May 1944, 4.

12 Imre Tamási Varga (19?–1944), physician and Zionist activist, one of the founders of the (Zionist) Jewish Working Group active between 1939 and 1942.

a chance to speak their minds face to face with the Council, the repository of absolute discretion over the internal affairs of the organization. Dr Varga spoke passionately. "Can't you see?" he said in great agitation:

> Don't you understand that our fathers, mothers, brothers, and sisters are being shoved into freight cars by the Gendarmerie at the point of bayonets, seventy of them at a time, to be dragged away into the unknown, into annihilation, smothered in human excrement? How can we stand for this any longer? How can we content ourselves with mere petitions and servile supplications instead of revealing it all to Christian society? We must shout out to the whole world that they are murdering us! We must resist instead of slavishly obeying their orders!

The executive meeting room was full. Everyone was carried away by Varga's sincere indignation and incitement to take a brave stance. His speech was accompanied by utter silence, and although the solemn promises made previously led one to expect further commentary, no one else rose to speak. The president replied calmly in a dry tone of voice:

> The Jewish Council is doing everything humanly possible. The news of the deportations has been relayed to every important official and clerical entity whose support we can count on. Unfortunately, the Germans are in command, and the Hungarian authorities cannot or dare not oppose them. Any resistance on the part of us Jews would only lead to futile bloodshed and would collapse almost instantly, aggravating the situation of others unimaginably. The Council has fulfilled its duty and will continue to do so.

His brief address finished, the president rushed out of the room. Those who remained entered into a heated discussion about Dr Varga's plea and possible ways of administering affairs with better results than the Council was capable of. The following day we learned that Varga had committed suicide in his despair over the inadequate reception to and impact of his speech. The Jewry of Budapest failed to replicate the Warsaw Ghetto Uprising, despite the similarity of circumstances in several respects. In both cities, it was the courage and life instinct of the youth against the prudent deliberation of the old, except that the Polish Jews were endowed with a lot more rustic verve and vitality than their Hungarian brethren.

Yet the movement in Hungary, once started, did not grind to a complete halt. At the Council's department of provincial affairs, two young Zionists, Dr Lajos Gottesmann[13] and Dr Sándor Braun, a physician,[14] remained fully engaged. Gottesmann in particular dedicated himself to the task of overseeing underground communications with the ghettos. As early as the beginning of June, he was busy fabricating fake birth certificates and other identity papers aiding the messengers to travel and the hunted to disappear.

Your humble author was personally in contact with Gottesmann, who one day decided that it was impossible to wait any longer: Christian society had to be enlightened to the deportations and the fact that the Jews were not being carried away to work, but to the gas chambers of Auschwitz. Before long, this led to the idea of publishing an underground pamphlet and distributing it in tens of thousands of copies. As I did not believe that the Council would ever bring itself to take such a measure, I approved of the plan and suggested that György Polgár[15] should be invited to participate in the action. Gottesmann brought Dr Braun with him to these meetings. I thought it best to render the document compatible with the tastes of Christian intellectuals, with content designed to move both the mind and the heart. The task naturally entailed no small amount of self-censorship, but in light of the goal we wished to achieve, I considered this style much more conducive than a harsh wake-up call. We had reason to fear that a sharply worded pamphlet would end up in waste-paper baskets before being read to the end. I was put in charge of drafting the text of the pamphlet, which I completed by the end of the evening. The next morning I was surprised to learn that Sándor Somló, the head of the Council's food department, had addressed a petition to the Council urging the publication of a manifesto conceived in much the same spirit. Somló then sent me a copy of his petition. The dice were cast. What official position will the Council assume? Are they going to hesitate still? What was there to lose? I burst into the president's room with Somló's proposal in hand and showed it to him. Károly Wilhelm, who happened to be around, asked to see the letter. "We must go ahead with this," he said when he finished reading, "come what may. Most of the

13 Lajos Gottesmann was a leader of Betar, the Revisionist Zionist youth movement, in Hungary.
14 No further information could be found on Dr Braun.
15 György Polgár was a senior official of the National Hungarian Association to Assist Jews (Országos Magyar Zsidó Segítő Akció, or OMZSA), an aid agency founded in 1939 to support Jews drafted for labour service and their families.

provinces have been herded away, the few people left are crowded together in ghettos and brickyards, and the rounding-up in Pest is around the corner to ready us for deportation. Nobody will escape his fate. The Council must undertake open confrontation." The president seemed willing to yield to Wilhelm's persuasion. He issued instructions to convene a session for the following morning, and asked me to draft the text of the announcement. "I have it ready, sir," I replied. Easily done when I had already worded the manifesto for purposes of illicit dissemination.

That next day was a Saturday. The entire Council showed up, with the exception of Károly Wilhelm, who was visiting with Bishop Ravasz[16] to enlist his intervention. The Council session was conducted in a sombre mood, with all participants evidently burdened by the weight of the impending critical decision, fully aware that the publication would be tantamount to the onset of open disobedience. The meeting began with my reading the draft out loud. I added that pushing this text through the censors of the Prosecutor's Office[17] would be an enterprise doomed to failure, meaning that the announcement had to appear uncensored, and everyone present had to accept responsibility for it. The Council president seemed extremely overwrought and vehemently opposed the publication. He refused to take part in anything illegal, and would not approve the publication unless we obtained the permission of the Prosecutor's Office (which, as I have mentioned, seemed practically impossible). Then almost every member of the Council spoke to the same effect as the president. Seeing the turn of the tide, I qualified the proposal by suggesting that we make a few thousand copies of the text signed by the Council and send them out in the form of a letter by regular post. I argued that, in this scheme, the sealed letter would no longer qualify as a pamphlet, allowing us to bypass censorship in good faith. Yet even this solution was not good enough for them. Finally, after much labour, they gave birth to a Horatian *ridiculus mus*[18] by resolving to turn to members of the government and disclose the true details of the deportations to them. The Council hastened to ensure that even the mere discussion of this matter be stricken from the session minutes.

16 See 131.

17 Under Regent Horthy, the Royal Hungarian Prosecutor's Office was responsible for censoring the press.

18 From Horace's *Ars Poetica* (*The Art of Poetry*) the full Latin quotation is "Parturient montes, nascetur ridiculus mus" ("Mountains labour and a ridiculous mouse is born"), used to describe great efforts that amount to very little.

Realizing that no results would be achieved this way, in concurrence with Gottesmann, I handed over the text to Dr Fábián Herskovits,[19] who revised a few sentences together with Somló. The document was then mimeographed on the machine of the Orthodox People's Kitchen.[20] Professors Fülöp Grünwald[21] and Jenő Grünwald[22] helped with the work of reproduction. The envelopes were addressed and stuffed in a secluded room of the rabbinate.

During the reproduction, several versions were made, some of which had to be abridged or consolidated for technical reasons in order to have the text fill exactly two or three pages. The following quotations are taken from one of the surviving copies of this pamphlet:

An Appeal to Christian Society
In the twenty-fourth hour of its tragic fate, Hungarian Jewry turns to Hungarian-Christian society with a plea. We turn to you as our fellow countrymen and women with whom we have shared for a millennium, for better or for worse, this homeland in which our fathers, grandfathers, and forebears have been laid to rest in the same dust.

We did not raise our voices when we were robbed of our property and lost our human dignity and respect as citizens. We even desisted from this measure of last resort when we were torn away from our family hearths. But now it is our very existence that has come under threat. Indeed – and how excruciatingly difficult this is to write

19 Fábián Herskovits (1907–1982), rabbi, university professor. He was one of the leading members of the Zionist resistance in Budapest. He served as the rabbi of the Dohány Street Synagogue after the war and emigrated to Israel in 1949.

20 The Orthodox People's Kitchen (officially, the Orthodox Jewish People's Table Association) was a charitable organization that provided food for impoverished Orthodox Jews. It was located at 13 Wesselényi Street.

21 Fülöp Grünvald (1887–1964), teacher, historian, employee of the Pest Israelite Congregation. During the German occupation, he worked for the Central Jewish Council's housing department. He survived the Holocaust in Budapest. After the war, he was headmaster of Budapest's Neolog Jewish High School (Pesti Izraelita Hitközség Gimnáziuma) and, from 1948 to 1959, headed the history department at the Rabbinical Seminary. As well, from 1933 to 1950, he served variously as curator, deputy director, and director of the Hungarian Jewish Museum.

22 Jenő Grünvald was Fülöp's brother and a teacher at Budapest's Neolog Jewish High School (Pesti Izraelita Hitközség Gimnáziuma).

– it is now only a portion of Hungarian Jewry whose lives remain
at stake.

We must alert Christian society to the fact that, for weeks,
hundreds of thousands of Hungarian Jews have been deported in
circumstances so tragic and cruel as to be unprecedented in the
history of the world.

From the first moment of the changes, the Jews of Hungary have
borne their afflictions in quiet resignation, but nevertheless the death
trains have rolled out from all parts of the country. Nearly 500,000
people have been deported so far.

Although the applicable government decree only provides for
the resettlement of Jews in segregated parts of the cities, in fact these
ghettos became horrendous internment camps, from which the Jews
of the provinces were carried away and crowded together in even
more abysmal conditions in brickyards and abandoned, dilapidated
mills outside the settlements.

From there, they were driven out by rifle butts, bayonets, and whips,
and stuffed into the freight cars of the deportation trains, often seventy
or eighty people per car. Inside the wagons, there was no air except the
little they could draw from the scant ventilation slots. Deprived of all
their belongings and money, without blankets or even straw on the
floor, these misfortunate souls journeyed for days inside the locked and
sealed wagons. All they were given to eat were a few loaves of bread. In
each wagon, there were two buckets: one filled with water, the other an
empty one for human needs. This is how they went off to an alien land.

We would have found a degree of comfort had the transports
consisted only of men fit to work. But the deportees crammed
indiscriminately together in the wagons included very old people and
babies. Often, hospital patients in a serious post-operation condition
and pregnant women were brought on stretchers and loaded into the
cattle wagons amid the most appalling atrocities. Obviously, these
people were not being hurried off to work!

On May 23, *Új Nemzedék*[23] published a report of three women
who died at the Szombathely station on board a "Jewish train"
arriving from Nagykanizsa. They were 104, 102, and 92 years old.

---

23 *Új Nemzedék* (*New Generation*), 1913–44. Originally a conservative Christian newspaper,
it served in 1944 as a platform for the extreme right.

The 102-year-old woman died of pneumonia. Obviously, these were not being dispatched to work, either. The sick, the elderly, and the infants would only mean more hungry mouths to feed in a foreign land. We can thus have no doubt as to the fate awaiting them: annihilation.

Hungarian society would certainly not sit around with indifference if they had known about these monstrous happenings. Yet experience has taught us that a significant part of the Hungarian public knows nothing about what is transpiring before our eyes, if only because the press has remained completely silent on these matters.[24]

How will it be possible to own up before the tribunal of history to the fact that 8 percent of Hungarian citizens, nearly one million people, were condemned to deportation and obliteration without a court hearing and a conviction?

Today, we have neither the time nor especially the opportunity to defend ourselves against one-sided accusations. Yet we stand with our heads high, ready to face those charges. If we have made mistakes, we are not solely to blame, for these mistakes arose from the system of production that has ruled Hungary and the world for a century, and which relied on all forces of production, including Christians and Jews.[25]

Those familiar with history will know that the nation is eternal while political trends come and go: today we accept one thing as political justice, tomorrow another. Yet within these various political trends there is the constant of human justice, and nobody who transgresses that principle will be able to stand before the judgment of our common almighty God, the lord of history.

It may be that the Hungarian nation considers it well advised to eject the Jewry from its bosom. But how could this ejection be construed by the always-chivalrous Hungarian nation as being equal to the ruthless extermination of powerless, unarmed people, including the helpless old, infants, and veterans blinded and maimed in war?

---

24 In fact, by this time, the extent and endpoint of the deportations were widely known in Hungary.
25 The author here alludes to widespread antisemitic tropes of Jews as greedy capitalists who were "overrepresented" in Hungary's economy. By "mistakes" he seems to be referring to the "excessive greed" of Jews, as if to pre-empt those antisemitic charges.

A way must be found, in collaboration with the neutral states,[26] to allow the remaining few hundred thousand Hungarian Jews to emigrate.

In the name of our children, our women, our elderly, and all of us facing final ruin, we now raise our voices to Hungarian-Christian society in supplication.

We trust in the Hungarian nation's sense of justice, just as it demands the same from other people of the world,[27] and which can neither desire nor condone the terrible devastation of innocent souls.

Should these pleas for mere survival fall upon deaf ears, we will only ask the Hungarian nation to end our suffering here in our homeland, forgoing the deportations with their accompanying horrors, so that we may at least be laid to rest in our native land.

When Kasztner's special group left the country in late June, they forgot to return to us the leftover copies of the pamphlets and the envelopes. They were found and destroyed by deputy clerks in the rabbinate's room.

The propagators of the pamphlet suffered badly for their involvement. In early August, a copy that had been sent to a Christian school mistress by Dr Dénes Láczer,[28] a religious studies teacher, was intercepted by the police, and Láczer was arrested. He was followed in detention by professors Fülöp and Jenő Grünwald and the rabbi Dr Fábián Herskovits. They were first taken to Svábhegy then transferred to the infamous investigative unit of the Gendarmerie in Csillaghegy,[29] where they were tortured. They had no choice but to confess to the dissemination of the pamphlet, and they identified Síp Street as the point of origin. Political detectives soon appeared on the third floor of the headquarters, and began to question your humble

---

26 Specifically, the neutral countries of Switzerland, Sweden, the Holy See, Spain, Portugal, and Turkey.

27 This is an intentional allusion to the slogan "Justice for Hungary!" used as a rallying cry against the punishing loss of territory imposed on Hungary in the Treaty of Trianon.

28 Dénes Láczer (1896–1944/45), rabbi, teacher of religious studies at the Pest Israelite Congregation. He was arrested during the rule of the Arrow Cross and deported to Buchenwald on 20 October 1944. Láczer perished in a German concentration camp.

29 Special unit of the Central Investigation Command of the Hungarian Gendarmerie, tasked with neutralizing left-wing resistance groups. It was stationed in the municipality of Csillaghegy, north of Budapest (today a part of Budapest's 3rd District).

author. A detective called Erdélyi[30] did quite a thorough job. He compared the pamphlet with some of my publications in print, pointing out striking similarities of phrasing in certain sentences. "These are commonplaces used by everybody," I answered by way of an explanation. The detainees owed their eventual escape to the fact that by then the deportations had been called off (the last incident was the well-known abduction of some of the people interned in Kistarcsa on July 17).[31] In the thawed climate of the Lakatos cabinet,[32] our friends were released from custody just one day before Rosh Hashanah.[33]

In accordance with its resolution,[34] on June 22 the Council lodged a submission with Prime Minister Sztójay,[35] with copies sent to a few other members of the cabinet. This historic document reads as follows:

On behalf of the Interim Executive Board of the Association of Jews in Hungary, at present the chief legitimate advocacy organization of Hungarian Jewry as per Government Decree 1520/1944. M.E., we wish to respectfully submit to Your Excellency and the Royal Hungarian Government our description of a most dreadful situation that

30   Probably Barna Erdélyi, police detective, member of the special unit responsible for the personal safety of Regent Horthy, and later of Prime Minister Döme Sztójay.
31   Despite the general decision of Regent Horthy to halt the deportations in early July, Eichmann's unit launched surprise attacks against the Kistarcsa and Sárvár internment camps on 19 and 24 July 1944, deporting more than 2,700 inmates to Auschwitz. See the Glossary entry on Kistarcsa and Sárvár.
32   Géza Lakatos (1890–1967), army general and prime minister of Hungary from 29 August to 16 October 1944. After Romania broke with Nazi Germany on 23 August and pledged loyalty to the Allied powers, Regent Horthy dropped the pro-Nazi Sztójay government and appointed the loyalist Lakatos as prime minister, with a secret mandate to prepare for a ceasefire and defection from the Axis – a brief period that led to the "thawed climate" referred to by the author. The hoped-for defection never happened. Instead, the Arrow Cross leader Ferenc Szálasi seized power in mid-October, whereupon Lakatos was arrested and imprisoned by the Germans. Later, in 1945, he was captured by the Soviets. He was not convicted of war crimes, but under Hungary's communist regime his pension was revoked and his land and other assets were confiscated. In 1965, he emigrated to Australia.
33   Rosh Hashanah, the Jewish New Year, began at sundown on 17 September 1944.
34   The Horatian *ridiculus mus* described on 142, in which the Council resolved to "disclose the true details of the deportations" to members of the government.
35   About Prime Minister Döme Sztójay, see 168.

threatens Hungarian Jewry in its very existence and fills us all with despair on account of the deportation of hundreds of thousands of Jews, both Israelite and Christian, that commenced in the month of May and has continued to this day. In the twelfth hour of our tragic destiny, in the name of the timeless ideals of humankind, we raise our pleading voice with a sunken heart to beseech Your Excellency and the Royal Hungarian Government to halt with special dispatch the deportation of hundreds of thousands of innocent people from our land.

In recent times, the Jews of Hungary have sustained a quick succession of fatal blows in meek surrender. Without so much as a murmur, we have bowed our heads as one government measure after another deprived us of our property, our family hearth, and our honour as citizens, and excluded us not only from the nation but practically from mankind. We only cried out when we saw that the Jews in the border regions, already dispossessed and gathered in overcrowded ghettos, were being taken to abandoned factory grounds and vacant lots, then deported without regard to age or gender. Initially confined to the northeastern areas of military operation and the southern border regions, the deportations then made inroads into the heart of the country, refuting the hypothesis that the removal of residents was necessitated by military logistics. We were also proven wrong in our hopes that these masses were being taken away for work. Such a purpose is hardly compatible with deporting everyone without regard to age, health, and gender. According to reports we have received, as of June 20, 427,100 Jews, or about half of the entire Jewish population in Hungary, have met their ghastly fate of deportation. This number is divided among the country's regions and settlements as follows:

SUBCARPATHIA	
Munkács[36]	26,000
Ungvár[37]	14,000
Beregszász[38]	10,000
Nagyszőllős[39]	8,000
Máramarossziget[40]	12,000
Huszt[41]	10,000
Felsővisó[42]	8,000
Szeklence[43]	5,000
Iza[44]	3,000
Bárdfalva[45]	3,000
Técső[46]	10,000

TISZAHÁT	
Nyíregyháza	20,000
Kisvárda	12,000
Szatmárnémeti[47]	24,000
Mátészalka	17,000

NORTHERN PROVINCE	
Kassa[48]	12,000
Sátoraljaújhely	15,000
Miskolc	21,000
Eger	9,000
Hatvan	12,000
Balassagyarmat	4,000
Salgótarján	4,000
Léva[49]	4,000
Komárom	8,000
Érsekújvár[50]	7,000
Dunaszerdahely[51]	8,000

TRANSDANUBIA	
Győr	5,200
Székesfehérvár	4,000

SOUTHERN PROVINCE	
Baja	8,200
Nagykanizsa	9,000
Barcs	2,500
Szabadka[52]	3,500
Szeged	4,000

TRANSYLVANIA	
Kolozsvár[53]	22,000
Dés[54]	10,000
Beszterce[55]	8,000
Nagyvárad[56]	36,000
Marosvásárhely[57]	6,000
Szászrégen[58]	8,000
Szilágysomlyó[59]	7,000

INTERNMENT CAMPS	
Bácstopolya[60]	5,000
Sárvár	1,000
Kistarcsa	2,000

TOTAL	427,400

36 Today Mukacheve, Ukraine.
37 Today Uzhhorod, Ukraine.
38 Today Beregovo, Ukraine.
39 Today Vynohradiv, Ukraine.
40 Today Sighetu Marmaţiei, Romania.
41 Today Khust, Ukraine.
42 Today Vişeu de Sus, Romania.
43 Today Sokyrnytsya, Ukraine.
44 Today in Ukraine.
45 Today Berbeşti, Romania.
46 Today Tiachiv, Ukraine.
47 Today Satu Mare, Romania.
48 Today Košice, Slovakia.
49 Today Levice, Slovakia.
50 Today Nové Zámky, Slovakia.
51 Today Dunajská Streda, Slovakia.
52 Today Subotica, Serbia.
53 Today Cluj, Romania.
54 Today Dej, Romania.
55 Today Bistriţa, Romania.
56 Today Oradea, Romania.
57 Today Târgu Mureş, Romania.
58 Today Reghin, Romania.
59 Today Şimleu Silvaniei, Romania.
60 Today Bačka Topola, Serbia.

While the applicable government decree only provides for the relocation of Jews into segregated parts of the cities, in fact these segregated districts (ghettos) became internment camps, from where the Jews of the provinces were carried away and crowded together in even more abysmal conditions in brickyards and in abandoned dilapidated mills outside the settlements.

From these internment camps, according to reports received by us, the physically and spiritually anguished people were taken, frequently after being questioned under torture and otherwise severely abused, and stuffed into deportation trains, seventy or eighty people per wagon. The wagons were sealed and there was no air inside except the little that could be drawn through the scant ventilation slots. Deprived of all their belongings and money, these miserable souls journeyed for days. All they were given to eat were a few loaves of bread. In each wagon, there were two buckets: one filled with water, the other an empty one for human needs. This is how all of them went off to alien land, women, men, infants, the old, and the seriously ill.

We have just learned, with the most profound shock, that the atrocities continue in Kecskemét, Békéscsaba, Szolnok, Sárvár, Debrecen, Szombathely, Szeged, and other parts of the country, where tens of thousands of hapless people have been consigned to transit camps on the outskirts of the cities, evidently with the aim of deportation.

Given the circumstances, we are filled with utter trepidation by reports that the deportation of Jews from the capital is expected to begin within the next few days in order to complete the wholesale "de-Judaization" of Hungary.

Your Right Honourable Excellency!

In the name of humanity and the divine command of neighbourly love, we raise our voice against the relentless and unremitting application of collective responsibility to one million Hungarian citizens – a doctrine rejected and condemned equally by the Scriptures and the Church.[61] As witnesses before man and God,

---

61 By "collective responsibility" the letter alludes to an assumption that the Jews of Hungary were somehow being collectively punished for the wrongdoings of certain groups of Jews.

we wish to invoke the proverbial sense of justice of the Hungarian
nation, which we trust will not deny itself at this critical juncture
of its history, and will not allow nearly one million citizens to be
condemned to deportation, an unspeakable punishment unheard of
in the Hungarian legal system, without a hearing and judgment by a
court of law. If there are individuals to blame among us – as there may
and will be in any human community – then let them be struck down
by the rigour of Hungarian law and the judgment of a Hungarian
court. Yet every righteous person, regardless of his religion, must
cry out in compassion when mothers carry their innocent children
and infants on their arms into annihilation; when the helpless sick,
the old, and pregnant women, crammed together and suffocating in
airless cattle wagons, without food, medical care, and proper clothing,
embark on what may well be their last journey. The children of many
thousands of Jews who distinguished themselves with their valour in
the First World War are being dragged away, as are the wives, children,
and parents of tens of thousands in labour service working in the
battlefield or in the hinterland of the present war. In some places, even
those exempt on account of their military or patriotic services have
not been able to avoid deportation.

According to the statistics disclosed in the foregoing, already
approximately half of Hungarian Jewry has been deported. Today, in
the last hour so to speak, as we plead for mercy for those remaining
in the country and for the lives of innocent children, may we invoke
the thousand-year history of the Hungarian Homeland as well as the
common lot that has united the country's Jews with the Hungarian
nation, for better or for worse, since the Conquest of the Homeland.[62]

Let us be allowed to quote Mr Lajos Szász, minister of industry,
from his speech delivered in Nyíregyháza,[63] which no doubt faithfully
represents the position of the Royal Hungarian Government:

"When searching for a solution to the Jewish question, we must
not look to hatred-fuelled antisemitism for guidance, but only and
exclusively to the cause of racial protection pervaded by love. What we

---

62   "Conquest of the Homeland" refers to the arrival and settlement of the Hungarian
      nomadic tribes in the territory of the future Kingdom of Hungary around AD 895.
63   See 138.

want is not to exterminate the people of poor Ahasuerus,[64] but that they finally find a homeland on this Earth after all their wanderings."

We remain staunch believers in the Hungarian nation's love of justice and knightly virtues, which cannot desire nor permit hundreds of thousands of innocent people to go to their ruin. We believe in the sacred humane ideal and the rule of the moral world-order of Christianity. We thus place our lives, and the lives of our parents, children, brothers, and sisters in the hands of the everlasting Hungarian nation.

In our heartrending predicament, it is in downcast spirit but hopeful expectation that we look to the responsible government of the country, humbly imploring you to end the horrors of the deportations with special expediency, and to use the working capacity of the Jewry in the service of nation building and domestic production.

With respect to the Jews already deported beyond the borders, we request Your Excellency to kindly ensure humane treatment for them, and allow them – as any other migrant workers – to earn a living for themselves and their families.

Recommending this petition for the preservation of hundreds of thousands of lives entrusted to our care to the munificent goodwill of Your Excellency and the Royal Hungarian Government, and reiterating the urgency of our humble request herein, we remain with the deepest respect sincerely yours,

The Interim Executive Board of the Association of Jews in Hungary.
Budapest, 22 June 1944

While the Budapest elite were making a last-ditch attempt to save the remainder of the Jewry in the provinces and trying desperately to forestall impending deportations from the capital, the concentration of the Budapest Jewry was already going on. I do not think that the history of the world can serve us with another instance when nearly 250,000 people in a city moved house or were forced to share their home with others in all of eight days. Yet this is precisely what happened between 17 June and 24 June 1944, in Budapest, the "citadel of civilization" and capital of a nation formerly celebrated for its "chivalry."

---

64   A reference to the mythical "Wandering Jew," cursed to walk the world over until the Second Coming of Christ. In some versions of the legend, he is given the name Ahasuerus.

Since the promulgation, on 28 April 1944, of the decree that authorized senior municipal officials and mayors to designate segregated residential areas (ghettos) for Jews around the country, ghettos had been springing up in the provinces at a great speed.[65] These examples left no doubt that sooner or later it would the capital city's turn and that the largest Jewish community in Europe after Warsaw would eventually be driven into "forced residence." At first, the Germans and Péter Hain[66] with his cohorts thought of setting up a single large ghetto in Budapest that would comprise the most densely populated Jewish streets from Rákóczi Street to Podmaniczky Street.[67] They made no secret of this plan when, on the occasion of requisitioning flats for bomb raid victims, they warned the Jewish Council to find accommodation for the evicted in this area. There were numerous hindrances to implementing this plan, notably the especially large number of Christians who would have to move away from this rather busy part of the capital. The Gestapo and their Hungarian underlings had always taken great pains not to hurt the sensibilities of non-Jewish residents, indeed to give them various bits of spoils in an attempt to make the anti-Jewish measures appear to have been designed in their favour. Eventually, though, the idea of the great Budapest ghetto capsized on the intimation that Allied bombers would spare Jewish quarters. For this reason – and only to save their own hides – the ghetto architects dropped that plan and embraced instead the concept of designated Jewish ("yellow-star") houses in locations scattered around the city, to serve as prison-houses for the Jewry. This solution was not unheard of in certain towns around the country.[68]

On May 17, Councillor Dr József Szentmiklóssy, the head of the city's 9th District Department of Social Policy,summoned to his office Dr István Kurzweil,[69] an official of the Jewish Council, and told him confidentially that László Endre was at work on the plan of ghettoizing the Jews of Budapest. There was talk that the Minister of the Interior would put the Councillor in charge of the implementation, but Szentmiklóssy considered the plan inhumane and unlawful, and was going to refuse the commission. The Jewish Council put the issue on the agenda immediately and decided that having Szentmiklóssy accept the appointment was preferable to having an unknown

---

65 See 74–5.
66 See 32.
67 That is, Budapest's 6th and 7th Districts.
68 For example, the architects of ghettoization followed the same pattern in Újpest and Kispest, cities to the north and east of Budapest (today, Budapest's 4th and 19th Districts).
69 See 54.

official who would likely be much less sympathetic to Jewish interests. Upon being advised of the Council's position, Szentmiklóssy received the Council leaders in his office, and made sure well in advance that no one other than his most trusted clerks was present at the meeting.

After these preliminaries, Szentmiklóssy agreed to accept the appointment, but pledged to do everything in his power to have the whole plan shelved or, failing that, to delay the concentration as long as he could. At the meeting, Szentmiklóssy outlined László Endre's ideas, and concurred with the Council on the points where certain concessions could possibly be achieved. Afterward, Szentmiklóssy kept the Council up to date almost daily. He showed them the draft of the decree and even made certain favourable changes in the text himself. In his report to the minister, he pointed out that it was absolutely inconceivable to carry out the concentration program in less than three months from the date the houses were designated, so he recommended this as the official deadline. He described specific risks that a speedier concentration process would impose on the Christian public, and in general did his best to put the emphasis on the complications that the concentration would entail.

Yet all his efforts proved to be in vain: As it turned out, he was left with no choice but to go ahead with the designation process. The actual plan, drafted by a dedicated department working under Szentmiklóssy and based on data obtained from the statistical office, proposed to designate any building, excluding retail spaces and office buildings, in which 50 percent or nearly 50 percent of the tenants were Jews. At first, László Endre insisted on implementing the concentration program in three days; it took no small effort on the part of Szentmiklóssy to extend the time frame to eight days.

Szentmiklóssy's office had already been a much-frequented place. With the publication of the decree, it was besieged by a massive flood of people, everyone determined to use their best connections to overturn the Jewish-star designation of certain buildings or, conversely, to designate others as Jewish buildings. As Szentmiklóssy himself was almost always out of his office in that period – at first, he huddled in the statistical office, then took a few days off – the complainants, mostly comprising the owners and tenants of the buildings in question, turned to the Ministry of the Interior. In a great many cases, Jaross and Endre sustained the complaints, repealing the star-designation of about eight hundred buildings, or a third of the buildings so designated by Szentmiklóssy and his team, leaving that much less total floor space for the Jews to occupy.[70] On behalf of the Ministry of the Interior, these complaints and appeals were processed by the Pest County notary named Puskás,[71] who had just been promoted to the helm of the housing department in consultation with the municipal prosecutor Dr Károly Kiss,[72] a stalwart member of the Arrow Cross party.

Endre's measure, whereby eight hundred previously designated yellow-star buildings were now barred from the Jews, wreaked further havoc. When the original concentration decree had been published, all the Jews had rushed to secure a residence in one of the designated buildings, and many had actually moved in by the time the new measure came out, forcing them, along with the long-time tenants, to move out again. By then, however, all the eligible apartments had been occupied, and these Jews were given only three days, instead of the originally approved eight, to find a place, move in, and prepare the mandatory inventory.

Rezső Müller, who was in charge of the housing office of the Jewish Council, had previously compiled his own statistics on the number of Jewish tenants in each building and any room remaining available in those buildings. In this way, by the time the notice was published, the housing office of the Jewish Council was ready to implement the program of moving families in together.

During the allotted eight-day period, the Council applied for an extension several times via Szentmiklóssy, citing the interruption of moving plans

70　The original decree, issued by the mayor of Budapest on 16 June 1944, designated 2,639 yellow-star houses, to which the approximately 200,000 Jews of Budapest were to be forcibly relocated by 8 p.m. on 21 June 1944. However, in response to petitioning by Christian residents who were required to vacate buildings designated for Jews, the authorities sharply reduced the number of yellow-star houses to 1,948 with a move-in deadline of midnight on 24 June. To accommodate everyone, families were forbidden from occupying more than a single room. (Warned the decree: "Where the size of an apartment or dwelling is greater than legitimate dwelling needs of Jews, other Jewish families will be moved into the excess rooms.") All designated buildings were required to be marked with "a six-pointed canary yellow star measuring 30 centimetres in diameter, on a 51 × 36 cm black background." For more about the ghettoization in Budapest, see Tim Cole, *Holocaust City: The Making of a Jewish Ghetto* (New York/London: Routledge, 2003), 101–5.

71　István Puskás, civil servant, deputy notary of Pest-Pilis-Solt-Kiskun County. In April 1944 he was promoted to the head of the housing sub-department (xxi/a) of the Ministry of the Interior.

72　Károly Kiss, deputy public prosecutor at the Budapest Municipal Administration (Székesfővárosi tiszti ügyészség).

by the retroactive measure of the Minister of the Interior. Jaross remained intractable, however. All he would do was promise to hold off raids until after June 25, so that people moving in on that day would not be harassed.

The last official day for completing the concentration was June 24, which fell on a Saturday. On that day, Budapest turned into an unprecedented, bustling scene, with the children of Israel hauling all their belongings, basic furniture, and household objects in horse-drawn carts, handcarts, wheelbarrows or – if they had no access to such conveniences – in bundles on their backs to the "designated" houses. One day later, when the curfew had entered into force, regular worship service was called off – something that had never before happened, not since the synagogues were erected. These events fulfilled the ancient gloomy prophecy about the sinful capital of Israel: "God shall put an end to the rest of Sabbath and the holidays in Zion."[73] On the last day, thousands of Jews were forced to break the sacrament of the Sabbath by shouldering the burden of their belongings. Had they not done so, they would have remained without a roof by the evening, providing the SS and detectives patrolling the streets with an excuse to round them up. It was a long summer evening. The last rays of the setting sun illuminated a handful of remaining outcasts as they hurried almost stealthily to their "new homes."

A radio announcement, aired before the end of the night and confirmed by the morning papers on June 25, brought news of a ban, effective immediately, prohibiting Jews from leaving their star-marked residences except between two and five o'clock in the afternoon, and then subject to proving adequate grounds for doing so. (This measure was later relaxed by an amendment allowing Jews to go out at eleven o'clock in the morning.)

On July 1, the Jewish Council sent a memorandum to Councillor Szentmiklóssy describing the process of the evictions and the housing concentration program in Budapest. The document ended with the following:

> It can be stated that those provisions of the decree that, given the circumstances, could be viewed as relatively favourable to the Jews, provisions which were proposed by Councillor Dr József

---

73 It is not clear where this quotation comes from. Assuming it is Biblical, perhaps the full or correct version is from the Book of Hosea, which warns: "I will also cause all her mirth to cease, her feast days, her new moons, and her Sabbaths, and all her solemn feasts" (Hosea 2:11 KJV).

Szentmiklóssy partly at our own initiative, were not upheld in actual implementation. It was not the fault of Mr Szentmiklóssy that the innumerable partial measures he endeavoured to incorporate in the decree for the benefit of the Jews were ultimately not put into practice. Because the current situation does not enable us to predict what lies in store ahead of us, we feel an obligation to establish this state of affairs for the record.

The memorandum was accompanied by a letter that reads as follows:

Dear Mr Councillor –
The segregation of the Jews of Budapest on the orders of the government now completed, we feel obliged to convey to you our heartfelt gratitude and appreciation for the goodwill and generosity to the embattled Jewry that you have steadfastly shown, within the limits of prevailing circumstances, just as you showed in conducting the housing affairs of the bombing victims. Allow us to present to you a memorandum we compiled on the relevant events. Trusting that you will kindly persist in your benevolence which the Jews of Budapest so badly need to fall back, we remain sincerely yours,
The Interim Executive Board of the Association of Jews in Hungary.

The last days of June brought a decisive turn in the life of the capital's Jewry. With the *aliyah* of Kasztner's group on June 29, most of the Zionist vanguard left the country and with them the group that viewed the situation most realistically, had the best foreign connections, and was more daring than all the others. On June 30, the rounding-up of Jews from the outlying districts of Újpest and Békásmegyer commenced, warning that the forces of deportation were standing at the city gates. Meanwhile, the notorious rooster feathers appeared in the inner city in squads of two or three.[74] The Jews were overtaken by an intense feeling of foreboding; barring divine intervention, most had lost all hope. During these days of waiting for a miracle, the role of the Christian churches came to the fore. In what follows, I shall examine this role in some depth.

---

74   A reference to the Hungarian Gendarmerie assigned to deport the Jews from Budapest. See 69.

6

The Role of the Christian Churches

*Hungarian Jewry and the Christian Churches – A queue
in front of the rabbinates – The stance of church leaders in
response to the anti-Jewish laws – Protests by the Calvinist
churches – Bishop Márton's speech in St Michael's Church
in Kolozsvár – Bishop Ravasz visits the regent – Horthy's
prior knowledge of the deportations – Protest by the Calvinist
Convention – The "voice of conscience" from Transylvania –
An ultimatum by the Protestant churches – The protest movement
of the churches – Conflicts with Jewish converts – Sándor
Török as spokesman for the churches – The "Christian Jewish
Council" – The letter of Reverend Éliás – The "Department
of Converts" – The Alliance of Christian Jews is formed*

The relations of Hungarian Jewry with the historic churches[1] had worsened since the counter-revolution of 1919.[2] During the decades of liberalism,[3] it was still possible to characterize those relations as amicable, so much so, in fact, that they even withstood the formation of the decidedly clerical

---

1   The "historic churches" refers to the Roman and Greek Catholic, Calvinist, Lutheran, Unitarian, and Greek Orthodox churches, those privileged "accepted religions," recognized by the state as *bevett vallás* (Hungarian) or *religio recepta* (Latin). In 1895, the Law of Reception (Act XLII) named Judaism a *religio recepta*, granting Jews equal status to Christians under the law, an honour that was formally rescinded with Law XVII of in 1942.
2   Led by Regent Horthy, the right-wing Christian regime that assumed power in Hungary in 1919 defined itself as "counter-revolutionary," positioning itself as the antithesis of the left-wing revolutions of 1918 and 1919.
3   That is, the era of the Austro-Hungarian Empire, 1867–1918.

Fig. 23   In Ungvár (today Užhorod, Ukraine), a man with a yellow star on his overcoat is followed by two boys. The photo was published in the pro-Nazi newspaper *Magyar Futár* (*Hungarian Courier*) on 31 May 1944 with the headline "Still life in Ungvár before the final act." During the last two weeks of May, Ungvár's ghettos and collection camps, located in the local brick and lumber yards, were vacated as more than 17,000 Jewish men, women, and children from the town and surrounding region were deported to Auschwitz-Birkenau.

People's Party[4] following the adoption of laws on clerical policy.[5] In many places, the estates of the high clergy had been successfully run by Jewish tenants to the great satisfaction of the owners. Provincial priests had nourished friendly relations with local Jewish shopkeepers. The teaching orders had gladly admitted the children of city-dwelling Jews, and the students absorbed the spirit of these schools. The so-called Christian Era[6] changed all

4   A right-wing party established in 1894 with the main objective of opposing the separation of church and state and the religious emancipation of the Jews. Originally the Catholic People's Party, in 1918 it merged with and was renamed the Christian Social People's Party.
5   These included Act XLII of 1895, making Judaism a *religio recepta*.
6   Munkácsi refers here again to the regime under Regent Horthy, which was in power from 1919 to 1944.

of this. That turn ushered in a shift toward displacing and stigmatizing Jews everywhere. The papers sponsored by the new direction began to churn out articles written by the lesser clergy with the purpose of inciting hatred against the Jewry, and several Christian priests sitting in the National Assembly between 1920 and 1924 distinguished themselves as ardent antisemites. The new ethos made fewer inroads into the ranks of the high clergy, where the liberal moderation of János Csernoch[7] continued to reign supreme, although the seething antisemitism of Bishop Prohászka[8] managed to make a breach in this bastion of gentility as well.

The large-scale conversion of Hungarian Jews to Christianity commenced in 1919. Few responded to the antisemitism superseding half a century of liberalism by avowing their Jewish identity; far more chose to blend in and swim with the tide. The summer and fall of 1919 witnessed the conversion of many pre-eminent writers, artists, public figures, and businessmen – the skimming off, as it were, of the *crème de la crème* of a Jewry that had gathered strength and refinement during the decades of peace.

During the "neo-baroque" period of the counter-revolution,[9] the so-called era of consolidation, these tensions eased somewhat, and many converts actually returned to the fold of the Israelite religion.

Then, with Hitler's rise to power, the conversion drive resumed with redoubled momentum. Although the Roman Church in particular had nourished an intense dislike for the "neo-paganists"[10] from the start, this did not prevent the positive Judaism camp[11] from sustaining severe losses

7   János Csernoch (1852–1927), Catholic priest, MP of the Catholic People's Party in 1901–08, archbishop of Esztergom, and the prince primate of Hungary from 1912 until his death in 1927. An advocate of denominational peace for the sake of national unity, he raised his voice against violent and radical forms of antisemitism.

8   Ottokár Prohászka (1858–1927), Catholic bishop, Christian socialist politician, theologian, member of the Hungarian Academy of Sciences. A renowned reformer, publicist, and orator, he was also one of the most influential advocates of antisemitic ideology in Hungary. For more on Prohászka and Csernoch, see Paul A. Hanebrink, *In Defense of Christian Hungary: Religion, Nationalism, and Antisemitism, 1890–1944* (Ithaca: Cornell University Press, 2009).

9   A reference again to the era under Regent Horthy, with its fondness for "neo-baroque" pomp and hierarchy. The description "neo-baroque" was coined by the leading Hungarian historian of the time, Gyula Szekfű (1883–1955), in *Three Generations*, his influential book published in a revised edition in 1934.

10 Meaning Nazis.

11 Possibly a reference to the theology of positive-historical Judaism, embraced by leading Jewish scholars in Hungary at the time. See Ferenc Laczó, *Hungarian Jews in the Age of Genocide: An Intellectual History, 1929–1948* (Leiden: Brill, 2016).

as many of their brethren, discouraged by what had happened in Germany and trusting in the influence of the Church, decided to receive the baptism anyway. In 1938, when the first anti-Jewish bill was submitted to the floor, the process assumed dimensions unprecedented in the history of Hungarian Jewry. The capital was hit particularly hard as lines began to form in front of the rabbinate in Wesselényi Street.[12] The masses realized how difficult it would be to adopt anti-Jewish laws on a purely racial basis in Hungary, and that the provisions would confer certain benefits and exemptions upon the converts. There were so many applicants that numbers had to be issued to help with the administration.[13] While the conversion movement gathered speed, the elders of the Jewish congregations did not sit around with their hands in their laps. A counter-movement took off in the Jewish press, from the pulpits, by means of clerical visits, and on many other fronts. Yet all these countermeasures proved ineffectual in the face of the sheer instinct of survival and, as is often the case in the course of history, they failed to produce any meaningful results. One of the most harrowing aspects of this process – and one that proved particularly ruinous for Hungarian Jewry – consisted of the fact that conversion against one's sincere convictions was ultimately a lie and therefore an immoral act. True enough, what the anti-Jewish laws stigmatized was not so much the Jewish race as the Jewish religion and its spiritual disposition. More or less recognizing conversion as a sign of assimilation and loyalty to the Hungarian nation, the anti-Jewish laws reaffirmed the perception that the converts, from the point of view of the nation, had chosen the righteous path. In this way, each and every instance of conversion aggravated the predicament of those Jews who stood by their religion. Ironically, and fatefully for the devout Jewry, most of the longstanding and recent converts came from the ranks of leading figures in politics, publishing, finance, industry, and commerce – those against whom the anti-Jewish laws had been created in the first place. Conversely, the anti-Jewish laws inflicted by far the most damage on Jews who chose to adhere to their faith. It was the converts I alluded to in a newspaper article published in 1939:

12 Specifically, 7 Wesselényi Street, just behind the Dohány Street Synagogue in Budapest's 7th District, a multipurpose building belonging to the Israelite Congregation of Pest.

13 As the author explains later in this chapter, Jews hoping to convert to Christianity were required to "opt out" of Judaism by completing "renunciation forms." Thus, the long lines of hopeful converts at the rabbinate.

They have been living in their new faith of choice for half a century or longer without ever having become "better," "assimilated," or more "Hungarian" ... Were it true that conversion is the only means of assimilation, the only solution to the Jewish question, there would be no Jewish question to talk about today. But that question exists and it continues to spread destruction among us, mostly on account of those who have long since settled or, rather, thought to have settled the issue personally for themselves.

Each anti-Jewish law triggered a new and broader wave of conversions. There were other contributing factors as well, such as the creation of the so-called white-band *musz*, or Jewish labour service companies. As part of such a company, whether one worked in the home country or was forced to work in Ukraine – virtually a choice between life and death – often depended on whether the company assumed Christianity or not.[14] The *en masse* conversions weakened Jewry spiritually and financially. Instead of constituting a homogenous whole, Jewry had always been split into multiple organizations and social classes, to name just a few lines of division. This inherent differentiation was only exacerbated by the rapidly spreading fever of conversion. During the time of the anti-Jewish laws, the number of Jewish converts increased to the point that they decided to set up their own organizations within their newly chosen church, particularly for purposes of social work and charity. This marked the inception of the Holy Cross Society and the Good Shepherd Mission.[15]

The conversion epidemic soon reached the re-annexed territories of the country.[16] Wherever Hungarian troops appeared, dissolution among the Jews

14 The "white-band" refers to the white armband that converts had to wear in Hungary's forced labour service (*Munkaszolgálat*), as opposed to the yellow armbands imposed on Jews. Initially, all labour servicemen wore military uniforms and armbands with Hungarian national colours. However, beginning in the summer of 1941, as a clear sign of their exclusion from Hungary's army and society, Jews had to provide their own clothes and wear a yellow armband. While many Jewish converts to Christianity were also sent to serve in labour forces at the front, thanks to the intervention of the Christian churches they tended to be treated more leniently.

15 The Good Shepherd Mission was a joint venture of the Hungarian Lutheran and Calvinist Churches, established in 1942 to provide Jewish converts to Protestantism with spiritual, legal, and material support. In 1944 it was involved in rescue activities as well. Its Catholic counterpart was the Hungarian Holy Cross Society (see note about József Cavallier, 90).

16 A reference to territories regained by Hungary from Czechoslovakia, Romania, and

quickly began, with the intellectual professions and big business claiming the lead in apostasy. Many came to regard the baptismal certificate as an entry ticket to chambers of medicine and law, or a voucher redeemable for a coveted trade licence.

It is hardly surprising that the Jews who stood by their religion developed a certain resentment against the others, because they felt that each and every instance of conversion delivered another blow to the moral fortitude of the community, and that those who turned their backs on the fold without any scruple gained advantage to the detriment of their loyal brethren.

The leaders of the Christian churches voted "yes" on the first and second anti-Jewish laws.[17] While they did criticize the bills and mount a degree of resistance within the House of Representatives for the amendment of the language of the second anti-Jewish law, this does not materially overwrite the fact that they ultimately approved these laws. Undoubtedly, this feeble resistance on behalf of church leaders influenced the attitude of millions of Hungarians to a significant extent. This is why it is especially important to take a closer look at what those leaders had to say about the anti-Jewish laws and, in general, about the Jewish question. Below is a characteristic excerpt from an address delivered in the Upper House of Parliament by Jusztinián Serédi, Cardinal and Prince Primate:[18]

As a premise, let me submit to you, the Honourable Upper House, that the need to reasonably curb the presence of Jews in public affairs, the economy, and other areas of life as a justified measure of national self-defence will be recognized by everyone who, like myself, has watched with mounting concern as a certain faction of the domestic Jewry, encouraged by the passage of the Law of Reception,[19] and bearing the tacit approval of the others, has questioned or discredited virtually everything understood as being Christian in nature, in all

---

Yugoslavia between 1938 and 1941 with the support of Nazi Germany. See the Glossary entry on Border Revisions.

17 Hungary's Catholic and Protestant bishops were in favour of the first and second anti-Jewish laws of 1938 and 1939; however, they opposed the third law of 1941 because, by defining Judaism as a race as opposed to a religion, the law affected thousands of Jewish converts to Christianity and undermined the jurisdiction of the churches. On the anti-Jewish laws, see the Glossary.

18 See 131.

19 See note about "historic churches" on 158.

possible forms – from religion and the Church itself, to marriage, family, and homeland – under the pretext of "art," including literature, poetry, theatre, motion pictures, music, and painting, despite ceaseless protests from the Catholics, even while being aided and abetted by the liberals and exploiting the press to its own ends, just as it has endeavoured to undermine Christian morals in agriculture, industry, commerce, finance – the sum total of the economy – as well as in our public affairs and private lives. I stress that these comments of mine apply to a certain portion of the Jewry only.

Speaking of the retributions against the Jews, the prince primate added: "The Church has never approved of repressive measures of this kind. It has always disapproved of them because its Christian doctrine of morality holds up everyone individually and separately against all internal and external standards of justice, and seeks to judge individual actions by taking all relevant circumstances into consideration." The following sentence is especially symptomatic of the attitude of the Catholic clergy: "I wish to emphasize to the Honourable Upper House that my aim here is not to protect Jews or Israelites, but first and foremost those Christians, and the followers of the Catholic faith in particular, who are not responsible for the excesses committed by the Jews." Cardinal Serédi ended his address by saying: "Far be it from us to cause difficulties to the Royal Hungarian government or to the nation. Indeed, the justified self-defence of the nation commands us to desire the reasonable and equitable containment of Jews." He nevertheless added his wish "that a means be found to extend protection to all those Christians who have done nothing to deserve this containment."[20]

Bishop Sándor Raffai's[21] position is well illustrated by this sentence: "This bill is not just an ordinary bill; it is entirely and most definitely vital. If we apply to this bill the same criterion that we must apply to any piece of legislation, namely the principle that we do not truly need a law unless it is called into being by the exigencies of life itself, then we have no choice but to say that this bill has been forced by life and nothing else." He concluded by admitting that: "It is with a certain anxiety of my soul, a certain

20 That is, less obliquely, Jewish converts to Christianity who, one is to understand, are not responsible for the alleged collective crimes of the Jews.

21 Sándor Raffai (1866–1947), Lutheran bishop and theologian, member of the Upper House of Parliament.

well-founded concern, that I approve this bill, let me reiterate, together with its amendments and certainly not without those amendments."

The bishop of Csanád, Gyula Glattfelder,[22] spoke, as the others generally did, mainly on behalf of the converted Jews, proposing during the committee hearings that "those who had been with us since before 1867 and later took the decisive step to break with their faith and, by virtue of that gesture, and in the most solemn form imaginable, united themselves with what we call the Hungarian nation – those should be assumed to have assimilated permanently." Glattfelder was also the one who suggested that those who had been baptized at least twenty years before and were able to show that their ancestors had lived in Hungary since 1848 should be exempt from the restrictions of the anti-Jewish laws.

Bishop László Ravasz[23] examined the Jewish question in remarkably minute detail. While he shed light on the crisis brought about by the wave of conversions and generously acknowledged the faithful Jewry as the people of the Old Testament, he ultimately decided to vote in favour:

> Based on the foregoing ... I must inevitably conclude that, in principle, I am unable to reject the anti-Jewish law ... For all its valuable traits, wit, and radiating intelligence, the Jewish spirit has developed a decadent, declining disposition that has alternately spread world-weary resignation, established itself as a cold, calculating intellect, or threatened erosion through arrogant relativism. In those of a more nervous and irrational temperament, it has become sheer blind demagoguery (remember the revolutions[24]) – the final outcome invariably being a fall from the ideal of sanctity. The people of sanctity have forsaken the principle of sanctity.

The scope of this book does not permit sufficiently detailed quotations from these high priestly arguments. In all fairness, though, I must point out

22 Gyula Glattfelder (1874–1943), Catholic bishop, and archbishop of Kalocsa in 1942–43.
23 See 131.
24 According to the popular antisemitic narrative of the time, the Jews had been responsible for Hungary's Bolshevik Revolution of March 1919, which resulted in the repressive Hungarian Soviet Republic (*Tanácsköztársaság*). In fact, while many leaders of this short-lived communist regime were Jewish, most notably Béla Kun, only a fragment of Hungary's Jewish community supported the communists, and the regime's victims included numerous Jews.

that Bishop Ravasz conceded that the Jewish soul is not inferior to nor any more worthless than the soul of the Germanic, Anglo-Saxon, or Hungarian peoples, and he even raised the idea that the law should provide for the compensation of Jews for the divestment of their rights. All the same, he regarded regulation by law as inevitable on the grounds that "the Jewish spirit is different from the Hungarian spirit, and one must draw conclusions from this difference, to the effect of finding legally binding ways to uphold the positive Hungarian spirit vis à vis any other alien spirit."

The third anti-Jewish law, the so-called Racial Protection Act, elicited greater resistance from the church leaders. Bishop László Ravasz, the pre-eminent orator of the Calvinist church, concluded his speech of rebuttal by reading a solemn declaration signed by all the bishops and four general superintendents protesting against the act. But it was too late. The process could no longer be stopped, and the German invasion pushed the Christian churches into a situation where they realized that certain critical decisions would have to be made.

The way a community responds to external attacks spells the difference between its being healthy or diseased. Internal unanimity – what the English call the "closing of ranks" – is the token of a community's viability, while dissension always heralds ultimate demise. It is a lamentable fact that a significant part of Hungarian Jewry responded to the German occupation by forming interminable lines in front of the rabbinate in Wesselényi Street to clamour for official recognition of their conversion amid tumultuous scenes in which emotions frequently got out of hand. The commotion did not go unnoticed by the German officers visiting the Síp Street headquarters, who demanded to know what was going on. Apprised of the situation, they threatened to put an end to these scenes by holding random raids, although they never made good on their word, and no brutalities were committed on this account.

As we have seen in connection with the anti-Jewish laws, the Christian churches entered the lists[25] primarily and specifically on behalf of converted Jews, and they continued to do so for some time during the German occupation. When the substance of the yellow-star decree was aired to official circles,[26] it caused great consternation among the churches, as the mandatory public stigmatization was conceived as being equally binding for long-time

25 That is, the lists of people exempted from the law.
26 Decree No. 1240/1944 on the distinguishing marks of the Jews was published in the official bulletin *Budapesti Közlöny* on 31 March 1944.

Jewish converts, people of Jewish extraction who were born Christian, and even Jewish Christians holding clerical office.

On April 30, Bishop Ravasz lodged a proposal with the Ministry of the Interior, requesting certain exemptions from the star-wearing requirement and its consequences. Promises were then made, but the decrees, when promulgated, redeemed those promises only in part, providing exemptions only for pastors, deacons, and deaconesses. On April 6, the Calvinist Convention and the Universal Evangelical (Lutheran) Church filed another petition urging the Minister of the Interior to broaden the eligibility for exemption. As a result, the exemptions were extended to include mixed marriages. Undoubtedly, this measure saved hundreds of families from persecution, but as a side effect it increased the number of conversions, as many Jewish spouses in mixed marriages rushed to receive baptism upon hearing the news. In his work, entitled *Hungarian Protestantism against the Persecution of Jews*, Albert Bereczky[27] mentions Bishop Ravasz's audience with the regent on April 12. In the first days of the German occupation, those close to the regent leaked the information that the regent considered himself captive and would refrain from taking any action as a means of expressing his disapproval of what was happening in the country. Before long, however, it became apparent that this position was untenable. The audience of Bishop Ravasz must be counted among the most momentous episodes of the great historic drama as it unfolded. Bereczky relates how, on this occasion, the bishop cautioned the regent to refrain from assuming any position on the Jewish question that might in the future shift the responsibility for the impending atrocities to him and link them to his name.

Before the end of April, Bishop Ravasz was informed by Zsigmond Perényi, the Speaker of the Upper House,[28] about the ghettos in the Subcarpathian region and the uncommon cruelty with which the local Jews were being

27 Albert Bereczky (1893–1966), Calvinist pastor, one of the key figures of the rescue and resistance activities of the Protestant churches in wartime Budapest. During the Arrow Cross rule, he went into hiding. After 1945 he became a member of the National Assembly as a delegate of the Smallholders' Party. He served as bishop between 1948 and 1958. In 1945 he published his account of the Protestant rescue activities, translated into English as *Hungarian Protestantism and the Persecution of Jews* (Budapest: Sylvester, 1945).

28 Zsigmond Perényi (1870–1946), conservative right-wing politician, one of the confidantes of Regent Horthy. He served as the regent's commissioner of Subcarpathia in 1939–40 and as Speaker of the Upper House of Parliament between 23 October 1943 and 3 November 1944.

carried off to concentration camps. (Perényi had been briefed by Samu Kahán-Frankl and Imre Reiner.) The following day, on April 28, Bishop Ravasz was received by Horthy, and reiterated the admonition that the regent should disclaim responsibility for the anti-Jewish atrocities and do his best to prevent them. Ravasz provided the following account of this dramatic interchange:[29]

> The regent listened to my proposals with a certain air of dissatisfaction, as if under the impression that I was overstepping my competence. Yet my boldness had ensued from the situation itself, and I had no choice but to undertake that risk. In reply, the regent told me that, as soon as he had heard about the atrocities in Nyíregyháza, he called the minister of the interior, raised hell with him, and immediately dispatched the two state undersecretaries,[30] who, as far as he knew, put an end to the outrageous treatment of the detainees. Then he talked about the Germans' demand for a large number of hands for labour service ... Consequently, a few hundred thousand Jews would be taken out of the country, but they would no more have the hair on their heads hurt than the hundreds of thousands of Hungarians who had been working in Germany since the beginning of the war. From this I was dismayed to conclude that the regent had been misled. I had barely stepped out the door when a young Gendarme lieutenant entered his room. I only found out later that it was Undersecretary László Baky.[31]

The document quoted above makes it unambiguously clear that Horthy, if nothing else, had prior knowledge that hundreds of thousands of Jews would be transported abroad, and yet he did nothing to prevent it.

The prime minister's[32] reply to the submission of the two Protestant churches was received on May 10. No less frivolous and perfunctory than any

---

29 Ravasz's quote is from the 1945 (Hungarian) edition of Bereczky's *Hungarian Protestantism and the Persecution of Jews*.
30 László Baky and László Endre.
31 On László Baky, see 72.
32 Döme Sztójay (1883–1946), army officer and diplomat, Hungarian ambassador to Berlin between 1935 and 1944, prime minister of Hungary and minister of foreign affairs from 22 March to 29 August 1944. During his brief tenure as prime minister, his cabinet issued close to one hundred anti-Jewish decrees and orchestrated the plunder and deportation to Auschwitz of practically all the Jews from Hungary's provinces. Sztójay was deposed at the end of August 1944, a consequence of Horthy's efforts to distance the country from the German orbit and exit the war. After the war, the People's Court found Sztójay guilty of war crimes. He was sentenced to death and executed.

other communication by the government from that period, the letter simply glossed over the true nature of the problem by pontificating that "Jewry is a race, and therefore the regulation of the Jewish question is a racial issue rather than a matter of religion." The prime minister's response also hinted at plans to set up a separate department within the Jewish Association[33] that would be in charge of administering convert affairs. This was hardly news to anyone. At the time the first Jewish Council was being organized, the Germans had expressed a wish to establish a department dedicated to convert affairs, and such a department did indeed exist on paper, if not in practice. When the government decree created the Jewish Association and talks began on its composition, Zoltán Bosnyák insisted that at least one member should be a converted Jew. The winning candidate, the writer Sándor Török,[34] was released from detention in Horthyliget[35] to take up this position.

The Calvinist Convention replied to the prime minister's letter on May 17, making two important statements. Firstly, it protested the segregation and ghettoization of Jews: "In connection with the segregation of individuals regarded as Jewish, we wish to state for the record our firmest disapproval of the fact of segregation, and are of the belief that it is not permissible to revive any such practice or tradition as Christian society may have pursued in the past." Second, the letter proceeded to unmask an even more abominable practice, that of deportation:

The other point we wish to bring up has to do with something that is not more than a misgiving and concern at this stage: Certain circumstances we are familiar with seem to suggest that, in addition to sheer segregation, preparations are under way for deportations across the country's borders. We feel obliged to bring the attention of Your Excellency to the analogy of sad incidents that culminated in the final deportation of Jews in other countries. We most emphatically request Your Excellency to do everything in your power to pre-empt such incidents, thereby averting responsibility for the same on the part of

33 The Interim Executive Board of the Association of Jews in Hungary (the Second Jewish Council), formed at the end of April 1944. See the Glossary entry on the Jewish Councils.

34 About Török, see 90.

35 Horthyliget was one of a cluster of internment camps located in the former Duna aircraft factory on Csepel Island between 3 May and the end of August 1944. Horthyliget's detainees were mostly Jews, including journalists and other prominent intellectuals.

the Royal Hungarian Government and thus of the Hungarian nation
as a whole.

It was May 17. By then, the interminable convoys of death trains had
been rolling out of the stations. But lo and behold, we suddenly saw a faint
light gleaming forth from the east – *ex oriente lux*.[36] It was in the capital
of Transylvania,[37] then the easternmost Hungarian territory, that the voice
of human conscience was first raised in public as a Catholic bishop in
St Michael's Cathedral on Korvin Mátyás Square confessed to the word of
the prophet: "Is it not the case that we were all created by one and the same
God, that we are all children of the same Father?"

Áron Márton was Bishop of Transylvania, a region split between two
countries by the Vienna Awards.[38] From his headquarters in Gyulafehérvár,
he would make occasional trips to Kolozsvár to attend to his pontifical
functions. On Ascension Day, he delivered a sermon in full pontifical dress
to an overflowing crowd of believers at St. Michael's Cathedral. This is what
the faithful heard that day:

> Loyal to the command of its divine founder and consistently embracing
> and promoting neighbourly love, the Church has always laboured to
> disseminate the notion that all members of the human race are united
> in one and the same extensive family. Beyond the affirmative call of
> neighbourly love, the views and steadfast practice of the Church have
> been informed by the fundamental doctrine of Christianity whereby
> we are all regarded as children of God and brothers in Christ. The
> world has repudiated both these doctrines in theory, and even more
> in practice. In the name of science, and by propagating sonorous and
> misleading theories, it has rejected the notion of childhood in God
> and especially the notion of brotherhood in Christ. By one-sidedly and
> inequitably over-extending certain interests rallied under various titles,

36 Latin for "out of the East, light," an idiom originally suggesting that wisdom and
     enlightenment arise from the Eastern world.
37 The city of Kolozsvár (today Cluj, Romania). See the Glossary entry on Border
     Revisions and the map on xvi–xxvii.
38 Gyulafehérvár (today Alba Iulia, Romania) was the seat of the Catholic bishop of
     Transylvania, a post held by Áron Márton (1896–1980) during the war years. For his
     firm stance against the persecution of the Jews, Márton was awarded the Righteous
     Among the Nations honorific by the State of Israel in 1999.

often in the name of the sacred words of the Scripture, it has sought to undermine the pre-eminence of neighbourly love.

We do not have the time, nor perhaps would it be appropriate for us, to put these presumptions on trial. Where one faces passion and prejudice, sober arguments are of little help, and the only effective cure for spiritual blindness is the mercy of God. Regardless of any claim on the part of their exponents that they will stand the test of time, theories come and go, one burying the other before it. However, for us, my brothers and sisters in Christ, the fundamental premise of our holy faith shall remain valid, and the open affirmation and implementation of the command of neighbourly love is even more of a moral obligation for us now than in times of peace. We are bound to this obligation, my brothers and sisters, by the very title of Christianity, a title that is so often abused nowadays in the form of a slogan subservient to any number of interpretations. He who sins against his neighbour puts in jeopardy one of the great achievements of Christianity in its two-thousand-year history, which is the thought of brotherhood among the people of the earth. That person will have acted in a heathen rather than in a Christian spirit and, knowingly or unwittingly, will have joined the forces that have split up people into races, social classes, and selfish alliances, pitting one against the other in irreconcilable hostilities.

Finally, my brothers and sisters, we are bound by our last inalienable asset: the honour of our people. People everywhere desire an order erected on justice, on laws applied to everyone equally without discrimination, and on universal love, because they know from an innate sense of equity and timeless experience that nothing else can provide life with the secure framework in which everyone can peacefully labour for himself, for his family, and for the benefit of the community. I have received word that my followers in Christ everywhere from the easternmost boundaries of the bishopric have been profoundly shocked by news that the freedom of certain well-known personages has come under restrictions and that their fate is now in doubt, just as they have followed with utmost concern the recent measures implemented against the Jews. I was pleased to take note of my followers' morally sound assessment, opinion, and judgment of these events. I am proud to mention this in my capacity as bishop, for I see such an assessment, opinion, and

judgment on the part of broad masses as an indication that the true
Catholic spirit remains deeply rooted and vitally active in the soul
of our people. When suffered in defence of justice and in the service
of love, persecution and imprisonment are not a disgrace but a
glorious triumph.

The speech of Bishop Áron Márton was mimeographed in the office of
the Holy Spirit Society.[39] The disseminated copies provided hundreds of
Christians with guidance and thousands of Jews with hope.

~ ~ ~

Great dramatic constructs often allow us glimpses of the heroic struggle of
individuals or communities. The true protagonist of the tragedy of 1944 is
the Jewish people, but the fall of the Hungarian Jewry went hand in hand
with other dramatic efforts. First to be mentioned are the courageous stances
taken by the Protestant churches and the worthy fight put up by certain
Christian priests, including József Jánosi and his associates,[40] now recorded
in the annals of history. However, it is not up to the Jewry of Hungary to
measure the results of this struggle. On 9 May 1946, in possession of the
requisite historic perspective, the council of the Hungarian Calvinist Synod
resolved the following:

[We] solemnly confess, in deep humility, our sin of insulting the glory
of God by failing to faithfully fulfill the divine office with which we
were vested by Him. We neglected to admonish the people and its
supreme leaders when both veered off the path dear to God, and we
failed to stand up sufficiently for the prosecuted innocent. We confess
that, as a Church, we did not carry our affairs as our King and Lord
would have expected us to carry them. We failed to guard the purity of

39   The Holy Spirit Society was a Catholic society whose main mission was supporting
     the activities of priests and monks. Established in 1924, the society was banned by the
     communist state in 1950.
40   József Jánosi (1898–1965), Jesuit theologian and monk, philosopher and university pro-
     fessor. From 1942–44, Jánosi was the chairman of the Holy Cross Society, about which
     see note about József Cavallier, 90. He was active in the rescue actions of the Apostolic
     Nunciature of the Holy See in Budapest. He emigrated to Austria in 1949 and later
     to Germany.

the sermon, grew idle in love, made compromises with the powerful, and made concessions to secular measures in the Church.

Indeed, had the churches evinced more verve, courage, and resolve, they would have been able to point the way out of the cataclysm for those Hungarians who had not been tainted by fascism. If that had happened, Szálasi's coup[41] of October 15 could not have been successful, and we would not have to stand alone bearing no one's sympathy before the People's Tribunal today.[42]

But the people of Hungary did not ride the chariot of fortune sagaciously and, in June 1944, instead of reaching its dénouement, the drama drifted along its escalating orbit toward disaster. As we have seen, the *démarche* of the Protestant churches of May 17 had already mentioned the reports of deportation.[43] These increasingly staggering reports kept reaching people in Budapest, among them the leaders of the Protestant churches, who responded by dispatching a pastor to Kassa to obtain first-hand intelligence. The envoy returned with reports of people being loaded into train wagons for deportation. The information prompted the Protestant leaders to make one last attempt to sway the government confidentially, without public exposure. Bishop Ravasz worded a memorandum which he had pastors deliver to the nine Protestant bishops around the country, all of whom signed the document. It was handed over to Prime Minister Sztójay on 21 June 1944 by a delegation consisting of Calvinist Convention president Jenő Balogh,[44] Lutheran superintendent Albert Radvánszky,[45] Lutheran bishop Béla Kapy,[46] and Calvinist pastors Gyula Muraközy[47] and Albert

41 The Arrow Cross coup of 15 October 1944.
42 This seems to refer to the 1947 Paris Peace Treaty, which forced Hungary to relinquish its territorial expansions of 1938–40 and retreat to the borders dictated by the 1920 Treaty of Trianon.
43 See the letter quoted on 169.
44 Jenő Balogh (1864–1953), politician, lawyer, superintendent of the Hungarian Calvinist Church from 1921 until his death.
45 Albert Radvánszky (1880–1963), landowner, lawyer, politician. He was the national superintendent of the Hungarian Lutheran Church from 1923 to 1948, and the deputy speaker of the Upper House of Parliament from 1935 to 1944. He took part in the rescue activities of the Swedish Red Cross in 1944.
46 Béla Kapy (1879–1957), Lutheran bishop, writer, member of the Upper House of Parliament from 1927 to 1939.
47 Gyula Muraközy (1892–1961), Calvinist pastor, writer, journalist.

Bereczky. The memorandum leaves no doubt that it is presented as a "last-gasp attempt," and that the churches are determined to go public if it fails to produce the desired result.

The memorandum reads as follows:

> In our submission of May 19, the deportation of Hungarian Jews to an unknown location was still discussed as an assumption or possible exigency. Since then, we have received information from reliable sources that, day by day, crammed into sealed wagons seventy to eighty each, large masses of Jews of different sex, age, and social position, Christians as well as Israelites, are being shipped out of the country and disappearing without a trace. Both the deportees and their families are convinced that their journey will end in annihilation. This solution to the Jewish question, as an act of defiance against the eternal laws of God, compels us to raise a voice of protest and supplication to the head of the responsible government. We cannot do otherwise. [A famous saying by Luther is quoted here,[48] suggesting that the authors of the memorandum were fully aware of the historic import of the moment.] We have been ordered by God to enunciate His eternal Gospel in this generation of ours and to attest to the immutable validity of His moral world order, whether people like it or not. It is by this divine office that we feel authorized, as humble sinners nevertheless determined to live up to the Word of God in the holy bond of faith and obedience, to condemn any practice that violates human dignity, justice, and charity, bringing the formidable judgment of innocently spilled blood on the head of our nation.

Later, as Hungary stood before the People's Tribunal, it was impossible not to recall this "formidable judgment of spilled blood," which had been prophesied, five or six years preceding the above memorandum, by submissions of Hungarian Jewry to the parliament: "The Jewry of Hungary may perish, but our destiny can only be thought of as part of the suffering of the entire nation. Indeed, our ruin is closely intertwined with that of the whole world." (This was what we wrote back then.)

---

48   Munkácsi is highlighting the statement *"Hier stehe ich; ich kann nicht anders"* ("Here I stand; I cannot do otherwise"), reputedly uttered by Martin Luther at the Diet of Worms in 1521.

Bishop Ravasz's memorandum continues:

> As bishops of the two Protestant churches, we raise our voice of
> protest upon seeing that fervent members of our Church, without
> regard to their attestation of Christian principles and morals, just
> because they happen to be considered part of the Jewish race, are
> being punished for the Jewish character with which they – in many
> cases, their ancestors – have solemnly broken their ties to and from
> which they have distanced themselves.

This sentence harks back to the warped vocabulary of the anti-Jewish laws
in that it speaks about a "Jewish character" with which some had "solemnly
broken their ties." The Lord punished the Churches' acuity of vision with
blindness. Even as they were trying to save the Jews, they managed to put
a stab in:

> Finally, as Hungarian citizens and Christian pastors, we reiterate our
> pleas to Your Excellency to put an end to the atrocities which Your
> Excellency has no qualms about condemning, thereby vindicating a
> statement by one of the members of your Government against the
> senseless and ruthless extermination of the Jews.[49] We do not mean to
> aggravate the political situation of Your Excellency. On the contrary,
> we wish to facilitate the performance of your undertaken duties as
> the process unfolds. For this reason, we are satisfied, for the time
> being, not to disclose this protest of ours before the general public,
> albeit we may be chastised and called to task for not doing so by the
> leading bodies of world Christianity. But if our voice goes unheard, we
> will be forced to go forth and testify before our believers and global
> Protestantism that we have not held back the message of God.
>
> As a last attempt, we are now appealing to the conscience of the
> Royal Hungarian Government by agency of Your Excellency's good
> Hungarian heart and Christian sentiment, trusting that you will
> rally behind a cause of which this document is the most painful
> proclamation in the history of our service of the nation.

---

49 The statement about the "extermination of the Jews" is a reference to Lajos Szász's
    speech about the "final and radical solution of the Jewish question." See 138.

On June 21, the day the memorandum was delivered, the Council of Ministers was convened to hear reports from Baky and Endre, the two undersecretaries in charge of the deportations, invited on the orders of the regent.[50] Endre read a detailed report which teemed with lies, as one would have expected. Based on what was heard in the Council of Ministers, Sztójay informed the Protestant delegation that deportations were out of the question; Jews were only transported out of the country to work because Germany struggled with a labour shortage. When a member of the delegation interjected that the transports included babies, pregnant women, and very old people, Sztójay explained that the Germans hesitated to separate families, given the strong family ties that Jews were known for. (This cynical and stupid lie was the brainchild of Adolf Eichmann, as revealed by Veesenmayer's testimony.[51])

The memorandum of the Protestant churches – their "last-gasp attempt" – went unheeded, so Bishop Ravasz a few days later drafted a text suitable for purposes of public protest, which was supposed to be delivered to every Protestant pastor in the country. This text describes the events leading up to the memorandum of June 21 which is referred to as a document "in which we pointed to the more than lamentable circumstances accompanying the segregation and deportation of Hungarian Jewry, whether they are Christian or not." The text goes on to reiterate the central idea of that memorandum:

> We have been ordered by God to enunciate His eternal Gospel in this generation of ours and to attest to the immutable validity of His moral world order, whether people like it or not. It is by this divine office that we feel authorized, as humble sinners nevertheless determined to evince the Word of God in the holy bond of faith and obedience, to condemn any practice that violates human dignity, justice, and charity, bringing the formidable judgment of innocently spilled blood on the head of our nation. We call the congregations to penitence and the entire Hungarian people to humility under the powerful hand of God and to eager prayer to Him, even as we beseech Him to turn his pity and preserving mercy toward our Hungarian nation.

50   For details on the special meeting of the Council of Ministers and the text of Endre's report, see Vági, Csősz, and Kádár, *The Holocaust in Hungary*, 115–17.

51   About Edmund Veesenmayer, see 132.

The text of the protest, finalized on the last Sunday of June, was then mimeographed, the envelopes addressed to two thousand ministries. The plan was to mail them from post offices in various parts of the country to prevent the circular from being seized by the always-alert Gestapo and its accomplices. Meanwhile, Prince Primate Serédi lodged his own protest with Minister of Culture István Antal[52] and State Secretary Miklós Mester,[53] warning that the Catholic church would no longer tolerate the laws of God and the laws of men to be trampled underfoot. The prince primate also made preparations for a public protest, but his encyclical was intercepted and withheld by the post offices. Having bought some time in this way, István Antal told the Protestant church leaders he wanted to speak with them. As a result, the public demonstration, scheduled for July 9, was held off. Two days later, on July 11, Bishop Ravasz was paid a visit on his sick bed by Minister István Antal, Secretary Miklós Mester, Bishops Szabolcs Lőrinczy,[54] Imre Révész,[55] and Béla Kapy, and Calvinist pastor Albert Bereczky. Antal said that the prince primate had agreed to rescind his charge in exchange for a promise to halt the deportations, observe humane standards in the segregation of Jews, and provide benefits for those who had converted prior to 1 August 1941. (News of the pact quickly leaked, and when posters appeared around the city announcing those Jews who been baptized before the specified date, a wave of conversions swept over the capital, even swaying Jews hitherto believed to be firm as a rock. At the same time, baptism certificates began to be forged to prove conversion prior to 1941.)

52 István Antal (1896–1975), lawyer and politician. He served as minister of propaganda in the Kállay government and minister of justice and minister of religion and education in the Sztójay government. The People's Court found him guilty and sentenced him to death in 1946. His sentence was commuted and changed to life imprisonment. Antal was acquitted in 1960.

53 Miklós Mester (1906–1989), historian, publicist, politician. MP of the Party of Hungarian Life in 1939–40, and the extreme-right Party of Hungarian Renewal in 1940–44. In April–October 1944 he acted as state secretary in the Ministry of Religion and Education. He opposed the persecution of Jews, participated in rescue efforts, and cooperated with the Zionist underground. He went into hiding after the Arrow Cross takeover.

54 Szabolcs Lőrinczy (1899–1970), ministerial councillor, head of the presidential department of the Ministry of Religion and Education. He was active in the rescue operations of Miklós Mester.

55 Imre Révész (1889–1967), Calvinist bishop, scholar, university professor.

Antal reasoned that, should the churches go ahead with their plans of public protest, Sztójay's cabinet would be forced to decide whether to undertake open confrontation with the churches or to resign, in which case the Arrow Cross would surely come to power under the German military occupation. These arguments persuaded the churches to accept the compromise, subject to being permitted to read a short message to every Protestant congregation the following Sunday. That Sunday was July 16, when the following message was announced as part of the regular service at all Protestant churches around the country:

> The bishops of the Calvinist church of Hungary and the Lutheran church of Hungary inform the congregation that the leaders of both churches have taken repeated action with the competent government authorities in connection with the Jewish question, and especially for the benefit of converted Jews, and that they are determined to continue these efforts in the future.

To restate the obvious: Not only did the Christian churches act principally on behalf of converts but they explicitly stressed this bias in their communications. As we will see shortly, this distinction between two subsets of the persecuted entailed grave circumstances. On the one hand, the differentiation certainly encouraged the masses of converts, bringing them the hope of support by a powerful patron, even if their act of conversion lacked any trace of genuine conviction. On the other hand, it drew distrust from the masses of Jews who remained true to their ancient faith in the shadow of impending doom, while everyone was waiting for a miracle. These loyal Jews did not seek deliverance from a new faith mastered at a crash course held in a bomb shelter, but from the ancient God of Israel, who had always led and would always lead his people through the deepest chasms over the millennia.

These divisions were not new. They had been very much in evidence when Decree No. 1520/1944 of April 19 consolidated under the jurisdiction of a single organization all Jews subject to the star-display requirement, be they Christian or Israelite of religion. For in vain did those subjects include a large number of converts – many of whom went their separate ways whenever they could and spared no effort in enjoying the benefits of belonging in the Christian fold – when the overwhelming majority of the leadership consisted of Jews actively practising their original religion, and the location of its headquarters on Síp Street hung gloomily over the entire organization. Nor did it matter that the converts had their own representative in the Jewish Council in the person of Sándor Török. With his amiable character, embracing humanity, and his consistent readiness to be at the service of everyone, this eminent writer did his best to alleviate the internal tensions, but with precious little result. Well-meaning Christian clerics saw in him someone who represented the interests of the new Christians – their own group, after all – but the Jewish Council was unable and unwilling to take such things into consideration. Under the circumstances, Török's position grew increasingly difficult as he could not escape being torn between the two groups. The internal struggle of the Jewry and its symptoms are illuminated sharply by a letter written to Török on May 24 by the pastor József Éliás,[56] one of the most avid members of the committee assigned by the Protestant church to the aid of the Jewry.

It is the view of our Protestant church – and one in which all Christian churches concur – that its members of Jewish descent should under no circumstances be placed under the administrative authority of another congregation, in the present case the Israelite congregation. We are now petitioning the Royal Hungarian Government to appoint, on the nomination of church leaders, a committee or a commissioner to the affairs of church members who are Christian in their religion but Jewish in their extraction. We cannot settle for having members of our church administered by an organization that is for the most part composed of members of the Israelite congregation. It is unfair, both in terms of the given proportions of representation and the sheer significance of the historic churches in Hungary, that only one member of the current nine-member administrative committee should be Christian by religion. Even if each of the three historic churches – Catholic, Calvinist, Lutheran – had its own member sit on that committee, meaning a bare minimum of three members, we would still not accept the jurisdiction over Christians of an authority that has an

---

56   József Éliás (1914–1995), Calvinist pastor of Jewish origin, scholar, and playwright. As
     head of the Good Shepherd Committee, Éliás was one of the most prominent actors
     of civil rescue and resistance in Hungary in 1944. See also 162.

Israelite majority. That being said, until such time as the wishes of the churches can be fulfilled, as law-abiding citizens, if nothing else, we will start from the premise established by the decree of His Excellency the Minister of the Interior, whereby you, Respected Editor Török, have been appointed to the nine-member administrative committee. In other words, we will support you as you go about your difficult tasks until a better solution is found, but we ask and expect you to kindly make known, stand by, and enforce our point of view, which is one and the same as the point of view of our church members of Jewish descent. It was the Central Jewish Council, which did not have a Christian member, let alone a member representing the Christian church, which vacated flats and imposed various financial burdens, not only on Israelites but on our members as well.

Conversely – and I am speaking from direct experience – when Christian Jews applied to the Council for some kind of aid or support, they were always turned down and referred to the Christian churches by the Council clerks. The Council neglected to notify the Christian churches about affairs with implications for the converts, nor did it seek their support in its own affairs on the same grounds, simply because it took its jurisdiction over converts for granted. This situation could be thought of as being self-evident in light of the official measures, yet it would appear far less self-evident if one considered the reverse scenario: Had the official measures placed under the jurisdiction of the Christian churches individuals professing to and insisting on their Israelite religion, the Christian churches would surely have officially notified the Israelite congregation to this effect. I would not bring this up if the Council operated as a people's organization appointed by the authorities and had treated its members of Jewish descent without discrimination, not only in burden-sharing but also in administering social care. As the case may be, the Council received its mandate as a people's organization but in practice operated as a congregational organization, giving us cause to resent the striking reticence it has shown toward the Christian churches and their competent bodies providing spiritual and social welfare services. I nevertheless realize that these trying times are not suitable for raising such remonstrations, so I will remain content to merely emphasize and maintain the need to change the current state of affairs as outlined above, and to deal with the situation in relative terms until such time as the wishes of the churches can be fully satisfied.

In closing, Éliás summarized the specific demands of the Churches as follows: The affairs of each Christian member should be heard and administered by Sándor Török; the Council should determine the number of converted Jews and ensure that they contribute to the sharing of burdens proportionately and have equal access to care and services; during the implementation of official measures, only Christian agents should be sent out to converts; donations from Christian individuals should be placed at the disposal of Sándor Török exclusively and used by him to the benefit of the new Christians; the Holy Cross Society and the Good Shepherd Mission will dispatch agents to serve as liaisons; in the organization, Christian Jews must be represented not by a single Council member but by one delegated by each of the three historic churches.

Török relayed Éliás's demands to the Council, but the prevailing conditions prevented any meaningful change. The group that mainly looked to the churches for the saving of the Jews – the group headed by Török during those days – was given its own official premises at Síp Street. The crowds seeking conversion swelled further when word got around that it was no longer necessary to opt out at the rabbinate; all one had to do was come to the "department of converts" on the third floor of the headquarters, where forms were handed out. The narrow corridors overflowed with thousands of applicants clamouring for renunciation forms amid the most disgraceful scenes. It was as if one's worst nightmare had come true: In the official headquarters of the Jewish community, where almost superhuman efforts were being mounted to save the Jewry, a quasi-official or even official agency engaged in the business of handing out forms used for the purpose of Jewish self-abnegation. At a crucial juncture of history, the two opposed factions of Hungarian Jewry[57] that had coexisted for nearly half a century found themselves in close proximity to each other, religious conservatives and proponents of Jewish identity sharing a building with the most extreme assimilationists and advocates of Baptism.

This situation was unsustainable for any length of time. The letter of Pastor Éliás makes it clear that the churches had called for an independent Alliance of Christian Jews as early as in May. However, this was not realized until July 12, one day after the government had made its deal with the Calvinist church, and plans for the first round of deportations from Budapest had been cancelled. The creation of the Alliance of Christian Jews was also linked to the agreement with the churches. The relevant government decree

57   A reference to the Neolog and Orthodox congregations.

(No. 2540/1944 M.E.), published in the July 14 issue of the official journal, ushered in a significant change by providing for an independent municipal and advocacy organization for Jewish converts to Christianity, under any congregation, who were required to display the yellow star. This organization was named "The Alliance of the Christian Jews of Hungary."[58] Incidentally, the decree, like every other regulation issued by the Sztójay cabinet, was a slipshod affair, in that it merely applied the relevant rules governing the Jewish Council to the internal administration of the Alliance of the Christian Jews of Hungary. The authorities quickly moved to appoint an administrative committee headed by Dr György Auer,[59] the well-known criminal lawyer, who had been relieved of his position as attorney general because he was Jewish. The committee was joined by Sándor Török, whose previous experience and hard work in Síp Street served him well in the new organization, where he remained a key figure in the movement of converted Jews.

From this point onward, two Jewish organizations existed side by side, at least on paper, with equal rights and obligations. In reality, the lion's share of the work continued to be shouldered by Síp Street, and the difficulty of drawing a precise line of demarcation between the two organizations gave rise to constant friction. From beginning to end, the Alliance of Christian Jews was an attempt at squaring the circle and its only claim to functional viability lay in its direct patronage by the Christian churches.[60]

These are the conditions that characterized the internal affairs of the Jews of the capital, while Obersturmbannführer Eichmann – aided by gendarme lieutenant colonel Ferenczy, Endre, and Baky, and having completed the work of purging the provinces of its Jews – was preparing to storm the yellow-star houses and round up the tenants for deportation.

58 Prime Minister's Decree No. 2540/1944 on the modification and extension of Prime Minister's Decree No. 1520/1944 on the self-government and representation of the Jews. See *Budapesti Közlöny*, 14 July 1944. See Glossary entry on the Jewish Councils.
59 György Auer (1888–1958), lawyer and university professor of criminal law, served as deputy prosecutor general in Budapest from 1933 to 1940 and prosecutor general from 1945 to 1948. He was chairman of the Interim Executive Board of the Alliance of the Christian Jews of Hungary in 1944 (see Glossary).
60 Indeed, during its relatively brief existence from 14 July to October 1944, the separate council for converts, the Alliance of Christian Jews in Hungary, was largely inactive and ineffective.

7

The Struggle to Save the Jews of Budapest

*A portrait of László Ferenczy, hangman of Hungarian Jews –
Talks with Jewish leaders – The trail of blood – The Council
of Ministers in session on June 21 and 23 – The summoning of
Endre and Baky – Neutral countries stirring – Jaross in denial,
Jurcsek on the offensive – A gathering movement to halt the
deportations – Sztójay and the deportations – Veesenmayer on
the deportations – Horthy and the deportations – The horrors of
the deportations from Szeged – Testimony of Móric Esterházy –
Jewish Council relations – The Crown Council of June 21 –
Crown Council resolutions in contempt – Foreign forces on the
move – Preparations for and cancellation of the deportations
from Budapest scheduled for July 6 – Baky scheming for a coup*

At the end of June, László Ferenczy,[1] commander of the gendarme units in charge of deportations, arrived in Budapest to handle the deportation of Jews from the city and its outskirts. Let us pause and dwell on this name for a moment. The heinous crime of the extermination of Hungarian Jewry in 1944 can be laid at the feet of four individuals: Adolf Eichmann, László Endre, László Baky, and the hands-on executioner, László Ferenczy. The first of the four came on Himmler's orders to perform his infernal assignment in Hungary based on the substantial experience he had accumulated across Europe. Endre and Baky supplied him with the knowledge of local conditions, the means of law enforcement, and a penchant for misleading virtually all actors in the political arena. But the man directly in charge of implementation was László Ferenczy, along with the gendarmes under

---

1   About László Ferenczy, see 96.

Fig. 24   In June 144, Budapest's 200,000 Jews were evicted from their homes and forcibly relocated to "yellow-star houses" – 1,948 crowded buildings, including this one at 8 Vay Ádám Street in the 8th District, that collectively served as a ghetto. The process of moving was traumatic, as men, women, and children hauled their furniture and household objects across Budapest in horse-drawn carts, handcarts, and wheelbarrows, or in bundles on their backs.

his command. As we shall see shortly, Ferenczy had not established direct contact with the Central Jewish Council before the second half of July; until then, Jewish leaders had only heard his name without ever seeing him. In fact, Ferenczy had served since March 28 as a liaison officer mediating between Eichmann's Sondereinsatzkommando and the Hungarian Ministry of Foreign Affairs.[2] His title of "liaison officer," however, was no more than a cover for his actual mission to procure from the Hungarian government the armed forces without which Eichmann's understaffed detachment would not have been able to handle the task of rounding up the Jews, forcing them into ghettos, and loading them onto wagons.

Ferenczy went about his business with methodical precision. He had a hand in everything and a habit of mysteriously appearing wherever Jews were to be deported. From early April to the end of June he spent most of his time working in the provinces, and few knew that this enigmatic figure maintained his offices in the Pest County Hall building on Semmelweis Street. Ferenczy must have had good reasons to set up camp in the most intimate proximity to the empire of his boss, László Endre. Every time Ferenczy was in Budapest, his shiny, spanking clean car, chauffeured by a rooster-feathered corporal, would be seen rushing back and forth between the Ministry of the Interior and the office on Semmelweis Street.[3] This ominous vehicle was also frequently spotted in front of the Goldberger Palace in Vörösmarty Square, where the former Union Club,[4] a velvet-cushioned hideout of the wealthiest, had been taken over by Bosnyák's sprawling Hungarian Institute for Research into the Jewish Question.[5]

In administrative measures, Ferenczy reported to and took hints from Endre; in matters of principle, he remained under the orders and tutelage of Zoltán Bosnyák. Whenever Ferenczy, tall, dashing, and sun-tanned, hurried down the corridors of the ministry storming into various offices busy making preparations for his horrendous crimes, everybody snapped to attention as he brushed past them, including police officers and civil servants. Everybody knew that this officer of the Gendarmerie, at the age of forty-six, commanded the ultimate power in Hungary, with uncontested discretion to lord over the life or death of hundreds of thousands of citizens. More than once a Jewish envoy, yellow star on his chest, would be waiting anxiously, torn between doubt and hope, between resignation and

2   This is a mistake: the author means the Ministry of the Interior.

3   The Ministry of the Interior was located in the Castle District of Buda, occupying the bloc at 26–32 Országház Street and 47–53 Úri Street. As sub-prefect of Pest-Pilis-Solt-Kiskun County until early April 1944, László Endre worked at the Pest County Hall building on Semmelweis Street. See also 19.

4   An exclusive club of wealthy industrialists, the Hungarian Union Club (Magyar Unió Klub) was located at 4 Vörösmarty Square in Budapest's 4th District.

5   About Zoltán Bosnyák and his infamous institute, see 72.

joyful anticipation, in the same waiting room where this mass murderer of Hungarian Jews darted through without glancing left or right. He had a habit of not looking anyone in the eye.

Another reason why the figure of Ferenczy towers above the tragic events of 1944 like a dark shadow is that he, alone among all the mass murderers, had been a part of those often very dramatic events from the start, in one capacity or another. As commander of the Gendarmerie in charge of deportations, he kept meticulous records of death-train departures and the number of Jews driven into annihilation, with the painstaking attention to detail of an experienced accountant.[6] In late June and early July, he carried out the extermination of Jews from the area surrounding the capital, and went on to prepare for the deportation of tenants from the yellow-star houses of Budapest. It was certainly through no fault of his own that these final plans fell through. Yet, at the very last minute this ferocious beast suddenly came to his senses, or so it seemed. What happened was that the regent, yielding to influence from various corners, called a halt to the deportations,[7] requiring Ferenczy to contemplate his fate if some brethren of the murder victims were left alive. What would come of him then? Harried by such uneasy thoughts, the chief executioner of Hungarian Jewry proposed talks with Jewish leaders, and on two occasions paid secret visits to the private residences of the presidents of the Jewish Council, the National Office, and the Pest Congregation. Ferenczy continued to play the game cleverly for a while. Two weeks later, acting on the regent's orders, he prevented the deportation slated for August 26, already the second date set for the extermination of the Jews of Budapest. When nobody in the government would dare tell the Germans that Hungary refused to obey the deportation order, Ferenczy did so. Then, during the fog-blanketed days of the fall of 1944, being one of those who correctly gauged the dwindling strength of Horthy and his sinking ship, he instantly reverted to his

---

6   For more on the so-called Ferenczy Reports, near-daily reports in which, for the benefit of his superiors at the Ministry of the Interior, Ferenczy meticulously documented the process of ghettoizing and deporting Jews from the Hungarian provinces, see Vági, Csősz, and Kádár, *The Holocaust in Hungary*, 105–11.

7   Regent Miklós Horthy ordered the deportations halted on 6 July, largely in response to international diplomatic pressure. Nevertheless, the deportations continued until 9 July. Thereafter, the deportations were stopped until the Arrow Cross takeover in mid-October, with two notable exceptions: on 19 July, approximately 1,200 Jews were deported from Kistarcsa and on 24 July, 1,500 Jews were deported from Sárvár.

murderous mission, which he had never really given up in the depth of his heart. He started by readying concentration camps, and on October 16 he again made his allegiance clear: this experienced executioner of the Jews of the Hungarian countryside reported to the new Arrow Cross rulers to complete the doom of the Jews of Budapest. The brickyard in Óbuda,[8] the detention centres in Teleki Square,[9] and the so-called Ferenczy Route[10] leading to the western border town of Hegyeshalom – each an infernally miserable memento to the losses sustained by the city's Jewry – were the fruits of Ferenczy's tireless endeavours. Eventually, he even succeeded in setting up the ghetto of Budapest,[11] designed to stifle and starve to death the elderly of the Jewish population, and he was the one who issued orders for transporting thousands of Jews gathered in "protected companies"[12] to Balf and Fertőrákos near the Austrian border. He managed to escape just as the iron ring of Russian troops was closing in around Budapest, and fled to the West, where he was captured by the Americans. Vitéz László Ferenczy, lieutenant colonel of the Royal Hungarian Gendarmerie, who wrote his name indelibly in the annals of Jewish history, was put through the wringer by the People's Court and ended his life on the gallows of the Markó Street prison. He was a worthy heir to the seventeenth-century Cossack leader Khmelnytsky, who had the innocent blood of tens of thousands of Polish Jews on his hands.

8   The Nagybátony-Újlaki Brickyard at 134–136 Bécsi Street in Budapest's 3rd District (Óbuda) served in the fall of 1944 as a transit camp for thousands of Jews. From there they were deported to Germany, mostly on forced marches.

9   Under the Arrow Cross regime, Jews were rounded up, forcibly gathered, and terrorized in several locations, including Teleki Square in the 8th District of Budapest. The building at Teleki Square 10, formerly designated a yellow-star house, was, along with several other surrounding buildings, converted into a house of terror where Arrow Cross militants brutalized Jews captured during their raids.

10 This refers to the so-called death marches that began on 6 November 1944, with several thousand Hungarian Jews forced to march nearly 200 kilometres from Budapest to the western border in seven or eight days in order to build fortifications along the frontier of the collapsing Reich.

11 In early December 1944, the Jews of Budapest were forced by the Arrow Cross to move from the yellow-star houses to an enclosed ghetto in the city's 7th District.

12 The Arrow Cross government handed over to the Germans tens of thousands of Jewish men to be used as slave labour, including labour-service members under the diplomatic protection of neutral embassies. See 218.

How did this man attain to such a bloody career? He came from the historic Hungarian middle class, in the notional sense of the word, rather than that of actual lineage. He was born in Felsővisó, a town in Máramaros County, and was only forty-six in the cataclysmic year of 1944. In his testimony he said that both his parents were Hungarian, a chief constable father and a mother from a family with roots in the judiciary. After attending schools in Máramarossziget and Nagyvárad, he fought with distinction in the First World War, and was decorated with a gold and a silver war medal. In the wake of the general demobilization that followed the Trianon Peace Treaty, he transferred to the Gendarmerie. He was awarded the title Vitéz[13] in 1929. He finished a staff officer course and was transferred to Kassa as chief investigative officer in May 1940, following the invasion of the Northern Province. However, in the summer before he took up his office in Kassa, he had had the honour of service at the Gödöllő Mansion[14] of the regent. It was evidently here that he made the acquaintance of the head of state, which boosted his self-confidence and was probably instrumental in his success in persuading the leaders of the Jewish Council, in the summer of 1944, to wangle him a privy audience with Horthy. (I will come back later to these meetings between Horthy and Ferenczy and the consequences they entailed.) During the war, Ferenczy began to conduct political investigations and entered into a confrontation with Police Chief Sombor-Schweinitzer. Meanwhile, he was also active in the military supplies field, particularly in Lemberg. Later, under the German occupation, his previous "estimable services" predestined him on 28 March 1944 to be entrusted with the post of liaison officer in Jewish affairs between the German security police and the Hungarian Gendarmerie. He soon presented his new credentials to Lieutenant General Faraghó, the superintendent of the Gendarmerie,[15] who

13 About the Order of Vitéz, see 77.
14 The Royal Palace of Gödöllő, a sprawling Baroque palace built in the eighteenth century, was used by Regent Horthy as a summer home between 1920 and 1944.
15 Gábor Faragho (1890–1953), army general and superintendent of the Royal Hungarian Gendarmerie. Faragho played a prominent role in the mass deportations from the Hungarian provinces. In the autumn of 1944, he was the key figure of Regent Horthy's negotiations with the Soviets for a ceasefire, as a result of which he was stripped of his rank by the Arrow Cross. He avoided being held accountable after the war, and even served as minister of public welfare in the democratic government of 1944–45. Later, the Hungarian Stalinist regime expelled him from Budapest and forced him to live in isolation in a village near Kecskemét.

instructed Ferenczy to personally report to him and keep him up to date on a regular basis. This ushered in the fatal chapter in Ferenczy's career.

Ferenczy's portrait would not be complete without a description of his character provided by his aide and interpreter Captain Dr Leó Lulay, who observed him more intimately than anyone else:

> Ferenczy was an extremely taciturn, distrustful man capable, by
> his very nature, of creating tension around him. He was impatient,
> impulsive, and extraordinarily tight-fisted. Due to his position in the
> chain of command, he implemented and enforced all instructions
> relayed or personally given to him, typically by László Endre, with
> a rigour and ruthlessness that left nothing to chance. My personal
> impression of him was of a narrow-minded officer with a rather
> limited intelligence who came off as a career fiend more than
> anything else.[16]

There is another character trait that goes a long way to explaining Ferenczy's course of action in July and August 1944. In his testimony, Lulay said: "His money-grubbing was a direct consequence of his miserly disposition. I pointed this out to three leading members of the Jewish Council, and I assume it was by exploiting this weakness in him that they managed to enlist his services during the summer months." Another witness made the point-blank assertion that Ferenczy's support had been purchased with a considerable sum of money, as admitted by the Council leaders themselves.

The scheduled date for commencing deportations from Budapest was July 6. Just before that date, five large groups of Jews had met their fate in the most tragic circumstances: From Szeged and Debrecen 40,505 persons were deported between June 25 and 28; from Pécs and Szombathely, 29,556 persons between July 4 and 6; and finally, between July 6 and 8, 24,128 persons from around Budapest. When these actions were completed, the only Jews remaining were in Budapest, except for the detainees in the Kistarcsa and Sárvár internment camps[17] and of course those hiding in the provinces with

---

16 Here Munkácsi quotes from the postwar testimony of Lulay, Ferenczy's former colleague. It is worth noting that to de-emphasize his own role, Lulay had an incentive to depict Ferenczy as negatively as possible. About Lulay, see 98.

17 See the Glossary entries on Kistarcsa and Sárvár internment camps.

false papers under assumed names. With the capital's Jews now methodically hedged in, and all the outposts fallen, the extermination of the heart of the country's Jewry on July 6 looked entirely inevitable.

Since the deportations had begun from regions of the country that had nothing to do with military operations, those with any clarity of vision had not entertained a modicum of doubt that the Jews of Budapest would be eventually taken, last though they might be on the list. Also without a doubt, this last act would be the most difficult for the Gestapo and the Gendarmerie to carry out. For various technical reasons, the herding of Jews into yellow-star buildings in Budapest had not been completed until June 24. The ruses and obfuscations that had worked reasonably well in the provinces had to be dropped in the case of the Budapest "mission," which had to be executed before the eyes of neutral embassies, central authorities, large masses of the proletariat, and the admittedly small faction of left-wing Christians who were sympathetic to the predicament of the Jewry. Furthermore, the numbers involved were an order of a magnitude greater than in any transit camp in the provinces. The largest of those was Nagyvárad with a head count of 35,000, whereas Budapest had nearly 250,000 Jews. No wonder that the "crowning moment" of Hungary's "de-Judaization" required extensive preparations. Yet even while Jews were being boxed in from all directions, resistance began to gather. This only made sense, in terms of sociology and history. The success of the deportations from the provinces lay in the smokescreen tactics and cunning lies of the Nazis, their obstruction of lines of communication, and the inescapable psychological fact that people do not like to take notice of news detrimental to them. However, the more tightly the noose of deportation was drawn around the city, the weaker grew the forces that tightened it. Clearly, the elderly, babies, lunatics, and hospital patients recently operated on could not have been brutally loaded into wagons and carried off under the watchful gaze of the Nuncio, neutral ambassadors, church leaders, and the central authorities. Concealing or even glazing over what was happening was definitely out of the question.

I have already spoken about the churches as one of the forces of resistance which, like the others, took a long time to deploy their ranks. The other major force consisted of the neutral foreign powers, which began to take action. Their influence on Hungarian politics is illustrated well by a speech delivered by Ambassador Mihály Arnóthy-Jungerth,[18] who, as

18 Mihály Arnóthy-Jungerth (1883–1957), diplomat, Hungarian ambassador in the
    Soviet Union from 1935–39 and in Bulgaria from 1939 to April 1944. From 6 April
    1944, Arnóthy-Jungerth served as a deputy minister of foreign affairs (under head of

permanent deputy to Foreign Affairs Minister Sztójay and practically in charge of the country's foreign affairs, was in the best position to gauge the impact of foreign governments. During the People's Court hearings, Arnóthy-Jungerth recalled that he had begun to deal with the affairs of Jews of Hungarian citizenship after he was alerted to anti-Jewish measures abroad and mounted a protest. Neutral foreign countries had started to pay attention to the Jewish question in Hungary in April and had censured the country in the most severe terms. The neutral foreign press condemned not simply the government but Hungarians on the whole as the most ruthless nation in all of Europe, who sent their Jews into ghettos, treated them like animals, stuffed them into cattle wagons seventy or eighty apiece, and waved them off to Germany, where the vast majority were gassed. (It is true that the deportation and extermination of Jews from the other European states – with the single exception of Denmark – were more successfully kept in secret or at least glossed over by the Gestapo. Because the operation in Hungary was to be the last and the Germans had to make quick work of it, the deportations here were even more comprehensive and vicious than elsewhere.) The ambassadors of neutral foreign countries showed up at the Ministry of Foreign Affairs one after the other; hardly a day passed without one paying a visit to protest. The Nuncio, the ambassadors from Sweden and Switzerland, and others took turns warning Arnóthy-Jungerth, the *bona fide* foreign minister, about what was happening in the country. He then called Sztójay to tell him that, as the official in charge, he was going to bring the issue of the deportations and atrocities under the authority of the Ministry of Foreign Affairs and asked permission to raise this measure in the Council of Ministers. Sztójay agreed to these demands.

At the session of the Council of Ministers, of June 21, Arnóthy-Jungerth described at length the prevailing foreign opinion of the government and the people of Hungary on account of the persecution and deportation of Jews, providing a detailed account of the facts relayed to him by the ambassadors.[19] Arnóthy-Jungerth had access to all the secret radio transmissions via MTI,

---

government Sztójay, who also acted as foreign minister). Critical of the brutal campaign against the Jews, he was arrested after the Arrow Cross takeover. In 1945 he was forced into retirement and later, under Hungary's communist regime, had his pension revoked and was expelled from Budapest.

19 Munkácsi's information is not entirely accurate here. There was no such discussion on 21 June 1944; however, similar discussions did take place at the 26 June, 28 June, and 5 July meetings of the Council of Ministers.

the Hungarian national news agency. There were at least thirty or forty reports about the persecutions daily. (One gets an idea of the thickness of the veil of secrecy that surrounded the brutal ghettoization and deportation of Jews from the fact that the head of the Hungarian Ministry of Foreign Affairs had to be informed thereof by foreign ambassadors, who obviously had no executive jurisdiction in the country. Under the circumstances, how much was the general public really expected to know?) Arnóthy-Jungerth also relayed news received from abroad and from the ambassadors about the Jews deported to Poland being taken to Auschwitz, where they were to be gassed and cremated. After the Swedish ambassador delivered a memorandum to Arnóthy-Jungerth divulging the horrors of Auschwitz, the deputy minister of foreign affairs cautioned the government that international opinion could no longer be ignored: "As a small nation, we will need all the friendship and goodwill of the big ones when the war is over. Conversely, by persisting in our ways we will lose the sympathy of all nations, and Hungary will be forsaken and left alone by everyone in its desire to reconnect with the economic and cultural life of the world." Currently, we are witnessing the verbatim realization of this prophecy, which anyone with a vestige of common sense could have foreseen. Concluding his speech, Arnóthy-Jungerth urged the government to call a halt to the deportations and bring an end to the atrocities.

The ministers of the Sztójay cabinet resented Arnóthy-Jungerth's lecture deeply and turned against the deputy minister of foreign affairs. The first to comment was Jaross,[20] the minister of the interior in charge of Jewish affairs. In response to the report, he expounded his view on the matter as follows:

> The claims of seventy or eighty people being locked in each wagon and other atrocities do not on the whole correspond to the facts, considering that the transportation of workers to Germany has proceeded methodically following appropriate preparations. As for the potential consequences in terms of the international reception of Hungary, the report is guilty of gross exaggeration. No miracle lasts forever. The world may protest with all its might as we speak, but one day it will be all over, and nobody will care about these things any more.

20 On Andor Jaross, see 72.

Jaross then yielded the floor to the other ministers, Imrédy[21] chief among them. Arnóthy-Jungerth was left with the impression that the other ministers were perfectly aware of what was happening to the nation's Jewry. Jurcsek[22] accused Arnóthy-Jungerth of "refusing to understand the viewpoint of the Germans, and presenting the entire Jewish question with a strong anti-German bias." As for the charge that the deportees included not only able-bodied men, but old people, children, and women, Jurcsek offered the explanation that Jews tended to work with greater dedication when they had their families around.

It is not inconceivable that this inexcusably cynical and inane rationalization from Jurcsek was very much welcome by the ministers, who then went as far as to demand that the Ministry of Foreign Affairs repeat it by way of an answer to the ambassadors. Arnóthy-Jungerth rejoined: "No ambassador of a foreign country will believe this, because a Jew will perform best at work when he knows his family is safely at home." The session ended with a resolution, on the initiative of Sztójay, to summon reports from the two undersecretaries of the Ministry of the Interior, Endre and Baky, who directly supervised ghettoization campaigns and deportations.

The two undersecretaries duly appeared before the Council of Ministers on June 23, where each read his statement.[23] Baky explained that each "measure of ghettoization" (that is, each act of preparing for deportation) was preceded by a meeting where "the parties thoroughly discuss what is to be done and how to go about it." Endre's report, which he read from his notes, was not much different. He said that having personally toured the ghettos around the country he found all of them "decently provided for" and the accommodations "acceptable." He saw no sign of abuse and, although

21   Béla Imrédy (1891–1946), economist, financial expert, extreme right-wing politician. He served as prime minister from May 1938 to February 1939. Imrédy played a key role in the preparation of the first and second anti-Jewish laws (Act xv of 1938 and Act iv of 1939) and was the leader of the extreme right-wing, antisemitic Hungarian Life Movement launched in January 1939. From 1940 he led the Party of Hungarian Renewal, which split off from the right wing of the governing party. Following the occupation of Hungary, Imrédy was the Germans' first choice for prime minister, but Horthy was unwilling to appoint him. From 23 May to 7 August 1944, he acted as minister without portfolio responsible for economic affairs in the Sztójay government. Convicted by the People's Court, he was executed.

22   On Jurcsek, see 37.

23   Actually, they gave their statements on 21 June 1944.

he did encounter "certain anomalies," he "remedied those on the spot." He further contended that the Hungarian Gendarmerie had practically nothing to do with the ghettos, let alone the deportations, as the gendarmes were stationed outside the camps; it was not the gendarmes but the Gestapo conducting the deportation; the gendarmes only provided security for the transport outfits.[24] (Obviously, the secretary and the former sub-prefect did not learn their lesson when the notion of "accessory" to a crime was taught in law school.) Endre and Baky read out loud their written reports in a cold, dispassionate tone befitting true bureaucrats. The others had no comments to make. Before dismissing the two undersecretaries, Sztójay repeated what the deputy minister of foreign affairs had said and admonished them to "implement the measures in a humane manner," whatever he meant by that. Before Endre and Baky left the room, Arnóthy-Jungerth sarcastically remarked, "Next thing you know, you'll regret not being Jewish because it prevents you from joining these excursions."[25]

The Council of Ministers' meetings of June 21 and 23 were followed by a session of the Crown Council[26] on June 26, convened by Horthy on the matter of the deportations. Before giving an account of this famous Crown Council, however, let us take a look behind the scenes and examine how Sztójay, and especially Horthy, related to the deportations, and how they reacted to the news thereof.

It is widely known that Sztójay was a sissy puppet whose sole ambition consisted of attending to the Nazis to their absolute satisfaction. This border-guard officer,[27] who served as head of the Hungarian government in the country's most desperate hour of need, represented the worst type of the KUK officer.[28] He chose to play a passive rather than an active role in

---

24 For the full text of Endre's report to the Council of Ministers on 21 June, see Randolph L. Braham, *The Politics of Genocide: The Holocaust in Hungary*, 2nd, rev. and enlarged ed. (New York-Boulder: The Rosenthal Institute for Holocaust Studies, Graduate Center/ The City University of New York–Social Science Monographs, 1994), 865–9.

25 If Arnóthy-Jungerth made this statement, there remains no record of it in the surviving minutes from this Council of Ministers meeting.

26 The Crown Councils were joint meetings of the Hungarian government and the regent.

27 A reference to Sztójay having been born (as Dimitrije Stojaković) into a family of Serbian border patrol officers in the Austrian Empire.

28 An abbreviation for *kaiserlich und königlich*, or "imperial and royal," denoting institutions of the Austro-Hungarian Monarchy.

the deportations, only because what really mattered to him was handing over Jews as a gesture of *captatio benevolentiae*[29] to the Germans. At least this much can be gleaned from various testimonies before the People's Courts.

Sztójay took it for granted that the deportation of the Jews would occur sooner or later. He claimed that no matter what country they happened to have occupied – be it Belgium, France, or the Netherlands – the Germans, especially their army, were known to get Jews out of the way, considering them enemy sympathizers who could hardly be trusted to keep ongoing military operations secret. "It is also common knowledge," Sztójay added, "if only from the events transpired in Germany, that the Germans regard the Jewry as enemy number one, well ahead of the Anglo-Saxons or anyone else." So it came to pass in Hungary, specifically in Subcarpathia, the first region of the country where Germany deployed troops and thus the first to be purged of Jews. According to Sztójay, the Council of Ministers did not address the issue of deportations, and had not in fact become cognizant of them until the transports were well underway. Sztójay claims to have been first briefed on this by Jaross, who told him that the Jews had been evicted from Subcarpathia and later from areas along logistics-supply routes, without being asked any questions. Sztójay then turned to Veesenmayer[30] and – as he testified – "called him to task." Veesenmayer, however, insisted that this was the army's business and therefore of no concern to him, and that in any case this was routine procedure for the German army, regardless of location. The testimonies make it clear that Sztójay then heard about the deportations from the regent himself.

When summoned and "called to task" by Sztójay once again, the German envoy explained that Germany simply needed more workers, and even had the nerve to add that "these people are really having a good time of it." Sztójay testified that he protested the Germans' course of action, but Veesenmayer kept citing higher orders, military exigencies, and Germany's great labour shortage due to the war. He pointed out that every country had contributed labour forces to Germany, and that Hungary also had already sent ethnic Romanian labour servicemen.[31] Sztójay stressed that he had not been aware of deportations from areas unaffected by military operations before Horthy

29 Latin phrase meaning "fishing for goodwill" (literally the "capture of goodwill") as practised by Roman orators at the beginning of an appeal to an audience.
30 About Edmund Veesenmayer, see 132.
31 Historians have found no evidence to support this statement.

later told him. He related how he received various propositions from abroad, including from the Swiss and American Red Cross, requesting Hungary's permission for the resettlement of Jews in Palestine and partially in Sweden and Switzerland. He was paid visits by the ambassadors of neutral countries to discuss the details, and Sztójay allegedly pledged his support for the cause. He testified that these plans were ultimately shelved when the Germans, despite repeated interventions on the part of the Hungarian government, rejected these proposals on two separate occasions. In his defence, Sztójay mentioned that later, in the process of deportations, he prohibited any Hungarian government agency from participating in those actions. (Jaross qualified this claim by saying that the prime minister's ban merely stated that they should not participate "if possible.") When the deportations from Transdanubia were brought to his attention, around June 21, he claimed to have issued an unambiguous prohibition of "any further action," "ordered things to be stopped with the Germans and stressed that not a single soul from Budapest was to be taken." Sztójay cited the regent's own strict ban on involvement by any Hungarian body of public administration in the deportations.

Overall, it seems that in his objections to, and subsequent prohibition of, the deportations, Sztójay obeyed suggestions and, later, orders from the regent. In his testimony, he did mention that the source of his information about atrocities committed in connection with the deportations was the regent's Cabinet Office,[32] which handled complaints. It was this intelligence that prompted him, on June 21, to propose that the Council of Ministers summon the two undersecretaries overseeing deportations. Sztójay testified that the session two days later concluded with the government not objecting to the fulfilment of the request of foreign countries (to wit, permission for the transport of Jews to neutral foreign territory) but simultaneously declaring a ban on further deportations. Jaross took exception to this account. He maintained that, upon hearing the reports of the two state undersecretaries, the ministers sent firm instructions to them that they had to prevent further atrocities under their purview, "but no resolution was adopted for the government itself to halt the deportations, because the Council of Ministers

32   Established in 1920, the Cabinet Office was responsible for the administrative and economic matters of the regent of Hungary. Headed by Gyula Ambrózy (1884–1954), an anti-Nazi expert on international law, the office played an important role in Horthy's necessarily cautious attempts to distance the country from Nazi Germany and re-establish contacts with the Allies.

had not yet found the strength to do so on its own discretion. It is true that the prime minister was personally against the deportations but, like the others, he felt that the government lacked the necessary power to enforce such a ban on its own."

This indecision on the part of the government compelled Horthy to convene the Crown Council three days later. It had taken a fatefully long process of incremental considerations and a specific constellation of various factors before the regent finally took the matter of ending deportations into his own hands.

Bishop László Ravasz made notes of his audience with the regent on April 27. These notes reveal that Horthy on that day had already known that the Germans were gearing up for the deportation of hundreds of thousands of Jews, and that he remarked that "they will be treated the same way as all the hundreds of thousands of Hungarian migrant workers employed in Germany for years." (!) Bishop Ravasz later recalled this crucial meeting in even greater detail before the People's Court, testifying that by then Horthy must have been aware that the transports would not be confined to able-bodied men fit for work. Ravasz related how he rushed to report to the regent as soon as he had received from Zsigmond Perényi, the speaker of the Upper House, the news of the ghettoization in Nyíregyháza, Kassa, and Marosvásárhely, and had received "outrage and despairing" letters stating that "men, children, and the elderly were herded together like livestock in a corral." Ravasz said:

[I] fervently beseeched the regent to oppose these developments with all his might instead of letting the perpetrators hide behind his name. My experience told me that people would have no qualms about using the regent's authority as an excuse in their own defense. My visit was not a pleasant one, for the head of state or myself, and it was never my habit to make such appeals. This was the first and last time I ever did something like this. The regent told me that those unfit for military service were being taken to work, along with their families so they could all stay together.

(The same line was fed by Veesenmayer to Sztójay – Why should the nation support those families when they have a breadwinner working abroad?) At this point, the president of the court asked Bishop Ravasz if he thought "the regent offered this explanation in good faith or, rather, in an effort to mitigate the seriously unpleasant nature and stark reality of the subject, and to alleviate his discomfort in having to face you on this matter." "It is my belief," Bishop Ravasz replied, "that the regent had been misled and just wanted to ease his conscience."

In examining Horthy's role in the deportations, it seems essential to look at the circumstances under which he appointed Endre and Baky to their positions as state undersecretaries. On the record, Sztójay denied having submitted any proposal to that effect. Jaross admitted to having made the proposals himself, and said Horthy voiced no objection whatsoever. In fact, Jaross quoted him as saying, "I concur; it is the right thing to do. Both served under me as officers in Szeged."[33] Bishop Ravasz painted an entirely different picture of Horthy's relationship with the two state undersecretaries who oversaw the deportations. He testified that, on April 28, the regent "was outraged to hear about the abuses," "raised hell," and "chased the undersecretaries all the way to Nyíregyháza to do something about these untenable conditions." Yet another angle on Horthy's feelings about Baky, and especially about Endre, was provided by the wife of the university professor Dr István Kovács,[34] who was a personal acquaintance of the regent's. She conceded that Endre had initially been well liked and supported by Horthy, but later he fell from grace. According to Mrs Kovács, by 1944 Horthy had formed a very bad opinion of Endre. She recalled how, in her exchanges with Horthy, she would always find a way to dwell on the subject of the ghettoization and the horrors of the deportations. The regent was incredulous and promised to "send for the minister of the interior Andor Jaross immediately to report to me." Thus summoned, Jaross denied that anything of the sort was happening and dismissed the news as unfounded rumours "spread by the Jews." When the atrocities had escalated further, Mrs Kovács visited the regent once again to deliver the news to him. According to her, Horthy burst out saying, "I don't know how to keep these people at bay anymore" and called them "sadist villains." He had a much better opinion of Jaross, whom he had made minister of the interior of the Sztójay cabinet himself. (Veesenmayer, the

---

33 Szeged, a city in southern Hungary, served as the headquarters of the counter-revolutionary National Army led by Miklós Horthy.
34 Probably István J. Kovács (1880–1965), professor of theology, leading member of the Hungarian Calvinist church, MP and deputy chairman of the Smallholders' Party. His wife was Irén Schulek (1888–1968), daughter of the renowned architect Frigyes Schulek.

creator of the cabinet, had been in favour of appointing Ruszkay,[35] but the regent had more trust in Jaross.) When he first received Jaross in his new capacity as minister of the interior, he saw him off with the words, "My dear boy. I hope I can count on your support in these difficult times." How wrong he was! Barely a few months had passed before he realized that Jaross was just another Nazi henchman. Nor did he make a secret of this discovery; he literally used that epithet to describe Jaross.

The account provided by Mrs Kovács details the abominable incidents she brought to the attention of the regent, which clearly influenced his decisions. Having personally witnessed these historic events, she described the deportations from Szeged and the horrific contribution of László Endre in these words:

> I made the trip to Szeged, where I was told that the Jews from Kiskunhalas had been moved. I had previously conferred with Ernő Bródy and Cavallier,[36] president of the Holy Cross Society, to discuss our options. They said that I as a woman had a better chance of gaining access to certain places. So I travelled to Szeged and there I spun a yarn to the gendarme in charge about needing to get inside the brickyard[37] to deliver a package to a doctor I was indebted to. The lieutenant colonel said this was out of the question; nobody was allowed to enter. Then he suggested that I talk to László Endre; if anyone had the authority to issue the permission, he was the man. I told the officer my husband was a good friend of Endre's. I did not dare to claim I knew him personally myself lest they find out the truth. Having continued conversing with the officer for an hour and a half, I managed to gain his confidence, and he told me about certain things. I told him that I found it impossible

35 Jenő Ruszkay (1887–1946), army officer, diplomat, pro-Nazi politician. He was a leading member of the Arrow Cross between 1940 and 1942. In March 1945, Ruszkay was appointed superintendent of Hungarian SS troops in the rank of Obergruppenführer. The People's Court found him guilty of war crimes and he was executed.

36 About József Cavallier, see 90.

37 On 16–17 June 1944, nearly nine thousand Jews from Szeged and nearby municipalities were herded into a makeshift ghetto, a brickyard on the outskirts of the town, which lacked even the most basic sanitary facilities. The inmates of the brickyard were deported in three transports between 25 and 28 June. The Gendarmerie commander in Szeged was Captain Imre Finta (1911–2003) who, having escaped prosecution in Hungary, emigrated in 1948 to Canada and opened a restaurant in Toronto. In 1987, Finta became the first person prosecuted under Canada's war crimes law, but was acquitted.

that the Jews of Budapest were to be passed over when all the Jews
of the provinces were being taken out of the country. This would be
unjust. The lieutenant colonel believed that I was on his side. "Come
now, Madam," he said. "We will begin removing the Jews from the
brickyard this evening and will finish by Wednesday to make room
for the Jews arriving Thursday from Budapest." "Nonsense," I answered.
"How can you possibly get them all out on such a short notice?" The
officer then told me that the trains were waiting in Óbuda at the edge of
the city, six thousand gendarmes had been transferred to Budapest, and
that Eichmann, the chief deporter who possessed substantial experience
in the field, had arrived in the capital as well. At that moment, an SS
officer entered the room, and I had to come clean. He said he was going
to have me arrested and thrown into the brickyard if I wanted to see the
inside of it.

Ultimately, Mrs Kovács did not obtain a permission to enter the brickyard,
although she was allowed to watch as the Jews of Szeged were dragged off.

The Jews were led away at half past one, amid much terrible abuse by
the Gendarmerie. The elderly were kicked around. The bystanders felt
sorry for them. "Sorry, eh?" the gendarmes replied to them. "You want
to go with them, is that it?" The rear was brought up by a big black
automobile carrying the SS colonel, another gentleman I did not
know, and someone wearing dark glasses whom I recognized as László
Endre. They all followed the whole scene until it was over. I was
standing among the crowd. As the black car rolled by slowly along the
narrow road, I crouched against the wall of a small peasant cottage
some four or five metres away.

Mrs Kovács continued her testimony by describing some of the atrocities
she witnessed:

One example was an elderly couple, the old man, who must have
been around eighty, apparently having a problem with a stiff neck
or something. The gendarme gave him a blow on the back with the
butt of his rifle. The old man fell over, and the gendarme kicked him,
probably in the face, because I could see his face was all bloody ...

Only old people were brutalized like that, as the young quickened their pace seeing what was happening, but the elderly could not keep up and had to be pushed along by kicks and rifle butts.

Mrs Kovács then returned to Budapest and delivered her report to the regent. "I arrived in Budapest on Sunday. At three o'clock on Monday I visited the regent, who responded to my narrative by summoning Andor Jaross, Lieutenant Colonel Ferenczy, and the police chief to his office at five o'clock to confront them about the atrocities in Szeged."

The testimony of Móric Esterházy[38] sheds light on the influence of Angelo Rotta, the Papal Nuncio. At the beginning of 1944, fleeing the air raids, most of the foreign embassies had moved to the provinces.[39] The nuncio holed up at Esterházy's estate in Csákvár, while the ambassador of Switzerland went to Vajna some 40 kilometres away. The Episcopal Bench assigned Apor, the bishop of Győr,[40] to the task of shoring up support for the Jews. Father József Jánosi[41] kept in touch with him and the nuncio, making daily visits to the Ministry of the Interior and bringing news directly from the Jewish Council. Esterházy was in contact with Apor as well as his guest, the nuncio. Rotta acted not simply in his capacity as envoy of the Holy See but also as the doyen of ambassadors based in Budapest. Esterházy asked the nuncio to intercede mainly on his own behalf and, on the side, to communicate regularly with his colleagues, particularly the ambassadors of Sweden, Switzerland,

38 Móric Esterházy (1881–1960), landowner, conservative politician, prime minister from June to August 1917, MP of the United Christian Party (Egyesült Kereszténypárt, or EKP) from 1939 to 1944. After the Arrow Cross takeover in October 1944, he was arrested for being a leading supporter of Hungary's exit from the war and was deported to Mauthausen concentration camp. After surviving the war, he was classified by Hungary's Stalinist regime as a politically dangerous element and, in 1951, was expelled from Budapest to the countryside. He emigrated to Vienna in 1956.

39 While certain embassy offices were moved out of Budapest in 1944, numerous foreign diplomats, including key actors in rescue missions, remained in Budapest, some even during the siege of the capital city.

40 Vilmos Apor (1892–1945), Catholic bishop of Győr, who sharply opposed the persecution of Jews in 1944 and personally intervened for Catholics of Jewish origin. In March 1945, while attempting to protect women from marauding Soviet soldiers, he was shot to death by a Soviet officer.

41 On József Jánosi, see 172.

and, while he was still in the country, the ambassador of Portugal.[42] This diplomatic mission unfolded in two directions. One was the effort to enlist the help of the government and the regent by divulging the inhumane atrocities to them. The second front consisted of persuading the ambassadors to inform their own governments in the deepest possible detail, leaving no doubt in their minds that the ongoing horrors perpetrated in Hungary could not be construed as anything other than a heap of heinous crimes. It was also by agency of the neutral ambassadors that the general public and the press of foreign countries were kept up to date. The regent received intelligence from the nuncio mainly through his son, Miklós Horthy Jr,[43] who was in turn informed by Verolino, the councillor to the ambassador.[44] (Esterházy himself would pay visits to the regent to discuss the atrocities.) The nuncio had a rather pessimistic outlook, to the point of declaring outright: "It is unlikely that any meaningful change will be achieved while Endre and Baky remain in charge." On one occasion, the nuncio, who made frequent trips to the capital, returned in a particularly dejected mood. Esterházy wanted to see him right away, but the nuncio kept him waiting for hours, saying he was exhausted and did not have the time. When Esterházy finally gained entry, he found the man deeply depressed. The nuncio then produced for him a memorandum he had just written in French. The last sentences of

42 Carlos Sampaio Garrido (1883–1960), the Portuguese ambassador in Hungary, actively protested Hungary's anti-Jewish laws and sought to protect the country's Jews. Recalled by Portugal in April, he did not leave Budapest until 5 June. After his departure, his rescue activities were carried on by his successor, chargé d'affaires (deputy ambassador) Teixeira Branquinho (1902–1973), until he too left Hungary at the end of November 1944. Sampaio Garrido was awarded the Righteous Among the Nations honorific by the State of Israel in 2010.

43 Miklós Horthy Jr (1907–1993), landowner, diplomat, son of Regent Miklós Horthy. He served as ambassador to Brazil in 1939–42. From January 1944, he headed the colloquially known "bureau to exit the war" (Kiugrási Iroda), which prepared covertly to make peace with the Western Allies, and maintained contact with anti-Nazi opposition. On the morning of 15 October, the day that Regent Horthy attempted to surrender, Miklós Jr was kidnapped by a German commando and used as extortion against his father. He was interned at the Mauthausen concentration camp and later, for shorter periods, at Dachau, Innsbruck, and Niederdorf. At the end of the war, he was arrested by the liberating US Army and held in custody for three months before being released. He later sought exile with his father in Portugal, where he died in 1993.

44 Gennaro Verolino (1906–2005), Italian Catholic priest and diplomat. As the secretary of Nuncio Angelo Rotta in 1942–45, he played a key role in the rescue activities of the Holy See in Budapest.

the document invoked "the historic chivalry of the Hungarian nation in the way it treated Poles, Frenchmen, and other prisoners of war. In stark contrast to those noble traditions, what is being perpetrated against the Jews cannot be excused before the international community, before history, or before the throne of God." After this, Esterházy proceeded to dictate a memorandum in Hungarian for the nuncio to take with him on his next visit to the regent, and also prepared for him an abstract of the French text. Later, Esterházy himself paid a visit to Horthy and brought up the issue of persecutions. At that time, the regent admitted that "Jaross is hardly up to the task of bringing order to the chaos in the ministry, never mind the country." He added that he was unable to keep the reins on his undersecretaries, who refused to obey his instructions. "The country must itself get rid of Endre and Baky," he concluded.

By then, the Jewish Council had forged its own connections to the regent. The messenger was none other than Miklós Horthy Jr, who had been contacted by Dr Ernő Pető[45] with the help of the regent's personal secretary, Dr Dezső Ónody. Horthy Jr set up a meeting and called Pető to Castle Hill one late afternoon at the end of May. There Pető was greeted by Ónody in front of the Ministry of Foreign Affairs and ushered through a small door and a square courtyard to the reception room of the regent's son. This was the first in a series of frequent meetings in which the messenger for the Jewish Council exposed various anti-Jewish measures, from the hardships of the concentration of Jews in Budapest to the deportations and ultimately to the gas chambers of Auschwitz. Horthy Jr would listen to these accounts in utter shock and pledged his help by relaying the information to his father. In some cases, though, he questioned the truth of the reports. As he said, his father had called Jaross and Winkelmann[46] to ask about the fate of the deportees, and both had dismissed the allegations as "sheer Jewish chimera." More than once, Horthy Jr also complained about his inability to produce results on account of the ministers, who lied to his father incessantly.

All these influences were detectable in the regent's conduct in the Crown Council session of June 26. The righteous Christian conservatives, the churches, the nuncio, the atrocities unveiled by the Jewish Council, and foreign opinion had all played a part in swaying Horthy to take a firmer stance at long last, particularly in the wake of the two sessions of the Council

45 On Jewish Council member Ernő Pető, see 18.
46 About SS-Obergruppenführer Otto Winkelmann, see 32.

of Ministers, on June 21 and 23, when he could no longer pretend that his government was able or willing to do anything to stop the mass murders.

According to the testimony provided by the former deputy minister of foreign affairs, Arnóthy-Jungerth, the Crown Council was convened by Horthy specifically to discuss the issue of the deportations. "He said he would stand for none of this any longer, and asked me for a report on foreign opinions. I then told the Crown Council the same thing I had already explained to the Council of Ministers, namely that the atrocities must be stopped, if only to protect the honour and reputation of Hungary." After hearing further statements by Sztójay, Imrédy, and Reményi-Schneller, the regent finally announced his decision to "end the deportation of Jews." He further called on the government to remove Baky and Endre from office. He then ran down a long list of data substantiating the atrocities against the Jews and asserted he would "no longer tolerate these things," reiterating his demand to have Endre and Baky relieved of their duties on account of the atrocities. Cowed into silence, none of the ministers dared to put in a word for the two undersecretaries. Later, answering questions in court during the criminal proceedings brought against him, Jaross conceded that the regent had indeed called for the removal of Endre and Baky, but claimed that Horthy later changed his mind and essentially settled for having them reassigned to another position. (Despite the certainty that the Hungarian resistance movement would have gathered much strength if the authorities had learned that the two masters of deportation were no longer around the ministry, this is indeed what happened.[47])

Let us now look at the events that followed. On June 26, the Crown Council moved to pass a resolution ending the deportations. However, the law enforcement agencies, the Gendarmerie chief among them, held this resolution in such flagrant disregard that, from the June 25 to 28, they carried on with the work of deporting Jews from the ghettos in Szeged and Debrecen, and then, in the next few days, as if nothing had happened, followed by stuffing freight cars with Jews from Pécs, Szombathely, and the outskirts of Budapest. The Germans, Endre, and Baky continued to rule!

---

47 After prolonged hesitation, it was only on 20 July that responsibility for "Jewish affairs" was officially taken from László Endre (though he was not formally removed from his position until 22 August). Meanwhile, László Baky resigned on 8 August.

When these events were brought up at the main hearing before the People's Court, the presiding judge[48] put the following question to Jaross in the most vivid terms:

> You have testified that, at the Crown Council session of June 26, the regent clearly stated that he did not consent to the continuation of the deportations. Why, then, did you, as minister of the interior, not instruct your state undersecretaries or direct the authorities and the public safety corps of Hungarian public administration to refrain from participating in any further deportation action?

Jaross failed to provide a satisfactory answer to this question, trying to cover his tracks by invoking the German influence and the vacillation behind the regent's orders. The presiding judge was perfectly correct in remarking:

> In any event, it was certainly within your power, at least your moral power, to issue such a ban – one that constituted a protest on moral grounds, if nothing else – to the administrative and public safety corps, to the effect of prohibiting their further participation in supporting the violent measures initiated by the Germans. Any government would have had the power to do that.

Of course, this is not how it had come to pass. The government of Hungary failed to take action for ten days. This inaction alone claimed another hundred thousand Jewish lives,[49] as the deportations from Pécs, Szombathely, and around Budapest began only after Horthy had issued the ban.

I have already mentioned that as the threat of deportation edged closer and closer to the capital, resistance pick up speed and foreign countries acquired more and more knowledge of the events. Following the Crown Council meeting, further details kept coming to light, making the regent realize that the government and the country would soon be held accountable for everything perpetrated against the Jewry of Hungary. The memorandum

---

48 Péter Jankó (1907–1955), presiding judge of the Budapest People's Court from 1945 to 1948.

49 In the two weeks between 25 June and 9 July 1944 alone, nearly 95,000 people were deported from Hungary.

of protest by US president Roosevelt,[50] a sharp speech of condemnation by the US secretary of state Cordell Hull,[51] and the warnings of British foreign secretary Eden[52] all had a very clear impact. But the most effective message was no doubt delivered during the morning hours of July 2 with the first large-scale daytime bombing of Budapest,[53] a destructive force that convinced even the most hardened skeptics about who was winning the war. At the same time, the raid served as retribution against the audacity of Endre and his cohorts in going through with the ghettoization in Budapest.

~ ~ ~

Among the main characteristics of Horthy's quarter-century rule was that he generally took a long time gestating major decisions and shunned sharp conflicts unless he felt that the very foundations of the regime were at stake. Such eventualities arose with the attempts of Charles IV to reclaim the throne[54] and with the appointment of Gömbös as prime minister[55] – the most vocal anti-restoration pretenders, at a time when in neighbouring Austria

---

50 United States president Franklin D. Roosevelt delivered an ultimatum, via the Swiss Legation in Budapest, to Miklós Horthy on 26 June 1944, threatening military retaliation if the deportations were not immediately stopped. Horthy did not reply.

51 At a 14 July 1944 press conference, Hull denounced the "cold-blooded tortures and massacres of Jews" in Hungary, stating: "The puppet Hungarian Government, by its violation of the most elementary human rights and by its servile adoption of the worst features of the Nazi 'racial policy' stands condemned before history." "Hull Says 1,000,000 Jews in Hungary Are Menaced; U.S. Will Continue Rescue Efforts," *Jewish Telegraphic Agency*, 14 July 1944.

52 The statement is misleading. Despite having information about the massacres at his disposal, British Foreign Secretary Anthony Eden did not speak out against them publicly.

53 The 2 July 1944 air raid was the largest attack by the US Air Force against Hungary. The attacks primarily targeted factories, oil refineries, bridges and railroads, but also claimed the lives of more than five thousand civilians.

54 Charles I of Austria and Charles IV of Hungary (1916–18), last ruler of the Austro-Hungarian Empire, made two unsuccessful attempts to reclaim his throne in Hungary in 1921.

55 Gyula Gömbös, a military man, leader of the right-wing opposition to István Bethlen (prime minister of Hungary from 1921 to 1931), and head of radical nationalist secret organizations, was prime minister of Hungary from 1932 until his death in 1936. Inspired by fascist examples, he intended as prime minister to establish a more modern authoritarian regime.

the balance of power had begun to tilt toward restoration.[56] This scenario was virtually repeated with the election of István Horthy, the regent's eldest son, as deputy regent,[57] when the task to be solved was one of succession (an eternal problem for aging rulers in non-hereditary systems). The deportation of Jews forced similarly crucial decisions on Horthy's government. The lessons of history, and especially the practice of twenty-five years in power, provided those close to the regent with enough experience to recognize that the extermination of Hungarian Jewry was an egregious international crime which, should the war be lost (as they well knew it would be), would cause them not only to fall politically but also to be held accountable under criminal charges in the spirit of the Atlantic Charter.[58] There is of course a causal relationship between the Normandy landings and the Russian approach to the Carpathians on the one hand, and the campaign launched by the regent and his men to halt the deportations on the other. Yet in all probability none of this would have sufficed to force that radical decision had it not been for a new exigency widely assumed to threaten the overthrow of Horthy's government: the fear of an impending coup by Baky.

Horthy and his government had all the reason in the world to be wary of the five thousand desperate gendarmes gathered in Budapest under Baky's command. These Hungarian versions of the SS had gotten drunk on the smell of blood. There was no horror, no cruelty, no inhumanity in which they would not have actively participated during the deportations of the Jews from the countryside. They had learned that the Jew's life is worth less than a dog's and they had seen the property of the deported Jews looted by the

56 The author is probably referring to the right-wing political shift in Austria, which led to the takeover of Engelbert Dollfuss's Christian Social Party in 1933–34 and ended the Austrian Republic.

57 István Horthy (1904–1942), mechanical engineer, first lieutenant of the Hungarian Air Force, Regent Horthy's eldest son. As part of his father's ambition to secure his claim to the regency, and thereby establish a ruling dynasty, he was elected deputy regent in 1942. However, only a few months later, István Horthy died in a plane crash while serving as a fighter pilot on the Eastern front.

58 Issued in August 1941, the Atlantic Charter was a joint declaration of the leaders of the United States of America and Great Britain, defining the plans and ideas of the Western Allies about postwar reconstruction and international security. It served as a principal conceptual basis for the establishment of the United Nations in 1945.

mob. The only ambition they had left was to crown their heroic deeds by deporting the Jews of the capital – an enterprise holding forth the greatest promise of all, in terms of the sheer numbers to be vanquished and the size of the booty to be plundered. But how was it possible to vacate thousands of yellow-star-marked apartment buildings in Budapest without Christians being caught up in the atrocities? And who could guarantee the government that, at the apex of its achievements, the "army of deportation" would stop at Jewish blood and property and not conspire with the Arrow Cross and the occupying German troops to dethrone a head of state already shaken in his authority and prestige, in order to grab power? There you have it – therein lay the true motivation behind the prevention of deportations from Budapest, as corroborated by the facts I describe below.

At the Pest County Hall, Endre held a meeting, as he was wont to do prior to each deportation mission. The meeting chaired by Endre resolved to carry out the deportation of Jews from the outskirts of Budapest on July 2, and to begin evacuating the Jews on July 6 from star-marked houses in the centre of the city. According to the testimony of László Ferenczy, Endre informed the meeting about his agreement with Baky and Lieutenant General Faraghó,[59] superintendent of the Gendarmerie, that the "de-Judaization" mission in and around the city would be executed with the full support of the Gendarmerie. Their campaign plan was based on the idea that the large numbers of gendarmes suddenly reassigned to Budapest should be somehow prevented from attracting attention and arousing suspicion. Their stratagem was to schedule a flag-dedication ceremony for July 2, wherein the Galánta Gendarmerie battalion would be awarded its own banners. The "Mother of the Flag" would be the wife of the regent. The rank-and-file would be given a "leave of absence" for three days (July 3, 4, and 5) following the ceremony. The real purpose of the leave was to dispatch the men to inspect the star-marked houses and collect intelligence that would help devise ways of intercepting any fleeing tenants. These meticulous preparations would have been followed on July 6 by the commencement of the deportation action itself. This, then, was the infernal plan. The gendarme battalions arrived in the city. The appointed commanders of law enforcement in charge of the missions in the outskirts and the city proper were gendarme

59 About Gábor Faragho, see 188.

colonels Győző Tölgyessy[60] and Tibor Paksy-Kiss,[61] respectively. They both reported to Lieutenant General Faraghó for a "briefing." Armed support for the actions outside the city was to be provided by the Galánta Battalion and, in Budapest, jointly by the Galánta Battalion and the Nagyvárad Recruit Training Battalion. It appears that the extreme horrors and choice brutalities of the Nagyvárad ghetto had earned an unusual amount of trust for the local Gendarmerie. (Nagyvárad had been the city in all of Hungary where relations between Hungarians and Jews had been the most solid and most sincere. Consequently, it was here that the Gendarmerie had to employ the most ruthless and bloodiest of methods to tear them apart when the time came to exterminate the Jews.) The detailed blueprint for the deportation of Budapest was finalized by Colonel Jenő Péterffy[62] in collaboration with Paksy-Kiss, based on the "experience" the former had gained in Nagyvárad.

As it happened, the Jews of the suburbs were taken away, but the deportation from the city proper never came to pass, for reasons we have already seen. Horthy did not like such a concentration of gendarmes in the city at all, particularly in view of reports he received about Baky scheming to overthrow him by coup. Under the circumstances, Horthy had reason to suspect that the battalions had in fact been reassigned to Budapest to lend armed support to the impending coup. No wonder the regent and his aides had frowned on the flag-dedication ceremony from the start, and at the last moment called off the event in Heroes' Square[63] on the pretext of imminent air raids. Specific news of the contemplated coup reached Horthy

60　On Győző Tölgyessy, see 97.

61　Tibor Paksy-Kiss (1892–1967), Gendarmerie colonel, was commander of Hungary's 9th Gendarmerie District from July 1942 until September 1944. In the spring of 1944 he was instrumental in orchestrating the deportation of Jews from Northern Transylvania (the 9th and 10th Gendarmerie Districts). In 1946 the Budapest People's Court sentenced him to fifteen years in prison (he was amnestied after serving ten years).

62　Jenő Péterffy (1899–1945), Gendarmerie colonel, commander of the gendarme cadet corps in Nagyvárad from 1 May 1943, and in Galánta after 20 August 1944. He actively participated in the ghettoization and deportation process, ordering his men to treat the Jews in the most brutal manner. According to Baky's and Endre's plans, Péterffy would have orchestrated and directed the deportation of the Budapest Jews in early July 1944. Following the Arrow Cross takeover, he was appointed head of the 9th Gendarmerie District (Kolozsvár), by then almost entirely occupied by the Soviets. Arrested after the war, he died in pre-trial detention.

63　Budapest's largest square, known in Hungarian as Hősök tere.

on Wednesday, July 5, prompting the regent to send for Faraghó and the officer corps of the two armed battalions. He addressed a speech to them and gave them instructions on how to return to their stations.

Yet suspicion must have lingered among the regent's followers. Was this gang really going to give up their craving for more blood and loot, and pack their tents? What if they attempted the coup anyway and managed to sideline the regent? On the night of July 5 and the next day, these doubts prompted a series of resolute measures that boded well for a rebirth of Hungarian national sovereignty and had been unprecedented in their firmness since March 19.[64]

That night saw a series of dramatic events take place. Colonels Tölgyessy and Paksy-Kiss, the anointed executioners of the Jewry, were staying at the Pannonia Hotel on Rákóczi Avenue,[65] coincidentally just a stone's throw from the centre of Jewish life in Budapest and the headquarters of the Jewish Council on Síp Street. Around two o'clock in the morning, a car from the Office of the Regent pulled up in front of the hotel. A high-ranking officer got out and brought Tölgyessy to the Royal Castle, where he had to report to Lieutenant General Lázár, commander-in-chief of the Royal Guards.[66] Lázár handed him orders made out specifically in his name, to the effect that the command of the consolidated law enforcement troops in Budapest had been transferred to Lázár by the regent. Around four in the morning, the car from the regent's office returned to the hotel and took Paksy-Kiss to the castle. In both cases, the vehicle was escorted by sidecar motorcycles armed with submachine guns. Paksy-Kiss was also given his personalized orders by Lázár. According to Ferenczy's testimony, at around three o'clock in the morning, Corps Commander Szilárd Bakay[67] – the same officer who would

---

64 The day German troops entered Hungary.

65 An elegant hotel that existed between 1891 and 1949 at what is today 5–7 Rákóczi Street, just a few blocks away from the Dohány Street Synagogue.

66 Károly Lázár (1890–1968), army lieutenant general, commander-in-chief of the Royal Hungarian Guards (*testőrség*) between 1937 and 1944. In early July 1944, Regent Horthy appointed him the commander of combined law enforcement forces of Budapest (*karhatalmi parancsnok*). A Horthy loyalist, Lázár was arrested by the Germans on 15 October and, along with Miklós Horthy Jr (about whom see 202), was taken to the Mauthausen concentration camp. Extradited to the Arrow Cross authorities in early 1945, he was forced to march to Bavaria toward the very end of the war. He was liberated by US troops and returned to Hungary.

67 Szilárd Bakay (1892–1947), army colonel general, commander of Army Corps I of Budapest and city commander of Budapest in 1944. A key figure in Horthy's plans to abandon Hungary's alliance with Germany and exit the war, he was abducted by the Gestapo on 8 October 1944 and taken to Mauthausen concentration camp. Liberated

be captured by the treachery of the Gestapo a few days before October 15 and would have played a key role in the days following the proclamation of the armistice – called the gendarme garrison by telephone and asked to speak with Lieutenant-General Faraghó. The officer on duty said he was out. Bakay then wanted to speak with the officers in command. The man on duty said they were out as well. After this, Bakay called the Gendarmerie Inspectorate and asked to speak with Faraghó and the same officers mentioned above, and was told they were not there. Finally, he reached Faraghó in his own home. According to Ferenczy, Bakay asked Faraghó what he was doing. "I would be sleeping if you hadn't woken me up," Faraghó replied. Thereupon, Bakay simply wished him good night and hung up. That night, the national defence forces were ordered to gather and stand by on the ready in case Baky went ahead with the rumoured coup attempt. The following day, army troops marched in and set up base in Budapest.

Meanwhile certain gendarme officers were replaced, and some of the Gendarmerie – and I stress only those whom Lázár and Bakay deemed unreliable – left the capital.

The deportation did not happen – not because anyone directly gave orders for it to halt, but simply because the Gendarmerie was no longer there to implement it. When the presiding judge of the People's Court asked Ferenczy whether the Germans alone would have been capable of carrying out the deportation, he replied: "The Germans would not have been able to pull it off, because it was scheduled for the sixth."

~ ~ ~

"Beheading is now postpon'd for this once" – this is how the famous dramatist Madách[68] would have described the situation. Yet the majority of the Jewry only had a vague inkling of these events without having access to any confirmed information. True enough, those "in the know" had heard about Baky's alleged coup attempt and the deployment of the Esztergom special response battalion,[69] and the dwindling numbers of the Gendarmerie in the city had been conspicuous. Even though any contact between Jews and

---

by US troops after the war, he returned to Hungary, where in 1946 he was arrested by Soviet authorities and executed.

68   A line from Imre Madách's 1861 play *Az ember tragédiája* (*The Tragedy of Man*), spoken by Lucifer.

69   The author refers to the 1st Armoured Division of Esztergom under the command of Staff Colonel Ferenc Koszorús, which was ordered to move to Budapest.

Christians had been relegated to secrecy and was widely regarded as an "embarrassment" – few in those days were on top of the compassion game – certain details about the sessions of the Council of Ministers of June 21 and 23 and the Crown Council did leak out. The Ministry of Culture and the churches had begun to circulate vague but encouraging news about "priority status" awaiting converted Jews, without acknowledging the impending deportation of the others. The announcement calling on the converted Jews to report to the authorities, along with the formation of the Alliance of Christian Jews, certainly seemed to confirm reports that the churches had reached an agreement with the government under which converted Jews were to receive more lenient treatment, and there was talk about their exemption from deportation. In addition to these rumours, there was the much more tangible and far more important knowledge that the thoroughly planned deportations had been cancelled, for reasons that remained unknown to the general public at the time. Some of the feared gendarmes retreated to their garrisons, while others, frustrated and empty-handed, returned by train to the provinces. In short, the much-talked-about miracle had happened. Naturally, those who had preached the coming of this miracle from the start could not stop bragging about their keen foresight: "See, I told you. Deportations may be carried out anywhere else, but not here. The evil will stop at the gates of the city." It was the miracle of Jericho[70] in reverse: All the bastions had fallen, but the Jewry behind the walls of the city was spared. There was an all-pervading sense of relief, but these feelings – as we have seen and will shortly see even more clearly – had no real foundation in fact. That said, the appearances did prove the miracle-thirsty masses right. Truth be told, even after the miracle had occurred, very few rushed to the temples to thank and praise the ancient God of Israel. On the contrary, apostasy made greater waves than ever before, as masses of Jews in Budapest began to turn to religions they hoped would help them in times of need.

---

70   A reference to the Battle of Jericho (Joshua 6:1–27), wherein the Israelites, after marching around the city seven times and blowing their trumpets, bring down the walls of Jericho.

8

Between Two Deportation Dates

The situation of Budapest's Jews after the first deportation attempt – "First-round victory" – The impact of the Bergen-Belsen aliyah – A new entity in Vadász Street – A frenzy of conversion – Raoul Wallenberg visits the Jewish Council – The Jewish "elite" occupy the legation buildings – The organization of foreign legations – Neutral legations under siege – Gestapo trust in Síp Street shaken – Eichmann persists in plans of deporting the Jews of Budapest – Ferenczy takes action in Budapest – Ferenczy to travel to Auschwitz to "gather information" – Ferenczy knocking on the regent's door – Ferenczy to evict Jews from Pozsonyi Street – Ferenczy embarking on the game of his life – The internment camp in Kistarcsa – The deportation of detainees from Kistarcsa – Kistarcsa as a household name – Eichmann's threats – The death train out of Kistarcsa shunted – Eichmann at it again – Dr Sándor Bródy brings a report – The Ferenczy mystery – Foreign climate – Ferenczy visits Samu Stern in his home – Meeting details – Horthy Jr eyes Ferenczy with suspicion – The regent receives Ferenczy – Memorandum on the situation of Jews at the end of July 1944 – Applications for work and emigration – Talks with the International Red Cross and the chargé d'affaires for Spain – A telegram from Tangier – The first major mission by Frigyes Born – The Hungarian government issues a statement – First meeting at the Spanish Embassy – The role of the International Red Cross – Hungarian authorities to deliver Jews to the Germans – A démarche from the International Red Cross – Jaross on the Jewish question – Rumours of a Jewish camp in Encs – Winkelmann and Veesenmayer on "supporting" the Gendarmerie – Delivery of a letter of protest refusing to carry out the deportation – Himmler's indifference – Veesenmayer's testimony – Fülöp Freudiger and his friends escape – Labour leaders take a stance – Fuss about the letter of protest –

Fig. 25   Colloquially known as the Glass House, this building at 29 Vadász Street in
Budapest housed the Swiss Embassy's Department of Foreign Interests, headed by
Vice-Consul Carl Lutz (1895–1975). From the moment it opened on 24 July 1944, the
office was mobbed by Jews desperate to obtain protective documents. Lutz, whose black
Packard sedan is in the foreground, issued thousands of protective documents, used Swiss
diplomatic immunity to create dozens of "protected houses" for Jews, and offered as many
as two thousand Jews refuge in the Glass House. In 1965 Lutz was recognized by the State
of Israel as one of the Righteous Among the Nations.

The contents of the letter of protest – Council leaders stripped
of their stars – August: a month of calamities – Timetable
of deportations from Budapest – August 26, the day of crisis
– Crowds in Síp Street – The night and the day after

It is undeniable that the first round of the battle to save the Jews of Budapest
ended in victory. For weeks after the failure of the deportation on July 6 –
from July 6 to 10, preparations would have been made, as the first trains were
supposed to roll out on the tenth – the internal situation of the Jewry was

determined by four factors: (a) preparing the ground for a new round of emigration to Palestine; (b) the orientation toward the Christian churches, with spasmodic waves of conversions, some lawful and most fraudulent; (c) the arrival in Budapest of Secretary to the Swedish Legation Raoul Wallenberg[1] and the attendant mobilization of neutral legations, along with the occupation of the legations by some of the Jewish elite; (d) the establishment of direct communications with László Ferenczy.

I have in the foregoing discussed the circumstances in which the first *aliyah* took place.[2] Apart from Ottó Komoly[3] and Rezső Kasztner, nobody had been privy to the actual situation, given that the hopeful emigrants had been detained in the *Sonderlager* of Bergen-Belsen, and that the Gestapo had mounted astonishing demands in exchange for their liberation.

Yet the *aliyah* was set in motion, and although the destination lay to the East, the emigrants headed for the West. This fact alone implied that the process would not be smooth sailing. Indeed, the emigrants' crossing of the Hungarian border was preceded by great agitation with telegrams going back and forth, and news concerning the emigrants from Bergen-Belsen was rather depressing during the first few weeks. The reports were delivered – probably not without self-interest – by Krumey,[4] the deputy head of the detachment in charge of "de-Judaization." Several members of the Jewish Council were personally affected by the enterprise on account of family members and friends.[5] Fortunately, the Bergen-Belsen hopefuls included certain prominent Zionists, and the Jewry of the West raised a concerted effort through the mediation of neutral countries to save the

1   Raoul Wallenberg (1912–1947?), Swedish architect and diplomat. Following an assignment by the War Refugee Board, an American governmental organization, he joined the Swedish diplomatic mission in Budapest and provided assistance to Jews. Following his arrival in Budapest on 9 July 1944, he soon became the main actor behind Swedish rescue operations, issuing thousands of protective documents and placing numerous buildings under Swedish protection. Through his professional network as well as personal efforts, Wallenberg managed to save large numbers of people from the Arrow Cross regime. Soviet authorities arrested him in January 1945 and took him to Moscow. Having previously denied involvement in Wallenberg's disappearance, the Soviet government issued in 1957 an official statement that Wallenberg had died in prison in 1947, supposedly due to "heart failure."

2   A reference to the Kasztner Train passengers, who initially set out to emigrate to Mandatory Palestine. See 68–71.

3   About Ottó Komoly, see 68.

4   About Hermann Krumey, see 16.

5   The author does not mention that he himself had fourteen family members aboard the Kasztner Train. See lxviii.

whole group. The anabasis of this group came to be thought of as a matter of great historic significance. When they had made it to Switzerland, their creditable eyewitness reports helped stir foreign public opinion to action on behalf of the Jewry of Hungary. They brought a fresh dash of colour to the camp of emigrants in Switzerland, and when most of them ended up in Palestine in 1945, they were instrumental in reviving the Olej Hungaria (the Hungarian expatriate community) there.[6] Many of them would never have given up their professions, had their lives not been threatened by clear and present danger, and most found urban employment in Palestine.

But let us return to the impact this *aliyah* had on the home country in 1944. The group certainly set an edifying example; ultimately, it was the tortures inflicted by the Gestapo and the Gendarmerie, the agonies of ghettoization, and the deportations that familiarized Hungarian Jewry with the historic vision of Jewish unification in a single nation and a single country, where they would not be humiliated, harassed, or imprisoned in ghettos. The dialectic of Zionism pushed the movement to a turning point reminiscent of Marx's notion of collapse, or *Zusammenbruch*. There was no choice left for these Jews other than to return to the homeland of their ancestors; either that or let themselves be herded into wagons like livestock and carried off to the gas chambers of Auschwitz-Birkenau – names that by then had acquired a familiar ring thanks to the notorious pink "Waldsee postcards."[7] There was no time left for thinking. A miracle may have bailed them out on July 6, but the sword of Damocles continued to hover over the Jews of Budapest.

These realizations literally moved masses of people. Word got around that the first transport would be followed by many others. Later, sources close to Miklós Krausz, secretary of the Palestine Office,[8] leaked the information

6   Hitachdut Olej Hungaria, a cultural and welfare organization facilitating the social integration of Hungarian Jews settling in Mandatory Palestine and later Israel, active from the 1930s to the present day.

7   From Auschwitz, numerous Hungarian Jews were forced to send home cheery post-cards postmarked "Waldsee" (literally "Forest Lake"), a fictitious town invented by the Nazis to mask the destination of deported Jews. The deception was unmasked when a member of the Jewish Council discovered that the word *Waldsee* was superimposed on a hand-written word that ended in "witz."

8   Miklós Krausz (1908–1985), Zionist activist. Between 1938 and 1945, Krausz headed the Palestine Office in Budapest, a Zionist organization that carried out rescue activities in collaboration with members of the foreign diplomatic corps in Budapest. In the second half of June 1944, Krausz managed to get a copy of the Auschwitz Protocol to Switzerland, an event that helped trigger Horthy's halting of the deportations.

that a deal had been made with the Germans to transport several thousand Jews to the Holy Land via Romania and the Black Sea, this time not in cattle wagons but in third-class passenger cars.

The first *aliyah* had included several prominent Zionist leaders who had single-handedly run individual programs, and their departure was tantamount to the termination or atrophy of certain departments of the Jewish Council. This was the end of the Department of Provincial Affairs (not that any Jews whose affairs needed to be looked after remained in the provinces) and of the Information Office on the ground floor of the Síp Street headquarters, which had served as a regular meeting place for Zionist *chavers*.[9] Yet the Zionist organization itself lived on and continued to work smoothly. Not only did it prove itself fit to survive but there were early signs that it was practically the only Jewish organization capable of ruling the darkness at the apex of our existential crisis. The departed were replaced by newcomers. The figure of Ottó Komoly began to loom large, with negotiating partners who encompassed a wide circle, from the Gestapo to the outposts of the Hungarian resistance movement, to the conservative state secretary Miklós Mester.[10] Working side by side with Komoly were some of the old vanguard of the Zionist movement, including Dr Fábián Herskovits,[11] Dr Artúr Geyer,[12] and Mihály Salamon.[13] A crowd of thousands, hoping to get a ticket for the second transport, kept the Síp Street building under siege. During the morning hours, the applications were processed in the *yichud* or seclusion room of the Dohány Street Synagogue, while in the afternoon the applicants were received personally by Komoly in the tax office. (Under German protection in those days, Komoly and Kasztner were staying at the Institute for the Deaf on Columbus Street.)

On 24 July, he joined the Swiss Embassy and established the Emigration Department for Representing Foreign Interests in Budapest's so-called Glass House (see 218). Following the war, Krausz emigrated to Israel, where he worked for the Ministry of Social Affairs.

9 Hebrew for "friend" or "member."

10 About Miklós Mester, see 177.

11 See 143.

12 Artúr Geyer (1894–1976), rabbi, lawyer, Zionist activist. He was the librarian of the Rabbinical Seminary and a teacher of religion at the Jewish Grammar School.

13 Mihály Salamon (1897–1991), Zionist leader, member of the supervisory committee of the Palestine Office. After the war, he was chairman of the Hungarian Zionist Alliance and vice-chairman of the Pest Orthodox Congregation. He emigrated to Israel, where he worked as an editor and journalist.

At the pleading of foreign Jewish agencies, the Swiss legation undertook to organize the mission on the international level, and set up a separate division for the representation of "foreign interests" in collaboration with Miklós Krausz. Just as people had thought of ties with the Síp Street organization as a life-saving affiliation in the early days of the German occupation, now a movement away from Síp Street – under the motto "*los von Síputca* [away from Síp Street]" – gathered strength as many sought more powerful bastions of defence, whether subconsciously or for very rational reasons. Partially as a result of this trend, foreign interests preferred to set up their delegations in separate offices elsewhere. One summer evening, Arthur Weiss, a good fellow and the congregation's agile deputy prefect of ceremonies, announced his decision to relinquish to the Swiss legation his glass-panelled business centre at 29 Vadász Street, where the representation of foreign interests could operate as a separate department.[14] This decision marked the birth of the "Vadász Street shelter," which was to save hundreds of Jewish lives. Thenceforth, *aliyah* applicants abandoned Síp Street and pressed on to the "legation building" in Vadász Street, which soon evolved into a gigantic organization that even managed to win for its Jewish officials an exemption from having to wear the yellow star. All these circumstances gave leverage to the organization in its dealings with the authorities, while the "Twilight of the Gods" set in around the Council headquarters at Síp Street.

Before long, the list for the second transport was compiled and professionally bound amid diplomatic formalities as a collective passport, no less. This second transport, however, never left the city, in part because the

14 Better known as the Glass House (*üvegház*), the building at 29 Vadász Street, in Budapest's central 5th District (formerly owned by the glassware wholesaler Artúr Weiss [1897–1945]), served as headquarters for the Swiss embassy's Emigration Department for Representing Foreign Interests headed by the Swiss diplomatic officer Carl Lutz. (Hungary's anti-Jewish laws had forced Weiss to abandon the business.) Opened on 24 July 1944, the Glass House quickly became a focal point for Jews desperate to obtain protection letters from neutral countries, immigration certificates to Mandatory Palestine, "Schutz-passes," or other protective documents (legitimate and forged), escape routes, and other support necessary to stay alive. Apart from housing the Swiss rescue operations and offices for multiple covert Zionist resistance operations, the Glass House, protected by diplomatic immunity, also served as a shelter for several hundred to as many as two thousand Jews in late 1944 and early 1945. Artúr Weiss, who himself took shelter in the Glass House, was murdered by the Arrow Cross on 1 January 1945.

responsible leaders did not want to send the applicants into the wide-open arms of the Gestapo at Bergen-Belsen, and in part because the Germans made the official permission to emigrate through Romania contingent upon the commencement of deportations from Budapest.

Although everyone was waiting for a miracle in those days, some Jews looked to the land of Israel for that miracle, while others expected Christianity to supply it for them. In all honesty, this latter expectation was far from unrealistic. After all, people remembered the government's promise that no convert would be deported. Accordingly, an announcement posted around the streets of the city called on Jews who had been baptized prior to 1 August 1941 to report to the authorities in short order. Everyone had reason to assume that this would make a world of a difference. With the formation of the Alliance of Christian Jews, directly after the fiasco of the Baky coup on July 10, the new Christians were differentiated from the Jews, now in organizational form. The reasons for this must have been obvious to all. No wonder that huge masses of Jews reported to the local parish to be baptized – superficially or earnestly, as the case might be. Some were content to obtain fake (and often backdated) certificates of baptism in their own names, providing ample business for the newly sprung-up document forgery shops. Others would beleaguer pastors to baptize them before the prescribed Bible study period was up, and they often succeeded in these efforts. In some houses, the bomb shelters became classrooms where crash courses in Christian theology were taught to neophytes. Other would-be converts handled their case with pious earnestness, properly reporting to the rabbi as required, and then to the pastor of their new chosen religion, observing all necessary formalities. They considered it a duty to attend mass or service each day during the hours when Jews were permitted to go out. In any case, all allayed any pangs of conscience by telling themselves they were doing it as a "life-saving measure." Under the circumstances, it is hardly surprising that a Jew with ear locks and a kaftan was not an uncommon sight in the crowds waiting in line in front of the rectories.

The ordeal of the mass conversions proved so overwhelming that it seemed to sweep aside all commandments of the Jewish religion. Clerks at the headquarters of the Jewish Council worked away on Saturday as if it were any day of the week, while Jewish temples – or, to be more precise, those that had not been converted into internment camps or garrisons for labour servicemen – were completely empty. The struggle for survival threatened to wipe out generations of Jewish culture.

One day, early in July, a young man without a yellow star, who did not speak Hungarian, was picked out of the throng by the ushers on the third floor of the Síp Street headquarters and escorted to the president's room. The tailoring of his blue suit and his general appearance suggested a Western European man, albeit clearly not a German. Modestly withholding his title, he introduced himself simply as Wallenberg and said he came from the Swedish legation to talk with the Jewish Council. He was hustled into the always-crowded room and introduced to the president. In a moment, the stranger noticed Dr László Pető, a member of the team responsible for government relations, and addressed him directly. After the two exchanged a few confidential words at the window bay, they announced that the gentleman from the Swedish legation wished to speak to the leader of the Council on a crucial matter, whereupon the premises were vacated instantly. This is how Raoul Wallenberg, envoy of the king of Sweden, made his entrance. Luckily, he had been known to Pető from their student days, when they had shared a dormitory room in Thonon-les-Bains on the shore of Lake Geneva.[15] The consultation lasted for hours. At the time, not much could have leaked through the cushioned doors, but now we know that the young diplomat carried a hand-written letter from the king of Sweden to Horthy, asking the regent most emphatically to bring a halt to the deportations. (The letter indisputably played a role in the cancellation of the deportations on July 6. Replying to the letter through official diplomatic channels, Horthy pledged to uphold all standards of humanity to the degree permitted by the situation in Hungary.[16]) After Wallenberg left, three senior officials of the Jewish Council, namely Stern, Pető, and Wilhelm, stayed behind to continue the discussion among themselves. In the outcome of this meeting they finally resolved to draft a memorandum for the king of Sweden before the night was over. Their appeal to the king, written in German, reads as follows:

15   Wallenberg and Pető both spent part of the summer of 1929 studying French in the town of Thonon-les-Bains, although there is no evidence that they lived together.
16   There is no evidence of a hand-written letter from King Gustaf V of Sweden; however, the king did send a telegram to Regent Horthy on 30 June 1944, which was handed over by Ambassador Carl Ivan Danielsson and Secretary Per Anger on 5 July, shortly before the arrival of Raoul Wallenberg in Budapest. For an English translation of the telegram and Horthy's reply, see: Vági, Csősz, and Kádár, The Holocaust in Hungary, 135–6.

Your Majesty!

In the first place, despite our profound despair, we wish to convey to you our deepest thanks for the truly majestic steps undertaken on behalf of Hungarian Jewry.

We turn to Your Majesty in deep reverence with the request that you would command and permit the emigration of the approximately 200,000 Jews who are still in Hungary at this time.

It is our firm conviction that the only possibility that still exists for the salvation of the remaining Hungarian Jewry lies in emigration.

The possibility exists, however, only if:

(1) the Royal Hungarian government gives its permission for emigration;

(2) the Romanian government makes possible the emigration by granting permission for transit and making available means of transportation;

(3) the International Red Cross, or another organization of similar reputation, makes ships available in the port of Constanța;[17]

(4) the belligerent states allied with the Anglo-Saxons agree to the request to allow the ships to proceed unhindered despite the blockade;

(5) the necessary material means are obtained.

If for any reason there is no possibility for emigration in this manner, we appeal to your Majesty and humbly request that the internment of the Jewish community remaining in Hungary be facilitated in a neutral European state (such as Sweden) for the duration of the war, and that the fate of the Jewish community interned in such a manner be determined at the end of the war.

In order to carry out the specified tasks we request the dedicated support of your Majesty; firstly, the intervention at the highest levels of the Royal Hungarian government, since without such intervention the Hungarian Jewish community that still survives is doomed to destruction.

The dangerous shortage of time is the reason for our pleading, may your Majesty be so gracious as to issue immediately the concrete orders required.

---

17 The Port of Constanța, in Romania, the largest port on the Black Sea, was the main departure point for ships going to Mandatory Palestine during the war.

The situation in which we find ourselves explains also our humble plea that our cry for help, which we have been so free to submit to your Majesty, not become public in any way, shape, or form, and that the names of the undersigned be kept separate from the petition.

Budapest, 18 July 1944.

With deep reverence: (a) privy councillor Samuel Stern; (b) (signature illegible); (c) Dr Karl Wilhelm (Stamp), the provisional executive committee of the Union of Hungarian Jews.[18]

The next day, the document was handed to the courier for the Swedish legation. A few days later, Wallenberg was notified by telegram that the letter was delivered to the Ministry of Foreign Affairs and the king of Sweden.

This was the inception of the Swedish legation's rescue mission spearheaded by Wallenberg, who also succeeded in enlisting the chargé d'affaires of Portugal.[19] As we have seen, the Swiss legation, yielding to the influence of international Jewish agencies, took it upon itself to organize the "emigration transports." The nuncio's establishment, taking advantage of its extensive church connections, had long been active in the rescue effort, which was soon joined by the International Red Cross and, over time, by the Spanish legation as well. As one of the main points of his original commission, Wallenberg had brought with him 630 personalized entry permits, made out by the responsible Swedish ministry for those whose relatives, friends, or business partners in Stockholm had specifically applied for such permits in their names, as well as similar permits for notable Jewish personages such as Immánuel Lőw,[20] chief rabbi of Szeged, and his family. What with the ghettoization, the concentrations, and the general wartime conditions, it was only natural that the home address of most recipients had changed, so these had to be located. Wallenberg handed the list of 630 names to the government with the request to notify them and make preparations for

---

18   Munkácsi's comment (included in the main text of the Hungarian original): "No original of this letter survives. The author of this book received a copy in 1947 from the cabinet office of the king of Sweden via the Swedish Ministry of Foreign Affairs."

19   About Portugal's deputy ambassador Teixeira Branquinho, see 202.

20   Immánuel Lőw (1854–1944), chief rabbi of Szeged, renowned scholar and scientist, representative of the Jewish community in the Upper House of Parliament from 1927 to 1939. In late June 1944, at the age of ninety, he was forced into the ghetto in Szeged, and then deported, despite the intervention of Catholic prelates on his behalf. Pulled off the train in Budapest, he died in a Budapest hospital on 19 July 1944.

their emigration. (Later on I will speak about the ensuing process, which led to the establishment of the "international ghetto" and the notion of the so-called protected houses.)

The actions undertaken by the neutral legations triggered a peculiar development in the life of the city's Jewry. All the foreign representatives involved were of the smaller "legation" type, with only a handful of staff rather than full-blown embassies. How were they supposed to handle the onslaught of thousands of Hungarian Jews each day who, taking heart from the Wallenberg List and the first *aliyah*, rushed to apply for entry permits of their own? The recording of minutes, the filing and issuing of documents, and later the issuing of protective passes required an enormous apparatus for which the legations had neither the room nor the staff. The exodus from Síp Street was underway. The Zionists moved into the "Swiss" building on Vadász Street and continued to work there on the next *aliyahs* as "legation officials." Those who were unable to gain access there, or who simply could not cope with the idea of emigrating to Palestine, or had suitable connections elsewhere, stormed the other embassies and offered to work for them for free – some even offered their villas in Budapest.

Some of the intellectuals who had assembled at Síp Street following the German invasion, particularly those who spoke foreign languages, quit the Council headquarters, which they had come to regard as insufficient as a protective bulwark, and reinvented themselves as officials working under the Swiss, Swedish, Portuguese or Spanish legations, and the International Red Cross. Most of those remaining at Síp Street had commitments or emotional ties to the place or had nowhere else to go. This trend was encouraged by the fact that the Germans had rescinded the Gestapo identity documents, replacing them with passes issued by the Hungarian police which allowed freedom of movement until eight o'clock in the evening. These passes, handed out indiscriminately, in large numbers, afforded no protection whatsoever, absolute or relative. By contrast, embassy papers conferred upon the bearer the highest degree of liberty a Jew could hope to attain in those days: Exemption from the requirement to display the yellow star. Those in possession of embassy certificates were free to come and go and travel as they pleased, go shopping, see a motion picture, or sit around in a café – in short, to enjoy all the luxuries of a bygone world. Small wonder, then, that the so-called "men of means" abandoned Síp Street in droves to find employment at one of the legations, or indeed at several legations simultaneously, as was often the case.

It is only natural that some of these "accidental" embassy officials were prone to occasional abuse. There were widespread rumours about how many things could be arranged with money. Learning their lessons from the example of the provinces, the newly appointed "legation officials" quickly moved out of the star-marked buildings, where they obviously felt unsafe, and either set up residence in houses unmarked by a yellow star or furnished their sleeping quarters in the legation buildings themselves. They went by the assumption that these buildings enjoyed diplomatic immunity and were considered off limits for both the Gestapo and the Hungarian police. Later, in the Szálasi era after October 15, this practice evolved into an immense, well-organized mechanism.

Access to such life-saving schemes was mostly the privilege of the well-to-do and the well-connected, although there were some exceptions. They were also more likely than others to be informed to some extent of events that had occurred and of the next scare of the day. The Germans' loss of trust in the Council after July 6 also contributed to the decline of Síp Street's authority. Until then, the Germans believed that, in a manner of speaking, the Council had been successfully duped. Now, in the wake of the events of recent weeks, it began to dawn on the Germans that the Council had kept in touch with certain Hungarian governmental circles, and that the Jewish leaders must have exerted an influence on the regent and his allies. The Gestapo must have had no difficulty in learning that the Auschwitz Protocols and various other underground pamphlets were in general circulation. This meant that the would-be victims knew their turn would come soon. Having realized this, the Gestapo in Svábhegy fell into conspicuous silence. Eichmann stamped his feet in fury over the botched coup attempt of June 10, but there was precious little he could do with his staff of only 160 SS men. Some of the Gestapo officers had gone away. Wisliceny, the commander-in-chief of deportations, was spending his "vacation" at Lake Balaton. Who knew for how long – days or weeks? The usual "service orders" from Svábhegy petered out. To all appearances, the Germans' trust had been shaken and something was in the works. At first, Eichmann had plans to deport Jews from the 7th, 8th, and 9th Districts of the city in several installments. Shortly thereafter, he would have settled for entraining ten thousand Jews.

Meanwhile the time came to seek out and locate the 630 individuals on Wallenberg's list. This provided Ferenczy, the bloody executioner of the deportations, with an opportunity to establish direct contact with the Jewish

Council for the first time. In his testimony, Ferenczy described the events following the failure of the first deportation attempt as follows:

A long period of stagnation set in. The Germans resorted to various tricks of intimidation to enforce the deportations from Budapest, for instance by threatening to commission a separate SS division and to initiate a full-scale occupation campaign placing the whole country under German protectorate. At about this time I delivered a memorandum to Minister of the Interior Jaross describing the atrocities and further plans of the Germans. On this occasion, I recommended that the minister of the interior relinquish the entire Jewish question and its solution to the Germans. Let them implement it! The minister of the interior said this was out of the question. If they allowed the Germans to take charge, the government would have to resign. There would also be the risk of the German action getting out of control to the point of affecting Christians, and it would all end in pillage and plunder, he said. Afterward, I provided much the same account to Prime Minister Sztójay, who received me in the company of István Antal, the minister of justice. I recall having reported to the prime minister at another meeting that was attended by Béla Imrédy, Bálint Hóman,[21] and Reményi-Schneller.[22]

Previously, I had requested that Eichmann allow me to travel to Auschwitz to look around and see with my own eyes how the Jews were sorted and put to work. Eichmann gave his unconditional consent to this plan. I related the meeting to Prime Minister Sztójay, who ordered me to go and, upon my return, to report to him on my experiences. I had also previously obtained the permission

21 Bálint Hóman (1885–1951), professor of history, member of the Hungarian Academy of Sciences, politician. Minister of religion and education of Hungary, 1932–38 and 1939–42, and an MP representing the governing party from 1932 to 1945, he was a staunch supporter of the anti-Jewish laws and of Hungary's alliance with Germany. Unlike most MPs, he continued to attend parliament meetings after the Arrow Cross takeover. After the war, having fled to Germany, he was captured by US troops and extradited to Hungary, where he was found guilty of war crimes and sentenced to life imprisonment in 1946. He died in prison.

22 See 73.

of Lieutenant General Faraghó for the trip. I then drafted a
memorandum for Prime Minister Sztójay exclusively on the subject of
the conduct and attitude of the Germans. Finally, I set about making
preparations for my trip. When all that was left to do was to set the
exact date of my departure, I put in my request to Eichmann, who said
he would approve my trip but not until thirty days after the arrival
of the last transport at the camp. From this it was obvious to me that
the widespread rumours about Jews unfit to work being executed
in crematoria had to be based in fact. I then asked Prime Minister
Sztójay to help me make an appointment with the regent. Sztójay
promised this but cautioned me against denigrating the Germans
too much, saying that Horthy was very angry with them as it was.
However, I soon realized that my audience with the regent was not
going to happen through this channel. With the Germans constantly
urging the deportation of the Jews from Budapest, I decided to find
another way to meet Horthy.

(We shall see later on how Lieutenant Colonel Ferenczy finally managed to
meet Horthy through the mediation of the Jewish Council.)

The Wallenberg List provided the mass executioner of Hungarian Jewry
with the opportunity to face the leaders of the same. Around the middle of
July, the Jewish Council received instructions by telephone to dispatch one
of its members for a hearing before Ferenczy. In those days, few details were
known about Ferenczy's activities, other than that he had been in charge of
Gendarmerie operations during the deportations from the Northern Province.
No one knew about his actual function as liaison officer between Eichmann's
Sonderkommando and the Ministry of the Interior. The telephone call
elicited shock and trepidation. Dr István Kurzweil[23] agreed to the meeting
on behalf of the Council, and promptly reported to Ferenczy at his office on
the ground floor of the Pest County Hall overlooking Semmelweis Street.
Ferenczy said that, under the terms of an agreement with certain foreign
legations and the German authorities, a certain number of Jews would be
allowed to emigrate to Palestine and some other countries. (The number of
Jews permitted to leave for Sweden was 630, the number on Wallenberg's
list, while the head count of the new group bound for Palestine was set at
two thousand.) He said that this emigration would take place shortly, and

23   About István Kurzweil, see 54.

the requisite number of train cars had been made available. The departures would be attended to and supervised by representatives from the foreign legations. In the meantime, as the preparations would take five to six days, the emigrants had to be provided temporary accommodation in yellow-star houses, with the proviso that nobody else – meaning non-emigrating Jews – was allowed to stay in those buildings during this period. According to Ferenczy, this latter measure was justified for reasons of security and law enforcement. Consequently, Ferenczy called on the Jewish Council to vacate houses in sufficient numbers to put up 2,500 emigrating Jews. He made it a point that these houses had better be modern and equipped with the latest amenities because, as he said, it was important for him to know that the Jews arriving in a foreign country would attest to the impeccable treatment they had received back home. One of his most strikingly dubious statements was that the relocation of the emigrants would cause no inconvenience at all in view of the temporary nature of their stay. For this reason, the Jews moving out of their star-marked houses should not bring with them anything but the most basic necessities, since they would be returning to their homes after the prescribed period ended. By the same token, it was not necessary to take an inventory of their possessions left at home, as there was no risk of anybody misappropriating anything from the owners, who were staying elsewhere temporarily.

Having considered Ferenczy's pronouncements, the Council immediately smelled massive peril. (It was readily apparent that allowing 2,500 persons to leave was an omen for the deportation of the Jewry of Budapest.) Accordingly, the Jewish Council resolved to stall for as long as it was possible. On the one hand, they realized that refusing Ferenczy's demands point-blank was out of the question, if only to protect the interests of the Jews allegedly on the brink of emigration. On the other hand, they were painfully aware of the great threat to life and property that the action implied, not to mention the fact that the departure of the city's protected Jews – who numbered a total of 2,630 at the time – would open the sluice gate for the deportation of the entire Jewry of Budapest.[24]

In hindsight it seems certain that the system of so-called protected houses had already occurred to Ferenczy and the Germans by then, as had

24 "Protected Jews" were those with certificates showing that they were under the protection of one of the neutral diplomatic missions in Budapest, a number that eventually increased sharply from the 2,630 cited here.

the idea of an international ghetto, which would come to be implemented later under Szálasi's rule.[25]

As it turned out, the Council's strategy of procrastination worked to some extent. A few days later, when Ferenczy called to find out if any progress had been made, he was told that the Council was unable to proceed in the absence of the requisite personal data, because it was inevitable, by the very nature of the plan, that those moving out to make room for the emigrating Jews, in what would later be termed "protected houses," would themselves have to be moved mainly into the homes those Jews had vacated. The Council pointed out that this solution could not be dispensed with, otherwise there would be no room for the emigrating Jews in the already overcrowded "protected" houses. Ferenczy acknowledged the quandary and promised to make arrangements for a list of names to be handed over. A few days later, Ferenczy did deliver the first Swedish list, and copies were soon made available on the desks in the Council offices for anyone to read the names of the fortunate holders of permits to enter Sweden, hopefully with the blessing of German and Hungarian authorities. The Swedish list of 630 names was thus in hand. But what about the two thousand slated to leave for Palestine? As everyone could see that the whole action was but a way of gearing up for the all-out deportation of the city's Jewry, the Council tried to buy more time by preventing the Palestinian list, supplied by Ferenczy, from reaching the Swiss legation, its intended recipient. But Ferenczy knew what he was doing. He grew impatient and began to marshal serious threats to lend weight to his demands. Finally, the Council notified Ferenczy of having designated a few tenement buildings in Pozsonyi Street for those leaving for Sweden, effectively laying the cornerstone of the so-called international ghetto that would later come to comprise buildings along Pozsonyi Street and the neighbouring streets of the Lipótváros district.

This, then, was how communications began between Ferenczy and the Jewish Council of Budapest. One day around the middle of July, Ferenczy, in a mood even more ferocious than usual, ordered certain members of the Council to appear and talk with him in person. When Dr Ernő Pető,

25 Beginning in November 1944, several apartment buildings – "protected houses" or "safe houses" – in what is today Budapest's 13th District were reserved exclusively for "protected Jews." This is the area that the author refers to here as the "international ghetto." In theory, Jews in protected houses were safer than those forced to live in the official enclosed Jewish ghetto of the 7th District; however, many "protected" Jews were also harassed and murdered by Arrow Cross squads.

Dr János Gábor, the Rabbi Béla Berend, and Dr István Kurzweil reported to his office, Ferenczy, with gendarme captain Leó Lulay in attendance, gave them a nearly four-hour-long diatribe against the Gestapo and its local agencies in Hungary, whom he said they were fighting "tooth and nail" while endangering their own lives. They asked the Council members present for the truth concerning the reports from Auschwitz, because they had been trying in vain to obtain permits to travel there to see for themselves. The Council members explained the point of view of the Jewry in detail. Dr Pető pointed out that the military winds had shifted, and it was conceivable that Germany stood to lose the war; if this were the case, the ensuing peace treaty could be extremely damaging to Hungary on account of its treatment of its Jews. As a result of this exchange, Ferenczy asked the Council to remain in contact with him as the official liaison between the Hungarian and the German authorities.

~ ~ ~

The village of Kistarcsa is located about 20 kilometres northeast of Budapest along the paved military thoroughfare to Gödöllő. If you are not new to these parts, you will recall the many abrupt dips and bumps on the road that make for a veritable rollercoaster ride. The village itself is situated on the edge of the Kerepes forest, from which you can see as far as the Danube. Ease of access and other advantages made the location suitable as a site for constructing a huge machine factory before the First World War. The large masses of workers lured to the area by the manufacturing industry had to be accommodated somewhere, and the managers of the factory chose to erect for them high-rise proletarian tenement buildings rather than family homes. The bleak grey walls of these buildings rise up to the sky menacingly, in stark contrast to the otherwise quaint rural environment. When the factory shut down in the 1920s, the workers scattered, leaving the apartment towers empty. They were eventually acquired by the state and put to a very different use in harmony with the spirit of the times: They were converted into a temporary detention centre for vagrants, in order to relieve some of the burden on the overcrowded Mosonyi Street facility in the city.[26] As part of the project, the former workers' towers of Kistarcsa were surrounded by high

26   The Royal Hungarian Police detention house on Mosonyi Street in Budapest's 8th District.

walls and a handful of small pavillions were built to accommodate offices and police staff. Finally, the walls were topped with barbed wire charged with high-voltage electricity and the entire facility was fortified with four tall watchtowers from which the guards could look out a great distance without losing sight of any escapees. The place did not require any major alteration to become the infamous internment camp of Kistarcsa, the source of innumerable grim memories for Hungarian Jewry.[27]

The camp was visited frequently by the legal-aid staff of the Pest Congregation and later by representatives from the Support Office[28] to provide their interned brethren with legal advice and provisions. Of course, in those days – this was the "Gömbös Era"[29] – large groups of Jews were taken to this camp on account of their political conduct or "unsettled" citizenship status. The envoys of the Support Office began to talk with the camp police on duty, and their relations became more and more friendly as time went by. The deputy rabbi of Kistarcsa lived just a few steps from the detainment facility and had complete access there.

These relations deteriorated and became tense starting in 1941 when approximately thirty thousand Jews were accused of not holding Hungarian citizenship, after which most of them were transferred to Galicia. By the summer of 1944, the village of Kistarcsa was entirely empty of Jews. Those unable to escape to the capital were deported, their property confiscated, and their personal belongings sold. The Gestapo established a horse stable in the local Jewish temple.

During this year of terror, Kistarcsa became a household word. Many notable figures of Hungarian Jewry served a prison sentence there, and thousands of families everywhere were no longer capable of uttering the name of Kistarcsa without an intense loathing. When the Germans began to apprehend Jews in the city on March 19, the detainees were sorted at the facility in Mosonyi Street; some were released from custody, but most were taken to Kistarcsa, where the head count increased daily.

The plans for deporting the Jews of Budapest from July 6 to 10 may have fallen through, but SS Colonel Eichmann, the overlord of the "de-Judaization" detachment, was not a man to resign himself to defeat. He carried on with

27 For more about Kistarcsa, see the Glossary.
28 The Support Office of Hungarian Israelites (Magyar Izraeliták Pártfogó Irodája or MIPI), created in 1938 to support people who lost their jobs due to the anti-Jewish laws.
29 Gyula Gömbös, prime minister of Hungary between 1932 and 1936.

his usual barrage of threats and demands, warning that, if the Gendarmerie deserted him, an entire SS division in Budaörs was only waiting for his command to entrain the Jews of Budapest. Ferenczy – whose relations with the regent will be discussed later in this book – ascertained that this was untrue: There were SS troops stationed just outside the capital, but far short of the numbers claimed by Eichmann. This meant that, absent the support of the Hungarian Gendarmerie, Eichmann was clearly powerless. However, he felt the obligation to uphold the authority of the Gestapo and act using the meagre forces that he had at his disposal.

Kidnapping the Kistarcsa detainees provided a natural segue into resuming the deportations. This was first attempted by the Germans on July 14. All detainees, except for those in Pavilion B where hostages were kept, were loaded into train wagons. Luckily, the Jewish Council learned about the incident in time to mobilize its connections to the regent. They also called Apor, the bishop of Győr,[30] asking for his urgent intervention on grounds of the agreement between the government and the churches. Horthy sent for the minister of the interior, who then instructed Ferenczy to establish the facts. Ferenczy found out that some 1,500 people had been entrained, including inmates from the facilities at Rökk Szilárd Street[31] and Csepel.[32] Horthy issued orders to stop the train and return the detainees to their respective facilities. The command caught up with the train near the town of Hatvan, and the Jewish internees were back in Kistarcsa before the end of the evening.

But Eichmann would not rest. Despite the "small number of individuals involved," the Kistarcsa deportation proved to be a test case for deciding the all-important question: Who was the boss in Hungary? Just as German tanks and armoured vehicles roared down the streets of Budapest to demonstrate the might of the *Herrenvolk* ("master race") a few days after Baky's failed coup attempt, so too did the master of "de-Judaization" feel that no sacrifice was too great for him to show who was in charge when it came to the Jewish question.

Five days later, on July 19, a telephone call early in the morning summoned every Council member to Gestapo headquarters in Svábhegy, effective immediately. The only personnel left in the Síp Street building were the

---

30 About Bishop Vilmos Apor, see 201.
31 See 35.
32 See 91.

clerical staff, who did not know what to make of this early-morning mobilization of their superiors. They were aware of the intense conflict between the regent's entourage and the Germans, and had heard the rumours about Baky's coup attempt. On the upside, their confidence had been strengthened by the increasingly self-assured stance of the regent, as evinced by his resolve a few days earlier to stop and shunt a deportation train bound for an unknown destination across the border. They believed that the Council members would return by noon, if not sooner. That time passed, and still no news came. Instead, something else happened.

Early in the afternoon, Dr Sándor Bródy,[33] who was assigned to maintain contact with Kistarcsa on behalf of the Support Office, burst into the office in a terribly agitated state, his hair damp with sweat, and blurted out that the detainees of Kistarcsa had been kidnapped by the Gestapo. Everyone in the camp, except for Pavillion B, had been loaded into trucks and entrained at the station in Rákoscsaba. The fiendishly brutal action was led by Sturmbannführer Novak[34] and, on behalf of the Hungarian Gestapo, Pál Ubrizsi, assistant draftsman of the police and commander of the prison on Rökk Szilárd Street. One detainee was so old and weak with disease that he could not climb up onto the truck's high step. Two SS thugs grabbed him and roughly hurled him onto the floor of the truck. By the time his body made contact, the old man was dead. Then there was a disabled man who wanted to take his wheelchair. "You are not going to need that any more," the SS told him with an evil sneer.

The appearance of Dr Bródy hinted at some kind of a link between the kidnapping from Kistarcsa and the summoning of the Council, but the breadth of the correlation remained hidden until the following day.

The Council members were let go late that evening. As it turned out, they had waited hours before being finally received by Hunsche, Eichmann's deputy,[35] who asked them questions about the most trivial matters. For instance, he wanted to know why Jews did not go to the movies and how it might be possible to improve their general mood.

---

33 The author probably means Ernő Bródy, see 89.
34 About SS-Hauptsturmführer Franz Novak, see 75.
35 Otto Hunsche (1911–1994), lawyer, SS-Hauptsturmführer, member of Eichmann's Sondereinsatzkommando in Hungary. In the 1960s, three consecutive trials were initiated against him and Hermann Krumey. In the first two trials Hunsche was acquitted, but in the third, in 1969, he was sentenced to twelve years in prison, a conviction upheld in 1973.

The next day, on July 20, everything became clear. Fearing that the Council would mobilize the regent as it had on the previous occasion, Eichmann and his buddies had called for the members to appear in Svábhegy. Meanwhile, the SS stormed the camp in Kistarcsa, cut the telephone lines, and carried out the deportation.[36] This proved that the Gestapo knew everything, including the Council's contacts and lines of communication.

A few days later, the Jews of the internment camp of Sárvár were deported in much the same way.[37]

By then, Ferenczy had taken over as the agent with executive powers overseeing Jewish affairs across the board. No longer having anything to do in the provinces, he now established himself in Budapest permanently. He saw many things. For one thing, it was plain to him that the regent had turned against the Germans. He felt that his career and thus also his life were at stake in the faltering action of which he, as the bloody executioner, had been put in charge. He had to do something. He harboured the ambition of becoming the plenipotentiary administrator of Jewish affairs – a position that seemed not impossible to attain now that Endre and Baky had been removed from the equation. The two had remained in office on paper, but without any real powers to act. At first, Ferenczy tried gaining admittance to the regent with the assistance of Sztójay. When this did not work out, he looked for another channel. He contacted the Jewish Council, selling himself as the "enemy" of the Germans, as we have seen.

The exact details of Ferenczy's about-face are yet to be uncovered. For now, relevant evidence includes the depositions of Council leaders before the police and the People's Court, which tally in most respects with Ferenczy's own testimony. There is also indirect evidence. In the summer of 1944, the author of this book had a conversation with Father József Jánosi[38] in the garden of the boys' orphanage. Jánosi had knowledge that, earlier that day, Ferenczy got to the regent through the mediation of the Jewish Council, and had high hopes for the outcome of his audience.

In the wake of his talks with senior Council officials, Ferenczy paid two visits to Samu Stern[39] in his home. Anybody present may have been

36 See the Glossary entry on Kistarcsa.
37 See the Glossary entry on Sárvár.
38 About the Jesuit priest József Jánosi, see 172.
39 About Jewish Council president Samu Stern, see 14.

reminded of a scene of farcical horror from a Grand Guignol show[40] as the man responsible for the deportation of 500,000 Jews from the provinces politely entered and took a seat in great decorum in the same room where, for the past decade and a half, the most vital issues of the Jewry had been debated. What a travesty! Here we had gendarme Lieutenant Colonel Ferenczy conducting well-mannered negotiations in premises where the aspirations and ambitions of Hungarian Jewry from bygone better times still lingered in the air.

In his testimony, Dr Pető described these meetings as follows:

> Dr Károly Wilhelm, Samu Stern, and myself had a series of meetings with Ferenczy and Lulay. I tried to convince them that, if the Germans insisted on trying to push through their deportation program, which we had reason to fear they would, but the Hungarian authorities resisted, the Germans would not risk a conflict in view of the changed military situation. We devised a plan whereby they and the Gendarmerie would pretend to remain committed to the deportations, but would ultimately step in to prevent the implementation if the Germans went ahead. They would bring five thousand gendarme troops to the city, replace unreliable officers, and mobilize the special response corps from Esztergom. Ferenczy said that would be more than enough to outnumber the SS forces, who were by then reduced to 1,800 men. At one of the meetings in the home of Samu Stern, Ferenczy, and Lulay came up with the idea that we should try to procure for Ferenczy an audience with the regent, sidestepping official channels.

Pető further testified that Ferenczy and Lulay insisted on the strictest confidentiality, stipulating that nobody must know about the matter apart from Stern, Wilhelm, and himself. Ferenczy and his men were supposed to make it appear in the eyes of the Germans as if, by ordering the Gendarmerie forces to Budapest, they were going about the preparations as planned. Then, at the very last moment, they would refuse cooperation and declare their willingness, should the Germans pursue the matter, to mount an armed resistance

---

40 Le Théâtre du Grand-Guignol (literally "Theatre of the Big Puppet"), in operation in Paris from 1897 to 1962, was a legendary "house of horror," with performances that mixed gruesome violence, comedy, and social commentary.

to stop the deportation of Jews. Pető informed Horthy Jr of these talks. At first, the regent's son voiced his misgivings about Ferenczy's involvement, owing to his "bad reputation." Pető defended him as someone who, although known to the Jewish Council to have perpetrated acts of villainy in the provinces, had come to form a more realistic view of the Germans' military position and was keen on "distinguishing himself" in the effort of rescuing Jews as a means of expiating his sins. Ferenczy and Lulay also insisted that the plan be concealed from the members of Sztójay's cabinet, arguing that its premature airing would thwart successful implementation.

It was after this, some time in August, that Ferenczy presented his wish that the Council persuade the regent to receive him and instruct him directly, in person, to prevent the deportation. Pető relayed the request to Horthy Jr the same afternoon. The following day, the reply came to the effect that "Ferenczy will be received by the regent at 4 p.m." Following the audience, Ferenczy and Lulay dropped by Samu Stern's residence to report on what had happened. Ferenczy said he had spent hours with the regent, revealing to him all the infamies of the Gestapo. Thereupon the regent issued clear-cut orders for Ferenczy to prevent the deportation of the Jews of Budapest, by force of arms if need be.

According to his testimony, Ferenczy had a face-to-face meeting with the regent on three subsequent occasions. On one of these occasions, Horthy gave him the task of feeling out the actual military capabilities of German forces stationed in Hungary. Ferenczy found that, early on in the occupation, Germany had maintained five divisions in Transdanubia for the purpose of holding the regent and the capital in check. However, this initial number then began to decrease rapidly. By the time Ferenczy reported to the regent on August 20, German military presence in Hungary had dwindled to the point that hardly any operational troops remained in the country apart from command staff, institutions, and training corps. By any reckoning, this intelligence must have had a major influence on the memorable speech the regent delivered at the Ludovika Military Academy on August 20, to which I shall return later in this book.

~ ~ ~

Before moving on to discuss the deportation crisis and the events that led up to August 27, we cannot avoid describing the climate in foreign circles and the actual state of the Jewry's internal affairs.

On July 20 the following sensational article appeared in the evening
edition of the *St Gallener Tagblatt*, the large-circulation Swiss daily:

The Chivalrous
The Red Cross action was a success, and quite a resounding one.
To date, they have managed to save the lives of probably more than
half a million people by interceding with the gentlemen running
Hungary today.

Yet, giving any of the credit to these gentlemen themselves, even
with a single word of gratitude or a single breath of appreciation,
would be far more praise than they deserve. After all, they had resolved
to consign half a million individuals, mostly citizens of their country,
to the fate of gruesome extermination – albeit not until after they had
been robbed and subjected to torture. And robbed and dispossessed is
what they all became, save perhaps for a few millionaires who had had
the foresight to rescue some of their fortune from the greed of their
callous homeland, and thus had the means, in foreign currency, to
purchase two aircraft from the Gestapo.[41] As to murder, that enterprise
only succeeded in respect of 400,000 people. [In fact, that number
was already higher by the time this article was published.] Has the
world ever seen a thing more hypocritical than that first semi-official
communiqué?[42] But what exactly had happened? "Nothing but what
all the other countries had agreed on: A transport of labour force,"
or so the official explanation went. It is only natural that Jews were
proffered for this purpose. In any event, Hungary, in all probability for
reasons of lacking gassing facilities of sufficient capacity and nothing
else, merely undertook "technical arrangements." A labour force, to
be sure – sometimes including trainloads, sixty wagons at a time, of
children aged two to twelve. True enough, no hard work was ever
expected of them – just a brief stroll to the nearby barracks!

The response of the Hungarian authorities to the intervention of
the Red Cross was clearly drafted by the same person who had worded
the communiqué. Yes, the deportations were going to be stopped.

41 A reference to the extended intertwined Weiss and Chorin families, who were among
    the leading Hungarian industrialists of the time. Blackmailed by the Nazis, the family
    handed over their assets to the SS (among them Manfréd Weiss Works, Hungary's
    largest armament complex), in exchange for which the Nazis allowed forty members
    of the family to leave the country.
42 It is unclear what "communiqué" the author is referring to.

But not a single word has been uttered about the life conditions – or, rather, death conditions – awaiting the survivors. No amendment has been made to the regulations that continue to keep entire families crowded together in a single room, prohibited from going out except for a few hours a day, or from receiving visitors, or even from earning an income of their own. How generous that they should be allowed to be sent food. It is indeed a "poignant concession," in that it enables the country to spare its own national food supplies for export to its poor neighbours. Children under ten are permitted to travel abroad, provided they possess valid visas. In the unlikely event that all these children are granted asylum outside their homeland, they will of course need transit visas as well, which will be not very easy to obtain, given the shortage of train wagons in the transit country. Wagons are only kept available for trips to Auschwitz, you see. And imagine that the Jews are even allowed to head out for Palestine! We are talking about hundreds of thousands of people graciously given the right to leave their country as paupers, and should England refuse to issue visas *en masse*, the cabinet of Sztójay will surely not be blamed for the resulting loss of so many lives in one way or another. It is by such manoeuvres that Messrs Sztójay and Imrédy (the latter of whom had just recently succeeded in sawing his Jewish grandmother off his family tree) have sought to silence foreign opinion, which continues to be regarded as a matter of some consequence in certain circles in Hungary, as well as to silence underground opinion within the country – the only brand of domestic discontent remaining, now that there is no open public opinion in Hungary any more to talk about. And it would be impossible to deny that these gentlemen have reason to expect to see some results here and there, for there will always be people eager and happy to reassure themselves. However, the rationalizations of Sztójay et al. will surely fall on deaf ears with those, in Hungary and elsewhere in the world, who have held on to a modicum of humanity and a trace of independent thought.

No country, least of all Hungary, has the right to appeal to the government of England, a country entrenched in the thick of a war, to admit masses of its citizens numbering in the hundreds of thousands. Even making the requisite "technical arrangements" for this admission would involve more people than the Hungarian citizens extradited by the Sztójay cabinet to Germany, including women, children, and the elderly.

The overlords of Hungary know all of this perfectly well, which is one reason why they look in vain for gratitude for temporarily being satisfied with 400,000 "deliveries." Hungary likes to be thought of as a chivalrous and brave Christian nation. They certainly used to have a more rightful claim to these epithets in the past. But how they really wish to be seen on their own turf today was illustrated with the most barefaced eloquence by a man named János Treitel in Budapest the other day.[43] This man and his gang had just days earlier burglarized two Jewish women before butchering them in the most bestial manner imaginable. "We only implemented the government's intentions, and should deserve a medal of honour for doing so," the murderer said later. Then, as if in an attempt to compensate Hungarian citizens for its inability to inform them on the true details of the "labour service" performed by the extradited Jews, the Hungarian press went on to describe the murders in the most lurid detail. Treitel and his cronies have been sentenced to death by hanging. He will not be entirely unjustified in asking why he has been singled out for this punishment. The whole issue will certainly survive him.

This splendidly sarcastic article in the Swiss paper left a deep impression on its readers.

During the last week of July 1944, the Jewish Council delivered a memorandum to influential men in authority and the churches which it hoped would help save the day. The document paints a vivid picture of the situation the capital's Jewry faced between the first and second deportation attempts. It read as follows:

Following the transportations in May and June of the entire Jewish population of the provinces, a total of 500,000 individuals, and the concentration in the transit camp in Budakalász and subsequent deportation at the beginning of July of the 20,000 Jews living in towns and settlements in the vicinity of Budapest, the problem of Hungarian Jewry has essentially shrunk to the approximately 200,000 Jews in Budapest who await the consummation of their fate amid a barrage of often contradictory news reports.

43 This story is probably apocryphal: no reference to János Treitel's crime or sentence could be found in archival documents or press reports.

The herding together of nearby resident Jews in the Budakalász transit camp early last month, along with the unspeakable circumstances accompanying that action and all the physical and spiritual suffering inflicted upon these miserable victims, culminating in their deportation from the Budakalász camp, have traumatized the Jewry of the capital, who feel that their own annihilation is just around the corner.

Various measures have been put forward to stop further deportations, and certain reassuring statements to this effect have been made by competent officials in the presence of high clergy.

News of the suspension of deportations in the first half of July has brought a measure of relief to the tense mood among the capital's Jewry. The large number of gendarme troops assigned to Budapest, which had assisted the deportations in the provinces and around Budapest by methods and means already known to the public, have now left the city, and there are other signs to suggest that the deportations have ceased for the time being.

For all these positive developments, on the 19th of this month the German authorities proceeded to entrain and send off the approximately 1,200 Jews held in Kistarcsa. The train was, however, returned to Kistarcsa on the orders of the government. In spite of this, it seems that the intention to halt the deportations did not work out. Only two days later, the German authorities – no doubt with the approval of certain Hungarian authorities – took the internees of Kistarcsa, some of them on foot, some loaded onto trucks, to the station in Rákoscsaba, where they were forced into wagons and dispatched to an unknown location outside the country.[44] In effect, this action overruled the decision to halt the deportations. The German authorities seem to be sticking to their deportation plans and thus to the overall scheme of liquidating the entire Jewry of Hungary, even as the Hungarian government itself appears to be divided on the issue.

The mounting apprehension among the Jews of Budapest has been aggravated by reports of new gendarme detachments arriving in the city

---

44 The memorandum is not quite accurate. It was on 14 July 1944 that Eichmann's men attempted to deport the Kistarcsa inmates, but were stopped by the Hungarian authorities who turned back the train. However, five days later, on 19 July, an SS unit under the command of Hauptsturmführer Franz Novak again raided Kistarcsa, sending 1,220 people to Auschwitz. See the Glossary entry on Kistarcsa.

and of the unexpected resumption of the deportation campaign in the near future. It is no wonder that, spiritually overwrought and physically exhausted by the torments they have had to endure in the past four months, the remaining Jewry is prone to lend credence to these reports.

The press reports describing the situation of those deported to Germany are widely held by the Jews to be manipulated and incredible, designed to allay fears and to reassure public opinion.

The rampant restlessness and trepidation is further augmented by the fact that the hundreds of thousands of deportees, with very few exceptions, have sent no sign of life for months.

Quite apart from this, the situation of the 200,000 Jews of Budapest, huddled together in 1,900 designated buildings, has been critical to say the least. First to be mentioned is the nearly brutal reduction of food rations without regard to the needs of children, the elderly, and the sick, which continues to slowly but steadily undermine the physical strength of the people, particularly the children and the old, who have already been exposed to higher risks of disease given their accommodation in such tight quarters.

A recent decree has placed restrictions on the free movement of Jews, preventing them from leaving their residences except between eleven o'clock and five o'clock in the afternoon. In one fell swoop, this regulation has eliminated the livelihood of large numbers of labourers and the few white-collar employees who had managed to hold onto their jobs, as they are now unable to report for work in the morning.

Moreover, the freezing of Jews' assets has plunged many families into the most severe predicament.

The revenues of Jewish social and other public-minded institutions have petered out almost completely, thwarting any welfare and charity work at a time when such services are most needed.

As per official regulation, Jews are no longer eligible for public aid. The overload of Jewish hospitals has presented the Jewish Council with insurmountable difficulties in administering proper care for the unusually large numbers of the sick, not least because the admission of Jewish patients to the city's public hospitals has been practically discontinued.

The situation of the Jewry is further exacerbated by the shuttering of Jewish-owned retail shops and enterprises, which has resulted in widespread unemployment among those living on wages and salaries, and even ruined many with independent means.

The Jews of Budapest with permitted cash on their hands use these funds to live on, but the number of those who have completely depleted their savings increases day by day. Barred from taking up employment, these people and their families are headed for utter disaster. The majority of the Jewry, who have always relied on their own physical or intellectual work to support themselves and have no reserves to fall back on, have for some time barely eked out a miserable living. To add woe to injury, the Jewish associations and institutions are unable to help them for the reasons outlined above.

This harsh predicament, which fills the Jewry of Budapest with despair, will not be alleviated until the restrictive measures are lifted, allowing Jewish employees and tradesmen to carry on with their professions, and the jobless to reoccupy their place in production in the appropriate manner. Not only would this serve the best interests of the country but it would rescue thousands of families from collapse.

The Jewry stands ready to accept any work assignment. Just the other day we saw the commencement of a project of clearing the ruins organized and manned by the Jewish Council and overseen by the Ministry of National Defence. The project employs two thousand people, and this number is expected to grow.

The leaders of the Jewry have developed and delivered to the government a detailed program for the employment of the Jewish workforce of the city. By so doing, we wish to demonstrate that the Jews of Budapest are willing to undertake any work, be it the hardest physical labour, in the interest of the country and in order to save their families.

It is to be mentioned that Jews aged eighteen to forty-eight have been serving in auxiliary military labour service. The children and parents of these servicemen as well as the women are ready to accept any work if it helps them avoid deportation.

Finally, the Jews of Hungary are ready to emigrate if necessary and will be glad to contribute to the organized execution of the emigration process as a means of averting the nightmare of deportation tormenting them and their children.

Budapest, 24 July 1944.

~ ~ ~

Meanwhile, the rescue mission began to show tangible results. Among the first achievements was the procurement of visas to Tangier for five hundred children.[45] While in terms of the absolute number of subjects involved this was a minor triumph, it managed to stir up some of the neutral diplomats based in the city and gave them an excuse to get in touch with the Jewish Council side by side with the authorities of the government.

On July 12, the following telegram was delivered to Síp Street:

Request meeting with Spanish embassy in Budapest in matter of visas for 500 children. Stop. We have sent list of 200 names, you can choose 300 children. Stop. Request immediate response. Committee for Assisting the Tangier Refugees.[46]

Upon receiving the telegram, which offered five hundred Jewish children the opportunity to emigrate to Tangier, the Jewish Council immediately dispatched an envoy to M. Saus Brios, chargé d'affaires for Spain,[47] who turned out not to have been notified by his government as yet. Brios nevertheless made himself available to the envoy and suggested the Council telegraph Tangier to ask the refugee assistance committee there to request the Spanish Ministry of Foreign Affairs to officially instruct him to issue the visas. The chargé d'affaires said he would be unable to execute the action within the competence of the Spanish legation, so he thought it best if the Council went through Mr Frigyes Born,[48] the Hungarian delegate of the International Red

45 Although the disputed territory of and surrounding Tangier, Morocco, had since 1923 been under the joint international administration of Britain, France, and Spain, the city was occupied by Spain alone during the Second World War.

46 In the original: "Bitten bei Budapester spanischen Gesandtschaft betreffend Visa für 500 Kinder vorzusprechen Stop Liste 200 Namen von uns abgesandt 300 Kinder können von Ihnen bestimmt werden Stop Bitten sofortige Antwort Comité d'Assistance aux Réfugiés Tanger."

47 The author means Ángel Sanz-Briz (1910–1980), diplomat and Spanish chargé d'affaires (deputy ambassador) in Budapest in 1942–44. In the autumn of 1944, Sanz-Briz issued 2,300 passports and protective documents to Hungarian Jews. Due to the approach of the Soviet Army, he was recalled by the Spanish government at the end of November. He received the Righteous Among the Nations honorific from the State of Israel in 1991.

48 Appointed to his position while on a trade mission in Budapest, the Swiss Friedrich Born (1903–1963) served as chief delegate of the International Committee of the Red Cross in Hungary between May 1944 and January 1945. Working closely with the Swiss Embassy and various Zionist resistance organizations, he issued thousands of protective documents to Hungarian Jews, set up numerous buildings under Red Cross

Cross, asking him to make his organization available for this purpose. As recommended by the Spanish chargé d'affaires, the Council promptly sent a telegram to Tangier, and on July 29, Dr György Gergely,[49] a member of the Council's department of government relations, paid a visit to Frigyes Born.

The chief delegate of the International Red Cross received Gergely in his office on Tulipán Street. Having been briefed on the details, he said the case was entirely new to him. In the first place, he would need to be officially contacted by the Spanish chargé d'affaires with a proof of his authorization to issue the visas. Next, he would have to receive the appropriate instructions himself from the Red Cross headquarters in Geneva. They agreed that the three of them (that is, Born, Gergely, and Brios) would hold another meeting on July 31. Born pledged to handle the matter confidentially and in complete isolation from other emigration initiatives. As he said, the transportation itself was a secondary consideration; if the visas were in order, the Red Cross could provide its own trucks if needed. The envoy of the Jewish Council concluded the meeting by repeatedly cautioning Born to act with the utmost discretion in his negotiations with the authorities because the Germans were extremely wary and watchful of any government communication with diplomats. "I have been reasonably careful of my own accord," Born answered, "even though I could not care less about the opinion of the Germans."

Born also said he was "perfectly well informed on the developments, including the incidents in the provinces, as he received his news directly from the headquarters in Geneva via diplomatic pouch. He mentioned that on July 18 the Hungarian government handed him a statement on the temporary suspension of deportations, along with plans to put the Jews to work in *Arbeitskompanie*,[50] the converts inside the country's borders, the Israelites possibly outside the country." Born related that a *Sonderkurier*[51] had recently brought a letter from the International Red Cross headquarters that had to do with the ceasing of deportations. The addressee was someone identified only as a Hungarian person "of influence." The *Sonderkurier* was still in town and would return to the headquarters in a couple of days.

---

protection, and housed as many as seven thousand Jewish children and orphans. He was awarded the Righteous Among the Nations honorific by the State of Israel in 1987.

49 György Gergely, lawyer and member of the Interim Executive Board of the Association of Jews in Hungary (the "Second Jewish Council"; see the Glossary).

50 German for "labour service companies."

51 German for "special envoy."

In the meantime, the Council's telegram was received in Tangier, where the committee made the necessary arrangements, and the Spanish Ministry of Foreign Affairs shortly instructed its envoy in Budapest to issue visas to the five hundred Jewish children plus their fifty to seventy adult escorts.

The meeting between the three men took place on July 31 as scheduled. The memorandum of the meeting, penned by Dr György Gergely, has survived in the original and provides a fascinating historical glimpse. I quote the document in full:

> As per previous arrangement, I reported to the Spanish legation at noon today. In attendance at the meeting were: the chargé d'affaires for Spain; Friedrich Born, delegate of the International Red Cross in Hungary; Schirmer,[52] envoy extraordinaire of the International Red Cross in Budapest temporarily; and myself.
>
> The subject matter of the meeting was the emigration of 500 Jewish children to Tangier. The Red Cross officials and the chargé d'affaires confirmed their authorization by the Spanish Ministry of Foreign Affairs to issue the 500 visas. The representatives of the Red Cross wanted the petition for the emigration to be lodged by the Spanish legation, concurrently with the German and Hungarian authorities. However, the chargé d'affaires pointed out that his mandate only extended to the issuing of the visas; if the gentlemen from the Red Cross insisted on direct intervention by Spain, he would not decline to concur, but he would need a separate specific authorization, which he could obtain by telegram. He nevertheless suggested that we not take that route in light of the precarious situation, and that the necessary steps should be taken by the International Red Cross.
>
> A lengthy discussion by the two Red Cross officials in *schwitzer dijtsch*[53] ensued, from which I clearly gleaned that they would have preferred direct intervention by Spain and regretted that the chargé d'affaires was unwilling to do that without special authorization.

---

52 Robert Schirmer, representative of the International Committee of the Red Cross in Berlin during the war. In the summer of 1944, as the Red Cross became more active in Hungary, Schirmer was dispatched to Budapest to help Friedrich Born.

53 More commonly spelled "Schwyzerdütsch," the phonetical spelling for "Swiss German" in dialect (*Schweizerdeutsch* in High German).

Finally, following a brief debate with the chargé d'affaires, they resolved that the Red Cross would draft the notice to the Hungarian and German authorities the same afternoon, which they would present to the Spanish legation tomorrow. The chargé d'affaires pledged that, once in possession of the *démarche* of the Red Cross, he would confirm the essence thereof by means of a *note verbale* to the Hungarian and German authorities.

I then made the suggestion, formulating it as a question, that it might be preferable to wait until we heard from the Hungarian authorities before applying to the German authorities. The two Red Cross representatives exchanged a telling glance. The chargé d'affaires replied that it was not possible to drop the plan of concurrent application, as the German authorities had just informed him that morning that the Hungarian government had relinquished to them complete oversight of the affairs of the local Jewry.

When I expressed my not inconsiderable astonishment, Born attempted to downplay the gravity of the intelligence by saying that this had been in the air for weeks anyway. I pointed out that what happened a few weeks ago was not the same as having the news confirmed officially today. The envoy extraordinaire replied by exhorting me to keep everything I heard at the meeting in the greatest confidentiality.

Born then proceeded to request that we urgently compile the names of the 500 children, to be selected by us as per the telegram from the Comité d'assistance aux refugiés, who would be accommodated until their departure in a camp under the aegis of the Red Cross.

We further agreed among us that the chargé d'affaires would petition the Spanish for permission to issue visas for 50 additional adults to escort the children. Should this not be allowed, the Red Cross, possibly the Spanish Red Cross, would make arrangements for escorts. He added that the Spanish legation reserved the right to designate 20 children and 15 adults at its own discretion. Born presented a similar claim on behalf of his organization.

In order to qualify for the list, children must be currently living in Budapest and not in internment. In what followed, the Spanish chargé d'affaires made exhaustive inquiries about the appalling details of the deportations to find out to what extent these reports were true.

He then pronounced the news he received himself to be positively gruesome and went on to dwell on the details at length.

Tomorrow morning I will report to Mr Born, who promised to place a copy of the letter at our disposal.

Nothing else to report. Dated 31 July 1946.[54]

Gergely attached to the memorandum a copy of the note from Friedrich Born to the minister of foreign affairs of Hungary, which reads as follows:[55]

The Spanish embassy in Budapest has announced that it has received instructions from the Spanish government that entry visas are granted for 500 Jewish children as well as the necessary attendants consisting of 50–70 adults.

The International Committee of the Red Cross is requested to take the necessary steps to escort the above-mentioned number of Jewish children together with the required attendants during their departure from Hungary and in the same way to facilitate their transit through other countries.

Would you be so kind, Mr Minister, to inform me whether the government of Hungary would give its consent that this undertaking to send the 500 Jewish children, together with the required attendants, be initiated and implemented.

Allow me, Mr Minister, to assure you of my highest esteem.

Friedrich Born, the Delegate for Hungary of the International Committee of the Red Cross in Hungary.

Gergely reported on their next meeting, on August 2, as follows:

On this day, as previously agreed, I went to see Friedrich Born at the offices of the International Red Cross, where I accomplished the following:

I handed over two copies of the note addressed to the Royal Hungarian Ministry of Foreign Affairs. I am to deliver a third copy to the Spanish legation tomorrow and call on the chargé d'affaires

54   This is a typo: The correct date is 31 July 1944.
55   In the first (Hungarian) edition of Munkácsi's book, the note is printed in its original German.

to have it confirmed by the *note verbale* he promised. The case will
be administered by Dr Arnóthy-Jungerth,[56] envoy extraordinaire
and permanent deputy to the minister of foreign affairs. He was
the recipient of the note from the Red Cross, and I must direct the
Spanish chargé d'affaires to him.

Born has not yet addressed a note to the German authorities. I did
not enquire about his reasons on purpose, because I think we only
stand to profit from this omission.

During the discussion, which lasted for an hour and a half,
as the previous one had, Born explained that even the first group
bound for Palestine would be unable to leave the country due to
impending incidents in Turkey. He then told us about his audience
with Jaross yesterday in the company of the envoy extraordinaire
of the Red Cross,[57] during which Jaross stated his willingness to
hand over 200,000 or 250,000 Jews to the International Red Cross.
He then embarked on a lengthy explanation of his position on the
Jewish question. Freidrich Born had the impression that, by getting
rid of the Jews, Jaross sought to acquire merit in the eyes of history.
Indeed, his views appeared so outlandish that we decided "it would
make no sense to enter into an argument with him." Jaross added,
for whatever it was worth, that he had no intention of tormenting
the Jews unnecessarily, and he gave the Red Cross almost free rein in
pursuing its charitable objectives.

Born then related that yesterday or the day before he had received
a visit from a Hungarian gentleman of high standing ("eine sehr
hohe ungarische Persönlichkeit") with the honorary title of "Your
Excellency."[58] At one point during their long conversation, the
gentleman asked whether the Red Cross would be willing, if the need
arose, to take action on behalf of Hungarians in the same manner it
was now committed to helping the Jews. The delegate replied that his
organization could not be accused of partiality and would obviously
be ready to act in case of a particularly pressing exigency.

Next I shared with Born certain hitherto unconfirmed reports
about the conditions in a Jewish internment camp set up in the

56 About Mihály Arnóthy-Jungerth, see 190.
57 Robert Schirmer.
58 The identity of this person is unknown.

village of Encs near Kassa, where the daily food ration was a measly 70 grams of bread and the interned were treated so brutally that about a thousand have died in the camp so far. They needed urgent help. I stressed that the intelligence should not be regarded as authentic, as the precise facts were yet to be established.[59] He asked to be notified as soon as the reports have been corroborated. That done, he will travel to the location immediately and set things right, using the authority vested in him by Jaross yesterday. He took notes of the data I had just given him. I took the opportunity to reiterate my warning against his citing the Executive Board[60] as a source for any of the information supplied by us. He acknowledged this demand and promised compliance. He added that he had been advised to exercise extreme caution in the matter by the envoy extraordinaire himself.

Of particular interest in this report by Gergely is its account of the exchange Born and envoy extraordinaire Schirmer had with the minister of the interior, Andor Jaross. The other curiosity consists of the fact that even the best-informed continued to believe in the existence of hidden Jewish camps around the country long after all the Jews from the provinces had been swallowed by the black hole that was Auschwitz. Indeed, the months of June and July saw several search parties dispatched to various parts of the country to seek out such hidden camps. Unfortunately, the widely circulated rumours invariably turned out to be unfounded.

~ ~ ~

Concurrently with these countermeasures to rescue the Jewry of the capital, Eichmann and the Sondereinsatzkommando in his command pressed for the commencement of the deportations and set August 5 as the new starting date. Wisliceny interrupted his Lake Balaton vacation, joined the Kommando stationed in Svábhegy, and ordered his men to revamp the camp in Békásmegyer[61] from which he had deported Jews living in the vicinity of

59 The reports were indeed false: by this point, with practically all Jews from Hungary's provinces having been deported, any ghettos or internment camps that had existed would have been empty.

60 That is, the Jewish Council (then formally known as the Interim Executive Board of the Association of Jews in Hungary).

61 A neighbourhood northwest of central Budapest, today the city's 3rd District.

Budapest to Auschwitz back at the beginning of July. Now he was ready for the crowning moment of his oeuvre. As we have seen, the German ambition to deport all the Jews was not so much "thwarted" as merely "put on hold," to use the precise terminology of deportation preferred by Ferenczy. The lieutenant colonel added: "Except that they [that is, Eichmann and his men] were also aware that law enforcement had been scuttled for reasons of internal policy, due to the coup attempt. They would not interfere with that, but insisted that the deportations be resumed at a later date."

It remains a nagging question whether the Germans would have been able to accomplish the deportation without the help of Hungarians. The same question was put by the People's Court to police colonel Winkelmann,[62] the chief commander of SS troops stationed in Hungary. "It is my conviction," Winkelmann answered, "that the German authorities would not have employed force on their own. When I received my instructions from Himmler, he said that he was indifferent to the matter." In his defence, Winkelmann stated that Himmler had promised in 1943 not to ever assign him to such cases. He recalled having reminded Himmler of his promise when he was dispatched to Hungary. It was in this context that Himmler made the above comment to him. Winkelmann further argued that Germany sought to avoid confrontation with the Hungarians under all circumstances, owing to its vested interest in leaving the territory open for the undisturbed transportation of oil.

The same reasoning is illustrated with astonishing verisimilitude by the following dialogue between the president of the People's Court and Veesenmayer,[63] who had served as Hitler's plenipotentiary commissioner in Hungary:

PRESIDENT: What consequences would the Hungarian government have incurred by refusing to satisfy the German demand for deportation?
VEESENMAYER: Then it would not have been carried out. There was a precedent. When Horthy announced that they were not going to go along with it anymore, nothing really was done.
PRESIDENT: In other words, you affirm that if the Hungarian government had said no from the outset, it would have been able to

---

62   About SS-Obergruppenführer Otto Winkelmann, see 32.
63   About Edmund Veesenmayer, see 132.

ensure that the Jews could carry on with their lives as if nothing had happened. Are you saying that, in that event, Germany would not have brought any coercive measures?

VEESENMAYER: They would have made an attempt to exert pressure, to be sure, but they did not have the means at their disposal to push things through.

PRESIDENT: How can you say that when Germany had the requisite means of power to occupy the entire country?

VEESENMAYER: The invasion itself only lasted for a brief period, and the withdrawal of divisions began almost immediately afterward. In addition, the task would have called for intervention by the police rather than the military, and police forces were scant.

PRESIDENT: In that event, would Germany not have had the means to assign a police force of sufficient size?

VEESENMAYER: I do not think it would. Another hindrance was that German police did not speak Hungarian; nor did they have knowledge of the country and its people.

PRESIDENT: And what about Poland? How did you go about solving the Jewish question there? Bringing in sufficient police troops was not a problem in Poland?

VEESENMAYER: I have never been to Poland, but I consider that country to have been an entirely different territory of operations. That was the first country we occupied, and that occupation was total. It had no government of its own. It was under broad-based and all-encompassing German administration.

PRESIDENT: That said, you were nevertheless able to implement the radical solution to the Jewish question there as you had envisioned it. Why were you not able to do so in Hungary, a much smaller country?

VEESENMAYER: 1944 was different. It was already a year under crisis.

PRESIDENT: Are you suggesting that by then such unlimited German forces had not been available?

VEESENMAYER: No. By then it would have been impossible to commit forces of that magnitude.

It goes without saying that such testimonies must be taken with a grain of salt. Both Winkelmann and Veesenmayer were keen to save themselves by downplaying the importance of their respective roles. On the other hand, there is plenty of conclusive evidence to prove that the deportation of Hungarian Jewry could not have been carried out except with the full cooperation of the Hungarian Gendarmerie.

~ ~ ~

By the first weeks of August the Jews of Budapest found themselves out on a limb, and the Jewish leadership had undergone considerable transformation. The president of the Orthodox office, Samu Kahán-Frankl,[64] had gone underground and was replaced in office by Dr Ernő Boda.[65] The departure of Orthodox congregation leader Fülöp Freudiger and the secession of Sándor Török[66] left two posts vacant. As a new member, the executive board appointed Lajos Stöckler,[67] who nobody at the time suspected would later come to play a role of historic significance.

Fülöp Freudiger and about seventy companions fled the country on August 10 using false Romanian passports.[68] As Freudiger had always been known as one of the best-informed members of the Jewish Council, his sudden departure led many to assume that doomsday was near. His escape had been planned meticulously and was being talked about on the third floor of the Síp Street headquarters just hours before he left. The next day everybody knew he had crossed the border successfully. Eichmann, who had

64   About Samu Kahán-Frankl, see 22.
65   About Jewish Council member Ernő Boda, see 21.
66   A reference to Török's appointment to the Alliance of the Christian Jews of Hungary. See 91.
67   Lajos Stöckler (1897–1960), industrialist, member of the Jewish Council from July 1944. During the Szálasi regime, he became the de facto head of the Council even as Samu Stern nominally remained president. In his postwar testimony, he presented himself as having been in solidarity with the masses, as opposed to the "elitism" exhibited by Samu Stern and other Council members. Indeed, Stöckler proved effective in organizing food supplies and providing protection for Budapest ghetto residents. After the war, he became president of the Pest Israelite Congregation and of the National Association of Hungarian Jews (Magyar Izraeliták Országos Irodája), and then, in 1950, was appointed head of the National Representation of Hungarian Israelites, the organization sanctioned by Hungary's communist regime. In 1953, as a result of the anti-Israeli anti-Zionist position of communist bloc countries, Stöckler and other Jewish community leaders were arrested by the secret police on false charges, including the absurd claim that Raoul Wallenberg was a victim of a "Zionist conspiracy" concocted by Stöckler and his associates. Stöckler was convicted, but then released. In 1956, he emigrated to Australia.
68   About Fülöp Freudiger, see 19.

learned the news himself, asked Dr János Gábor, who happened to be in his office, what he knew about the affair. Gábor admitted that there had been rumours, so he had heard about the plan like everybody else. Eichmann yelled at him, saying he should have reported the "escape conspiracy" as a matter of duty, and placed him under arrest. Gábor was then brought to Síp Street by four detectives on the evening of August 11. They took the opportunity to intimidate Dr Imre Reiner[69] with threats over the escape of the Council member. Gábor was shortly taken to the jail of the Pest District Law Court and then to Kistarcsa. He was only freed in September when the Lakatos cabinet released a large number of detainees.

Dr Gábor was known for his exceptional ability to talk the Germans into things with more success than any of us. That even he could not escape his fate was a lesson for all of us. Now the only way out was to shake up the Hungarian authorities and mount resistance. During the talks with Ferenczy, certain misgivings emerged, suggesting that the Germans might succeed in rallying the Arrow Cross behind them. The Council leaders tried to reassure Ferenczy that, if it came to open confrontation, the organized workers would brave it out and could be persuaded to take sides with the Jewry. Ferenczy doubted this and asked the Council if they could present someone to substantiate the proposed scenario. The Council then offered to bring in one of the leaders of Social Democratic workers, Lajos Kabók.[70] In the subsequent talks between Kabók, Dr László Bánóczy, and Dr Pető, Kabók asked to be joined by Karácsonyi, then the head of the iron workers' trade union.[71] Kabók and Karácsonyi then held a meeting with Ferenczy which lasted for hours. They explained the workers' readiness to collaborate in the resistance, thereby strengthening Ferenczy in his resolve to support the regent's efforts to repudiate and prevent further deportations.

Meanwhile Horthy made his own decision. Ferenczy's deposition before the police describes the process in dramatic detail:

As far as I can recall it must have been at the end of July or during the first days of August when I first got to see the regent on this

69 About Jewish Council member Imre Reiner, see 27.
70 Lajos Kabók (1884–1945), engine fitter, trade union leader, MP of the Social Democratic Party in the years 1922–35 and 1939–44. He was arrested and murdered by Arrow Cross members in early January 1945.
71 Sándor Karácsony (1892–1944), trade union leader, member of the Social Democratic Party and the Municipal Committee of Budapest from 1940 to 1944. He was murdered by members of the Arrow Cross in December 1944.

matter, through the mediation of Horthy Jr. I informed the regent in full detail of what I knew, and told him that a categorical refusal regarding the Jewish question could be counted on to bring results against a Germany that had seen its forces in Hungary dwindle due to the military operations in the Carpathians.[72] This was when the regent gave me orders to find the exact size and location of German forces stationed in Hungary. Pending the results of such a survey, he agreed that he would refuse to extradite the Jews to the Germans. On the occasion of this first audience, I gave him a protest note I had drafted in five points. The regent accepted the document with the proviso that it would have to be reworded in diplomatic idiom. From the way he acted, it was obvious to me that he feared a wholesale German invasion.

The protest note was edited in accordance with diplomatic style by foreign ministry councillor Dr Csopey,[73] with the knowledge of deputy minister Arnóthy-Jungerth. The latest date the Germans had set for the deportation was August 26. The government was supposed to submit the letter of protest on the same date, a Saturday. What happened instead was that the regent personally gave a copy to Veesenmayer, the German envoy, who had come to see him about a different matter. The degree to which the government dreaded the idea of delivering the document became obvious when it failed to hand it over even after having received the reply from the Germans. It turned out only later that the regent had already handed over the letter of protest to Veesenmayer. In the letter, the government undertook the commitment to detain the Jews in the provinces, provided that it be permitted to solve the Jewish question at its own discretion and with its own resources. Under no circumstances would the Jews be extradited to a foreign power.

Ferenczy's testimony before the People's Court sheds an even keener light on the history of the diplomatic note as a document in which the Hungarian government refused to continue the deportations. The letter was drafted by

72 A reference to the Soviet offensive against German and Hungarian lines of defence in the northeastern Carpathians.

73 Dénes Csopey (1907–?), diplomat, head of the secretariat of the Ministry of Foreign Affairs. On 22 March 1944, Csopey was appointed head of the Political Department of the Ministry of Foreign Affairs. He continued to serve in the ministry after the Arrow Cross takeover in October 1944. In 1945, Csopey fled to Italy.

Ferenczy and consisted of five points. He showed a first draft to the Jewish
Council and had them translate it into German. Under the first point, the
government expressed its readiness to resettle the Jewry of Budapest in
the provinces using its own law enforcement resources. The government
would not, however, accept any further transportation of the Jews by the
Germans, as they had not been extradited. For the rest, the letter demanded
the departure of Eichmann's detachment, the handing over of detained
politicians and members of parliament to the courts, the return of the Pest
District Jail to Hungarian administration, and the return of Jewish property
and warehouses confiscated by the Gestapo. In exchange, the government
was willing to accommodate the Jews in camps in the provinces and put
them to work there. Ferenczy described this undertaking as only a pretext
for buying time. As he said, "We had to give the Germans something or it
would have been impossible to obstruct further deportation."

The letter of protest was typed in seven copies, one of them for the Jewish
Council. On August 26, Veesenmayer reported to the regent for an interview
in connection with his *démarche* to the Hungarian government concerning
Romania's defection from the Axis.[74] Horthy jumped at the opportunity
and handed over the letter of protest himself to the plenipotentiary envoy
of the Reich.

The ten days from August 17 to 26 marked a period of dramatic face-off
and crisis. Although Horthy's so-called exemption decree was not published
in the official journal until August 22 – I will discuss the substance and
outcome of this decree later – it was already common knowledge that
there were ways for some people, by going through the Prime Minister's
Office or the Cabinet Office, to win exemption from certain provisions of
the anti-Jewish laws, most notably from the requirement of wearing the
yellow star. Among the first to receive such exemptions were assimilated
Jews who had served as senior government officials in the liberal world,[75]
as well as scientists and artists and their relatives. (We will see shortly how
far this process was later extended.) In the attendant public mood, it was
a striking sight when, at around five o'clock in the afternoon of August
17, three leaders of the Jewish Council entered the bustling Síp Street

---

74 On 23 August 1944, a military coup led by Romania's King Michael I overthrew Prime
    Minister Ion Antonescu, and Romania switched from an alliance with Nazi Germany
    to the Allied forces.
75 The author is referring to the era of the Austro-Hungarian Monarchy before 1918.

headquarters without yellow stars. Rumour was that they had received the exemption granted by the regent directly from Secretary of State István Bárczy.[76] It may be that the stripping of stars from three high-profile Council members should not have had the impact it did, given that some others, such as the Zionist leaders Ottó Komoly and Rezső Kasztner, never had to wear the stigma to begin with, courtesy of their German papers. Yet this change in the external appearance of the three Council members left a deep impression in the tense atmosphere. For weeks, everyone had been talking about the deportations. The first question of every Jew at one meeting or another was whether fate would soon catch up with the Jews of Budapest. No wonder, then, that many interpreted the starless status of the Council members as a sign of impending deportations. The general astonishment was only amplified by the events of August 18.

In the evening of that day, Stern, Pető, Wilhelm, and their families were captured and hauled to Svábhegy by the Gestapo. From there, they were taken during the night to the German-run jail of the Pest District Law Court. Their interrogation focused on trifling details, and they were given no idea of why they had been arrested. At the very same hour, a detective of the Hungarian Gestapo from Svábhegy was searching for the author of this book. One did not need much imagination to see the correlation. Next morning, on Saturday, August 19, upon the strenuous intervention of the regent, Stern, Wilhelm, and their families were released; the Germans promised to free Pető the following Monday, August 21. When I called on Samu Stern around noon on August 19, I found him in bed with a fever and apparently still suffering from the calamities of the night before. He was being attended to by his next of kin. When the question repeatedly came up as to why they were arrested, the Council president insisted fervently that it must have been because of Fülöp Freudiger's escape.

Since then, a number of other explanations have been put forward, including the more plausible one that the Council members had to be sidelined for the time the deportations were supposed to begin. These suppositions were fuelled further by the conspicuous star-waiver legislative scheme, which the Germans obviously frowned upon as being detrimental

76 István Bárczy Jr (1882–1952), lawyer and civil servant. He served as administrative state secretary of the Prime Minister's Office from 1928 to 1944, and as the notary of the Council of Ministers and Crown Council meetings from 1921 onwards. After the war, Bárczy Jr emigrated to France.

to their plans: Absent their yellow stars, the Council leaders would have found it easy to go underground and continue to manage affairs from there. But this is all conjecture. The fact remains that Samu Stern unambiguously identified Fülöp Freudiger's departure as the cause for his arrest.

Dr Pető was handled separately and, in fact, physically abused after a document from the Swedish legation was found on him. He was interrogated about his relationship with the regent, about how the regent knew him, and was given to understand he was only being released on orders of the regent. When they let him go on August 21, they instructed him to compile and deliver in urgency to the Svábhegy Kommando a list of the Council members and all payroll and voluntary staff in the Council's administration. These demands were accompanied by severe threats.

The Gestapo action described above signalled the commencement of the deportation. The Council prepared a list of the names of the more than a thousand employees working within its organization but, feigning naïveté as to the intended use of the list, withheld home addresses. After a pause of one day, confirming the worst nightmare of hundreds of employees as they held their breath, the order came from above to supplement the list with the addresses. There was no doubt anymore as to what lay ahead. The same day, Ferenczy told Wilhelm and Pető that, as per Eichmann's instructions, the first to be deported were members of the Council, officials within the organization, and their relatives. Ferenczy also showed them the timetable specifying the settlements around the city where, from each section of the capital, the tenants of yellow-star houses were to be taken, as well as the times for boarding Jews from specific settlements on the deportation trains. The deportation process itself was to take place from August 27 to September 18.

These plans were quickly leaked to the public, intensifying the already rampant panic to the point best described as an endemic frenzy that threatened to break out of control at any minute. Practically nobody remained immune to insanity in this hour of utter despair, some waiting in apathy, others in sheer madness, for destiny to knock on their door.

This is how we edged closer and closer to Saturday, August 26, the darkest day of the crisis. Early in the morning the command came for the list of Council members and officials, complete with names and addresses, to be delivered to Svábhegy within the next few hours. The list was presented to the Gestapo by the attorney Dr E.R., a member of the government relations team,[77] in an act that obviously heralded the inception of the deportations. The

---

77   Dr E.R. could not be identified.

Council leaders were torn between hope and despondency. Nobody knew if Ferenczy, making good on his word, was going to take control of the situation and gain the upper hand of a predatory and bloodthirsty Gendarmerie who had been swarming Budapest in droves for the past few weeks, and whose members were ultimately his own accomplices and accessories. In any case, the Council members did what there was to be done, and went to the Castle district late in the morning. The author of this book alerted State Secretary Mester,[78] who maintained direct contact with the cabinet chief.

During the morning hours, thousands upon thousands inundated Síp Street to learn of news that would spell doom or deliverance for us all. In the event of news confirming the start of deportations, many entertained the idea of suicide; others thought the time ripe to take the risk of escaping from their star-marked residences to go into hiding with Christian papers. Before the morning was over, a large group assembled on the third floor, occupied the president's room (most of the Council members had left by then), and held a sort of makeshift meeting in a sizzling atmosphere. It was a dead ringer for the demonstration led by Dr Varga[79] back in June. Speakers fulminated against the Executive Board,[80] which they said had abandoned them, secure in their newfound starless privilege, in stark contrast to the stigmatized masses. The Council leaders returned to the building around two o'clock in the afternoon, directly from a meeting with Ferenczy, declared the rumours of the deportations to be unfounded, and described the situation as being no worse than it had been a week or two previously. In reality, they had just learned that morning that Horthy had given Veesenmayer the letter of protest, which they interpreted as a sign of firm resolve on the part of the regent. News of the letter of protest immediately sent one of Eichmann's men flying to Berlin to receive further instructions from Himmler. In a telegram sent to the Hungarian Ministry of Foreign Affairs, Himmler consented to the deferral of the deportations.[81] Ministry of Foreign Affairs

78 About Miklós Mester, see 177.
79 About Dr Imre Tamási Varga, see 139–40.
80 The Interim Executive Board of the Association of Jews in Hungary (the Second Jewish Council).
81 In a telegram of 25 August 1944, from Heinrich Himmler, Reich Leader of the SS, to Otto Winkelmann, chief of the SS and police forces in Hungary, all deportations to Germany were ordered halted effective immediately. [Political Archive of the Federal Foreign Office (PAAA) Abt. Gruppe Inland II. Geheim 58/3. *Juden in Ungarn.* 5795/E. 422181.]

councillor Dr Moór[82] and Zsigmond Székely-Molnár,[83] who was in charge of Jewish affairs in the Ministry of the Interior at the time, relayed the news to Pető and Wilhelm. (Ferenczy testified that Himmler's reply was received on August 28.)

Ironically, very little of this reassuring news reached the Jewish masses. That Saturday remained etched in the memory of the city's Jews as the first truly severe blow that shook them head to toe. Remembering the precedents of the provinces, many packed their belongings, kept handy a rucksack and, in some houses, even set up a kind of guard to put up a fight should they come under attack by the Gendarmerie. Many people spent a sleepless night, keeping vigil as so many of their ancestors had in the hours of darkness throughout the history of Israel.

The sun dawned on a beautiful summer day, suffusing the city with warmth. Come the official hour allotted for them to leave their homes, the Jews of Budapest flocked into the streets, drawing deep breaths of fresh air, wondrously relieved to still be around. This is how the deportation scheduled for August failed, and the Jews of the capital were saved a second time.

Suddenly, it was impossible to silence the optimists, who roared at the top of their lungs, "I told you there will be no deportations from Budapest!" Few realized the actual situation and the immutable truth of history that, while skirmishes may be won, while we may get away with the worst for a time, victory can only be claimed by those who prevail in the last battle. This was the single greatest predicament remaining to be solved by the Jews of Budapest.

---

82 Oszkár Moór (1891–19?), ministerial councillor, head of the Registration Department of the Ministry of Foreign Affairs. On 15 October 1944, he was arrested by the Arrow Cross.

83 On Zsigmond Székely-Molnár, see 72.

9

In the Shadow of Destiny
under the Lakatos Cabinet

*The formation and influence of the Lakatos cabinet – Endre and
Baky vanish from the Ministry of the Interior – Ferenczy receives
instructions and sets people "to work" – The "conscription"
of the Jewry of Budapest – Preparations for concentration
in the provinces – The International Red Cross informed –
The regent's exemptions and their influence – Instances of
maladministration – The first Schutz-passes handed out – Horthy
receives Samu Stern – Jewish holidays in the fall – The shadow
of Arrow Cross terror – A last attempt to arm labour servicemen
– What happened on the night of October 14? – October 15 –
October 16: The wrath of God – Jewish fate comes to Budapest*

The next period, from August 27 to October 16, was determined by the
events I describe in this chapter.

On August 30, at the regular inauguration of officers at the Ludovika
Military Academy,[1] Horthy's address included a sentence that caught everybody's attention. This speech no longer bore any trace of the old delusions
of glory, the usual and unfounded propaganda of the "final victory." Speaking
to the crowd in a rather gloomy atmosphere, Horthy exhorted the new
officers: "Make chivalry your priority above all else. This is how we have
always been known to the world, and if we have incurred a blot on our
escutcheon through ignorance of the situation we shall regain our good
reputation." It was impossible not to make a connection between Horthy's
speech and the article "The Chivalrous," that had appeared in the *St Gallener
Tagblatt* four weeks earlier.[2]

---

1   Actually, the inauguration ceremony took place on 20 August 1944.
2   For the referenced article, see 235.

Fig. 26   On 16 October 1944, the far-right Arrow Cross party took control of Hungary,
imposing on Budapest a new reign of terror. Freebooting Arrow Cross militias conducted
arbitrary raids, rounding up, terrorizing, and killing Jewish men, women, and children.
"Stunned Jews gasped under heavy blows as the takeover was celebrated with piercing cries
of debauchery, cheering, and vengeance," is how Ernő Munkácsi remembered October 16.
"As I stepped out on the street late in the evening, I found myself face to face with such a
mob. Rhythmic yells of 'Hit them high, hack them low!' were periodically interrupted by
a refrain of volleys as the henchmen fired into the surrounded crowd. The ensuing groans
and wailing were stifled by the tormenters' fierce rallying cries." Here, bystanders look on as
German soldiers herd Jews into the City Theatre on Tisza Kálmán Square (now Pope John
Paul II Square) in Budapest's 8th District, 17–18 October 1944.

The other key factor influencing the psychological state of the city's
Jews was the formation of the Lakatos cabinet on August 29.[3] For all intents
and purposes, Sztójay could be regarded as fallen since the failure of the
first deportation attempt when Baky's coup had been forestalled. Indeed,
Horthy had been in correspondence with Hitler since mid-July over the
appointment of a military-caretaker government. Even though the formal
dismissal of the Sztójay cabinet had been preceded by widespread rumours
that seemed authentic, the radio announcement in the evening of August 28

3   About the Lakatos cabinet, see 147.

of the appointment of a new government still came as a surprise to everyone. The Jewry of Budapest sighed a sigh of relief. The crisis of August 27 had been put behind, and many had high hopes for the new cabinet. All the horrors of the deportations had been associated with Sztójay's puppet regime, and the permanent departure of Endre and Baky from the Ministry of the Interior after the appointment of the Lakatos cabinet carried more than just symbolic significance. Although their powers of discretion in Jewish affairs had been rescinded as of the beginning of July, it took two full months to remove them from office conclusively, and this made all the difference. As long as these two chief executioners held office, those on the right still eyeing the spoils had reason to look forward to the resurrection of their principals. (And this resurrection, of both Endre and Baky, did come to pass after October 15.[4])

As soon as the Lakatos cabinet was sworn in, it entered into an agreement with the Germans that was supposed to finally settle the Jewish question. Under the agreement, full discretion over Jewish affairs devolved to the Hungarian government. Germany made a commitment to cease direct contact between the *Sicherheitspolizei* and the executive board of the Alliance of Hungarian Jews, and to progressively phase out internment camps in its purview.[5] In return for these promises, the Hungarian government obliged itself to carry out the complete "de-Judaization" of Budapest and to put what was left of Hungarian Jewry to work.

Accordingly, gendarme lieutenant colonel Ferenczy gave the Jewish Council a document confirming his exclusive purview of Jewish affairs. Contact with the Sondereinsatzkommando in Svábhegy had been fading since July 6; now they were reduced to a bare minimum. Eichmann and his team retained discretion in certain matters, such as their control of the facility in Dob Street,[6] but overall, they retreated into passivity. They neither gave up nor waved good-bye, as if they only had shut down operations temporarily; they were clearly waiting for something, and only they knew what that something was. Eichmann was rumoured to have been reassigned to the frontline. (As we shall see, he would reappear in Budapest just before

4   In fact, neither Endre nor Baky regained significant positions of power after the Arrow Cross takeover of 15 October.
5   The Kistarcsa internment camp was finally closed on 27 September 1944. The Sárvár camp continued to operate into 1945.
6   The Orthodox Congregation's complex of buildings at 31 Dob Street was occupied by the Germans. See 34.

October 15.) Several of his lieutenants had also vanished, only to resurface
on October 16, when their time had come.

On September 7 and 8, the daily papers ran two official communiqués on
the government's intention to enlist Budapest resident Jews aged fourteen
to seventy for the "total manpower recruitment effort," while those unfit to
work were to be assembled in various locations in the provinces. The first
communiqué read as follows:

> A Report by the Hungarian News Agency:
> Recent statements by the government have left no doubt that, in
> these days of hardship, all available manpower must be utilized to its
> utmost capacity. Under the circumstances, it is obvious that measures
> must be taken to remedy a situation in which thousands of Jewish
> men and women have been without work and income for months
> even as the country struggles with a shortage of labour. Pursuant to
> the National Defence Act, everyone between the ages of fourteen
> and seventy, without regard to sex, may be enlisted for public works
> of the kind suited to his or her physical and mental abilities. This
> work obligation applies equally to non-Jews and Jews. The Hungarian
> government wishes to avail itself of the Jewry's capacity and obligation
> to work to the full extent of the law. Therefore, the government is
> going to retain for national defence works all Jewish men and women
> aged fourteen to seventy living in the country who have been found
> fit to perform such work by the appropriate examination. Considering
> that the public employment of Jews will be subject to the provisions
> of the National Defence Act, which is universally binding, the work
> obligation will apply equally to Jews in possession of any exemption
> or waiver.

The second communiqué went on to address the details of the process
as follows:

> Yesterday's official communiqué emphasized that the government
> wishes to use its work obligation option to the fullest extent permitted
> by law, and will thus retain for national defence works all Jewish men
> and women aged fourteen to seventy living in the country who have
> been found fit to perform such work by the appropriate examination.
> According to competent officials, the Jews will take up work

under the National Defence Act in accordance with the following procedure: Every morning, Jews will be sorted per block of buildings by a joint committee, assigning each individual to specific details under the national defence work scheme as appropriate to his training and qualifications. Individuals found fit to perform national defence or military labour service[7] will be assigned to job descriptions appropriate to their training and usefulness. Those selected for work will be issued their allowance (stipend) at the usual rates. Jews deemed unfit for national defence or military labour service will be moved to camp facilities in the provinces furnished by representatives of the Jewry with the cooperation of the Hungarian Red Cross. Once there, these individuals will be employed in various domestic occupations such as feather plucking, basket weaving, and corn husking, or in other industries, possibly in various production facilities in the area. Jews selected for national defence labour service will be employed mainly in the armaments industry and will be accommodated in yellow-star houses close to their place of work. For the most part, their food provisions, medical care, and other services will be overseen and administered centrally by the Hungarian Red Cross. Children younger than working age will be cared for and supervised also by the Hungarian Red Cross in its own institutions. Jewish individuals incapable of work, including the sick and the elderly, will be quartered in Budapest, possibly in the Jewish Charity Hospital. In view of the government's commitment to organize the effort under the universally binding provisions of the National Defence Act, the work obligation will apply to all Jews irrespective of any exempt or privileged status.

Needless to say, the repeated reference to the National Defence Act was just another legal subterfuge of the kind routinely invoked since the adoption of the anti-Jewish laws, since the National Defence Act contained no provision that would have permitted the first-priority use of labourers belonging to

---

7   National defence labour service (*honvédelmi munkaszolgálat*) was a form of obligatory work imposed on all adult male members of civil society irrespective of their religion or background, as prescribed by the Act on National Defence (Act II of 1939). Introduced by the same act, military labour service (also known as *közérdekű munkaszolgálat*, or public-interest labour service) meant unarmed service in the military for those deemed "unfit" for armed service, meaning primarily Jews.

any one religious or ethnic group over any other member of society. An even more flagrant violation was in the attempt to assemble Jews deemed unfit to work in concentration camps in the provinces, without regard to sex or age. Of course, the National Defence Act contained no provision authorizing the government to do this; nor was there any executive decree to that effect. Incidentally, the government did not care much about the implementation of the Jewish work program, obviously regarding it as a mere gesture toward the Germans. Ferenczy took the thing all the more seriously. He was eager for "something to do," and went to great lengths to make sure that at least the so-called concentration, if not the deportation itself, be implemented.

The publication of the communiqués on September 7 and 8 marked the beginning of the process officially dubbed as "putting the Jews to work."

The Jewish Council was visited by Colonel János Heinrich[8] on behalf of the Ministry of Defence to talk over the steps to be taken. Subsequently, pursuant to Decree of the Minister of Defence No. 152.880 (XI/1944), the command of the 1 Army Corps issued instructions for the conscription of all Jewish men born between 1874 and 1930 for purposes of defence works projects.[9] In accordance with the order, draft boards were set up in several districts of the capital, and the air-raid warden of each building was given written instructions, signed by the commander of the 1 Army Corps, to have would-be draftees lined up for conscription. The detailed instruction, signed by a captain named Ede Gobbi,[10] was issued on September 23. The nine draft boards were located in the following facilities: For 5th District residents, in the synagogue at 3 Csáky Street; for 6th District residents, in the premises of the Travel Association at 4 Jókai Street; for inner 7th District residents, in the premises of the Children's Garden Society at 32 Akácfa Street; for outer 7th District and 8th District residents, in the synagogue at 2 Bethlen Square; for 12th and 9th District residents, in the Páva Street Synagogue; for 13th District residents in the synagogue at 55 Aréna Street; for 14th District

8   János Heinrich, army colonel, engineer, head of department no. 44 of the Ministry of Defence responsible for the equipment and budget matters of military labour service.
9   The decree stipulated that all able-bodied Jews between fourteen and seventy, includ-ing converted and exempted Jews, were obliged to perform military labour duty. The decree was announced in the *Journal of the Jews in Hungary*, 7 September 1944, and is available in Hungarian in Elek Karsai (ed.), *"Fegyvertelenül álltak az aknamezőkön…" II.* (Budapest: MIOK, 1962), 627–8.
10 Ede Gobbi (1881–1963), businessman, reserve army captain, organizer and commander of labour servicemen. Gobbi rescued hundreds of Jews by distributing forged documents.

residents, in the camp at 46 Columbus Street; for residents of the 1st, 2nd, 3rd, 11th, and 13th Districts, in the synagogue at Öntőház Street; and for 10th District residents, in the Cserkesz Street Synagogue.

The exact procedure of lining up the draftees as per the instruction is worth putting on record for history:

> The day preceding the draft, block residents are notified by delivery of three copies of the order into the hands of the air-raid warden and the concierge. Delivery of the notices is the responsibility of the Rubble Clearing Organization, by agency of the Royal Hungarian Police. One copy is to be kept by both the air-raid warden and the concierge, with the remaining copy posted in the doorway in a conspicuous location. The air-warden then prepares a list of all male tenants in his purview born between 1874 and 1930 who are required to wear a distinguishing mark or exempt thereof for any reason. Concurrently, the air-warden issues a reporting card for each individual on the list. On the day of the draft, individuals eligible to be drafted are prohibited from leaving their homes, whether or not they are obliged under other measures to report for work. The air-raid warden shall line up all tenants of the building at the specified time, walk them in tight formation to the draft board of competence in the given district, hand over the list of names to the officer in charge, and distribute the report cards to the draftees. Bed-ridden individuals do not need to be presented to the draft board in person, but must be listed separately for examination in their homes by the assigned medical officer or army surgeon.

The decree listed fourteen categories of exemption as follows:

> (1) exempt military personnel; (2) invalids with over 50 percent disability (disabled veterans); (3) retired and non-committed military personnel; (4) foreign citizens; (5) independent tradesmen, subject to furnishing proof from their industry chamber that they are actively pursuing their trade at present, except trades unassociated with wartime interests; (6) members of the Rubble Clearing Organization as well as bearers of identity papers issued by Departments 43 and 44 of the Ministry of Defence; (7) employees of the Association of Jews in Hungary and the Alliance of Christian Jews of Hungary, provided they hold a free movement pass from the police; (8) provisionally, workers of the Popular Records Office. Eligibility to be ascertained.

In this category, the words "provisional exemption" must be indicated conspicuously. (9) workers for various public utilities such as City Hall and MÁV,[11] etc.; (10) workers used by the Germans, provided they possess a pass signed by Colonel Neuer, head of the Todt Organization; (11) workers in the defence industries; (12) officials in religious function; (13) engineers, pharmacists, physicians, veterinaries, priests, teachers, schoolteachers; (14) those granted exemption by the regent. However, in case of a "fit to work" qualification, these must be assigned to the staff of the labour organization.

Concurrently with the conscription, in the middle of September, Ferenczy instructed the Council to set up a draft board for Jews living on Pozsonyi Street and Szent István Park, and called a Council representative to his office to discuss the details immediately. The Council sent Ferenc Schalk[12] to this meeting, which was attended, aside from Ferenczy himself, by Gendarmerie captain Lulay,[13] Captain Jankovich[14] from the Ministry of Defence, and medical officer Dr Doby on behalf of the city.[15] As per Ferenczy's instructions, every man and woman between the ages of fourteen and seventy had to be presented to the board for an examination. Ferenczy ordered eligible individuals to be handed over to the work organization, while he had plans to send those aged fourteen to seventy to the provinces. Pursuant to the instruction, vacated apartments were supposed to be relinquished to Jews in possession of a Swedish safe-conduct pass.[16]

By any account, Ferenczy was the man who devoted the most energy to the process of drafting and executing the agreement with the Germans: the work of concentration. He settled on the castle of Tura,[17] where, for starters,

---

11 MÁV stands for Magyar Államvasutak, the Hungarian State Railways.
12 Ferenc Schalk was a retired army captain, a veteran of the First World War, and the Jewish Council's representative on the Recruitment Committee, which organized and oversaw Jews mobilized for defence-related labour. Schalk aimed to delay the committee's recruitment efforts.
13 About Leó László Lulay, see 98.
14 Captain Jankovich could not be identified.
15 József Doby was a health officer serving in the municipality of the 5th District of Budapest.
16 About the Swedish "protected Jews," see 227–8.
17 Also known as the Schossberger Castle after its original owner, Zsigmond Schossberger, a Jewish landowner who had the palace built in French Renaissance style back in 1883. Tura is northeast of Budapest, in central Hungary.

he intended to send thousands of children, old people, and others found unfit to work. However, as the official declaration of the government provided for the concurrence of the Red Cross in designating any such holding facility, the Council managed to forestall the plan through the involvement of Dr Lajos Langman, the head physician of the Red Cross. This was critical in view of the precedents set by Kistarcsa and Sárvár, where concentration had quickly turned into deportation. I am quoting from a letter of orientation sent to Langman by the Jewish Council, a historic document that illustrates the whole situation:

> Background. In connection with the setting to work of the Jewry of Budapest, the idea of relocating those deemed unfit to work to the provinces goes back to certain historic precedents. Initially, under the terms of an agreement following the German invasion, the Hungarian government relinquished full discretion over the Jewish question to the Germans. It was on the grounds of this agreement that the German and Hungarian authorities performed the comprehensive deportation of Jews from the provinces. When practically only the Jews of Budapest remained, systematic deportations were suspended on July 10. Since then, deportation actions have occurred sporadically, without the knowledge and approval of the Hungarian authorities, and sometimes in blatant contempt of their explicit instructions. Two cases in point were the camps in Kistarcsa and Sárvár, from which the Germans deported 1,400 and 1,500 individuals, respectively, at the end of July and in early August. In both cases, the Germans showed up unexpectedly, surrounded the camps with armed guards, cut the telephone lines, and, disregarding the protests of the camp commandant, herded the detainees into wagons that were at the ready, and hurried the transport out of the country.
>
> Bowing to protests from leading Hungarian personalities and pressure from the entire international community, at the very end of August Hungary signed another agreement with Germany that reassigned the Jewish question to the competence of the Hungarian government. In return, the Hungarian government obliged itself to put to use Jewish manpower for the benefit of the country, and to resettle Jews unfit to work in camps in the provinces.
>
> On September 3, Lieutenant Colonel Ferenczy made the official statement that the work program would proceed as planned, but the

concentration in the provinces had been cancelled. On September 4, he issued instructions to commence the conscription, and on September 5 he announced that those unfit to work would be taken to camps in the provinces after all; the drafting for that purpose would begin on September 7. The drafting has been in progress since that date with the participation of the Hungarian Red Cross as required by the communiqué. To the extent that this can be gleaned from the communiqué, the contribution of the Red Cross will be focused on preparing the grounds for receiving the transports. The Red Cross will also be responsible for the "care, supervision, nutrition, and medical care" of children under working age. From these provisions, we can infer that the Red Cross is to play a central role in: (1) choosing the locations; (2) furnishing the facilities; (3) making arrangements for living quarters; (4) providing food; (5) organizing medical care; and (6) providing welfare and social services.

Considering that the entire action has been devised under German pressure and, presumably, not exactly to the liking of the Hungarian government or in harmony with the collective interests of Hungary as a nation, it would seem especially desirable to proceed with utmost care, fully observing the massive time requirements of prudent implementation. In this respect, the involvement of the Red Cross presents the following opportunities in terms of the duties outlined above: (1) For preference, the sites of choice should be located in major provincial centres, to prevent another disaster along the lines of Kistarcsa; (2) The camps must be equipped with the appropriate amenities to meet all humanitarian standards and sanitary requirements, with sufficient supplies of drinking water, adequate kitchens, canalized bathrooms and toilets. If the sites chosen do not already possess these facilities, the construction work to provide them must be started. If the required remodelling turns out to be large-scale and time-intensive, this should not discourage or deter implementation ... ; (3) In designing the accommodations, what is stressed is to avoid crowded conditions and enable families to stay together; (4) Overseeing food provisions is one of the most important functions of the Red Cross. Organizing the appropriate sources and allowing the resettled to obtain food supplies on their own will go a long way toward improving living conditions; (5) Medical care could be provided by doctors established on location, with the Red

Cross only retaining the role of general supervision. Of course, a hospital and necessary medical equipment and supplies are a must; (6) By social care, we primarily mean the monitoring of employment conditions, including work hours, as a means of preventing children, the sick, and the elderly from being worked beyond their physical capabilities and thus being exposed to harm to their health. This type of care also includes making arrangements for receiving visitors and a postal service for family members stationed in different camps and between the provinces and the city.

For the rest, the Background introduces to Langman the officers with whom the doctor is expected to interact. The way the document describes these individuals, in September 1944, is not without interest.

Lieutenant Colonel Ferenczy: Head of the Jewish committee, the chief Hungarian administrator of deportation affairs. The entire plan of the concentration is his brainchild, which makes it likely that he will insist on its implementation, or at least a semblance of implementation. Formerly, he had excellent relations with the German authorities, but has lost some of their confidence since he turned against the deportations. Captain Lulay: A member of the Jewish committee, who sees eye to eye with Ferenczy on everything, and considers it his mission to restore the good reputation of the Gendarmerie. Obersturmbannführer Eichmann: German officer entrusted with the task of solving the Jewish question in Hungary. The man fundamentally responsible for the liquidation of European Jewry, he is extremely strong-minded, undaunted, and ruthless. Currently reported to be away from Budapest. Obersturmbannführer Krumey: Eichmann's deputy. Unlike his superior, he is an amiable, smooth-talking man, but he has exactly the same mentality.

In closing, this rather confidential memorandum warns that, "It is true for all these German gentlemen that, whenever possible, their statements must be solicited in writing, lest they should forget everything they have said further down the line."

With the drafting in progress, the internal affairs of the Jewry were defined by two major tendencies: the drive to obtain exemption directly by authority of the regent, and the movement to go underground with Christian papers.

Exemptions from the effect of Sztójay's anti-Jewish laws (such as the waiver of the yellow-star-wearing requirement and the permission to maintain residence in Christian tenements) had been granted since May in certain exceptional cases, mainly to the well-connected. These papers were issued by the Ministry of the Interior, courtesy of Councillor László Szilágyi[18] – God only knows how, to whom, or on what grounds. The process later became a regular affair in the hands of the Cabinet Office, where some of the most celebrated Jewish writers, artists, university professors, and the like applied for, and frequently received, exemptions. Of course, the true purpose behind granting such exemptions on behalf of the regent was to save the privileged recipients from deportation. However, by the time this case-by-case favour became a routine substantiated by force of law, on August 22, the threat of deportation had faded, rendering the relevant statutory provision, like so many other rescue measures, pretty much out of date. The decree published in the official journal of the government provided that:

> In general, the effect of the provisions concerning the Jewry does not apply to individuals who have been exempted by the regent on the recommendation of the ministry in recognition of their merits in serving the country in the fields of science, art, or commerce, or for other reasons deserving of privileged consideration. The exemption shall not in any manner prejudice the force of racial preservation provisions enshrined in Act xv of 1941, and shall affect the provisions governing the property rights of the Jewry only to the extent expressly specified by the grant of the exemption.

It was on the grounds of this government decree that the authorities issued the stamped papers bearing the following text:

18 László Szilágyi (1897–1978), lawyer, civil servant, ministerial councillor, head of sub-department 11/a. of the Public Law Department of the Ministry of the Interior. Szilágyi was assigned to deal with the question of exemptions, and his office issued hundreds of exemption documents to Jews, including prominent scholars, artists, sportsmen, and business leaders and their families. With the front approaching Budapest, the office was evacuated from the Hungarian capital along with the apparatus of the ministry in early December and was eventually moved to Germany. Szilágyi was captured by US troops at the end of the war. He returned to Budapest in 1946, and continued to work for the Ministry of the Interior until 1950, when he retired.

Letter of exemption. His Excellency the Regent of Hungary, by force of his supreme resolution dated … 1944, has extended to … of … religion and resident at … exemption from the effect of provisions applicable to the Jewry pursuant to Section 1 of Decree of the Prime Minister No. 3040/1944,[19] with the provision that this exemption shall not prejudice the effect of racial preservation provisions set forth in Act xv of 1941[20] or of the provisions governing the property rights of Jews.

These papers were issued by Balla, head of the ministry department in the small palace occupied by the prime minister on Úri Street,[21] formerly headquarters of Imrédy's consolidated Ministry of the Economy.[22] Those who strolled down this main street of the Castle District following the promulgation of the decree witnessed a tumultuous scene with a police officer clad in full Attila uniform[23] and helmet, trying to keep at bay a throng bent on making an entry. Some in the crowd had already been proposed to the cabinet office for exemption by various ministries, mainly that of religion and public education, among them the relatives of nearly all the Jewish artists, celebrated members of the theatres of Budapest, scientists, and university professors, as well as former senior public servants now in retirement – all of them familiar names and faces. There were also the well-known and well-connected from the top echelons of finance, who arrived in automobiles. Lo and behold, the heavy oak door opened to them, as if by dint of a secret password, while the aged men of science and letters stood in line for hours in the blazing sun.

The number of applications for exemption escalated exponentially by the day. Of course, nobody could be blamed for mobilizing all of one's

19 The Decree of the Prime Minister No. 3040/1944 concerned the scope of persons exempted from the implications of the anti-Jewish laws and decrees.
20 Act xv of 1941, known as the third Jewish law or Race Protection Law, banned marriage between Jews and Christians and forbade sexual relations between Jewish men and non-Jewish women. See the Glossary on anti-Jewish laws.
21 István Balla was head of the ministry department in the Prime Minister's Office. The block of houses in question is 18 and 20 Úri Street in the Castle District. The original two medieval buildings were renovated and merged into a single building in 1912. In 1939, the Prime Minister's Office purchased the building for use as offices.
22 See 193.
23 Ceremonial jacket, elaborately decorated with braid cord and lace, originally the sixteenth-century uniform of the elite Hungarian light cavalry, the hussars. In the early nineteenth century, it became widely used by civilians as a symbol of patriotism.

connections in the attempt to regain one's human rights. The processing of the applications, for which a great number of family documents had to be filed, required a large and continuously swelling apparatus, but the workload remained overwhelming. Incidents of flagrant injustice further contributed to the heated atmosphere, as businessmen with money and friends in high places were issued their exemptions promptly, while disabled war veterans and white-collar employees milled around, almost losing hope while waiting in line for their turn.

The other parallel development was the formation of an underground Jewish community. By mid-September, everybody realized that the game was nearing its conclusion. This gave rise to the widespread premonition that the murderers and traitors would not surrender without a fight, but force a bloody and fearsome confrontation to the end. With this scenario in mind, many purchased authentic or forged Christian papers and either kept these handy in case bad came to worse, or used them to disappear from the yellow-star houses and, typically, resurface in the guise of refugees from the provinces, seeking and often finding shelter in Christian households willing to help. The process gained further momentum from the replacement of government. The more sensible part of Christian society began to seriously consider the possibility that the country would lose the war and they would have to pay their dues sooner or later. As a sign of the times, more and more people were willing to accept Jews in their homes, along with the risks such hospitality entailed. Interestingly, the exemptions themselves gave added impetus to going underground by making it easier for Jews to move out of their star-marked homes.

The general sense of the war drawing to a close was amplified by news from the front of the headlong withdrawal of German troops in the wake of Romania's defection from the Axis. The situation in the battlefield was best assessed in its full reality only by the neutral foreign legations that had for some time reckoned on the impending fall of the Horthy regime, followed by a reign of terror and, ultimately, a siege of Budapest. They took their steps accordingly. The rescue effort led by Sweden and Switzerland was joined by the Portuguese legation in September, but the driving force of the mission continued to be supplied by Papal Nuncio Rotta,[24] who frequently spoke out in very harsh words against the sadistic atrocities the Germans perpetrated against the Jews.

24 About Angelo Rotta, see 131.

This was when the Swedish Schutz-passes[25] began to be issued in great numbers. It was no longer just about the 630 individuals on the list sent by the Swedish Ministry of Foreign Affairs via Wallenberg, but about anyone with any Swedish connection at all, and often people who simply had to be saved from a clear and present threat to their lives. Having thus become masters of life and death, the foreign legations faced the need to find ever-larger official premises and to commit more and more staff to handle the workload.

During the same weeks, the International Red Cross came into its own with a department "A" for the rescue of Jews organized by Zionist president Ottó Komoly in the building under 4 Mérleg Street.[26] Working with him was Frigyes Görög,[27] who dug into the management of affairs on behalf of the International Red Cross. This was tantamount to a program of rescuing Jews at a time when everyone with any clarity of perception had to anticipate the need to use "cover names" in the period that lay ahead. The International Red Cross and the foreign legations provided such covers or guises. Ottó Komoly maintained contact with the leading secretary of the Ministry of Culture while simultaneously attending meetings of the Jewish Council and collaborating with Rezső Kasztner on their own covert mission. His activities were manifold and comprehensive indeed. The fulcrum of Jewish administration shifted to Mérleg Street. Many nurtured the presentiment that Síp Street would soon be turned into a ghetto, while Mérleg Street would remain a power in disguise, to be reckoned with even in a ghettoized world.

That said, many continued their visits to Síp Street all the same, mainly to report for a draft-related examination or to take care of affairs pertaining to their star-marked homes.

Around the middle of September, Horthy received Samu Stern, the president of the Jewish Council. The circumstances that led to the audience remain unknown, but they must have had to do with an effort to prevent the concentration in the provinces and with plans to relinquish control of the labour service recruits to the Germans. At dusk on a fine September day,

---

25 Issued by Wallenberg, these official-looking protective passes (*Schutz* is German for "protection") were actually false passports identifying the holder as a Swedish subject.

26 About Ottó Komoly, see 68. From September 1944, about three hundred people worked in the so-called Section A division of the Red Cross, mostly on the aid and rescue of children, but also to provide Jewish institutions with food and medicine.

27 See 5.

the automobile of the Jewish Council was seen rolling into the courtyard of the Royal Castle. The passenger who got out was none other than the head of Hungarian Jewry, wearing a plain grey suit. A haggard old man by then, Stern stepped into the room of Ambrózy, the cabinet chief,[28] who led him surreptitiously up the back steps to the regent of Hungary. For now, not much is known about the conversation that transpired between the two, other than the following details. "I have freed you all, have I not?" Horthy asked by way of prompting a report on the current state of affairs. President Stern then briefed him on the situation, placing special emphasis on the danger of concentrating Jews in camps in the countryside. Stern explained his view that, once the Jews had been hauled to the villages, the government would be powerless to defend them against the Germans, despite all best intentions. Horthy was persuaded by these arguments, and promised Stern he would call off the concentration.

This is all the information available about the famous meeting, which clearly represented a milestone on the road of Jewish destiny. While I do not pretend to have the ability to read minds, it seems inconceivable to me that Horthy – who, by then, had made all necessary preparations for negotiating an armistice and was aware that World War II pushed Hungary to the brink of final ruin – did not give thought to the ultimate consequence of the "Szeged Concept,"[29] which first reduced the noble adjectives of "Christian" and "national" to drunken slogans and later culminated in the repudiation of the rights of God and man through the adoption of the *numerus clausus*[30] and other anti-Jewish laws. At this juncture, when his entire political system had failed and his throne had begun to crumble, Horthy found himself face to face with this elderly Jew, the beacon of a Hungarian Jewry of whom hundreds of thousands, quite possibly the best, had been driven by Hungarian gendarmes to board a train to their death – by troops, mind you, who bore the

28 About Gyula Ambrózy, see 196.

29 The "Szeged Concept" is shorthand for the founding ideas of the right-wing "counter-revolutionary" Horthy regime that emerged upon the defeat of the Hungarian Soviet Republic (AKA Republic of Councils) in 1919. The concept was for-mulated in the southern city of Szeged, where the new leadership first gathered before taking power.

30 The popular name for the anti-Jewish Law XXV of 1920, which indirectly imposed quotas on the number of Jews permitted to attend institutions of higher education. See the Glossary entry on anti-Jewish laws.

epithet "Royal Hungarian" and wore on their hats the nation's crest coronet. Did it not, at that point in time, occur to the supreme commander of the nation that he was witnessing the fulfillment of the prophecy – "Our ruin is tantamount to the downfall of the entire country!" – that the Jews had written in protest against the laws created against them? And did not these same thoughts occur to the Jewish leader as he reported on the cold-blooded massacre of the vast majority of Hungarian Jewry, and begged mercy for those who survived?!

The great holidays of the fall season arrived. Early in the summer, on Shavuot,[31] the Day of the First Fruits, the Jews of Budapest hardly had had reason to hope for another celebration in their favourite temples. Now, they could prepare for the holidays according to their old traditions, to be celebrated in what remained of the temples. Most of the district temples and the Lágymányos district synagogue of the Buda community had been converted into internment camps or sleeping quarters for labour service companies. The day before New Year[32] a bomb hit the temple of the Boys' Orphanage, completely demolishing the magnificent building.[33] The celebration of Rosh Hashanah was interrupted by repeated air raids. The believers displayed no small courage in coming to the temple to pray, as there were no bomb shelters nearby. Incidentally, the government had lifted some of the curfew, enabling worship service to be held in accordance with custom. When the organ of the Dohány Street Synagogue began to pump out the traditional melody of *Unetaneh Tokef*,[34] and the cantor recited the ancient text, backed by a choir – "It is true that you are the one who judges, and reproves, who knows all, and bears witness, who inscribes, and seals, who reckons and enumerates," and "How many shall pass away and how many shall be born, who shall live and who shall die" – tears flowed down the cheeks of thousands. Never before had they felt the truth of this prayer and the nearing of the day of judgment as they did on that day.

---

31 Also known as the Feast of Weeks, the Jewish holiday Shavuot had begun on the eve of 27 May 1944.

32 The Jewish New Year, or Rosh Hashanah, began at sundown on 17 September 1944.

33 The building that housed the Boys' Orphanage and synagogue was located on Vilma királynő Street (today 25–27 Városligeti fasor Street).

34 An eleventh-century Hebrew poem traditionally recited on Rosh Hashanah and Yom Kippur.

On New Year's Day, Chief Rabbi Benjámin Fischer gave a sermon in the Rumbach Street temple.[35] On the eve of Kol Nidre,[36] the pulpit was taken by Izsák Pfeiffer, the pride of the Hungarian rabbinate – a man well versed in science and poetry, who had been saved from deportation from Monor by being transferred to the camp on Columbus Street.[37] In his poignant sermon, the grey-haired rabbi spoke about a return to faith and ethnic identity as an indispensable condition for Jewish renewal in Hungary. He finished his delivery by offering a prayer for those who sacrificed their lives for the sanctification of the name of God after enduring the horrors of the brickyards and the extermination camps. Pfeiffer was the first to explicitly mention brickyards and death camps before a congregation of believers. Did he have an intimation that, barely a few weeks later, he would share in the fate of the other martyrs and end his life in Dachau after months of slave labour? In the Dohány Street Synagogue, Chief Rabbi Hevesi[38] stressed the importance, especially in view of the approaching cold weather, of sending packages to our deported brethren, and urged everyone to pressure the government for permission to do so.

By the time the Festival of Booths came around,[39] the nights had turned nippy and there was fog in the mornings. On one of those foggy mornings, tiny slips of paper appeared on lamp posts and walls in the outskirts of the city that said: "We want peace!" and "Peace with the Soviets!" This was the first sign of a resistance movement ready to undertake open confrontation. Arming the labour service companies would have been crucial for the envisioned struggle between the Germans and the Hungarian government. Talks to

---

35 Rumbach Street Synagogue, the main religious centre of the Status Quo Ante Jewish congregation in Hungary, erected in the 7th District of Budapest in 1872. Benjámin Fischer (1878–1965), the last rabbi at the synagogue, served there from 1926 onward.

36 A reference to the eve of Yom Kippur, when the Kol Nidre is recited or sung in synagogue.

37 Izsák Pfeiffer (1884–1945), rabbi of Sümeg, Pécs, and, as of 1922, Monor, and poet under the name Izsák Pap. Captured by Arrow Cross militia on 25 October 1944, he was deported and died in Dachau concentration camp on 3 May 1945. About the Columbus Street camp, see 50.

38 Simon Hevesi (1863–1943), rabbi and scholar, professor of the Rabbinical Seminary, founder of the National Hungarian Israelite Cultural Society, and editor of various cultural and religious journals.

39 The Festival of Booths, also known as Sukkot, began on 2 October 1944 and ended with the holiday Simchat Tora on 9 October.

that end began, but the results were eventually frustrated by procrastination and sheer bad luck. These talks form the subject matter of three reports by Dr György Gergely,[40] which provide a clear outline of the events.

Report 1 – 30 September 1944
Bearing a letter of recommendation from József Pálffy,[41] on this day I went to the Castle and presented myself to Lieutenant General Károly Lázár,[42] commander of the Budapest corps. I had to wait a long time, until about 12:30, but then I was able to spend about forty minutes with him.

First of all, I informed him that I had been in the service of the Jewish Council since March 19, enjoying a position of trust, but I stressed that my visit today was not in that capacity but strictly as a civilian. I asked the lieutenant general what he thought the masses of Jews had to do to rejoin the life of the nation. Although I was curious to hear his answer, I posed the question by way of an introduction before I went on to explain concerns over the fate of the capital's Jewry.

Distrustful at first, the lieutenant general replied that this was a matter for politicians to decide and declined to comment for lack of competence. Then he suggested that we talk about specifics instead of remote political considerations, and hit me with the question: "What do you think the Jews of Budapest would do if they were attacked by extremists tonight?" I answered that the Jewry would be utterly helpless, especially now that those in active age among us had been removed from the city, and thanked him for helping me to get to the very point of my visit. He said he had been told by labour leaders that, in the event of being attacked, the Jews would immediately cast away their yellow stars, strip them off the houses as well, and

40 About György Gergely, see 243.
41 József Pálffy (1904–1988), Austro-Hungarian aristocrat and landowner, MP between 1939 and 1944, who opposed Hungary's involvement in the war. In October 1944, Pálffy became the founding president of the Christian Democratic People's Party, whose ambition was to have the country exit the war. He was replaced as party head by the more progressive István Barankovics in 1945, and Pálffy's more conservative faction was not allowed to compete in the elections. In 1947 he emigrated to Austria.
42 About Károly Lázár, commander-in-chief of the Royal Hungarian Guards, see 210.

scatter in all directions. I retorted that expecting any such attempt as
self-defence would be illusory because the list of marked houses had
been published in print as an annex to the applicable decree and was
thus available to everyone. Consequently, it would make no sense to
take the stars off the buildings. As for the rest, I proposed that 190,000
people could not just "scatter in all directions," not to mention the
curfew that kept everyone at home anyway – unless they wanted to go
against the law at risk of internment.

Then he asked about our relations with labour. I answered that,
inasmuch as there were any such relations, these certainly could not
be termed organized. At best, one could talk about a few shots in the
dark that had nothing to do with official Jewish bodies. But even if it
were not so, we would have no reason to trust that the workers would
take up arms on our side, if only because they had no arms to take up.
Therefore, if the authorities wanted to support the Jewry in their self-
defence, they should return the Jewish labour companies to Budapest or
at least to a location near the city.

The lieutenant general shrugged and spread his arms. "Sure ... If the
labour service units were here," he said, "at least we would have some
troops we could rely on." He added that rallying the labour service
units in Budapest would generate such political shock waves that only
the prime minister could do it, and even he would have a difficult
time of it. I suggested that this was obviously the case, due to the three
German armoured divisions. He replied without hesitation that he was
not concerned about the German forces, as the Germans only had two
brigades around the city, not three divisions, and even these were in the
process of being replenished. Then he said the following:

Under the circumstances, he thought it best if the Jews settled in
for self-defence. Each building should have a night watch to keep out
anyone unauthorized to enter. If they had unwanted visitors, they
should immediately notify the nearest police station in some way, by
telephone or messenger. These measures should be provided for in
advance. When I asked if we could count on the police, he answered
in the affirmative. He added that all precautions had been taken to
prevent any atrocities, and that he "hoped they would not be able to
gain the upper hand." This statement only confirmed my suspicion
that emerged from the entire conversation between us; i.e. that the
lieutenant general was wary of a specific and clearly present danger.

Before I took my leave, he asked me to find out for him the exact locations where the labour companies were stationed, if I had the capacity. The matter was urgent. He assured me of his willingness to talk with me about other affairs in the future, but now he could barely keep up with his busy schedule and had a conference to attend.

Report 2 – 4 October 1944

I went to the Castle today, on 4 October 1944, where I had to wait a long time again before Royal Guards Lieutenant General Lázár could see me. This time, I spent about thirty minutes in his office.

I handed over to him a sealed envelope containing the list of some 520 labour companies according to the records kept by the Veterans' Committee, indicating the serial number and station location of each company as best as we could. He opened the envelope and asked some questions, whereupon I had to admit that the list was incomplete. The official records did not allow us to determine the locations where the companies were kept; all we had to go by were certain informal reports by labour servicemen applying to us for donations of clothing.

I wanted to know what would happen to the list I had delivered to him.

He said that the decision on bringing the labour companies to Budapest was the sole responsibility of the prime minister, and even he would have to demonstrate specific reasons for doing so. His own idea was to have certain rapporteurs report to the prime minister on the urgent need to procure labour for certain projects in the city, where the requisite manpower was unavailable. The lieutenant general hoped that this would be a sufficient excuse for the prime minister to order the labour companies to Budapest.

I told him that the drafting of the Jewry of Budapest proceeded under the command of a captain named Gobbi,[43] who showed uncharacteristic goodwill to us and did his best to surmount the difficulties. We had not talked with him about this issue specifically, but I did not think it impossible that we could count on his support in bringing the labour companies to Budapest. I emphasized that this was my own personal impression and asked for permission to feel out Gobbi's inclinations.

---

43 About Ede Gobbi, see 264.

Lázár passed over my question without giving a straight answer, other than to say that he had not heard of Gobbi but would think it entirely impossible for him, whoever he was, to make a difference in a matter of principle and political consequence such as the rallying of labour service units around the capital. Seeing the firmness of his stance, I resolved not to press the matter further.

I then told him about our ongoing efforts to set up a guard in Jewish buildings as per his recommendations. He nodded in approval, adding that house guards would really need to be on duty only when it became known that the Budapest garrison had been put on the alert. When I asked him if such an alert was in force at present, he said that a certain measure of readiness was being maintained but the full alert had been cancelled. He suggested that, since the last time we talked, for the time being, the tension had eased considerably.

I explained our concerns over the suspension of passenger railway services as a possible sign of large numbers of German troops being shipped into the country. After a moment of hesitation, he said that the service restrictions had been imposed for two reasons. On the one hand, the Germans were pulling out their exhausted troops from the Transylvanian front lines to "prevent the slackening of discipline." On the other hand, they were indeed bringing in fresh troops and reserves to replenish their diminishing numbers. Most of these convoys, however, had been redirected to the Banat[44] and Belgrade, after the Russians had all but stopped in their tracks in Transylvania and turned their columns south. Obviously, the next major battle was expected to take place in the Banat or around Belgrade.

After this I came back to the political situation and informed him that SS Obersturmbannführer Eichmann had returned to the city. Lázár said that the signs of relaxation were nevertheless undeniable. Veesenmayer had gone to see Hitler, but the Führer refused to see him – evidently, he was ill. Veesenmayer also paid a visit to Prime Minister Lakatos, but talked to him in a surprisingly mild tone of voice without a trace of intimidation.

The lieutenant general then asked to be briefed on the circumstances of the deportations, specifically inquiring about the number of Jews taken from Budapest thus far. I told him that

44   A historical region today at the crossroads of Romania, Serbia, and Hungary.

number was impossible to guess, given that we did not have a chance or the means to collect data. What he said in reply to this was very interesting, in that it really came off as an apology: That is, that the Germans informed Castle Hill that everyone deported from Budapest was a foreign citizen in hiding. I countered by describing the haphazard manner in which people had been rounded up from the streets without any pretense of a proper investigation. Even if the nonsensical claim that these were foreign citizens were true, this could not have been conclusively determined and ascertained by anyone in the absence of an investigation. I related to Lázár a conversation I had once had with SS Obersturmbannführer Bethge,[45] which concluded by my learning that the children and the elderly from each deportation transport would be subjected to *Sonderbehandlung* or "special treatment." He pretended to be hearing about such horrors for the first time in his life. He declared he had never been an antisemite (nor a philosemite, for that matter). In any case, it was his conviction that the laws of God should never be contravened, and could certainly not be transgressed without incurring repercussions.

As I made for the door, I asked him to treat the list I gave him confidentially, which he promised to do.

Report 3 – 15 October 1944
On the evening of October 14 quite a crowd gathered at the agreed location.

Those present included Pálffy as well as Pallavicini,[46] who said that serious developments were in the wings and he expected everyone to take action the following day. He had sent his own brother to Castle Hill to be available as a guard there. He declared that the arming of the labour service units could not be delayed any longer, and instructed me to draft a solemn proclamation to the labour service companies. The next day, October 15, I was supposed to bring the text to the office at 1 Apponyi Square by nine o'clock in the morning,

45 Friedrich Bethge (1891–1963), poet, playwright, dramaturg who enjoyed great artistic success in Nazi Germany. Bethge joined the Nazi Party in 1932. He joined the SS in 1936 and was promoted to SS-Obersturmbannführer in 1941. He was in American captivity between 1945 and 1947.

46 Count György Pallavicini (1881–1946), landowner, Habsburg legitimist and anti-Nazi politician, member of the Upper House of Parliament.

where I would be given the address of the military barracks, as per instructions of Lázár, where the labour servicemen were to pick up their arms. He ordered me to have twenty men ready by the next day to deliver to the companies copies of the proclamation and the addresses of the barracks. He himself would visit Árpád Szakasits[47] during the night. Prompted by my question, he said that the entire executive staff of the Hungarian Front was aware of these plans.

When the meeting was over, I rushed to search for my friend Dr György Heltai, who headed the political department of the Ministry of Foreign Affairs.[48] I found him in the home of Dr János Beér, the city attorney.[49] Beér agreed to put the men at my disposal, while Heltai promised to wait for me starting at nine o'clock the next morning at the Café Presto near Apponyi Square.

It was getting late, so I hurried home to draft the solemn proclamation as requested.

At nine o'clock the following morning I presented myself at the office in Apponyi Square to get the addresses of the barracks. A long time passed without anything happening. Then Ottó Dragsitz, Pallavicini's secretary, showed up and told me in despair that Pallavicini had been arrested the night before and Lázár was nowhere to be reached. In this way, nobody could tell the companies where to go for the weapons, and the entire plan failed in half an hour.

~ ~ ~

This last report concerns the events that occurred on the morning of October 15, a historic turning point for Hungary and Hungarian Jewry.

47 Árpád Szakasits (1888–1965), leader of the Social Democrats, journalist, state secretary from 1945 to 1948, president of the Republic of Hungary (1948–49), and first chairman of the Presiding Council of the Hungarian People's Republic, 1949–50.

48 György Heltai (1914–1994), lawyer, member of the anti-Nazi resistance in Budapest, head of the political department of the Ministry of Foreign Affairs from 1945 to 1948. He was arrested in 1949 and sentenced to ten years in prison after a show trial, but released in 1954. In 1956, he served as deputy minister of foreign affairs in Imre Nagy's short-lived revolutionary cabinet. After the Soviet invasion, he emigrated to Brussels and later to the United States.

49 János Beér (1905–1966), lawyer, Budapest City Attorney from 1945 to 1948, university professor.

An eerie silence had descended on Síp Street. Dr Zoltán Kohn,[50] who was nominally still in charge, had long relinquished the actual work of administration to Rezső Müller,[51] who held uncontested sway in all the powers and competencies left in the hands of the Council – by then, mainly housing and employment affairs.

It was a splendid sunny day that Sunday, but the warmth – as everything else – turned out to be treacherous. Yellow leaves fell from the trees and drifted in the breeze, as if to signal that the season had ended, and gone with it was an entire world as we knew it. Around noon, I listened in awe and trepidation as the radio broadcast the announcement of Horthy's resignation. From the foggy distance of a quarter of a century I had a flashback of the Aster Revolution of 30 October 1918.[52] I reflected that, in the span of a single generation, this was the second time I had experienced the ending of a world war, and that now, as then, we stood on the cusp of a new era. But where were the overjoyed crowds of people throwing their arms around one another? Where were those who, in 1918, had kissed unknown soldiers and adorned them with chrysanthemums? Horthy's proclamation only elicited panic-stricken hurry-scurry. Everyone knew that the beast had not yet taken its last breath. The concierges watched uneasily as Jewish tenants removed the yellow stars from their doors and gates, doing away with the tell-tale sign of their stigmatization and manifest destiny. The concierges – these prison guards eternally on the alert – were bitterly antagonized by the thought that their prisoners were slipping from their hands, wiping out the joyous prospects of deportations and the free-for-all looting of Jewish property, the reward with which the Arrow Cross party had beguiled them for months. German tanks and armoured vehicles were roaring down the boulevards of Budapest and along the roads leading to settlements around the city.

By the early afternoon the Jews had torn off their yellow stars and taken to the boulevards *en masse*, walking about in the slanting rays of the autumn sun. The Jewry of Budapest believed they had recouped the promise of life,

50 About Zoltan Kohn, see 76.
51 About Rezső Müller, see 58.
52 Also known as the Chrysanthemum Revolution, a democratic revolution that overthrew the Austro-Hungarian Monarchy and established the short-loved Hungarian People's Republic under Count Mihály Károlyi. The name "aster" refers to the flowers (chrysanthemums) that Hungarian soldiers returning from the front used in place of the imperial insignia on their caps.

when in fact they had never been so close to death. At around four o'clock the military marches petered out on the radio, yielding the ether to ominous news. By the time dusk settled, all the Jews in the city knew that they had fallen prey to the Nazis and the Arrow Cross.

October 16 dawned on us without a trace of sun, heavy with darkness and gloom. It was the day of the wrath of God: *Dies irae, dies illa.*[53] Stunned Jews gasped under heavy blows as the takeover was celebrated with piercing cries of debauchery, cheering, and vengeance. The streets of Budapest opened wide to the pogrom-mongering armies, fulfilling the pipe dreams the villains had nourished for months, years, and decades. Interminable marches gathered everywhere as the Jews, evicted from their star-ridden houses, were herded, hands held high, toward the Tattersall.[54]

As I stepped out on the street late in the evening, I found myself face to face with such a mob. Rhythmic yells of "Hit them high, hack them low!" were periodically interrupted by a refrain of volleys as the henchmen fired into the surrounded crowd. The ensuing groans and wailing were stifled by the tormenters' fierce rallying cries.

The fateful date of 16 October 1944 saw the fall of the so-called Historical Hungary, and heralded a turning point in the history of the country's Jewry. The last bastion of our kind was shaken to its very foundations to clear the ground for a small remaining minority that was spiritually purer, morally more upright, and stronger in its convictions and adherence to the flock: The last vestiges of the once-grand Hungarian Jewish people. This is how the destiny of Jewish history came to Budapest, redeeming prophecies old and new. The words of Jeremiah about a depraved and sinful Jerusalem, and what Herzl[55] predicted lay in store for the blinded Jews of Hungary, now stood proven:

> For thus saith the Lord concerning the sons and concerning the
> daughters that are born in this place, and concerning their mothers

---

53 Latin for "the day of wrath and doom impending," the first line of a medieval religious poem that became part of the Requiem Mass in Catholic liturgy.

54 A horse-racing track in Budapest's 8th District, Tattersall was used as a temporary detention site for Jews rounded up by the Arrow Cross in October and November 1944.

55 Theodor Herzl (1860–1904), the Hungarian-born father of modern Zionism, predicted that without a state of their own, the Jews would be doomed; efforts to combat antisemitism in Europe would prove futile, he argued.

that bare them, and concerning their fathers that begat them in this land; They shall die of grievous deaths; they shall not be lamented; neither shall they be buried; but ... they shall be consumed by the sword, and by famine. (Jeremiah 16: 3–4)

Destiny will catch up with the Hungarian Jews too, the more brutal and harsh, the longer it takes, the more influential they are, the further they will fall. There is no escape.[56]

But it did not take a prophet to foresee the future. In the late 1930s and at the beginning of the 1940s, the author of this very book wrote these lines admonishing his people:

The Jews of Hungary have not understood their fate and position, and they remain immune to these considerations as we speak. They have failed to recognize that, in the world we live, the only hope for the survival of the Jewry is the return to its own identity, to the moral calling implicit in Jewish existence, by levelling discrepancies of wealth and organizing its own ranks. The community incapable of attaining these goals today is doomed to fall tomorrow. (*Years of Struggle*, 8)[57]

56 This passage is from Theodor Herzl's letter to Ernő Mezei, 10 March 1903.
57 Ernő Munkácsi, *Küzdelmes évek* ... [Years of Struggle ...] (Budapest: Libanon, 1943).

Glossary

Ferenc Laczó and László Csősz

ANTI-JEWISH LAWS OF HUNGARY

In 1920 Hungary introduced a *numerus clausus* law (Law xxv), limiting the number of Jews permitted to enroll in the nation's universities. Consequently, Hungarian universities rejected two-thirds of Jewish applicants, even while "Christian Hungarians" could not fill all the positions reserved for them. The years 1938 to 1941 then saw a sharp, steady escalation of antisemitism in Hungary, with a growing number of legal and bureaucratic measures, as well as downright illegal activity, designed to ostracize Jews and constrict their rights and opportunities. Of particular note are these three major laws, all of which are often referred to by Ernő Munkácsi:

Law xv of 1938, officially called "To More Effectively Ensure the Balance of Social and Economic Life" (aka the "first Jewish law"), limited to 20 percent the proportion of Jews in the liberal professions (lawyers, doctors, engineers, etc.) and in trading, financial, and industrial companies with more than ten white-collar employees. Allowing for a number of exceptions, the law broadly defined Jews as including those who had converted after 1 August 1919 (the end of the Hungarian Republic of Councils), thereby adding a politically charged racial element to what was primarily discrimination based on religion.

The law of 1938 was meant to be enforced over a period of five years; however, it was quickly followed by Law iv of 1939, officially called "Limiting the Jews' Conquest of Space in Public Life and the Economy." This "second Jewish law" added significant new restrictions: now, the proportion of Hungarians defined as "Jews" could not exceed 6 percent in the liberal professions. At the same time, Jews were entirely banned from working in the state administration, the apparatuses of justice, and secondary schools. Several further restrictions on the proportion of Jewish employees at companies were introduced while the *numerus clausus* law on university enrolment was formally reintroduced, having been nominally withdrawn under international pressure in the late 1920s. Notably, while allowing for certain exceptions, the 1939 anti-Jewish law endorsed an even broader racial definition of Jews, defining anyone with, for instance, at least two Jewish grandparents as Jewish, no matter his religion. The law brought widespread misery to the Jewish middle and lower-middle classes, resulting in approximately ninety thousand people losing their jobs.

It took just two more years for Hungary to adopt a law modelled on and using similar racial terminology to Germany's infamous Nuremberg Laws of 1935. Hungary's Law xv of 1941, officially "Supplement to and Modification of the Marriage Law (Law xxi of 1894) as well as Related and Necessary Measures of Racial Protection," banned marriages and restricted extramarital sexual relations between "non-Jews" and "Jews," with a curious double standard that allowed Gentile men to carry on love affairs with "Jewish" mistresses while forbidding "Jewish" men from having affairs with Gentile women. Hungary's "third Jewish law" of 1941 was seen as an important step in aligning Hungary's official ideology with that of its ally Nazi Germany.

AUSCHWITZ PROTOCOLS

The first of the Auschwitz Protocols of April 1944, also known as the Vrba-Wetzler report, was the first reliable detailed eyewitness account of the Auschwitz-Birkenau camp complex. Dictated or handwritten by Rudolf Vrba (originally Walter Rosenberg) and Alfred Wetzler, Jewish prisoners who escaped from Auschwitz in early April 1944, the report not only attempted to quantify the number of people imprisoned and killed in this major Nazi camp complex, but it also explained precisely how prisoners were "selected," murdered, and cremated, and included sketches indicating the layout of the gas chambers and crematoria. After reaching Žilina, Slovakia, in mid-April, Vrba and Wetzler told their story to members of the Jewish Council of Slovakia, who in turn typed up the report. The Auschwitz Protocols, completed in late April, was translated from Slovak into German and then Hungarian almost immediately. It was narrowly circulated in Budapest as Hungary's Jews were being deported to Auschwitz *en masse* between May and July 1944. The political leaders of Hungary, including Regent Horthy, received the Protocols after it arrived in Budapest in 1944, but the precise date they received it remains a matter of dispute. Equally controversial is that while certain Hungarian Jewish leaders, including members of the Jewish Council and prominent Zionists, knew of the contents of the Vrba-Wetzler report (possibly even earlier than their Hungarian persecutors), they refrained from making the information public.

The first English version of the report, which combined the Vrba-Wetzler report with shorter reports by other Auschwitz escapees (Arnost Rusin, Czeslaw Mordowicz, and Jerzy Tabeau), was published on 25 November 1944 by the United States War Refugee Board under the title "German Extermination Camps – Auschwitz and Birkenau." The joint reports, known colloquially as the Auschwitz Protocols, were used as evidence during the Nuremberg Trial. With the 1947 publication of *How It Happened*, Ernő Munkácsi was the first to make public one of two Hungarian versions of the Vrba-Wetzler report, translated by Mária Székely in 1944 under the auspices of the Reformed Church's Good Pastor Committee headed by József Eliás. (The other, prepared by the Jewish Council of Slovakia in 1944, has been lost.) In his book, Munkácsi reprinted an abridged and slightly modified version of Székely's translation, leaving out certain sections and correcting mistakes. That said, his version still includes a number of inaccuracies (as well as stylistic infelicities). It is worth noting that Munkácsi's version differs, significantly in some cases, from the better-known 1944 English translation of the Protocols.

BORDER REVISIONS, 1938–1941

Tormented by the humiliating loss of two-thirds of its territory and more than half its population after the First World War, Hungary in the interbellum years was determined to revise the terms of the 1920 Trianon Peace Treaty (see separate entry below). This ambition was a prime motivation for Hungary to ally itself with Fascist Italy and Nazi Germany and to fight on the side of the Axis powers during the Second World War. Thanks to this alliance, in four steps between 1938 and 1941, Hungary regained about 40 percent of the territories it had lost at the end of the First World War. However, the price for this bargain was tragically high: Hungary became a fully committed ally of Nazi Germany.

First, under the terms of the First Vienna Award on 2 November 1938, Hungary re-annexed from Czechoslovakia the southern strip of the Upper Province (today in Slovakia), where a majority of the population was ethnic Hungarian. Second, following the dismemberment of Czechoslovakia in March 1939 and Hungary's armed conflict (AKA the Little War) with the newly established Slovak state, the Hungarian Army occupied Subcarpathia (today in Ukraine) and a small strip of Eastern Slovakia. Third, under the terms of the Second Vienna Award of 30 August 1940, Hungary took back from Romania the region of Northern Transylvania, including the historic Szeklerland in the east. Finally, on 6 April 1941, Hungary joined the German invasion of Yugoslavia and annexed the regions of Bácska (today Bačka, Serbia), Muravidék (today Prekmurje, Slovenia), Muraköz (today Međimurje, Croatia), and the Baranya triangle (today Baranja, Croatia).

With its newly annexed territories, Hungary's population swelled from less than 500,000 Jews during the antebellum years to more than 700,000 by 1941. Denied rights by the Hungarian authorities, hundreds of thousands of Jews in these newly annexed territories faced brutal attacks as Hungary implemented increasingly extreme anti-Jewish policies. The 1941 expulsion of Jews with "unsettled citizenship" from Subcarpathia and the 1942 raid in Bácska both resulted in mass murder and served as precursors to the wholesale deportation of Hungary's Jews, which began in the spring of 1944 in the recently re-annexed Northern, Northeastern, and Southern parts of the country before extending to Hungary's "core."

After the war, in accordance with the Paris Peace Treaties of 1947, Hungary was forced to retreat once again to its pre-1938 borders, with minor modifications. Thus, as many as half of the victims of the Holocaust in Hungary were citizens of neighbouring countries between 1920 and 1938, and again after the Second World War their hometowns were not in Hungary.

JUDENRÄTE (JEWISH COUNCILS) IN HUNGARY
In the spring and summer of 1944, following a pattern established in other occupied countries, the Nazi Germans and their Hungarian allies established approximately 150 *Judenräte* or Jewish councils in Hungary. These Jewish councils functioned as administrative bodies responsible for the internal affairs of persecuted Jews. Any official contact between the Hungarian or German authorities and the country's Jews had to pass through the councils, whose task overwhelmingly involved the implementation and enforcement of ever-more restrictive measures against the Jewish population. Due to the swift deportation of Hungary's Jews, including members of the councils, the councils outside Budapest typically ceased functioning within a few weeks. By contrast, the Budapest-based Hungarian Central Jewish Council, whose sphere of authority was effectively restricted to the capital city, continued to act from 20 March 1944 until the liberation of the remaining Jews of Budapest in January 1945.

The Hungarian Central Jewish Council, for which Ernő Munkácsi served as secretary, was founded on the direct order of Adolf Eichmann's special operations unit (Sondereinsatzkommando Eichmann) almost immediately after the Nazis entered Budapest on 19 March 1944. The Eichmann commando did not appoint specific individuals to the Council; however, to give the administrative body a veneer of legitimacy, it insisted on the participation of community leaders, well-respected Jews drawn not only from the populous Neolog and Orthodox communities, but also Zionists and later, to a lesser extent, Jews who had converted to Christianity. Scholars typically distinguish four phases of the Jewish Council. The "First Council" began with the formation of the Jewish Council in March 1944 and was headed by Samu Stern, who largely controlled the Council with his two deputies, Ernő Pető and Károly Wilhelm. The "Second Council" was established toward the end of April when the Jewish Council, now officially recognized by and brought under the purview of Hungarian authorities, was renamed the Interim Executive Board of the Association of Jews in Hungary. A few new members joined at that stage. The date of 14 July 1944 marked the beginning of the "Third Council," when the group was expanded and modified with the addition of a separate Interim Executive Board of the Alliance of Christian Jews of Hungary, consisting of nine members, which was created to represent converts to Christianity. György Auer was nominally head of the Alliance of Christian Jews, but Sándor Török, who had been the representative for converts on the primary Jewish Council since May 8, emerged as its de facto leader. The final phase (the "Fourth Council") started with the Arrow Cross Party's seizure of power in mid-October 1944.

While the Council went through various phases, operating under different names with different personnel, its basic mandate remained unchanged throughout its existence. At times, certain members of the Jewish Council engaged in underground activities, but as a whole its chief strategy consisted of compliance and petitioning. Of the altogether twenty-five men who served on the Hungarian Central Jewish Council, twenty-two survived the Holocaust. After the war, they were accused of collaboration with the Nazis and betrayal of their fellow Jews, and forced to justify their wartime activities. None were found guilty, but controversies surrounding the actions of the Jewish Council during 1944 persist.

KISTARCSA INTERNMENT CAMP
In 1930 the Royal Hungarian Police converted the site of a former mechanical factory in the village of Kistarcsa (Gép és Vasútfelszerelési Gyár Rt., founded in 1907) into an auxiliary detention centre for political prisoners and common criminals. Due to its proximity to Budapest – Kistarcsa lies a mere 8 kilometres from the administrative borders of the capital city – and the excellent railroad connection, the site developed into the largest internment

camp in wartime Hungary. Upon Decree No. 79.630/1939 of the Ministry of the Interior, the complex, surrounded by watchtowers, concrete walls and barbed wire, was expanded to cover 10 hectares (close to 25 acres) in the very heart of the village. In 1944 the overwhelming majority of detainees held in Kistarcsa were Jewish. Right after the German invasion of 19 March 1944, using lists that had been prepared in advance, the Gestapo and Hungarian police arrested and interned at Kistarcsa thousands of Jews considered hostile to the Reich, many of them prominent industrialists, journalists, scholars, and political figures. Also, Kistarcsa served as a prison for numerous Jews swept up in random street raids. During the month following the Nazi invasion, more than seven thousand men and women were locked up at various detention facilities and prisons, including Kistarcsa.

The Jews detained at Kistarcsa became the first victims of the 1944 deportations from Hungary: on 28 April 1944, 1,800 inmates were deported to Auschwitz-Birkenau. Most of them were murdered immediately upon arrival on May 2. On July 19, in contravention of Regent Miklós Horthy's July 6 order to suspend deportations, an SS unit under the command of Hauptsturmführer Franz Novak raided Kistarcsa and deported another 1,220 people to Auschwitz-Birkenau.

SÁRVÁR INTERNMENT CAMP
Initially, in the fall of 1939, this former silk factory (Sárvári Műselyemgyár Rt., founded in 1904) in the small town of Sárvár in Western Hungary was used as an internment camp for Polish soldiers who had escaped to Hungary. Then, after the Hungarian invasion of Yugoslavia in April 1941, Sárvár was used to detain prisoners of war and civilians resettled from the annexed Yugoslav territories, primarily Serbs. It was only in early May 1944, as a result of the mass arrests of Jews in Budapest, which had led to the overcrowding of local prisons and detention facilities, that the former silk factory officially became an auxiliary detention house of the Hungarian Royal Police under Decree No. 146.626/1944 of the Ministry of the Interior. It soon became the second-largest internment camp in Hungary, with about 2,500 inmates. Most detainees were Jews, but trade unionists and other political prisoners were also imprisoned at Sárvár. As well, the camp also served as a transit site for Jews deported from the vicinity of Sárvár to Auschwitz-Birkenau. On 24 July 1944, in what would be the last major deportation of Hungarian Jews before the Arrow Cross takeover in October, the SS raided the Sárvár

internment camp and transported approximately 1,500 of the camp's inmates to Auschwitz-Birkenau. At the end of March 1945, with the front approaching, the Sárvár camp was evacuated and its prisoners were transported to Austria.

TRIANON PEACE TREATY

As a result of the Trianon Peace Treaty, signed in the wake of the First World War on 4 June 1920, Hungary, one of the successor states of the defeated Austro-Hungarian Monarchy, was forced to cede two-thirds of its territory to neighbouring countries, most prominently to Romania, Czechoslovakia, and the Kingdom of Serbs, Croats, and Slovenes (later Yugoslavia). Hungary's territory shrank from 282,000 to 93,000 square kilometres (109,000 to 36,000 square miles) and its population was reduced from 18.2 million to 7.9 million. Moreover, Hungary lost its access to the sea, most of its natural resources, and suffered a drastic cut in the size of its armed forces. Not surprisingly, the Hungarian public of the interbellum period, including Jews, bitterly opposed the terms of the Trianon Treaty (see "Border Revisions" above). Today, Trianon is considered one of the nation's greatest tragedies.

Contributors

NINA MUNK is a journalist and author whose work has been published in *Vanity Fair*, the *Atlantic*, the *New Yorker*, the *New York Times Magazine*, and *Fortune*, among other publications. Her book *The Idealist: Jeffrey Sachs and the Quest to End Poverty* (Knopf Doubleday, 2013) was nominated for the Lionel Gelber Prize and was a finalist for the Governor General's Award and the National Business Book Award. She is also the author of *Fools Rush In: Steve Case, Jerry Levin, and the Unmaking of* AOL *Time Warner* (HarperCollins, 2004) and *The Art of Clairtone: The Making of a Design Icon* (McClelland & Stewart, 2008). She is a descendant of Ernő Munkácsi.

LÁSZLÓ CSŐSZ is a historian and senior archivist at the National Archives of Hungary in Budapest who holds a PhD in history from the University of Szeged. He is the co-author, with Gábor Kádár and Zoltán Vági, of *The Holocaust in Hungary: Evolution of a Genocide* (AltaMira Press–United States Holocaust Memorial Museum, 2013).

FERENC LACZÓ is an assistant professor of European history at Maastricht University who holds a PhD in comparative history from Budapest's Central European University. His most recent book, *Hungarian Jews in the Age of Genocide: An Intellectual History, 1929–1948*, was published by Brill in 2016.

PÉTER BALIKÓ LENGYEL is a Hungarian writer and translator who earned his master's and PhD candidacy in English literature from the University of California, Santa Barbara.

SUSAN PAPP is a PhD candidate at the University of Toronto in European History. She is an award-winning documentary filmmaker and author of *Outcasts: A Love Story* (Dundurn, 2009).

Index